Corporate Policing, Yellow Unionism, and Strikebreaking, 1890–1930

AF694401

This book provides a comparative and transnational examination of the complex and multifaceted experiences of anti-labour mobilisation, from the bitter social conflicts of the pre-war period, through the epochal tremors of war and revolution, and the violent spasms of the 1920s and 1930s.

It retraces the formation of an extensive market for corporate policing, privately contracted security and yellow unionism, as well as processes of professionalisation in strikebreaking activities, labour espionage and surveillance. It reconstructs the diverse spectrum of right-wing patriotic leagues and vigilante corps which, in support or in competition with law enforcement agencies, sought to counter the dual dangers of industrial militancy and revolutionary situations. Although considerable research has been done on the rise of socialist parties and trade unions the repressive policies of their opponents have been generally left unexamined. This book fills this gap by reconstructing the methods and strategies used by state authorities and employers to counter outbreaks of labour militancy on a global scale. It adopts a long-term chronology that sheds light on the shocks and strains that marked industrial societies during their turbulent transition into mass politics from the bitter social conflicts of the pre-war period, through the epochal tremors of war and revolution, and the violent spasms of the 1920s and 1930s.

Offering a new angle of vision to examine the violent transition to mass politics in industrial societies, this is of great interest to scholars of policing, unionism and striking in the modern era.

Matteo Millan is associate professor of modern and contemporary history at the University of Padova, Italy. He worked as a postdoctoral researcher in Oxford and Dublin. In 2015 he obtained a major grant from the European Research Council. He has published extensively on Italian fascism and pre-1914 armed associations.

Alessandro Saluppo is an ERC postdoctoral researcher at the University of Padua, Italy. His current research is devoted to private industrial policing, strikebreaking and anti-labour violence in the United Kingdom before the First World War.

Routledge Studies in Modern History

69 The United Nations and Decolonization
Edited by Nicole Eggers, Jessica Lynne Pearson and Aurora Almada e Santos

70 The Grand Strategies of Great Powers
Tudor A. Onea

71 Ruler Personality Cults from Empires to Nation-States and Beyond
Edited by Kirill Postoutenko and Darin Stephanov

72 Embassies in Crisis
Studies of Diplomatic Missions in Testing Situations
Edited by Rogelia Pastor-Castro and Martin Thomas

73 Redefining Propaganda in Modern China
The Mao Era and its Legacies
Edited by James Farley and Matthew D. Johnson

74 War and Semiotics
Signs, Communication Systems, and the Preparation, Legitimization, and Commemoration of Collective Mass Violence
Edited by Frank Jacob

75 German-East Asian Encounters and Entanglements
Affinity in Culture and Politics Since 1945
Edited by Joanne Miyang Cho

76 Corporate Policing, Yellow Unionism, and Strikebreaking, 1890–1930
In Defence of Freedom
Edited by Matteo Millan and Alessandro Saluppo

For more information about this series, please visit: www.routledge.com/history/series/MODHIST

Corporate Policing, Yellow Unionism, and Strikebreaking, 1890–1930

In Defence of Freedom

Edited by Matteo Millan and Alessandro Saluppo

Routledge
Taylor & Francis Group
LONDON AND NEW YORK

First published 2021
by Routledge
2 Park Square, Milton Park, Abingdon, Oxon OX14 4RN

and by Routledge
52 Vanderbilt Avenue, New York, NY 10017

Routledge is an imprint of the Taylor & Francis Group, an informa business

© 2021 selection and editorial matter, Matteo Millan and Alessandro Saluppo; individual chapters, the contributors

The right of Matteo Millan and Alessandro Saluppo to be identified as the authors of the editorial material, and of the authors for their individual chapters, has been asserted in accordance with sections 77 and 78 of the Copyright, Designs and Patents Act 1988.

The Open Access version of this book, available at www.taylorfrancis.com, has been made available under a Creative Commons Attribution-Non Commercial-No Derivatives 4.0 license.

Trademark notice: Product or corporate names may be trademarks or registered trademarks, and are used only for identification and explanation without intent to infringe.

British Library Cataloguing-in-Publication Data
A catalogue record for this book is available from the British Library

Library of Congress Cataloging-in-Publication Data
Names: Millan, Matteo, editor. | Saluppo, Alessandro, editor.
Title: Corporate policing, yellow unionism, and strikebreaking, 1890–1930: in defence of freedom / edited by Matteo Millan and Alessandro Saluppo.
Description: Abingdon, Oxon ; New York, NY : Routledge, 2021. | Series: Routledge studies in modern history | Includes bibliographical references and index.
Identifiers: LCCN 2020039951 (print) | LCCN 2020039952 (ebook) | Subjects: LCSH: Labor unions—History—20th century. | Labor movement—Political aspects—History—20th century. | Strikebreakers—History—20th century. | Police, Private—History—20th century. | Political violence—History—20th century. | Democracy—History—20th century.
Classification: LCC HD6476 .C67 2021 (print) | LCC HD6476 (ebook) | DDC 331.89/409041—dc23
LC record available at https://lccn.loc.gov/2020039951
LC ebook record available at https://lccn.loc.gov/2020039952

ISBN: 978-0-367-37412-9 (hbk)
ISBN: 978-0-367-70117-8 (pbk)
ISBN: 978-0-429-35424-3 (ebk)

Typeset in Times New Roman
by Apex CoVantage, LLC

Contents

Tables

Figures

Contributors

Editors

Matteo Millan is associate professor of modern and contemporary history at the University of Padova, Italy. Before coming to Padova, he worked as a postdoctoral researcher in Oxford and Dublin. In 2015, he obtained a major grant from the European Research Council to lead the broad comparative project "The Dark Side of the Belle Époque. Political Violence and Armed Associations in Europe before the First World War". He has published extensively on the history of fascism and pre-1914 armed associationism in Europe.

Alessandro Saluppo is an ERC post-doctoral researcher at the University of Padova. His current research is devoted to private industrial policing, strike-breaking and anti-labour violence in Europe before the First World War. His works on armed groups, paramilitaries and militias, with respect to both the pre-war and interwar periods, have been published on peer-reviewed journals and edited volumes.

Contributors

Prerna Agarwal was a postdoctoral fellow at the Economic History Department, London School of Economics (LSE) (2017–19). In July 2018, she received her PhD in history and contemporary India at King's College London. She is currently based in New Delhi and working on editing her PhD thesis into a monograph, which relates to trade unions and political cultures in Calcutta's docklands.

Erik Bengtsson is an associate senior lecturer in economic history at Lund University in Sweden. He got his PhD from Gothenburg University in 2013 with the dissertation *Essays on Trade Unions and Functional Income Distribution*. His research concerns historical political economy and income and wealth distribution, in the eighteenth to twentieth centuries. At present, his research focuses on (a) a project on farmer politicians in Swedish modernisation c. 1770–1950 and (b) a project estimating the Swedish income distribution 1862–1970, building on a new dataset.

Thanasis Betas graduated from the Department of History and Archaeology, School of Philosophy, Aristotle University of Thessaloniki. He continued postgraduate studies and obtained a master's degree from the University of Crete. He received his PhD, with his dissertation entitled "Matsagos Cigarette Industry in Volos, 1918–1972, Labour and Survival in Volos" – on a scholarship from the European Program "Heraclitus II" – at the University of Thessaly. He has worked in research programs at the University of Thessaly, the Cultural Foundation of Piraeus Bank and the International Institute of Social History (The Netherlands). His current research project entitled "Filter-Cigarettes . . . Business Strategies, Technological Changes and Organisational Innovations in the Greek Tobacco Industry Between 1945–1973" is financed by the Research Centre for the Humanities (RCH, Athens). He is currently working as a research fellow in the rescue and recording of the Historical Archive of the General Confederation of Workers of Greece (Athens). He is a member of the Greek Economic History Association, the Greek Network for the History of Labour and Labour Movement, the Portuguese Economic and Social History Association and the Oral History Association of Volos.

Assumpta Castillo Cañiz is a PhD candidate at the University of Padua working on the Spanish and the Portuguese cases within the ERC project "The Dark Side of the Belle Époque. Political Violence and Armed Associations in Europe before the First World War". She has participated in several international conferences and has also published several works on the revolutionary process and the intra-community violence in the Republican rearguard during the Spanish Civil War, including "El forastero en la guerra civil española. Las dinámicas intra y extracomunitarias de la violencia en la retaguardia republicana" (Revista Universitaria de Historia Militar, 2014), and "Anarchism and the countryside: Old and new stumbling blocks in the study of rural collectivization during the Spanish Civil War" (*International Journal of Iberian Studies*, 2016). Her main research lines include the study of political violence between the late nineteenth and early twentieth centuries, the exploration of responses and alternatives to the Western capitalist model and the development of anti-democratic political cultures both in their practical and cultural forms.

Amerigo Caruso is an assistant professor of modern and contemporary history at the University of Greifswald (Germany). His current research project investigates how different political regimes reacted in times of turmoil and widespread insecurity during the nineteenth and early twentieth centuries. He has published widely on political history, the history of ideas, nationalism and social conflicts. His recent publications include *"Blut und Eisen auch im Innern". Soziale Konflikte, Massenpolitik und Gewalt in Deutschland vor 1914* (Campus, 2021) and a guest-edited issue of the *Journal of Modern Italian Studies* on historical identities and the process of nation-building in nineteenth-century Italy and Germany.

Martin Conway is professor of contemporary European history at the University of Oxford and is a fellow of Balliol College. He has published a number of books on aspects of the history of mid-twentieth-century Europe, and his most recent book is *Western Europe's Democratic Age 1945–68* (2020).

Pierre Eichenberger is permanent lecturer at the University of Lausanne. He carried out research and taught at the universities of Zurich and Yale and at the Robert L. Heilbroner Center for Capitalism Studies, New School for Social Research (New York). He is the author of *Mainmise sur l'État social: Mobilisation patronale et caisses de compensation en Suisse (1908–1960)* (2016).

Geoff Eley is Karl Pohrt Distinguished University Professor of Contemporary History at the University of Michigan, where he has taught since 1979. He previously taught at the University of Cambridge (1975–79). Trained originally as a modern German historian, he also works in modern British history, as well as on a general European front. He is interested in both the history of the left and the right; history and film; historiography; and history and theory. He has recently begun teaching a large new undergraduate course on the history of terrorism. His earliest works were *Reshaping the German Right: Radical Nationalism and Political Change after Bismarck* (1980, 1991) and (with David Blackbourn) *The Peculiarities of German History* (1980, 1984). More recent books include *Forging Democracy: A History of the Left in Europe. 1850–2000* (2002); *A Crooked Line: From Cultural History to the History of Society* (2005); (with Keith Nield) *The Future of Class in History* (2007); and *Nazism as Fascism: Violence, Ideology, and the Ground of Consent in Germany, 1930–1945* (2013). He co-edited *German Colonialism in a Global Age* (2014), *German Modernities from Wilhelm to Weimar: A Contest of Futures* (2016) and *Visualizing Fascism: The Twentieth-Century Rise of the Global Right* (2020). He is writing a general history of Europe in the twentieth century and a new study of the German right, *Genealogies of Nazism: Conservatives, Radical Nationalists, Fascists in Germany, 1860–1930.*

Charles Bégué Fawell is a doctoral candidate in history at the University of Chicago, where he is currently teaching and writing his dissertation, "In-Between Empires: Transit and Sovereignty along the Maritime Highways of Imperial France and Britain, 1870–1930". Based on archival research in France, the UK and Vietnam, the project re-examines the everyday histories of steamship voyages between West Europe and East Asia during the era of High Imperialism. Steamships of the colonial era, it argues, were both microcosms of empire and floating borderlands, where mobile encounters revealed the fault lines of imperial sovereignty and a nascent regime of global governance.

George Gilbert is lecturer in modern Russian history at the University of Southampton. His publications include *The Radical Right in late Imperial Russia* (2016), and, as editor, *Reading Russian Sources: A Student's Guide to Text and Visual Sources from Russia's History* (2020). He has also written a number of articles on various aspects of the social, cultural and political history of Russia's late Imperial period.

Vilja Hulden is instructor of history at the University of Colorado Boulder. Her work focuses on early twentieth-century employer organisations, especially on publicity and lobbying, a topic on which she is currently completing a manuscript tentatively entitled *Individual Rights and Collective Action: Employers, Workers, and the Closed Shop*, under advance contract with the University of Illinois Press. Her new project, *Speaking to the State*, analyses patterns in who appeared as witnesses at congressional hearings.

Volodymyr Kulikov is a historian and postdoctoral fellow at Central European University. Besides CEU, he teaches at the Ukrainian Catholic University in Lviv and at the Karazin Kharkiv National University, Ukraine. He specialises in the business history of Eastern Europe, with a particular interest in the history of enterprises, collective action problem, big business and industrialisation in the Russian Empire. In 2019, he received a research grant from The Shevchenko Scientific Society in the USA, which was partly used to collect archival materials for the research presented in this book.

Claire Morelon is ERC-postdoctoral research fellow at the University of Padova working on Austria-Hungary within the project "The Dark Side of the Belle Époque". Her publications include "Sounds of Loss: Church Bells, Place, and Time in the Habsburg Empire during the First World War", *Past & Present* (2019) and the edited volume *Embers of Empire: Continuity and Rupture in the Habsburg Successor States after 1918* (2018).

Chad Pearson teaches history at Collin College. He is the author of *Reform or Repression: Organizing America's Anti-Union Movement* (2016) and co-editor with Rosemary Feurer of *Against Labor: How U.S. Employers Organized to Defeat Union Activism* (2017). He is currently writing a book tentatively titled *Capital's Terrorists: Anti-Labor Violence in the Long Nineteenth Century.*

Irina Shilnikova obtained a PhD in history in 2001 at the Yaroslavl State University in Russia. She is an associate professor at the Russian Presidential Academy of National Economy and Public Administration in Moscow. She worked as a leading researcher at the Yaroslavl State Archive, and later as assistant professor at the Russian State University for the Humanities, Moscow. Between 2008 and 2019 she held the position of assistant professor at the Higher School of Economics. Her research interests include the economic and social history of the late Russian Empire, labour history and cliometrics. She has authored and co-authored four monographs as well as numerous articles on the labour and business history of the Russian Empire and Soviet Russia (the 1920s and 1930s).

Acknowledgements

This volume came out of the workshop "Industrial vigilantism, strikebreaking and patterns of anti-labour violence, 1890s–1930s. A comparative and transnational perspective" held at the University of Oxford in October 2018. The event was organised under the auspices of the Department of Historical and Geographical Sciences and the Ancient World of the University of Padua, the University of Oxford's Faculty of History and the Oxford Centre for European History (OCEH). We are hugely grateful to all of them.

The workshop was one of the first outcomes of the European Research Council (ERC)-funded project "The Dark Side of the Belle Époque. Political Violence and Armed Associations in Europe before the First World War". During the workshop, we were surprised to find how much the research we were (and are still) conducting on Central-Western Europe shared communalities and interests with that of scholars working in other parts of the globe. Thus, we decided to collect various contributions on the significantly underestimated, though crucial, phenomenon of anti-labour militancy from the late nineteenth century to the 1930s. We would like to personally thank all the contributors of this volume for having accepted such an endeavour: some of them are colleagues in Padova, while others come from other institutions. It was a great pleasure and was surely academically and scientifically stimulating to work with all of them.

Martin Conway has been an indispensable and invaluable collaborator in getting the manuscript shaped. It has been an extraordinary privilege to work with him. We are also much indebted to Geoff Eley who has served as a keynote speaker at the Oxford workshop and generously accepted to write the preface for this volume. We benefitted greatly from the help of Giulia Albanese who has offered her treasured comments and insights throughout the trajectory of this project. We are also thankful to Tom Buchanan, Patricia Calvin and Marc Mulholland for trying out the arguments of this book at the workshop. In connection to the workshop, we owe a large debt of gratitude to Laura Jimenez Aguado, Gianluca Marchiori, Matthew Myers, Romain Bonnet and Marco Maria Aterrano. Finally, we would like to thank Rob Langham and Max Novick for having believed in this book project before it was even conceived.

The book has received funding from the ERC under the European Union's Horizon 2020 Research and Innovation Programme (G.A. 677199 – ERC-StG2015 "The Dark Side of the Belle Époque. Political Violence and Armed Associations before the First World War").

Foreword

Coercion at work, violence in politics: what changed between 1890 and 1930?

Geoff Eley

Dimensions of violence

The years covered by the extremely rich studies presented in this volume formed a vital watershed in the shifting relationship of violence to the structure and conduct of politics. The character and meanings of violence itself are anything but transparent and straightforward. Any full and persuasive treatment would require the kind of elaborate conceptual work that exceeds the modest scope of these observations. Definition would proceed on multiple fronts. The first would separate *agency* from *structure*, distinguishing "physical assault" and the "use of physical force".[1] On the one hand, there is violence as the visible, tangible, directly experienced or witnessed material damage to persons or property, the actual blood, pain and shock, and the sensory horror or thrill of wreckage and destruction that such damage produces; on the other hand, there is violence as the more abstracted, distanced, mediated application of physical force to produce damage and harm elsewhere, and through it the securing of social and political objectives.

This distinction moves from the immediacy of the particular act to the more complicated chain of agency involved in the designing of policy, the implementing of plans, the sending of an order or the pressing of a button. It is this distancing effect, or displacement effect, that shapes violence as we move down the twentieth century. Clearly there were instances earlier, but during the last century the scale, speed, logistical effectiveness, applied technologies and general normativities of politically motivated violence become ratcheted so relentlessly higher, especially when perpetrated by states. One version of that story travels from the trenches of the First World War; another version runs from the bombing of Iraqi villages in 1920 through the Strategic Bombing Offensive, Hiroshima and Nagasaki, all the way down to 2003's "Shock and Awe".

Equally important are the concepts of *structural* or *systemic* violence and their cognate proposition of *symbolic* violence. These further elaborate the aforementioned displacement effect – the production and productivity of violence elsewhere, its projection and transference *outside* and *beyond* the immediately encountered everydayness of the practical circumstances where the particular act happens to land. "Structural violence" has been classically studied in its colonial settings. Thus South Asian historian Gyan Pandey refers to the "routine violence" that becomes endemic to the structural circumstances and mundane dynamics of the effects of a public power on its society (say, British rule in India). He sees violence *not* as an exceptional event – as something that is *not* "temporary, occasional, even abnormal", *not* an "interruption", *not* "merely transitional, a birthmark, or a departure" and *definitely not* "premodern", a trace of earlier practices, or a cultural formation that ought to have been superseded. Instead, Pandey argues, violence is "a much more general and continuous aspect of modern life".[2]

Originating with Pierre Bourdieu, symbolic violence was used by Alf Lüdtke in re-grounding an argument about nineteenth-century Prussian militarism in the social practices of policing in everyday life.[3] It describes the latent and unspoken, habituated or unconscious modalities of domination deeply and insidiously inscribed in everyday social practices and relations. It considers how generally distributed forms of injury or damage, like class rule, gender domination, ethnocultural "othering" or racism, work to ensure the "misrecognition of power relations". It describes the foisting of modalities of perception onto subordinated subjects who then accommodate to the given terms of the social order, naturalise it and come to believe in its necessity and justice. As such unreflected normativities become reproduced, given relations of domination get secured. The governed participate in the justice of their own naturalised subjection. Symbolic violence may even be more efficacious, precisely by *grounding* the social order's legitimacy in this imprinting of power relations on the very practices and habits of cognition of individuals.[4] Another version of this radically culturalist understanding of the political consequences of violence – of how popular acquiescence in a form of rule may become naturalised under the *threat* of physical violence as much as its actuality – can be found in post-Foucauldian treatments of governmentality and surveillance.

To grasp the full complexities of the violence of early twentieth-century labour history, these wider socio-cultural meanings will certainly be needed. In reconstructing the cultures of conformity and coercion, order and acquiescence, incentives and intimidation, whose consequences structured the management of labour markets and the labour process in the widely varying contexts covered by this volume, the socio-cultural perspectives enabled by concepts like "structural" and "symbolic" violence will have to be explored. In grasping the prevalence and efficacy of strikebreaking and vigilantism, or the two-way dynamics of workplace discipline and shopfloor practices, we surely will need the same.

In what follows, though, I approach issues of violence during 1890–1930 as a problem for democracy in the normative sense – as a wilful political challenge to the functioning and legitimacy of the emergent political forms and practices of those years. Relevant here is that classic claim to the monopoly over the legitimate use of political force seen by Max Weber as a hallmark of statehood and vital for the European state-making of the later-nineteenth century. I complicate that story by a two-step argument: first, by emphasising aspects of its unevenness before 1914, especially its contested and unfinished character; second, by showing how the turmoil after 1918–19 threw that process of the monopolising of the legitimate use of force drastically into question. If the extensive repertoire of anti-labour violence forms a prime feature of the pre-1914 histories, then fascism supplies the framing for what follows. In a nutshell: the prevalence of political violence in the 1920s and 1930s signifies a breakdown in the norms and ideals of democracy, publicness and civility whose efficacy became cumulatively established after the 1860s.

Expanding civility, 1860 to 1914: violence constrained

At the largest scale of analysis, two interconnected questions defined this terrain:

- What were the processes, under conditions of constitutional democracy, that enabled the large-scale use of political violence for the purposes of sustained collective mobilisation aiming at democracy's destruction?
- What was the relationship between the forms of anti-labour violence and this larger context of violence at the level of the polity and the state?

In the workplace, in labour markets, in the economy more broadly, anti-labour violence was constitutive for the rise of political movements demanding authoritarian rule and dismantling of democracy. At the same time, the precise forms and varying prevalence of anti-labour violence, society by society, were directly connected to the strength or weakness of each society's democratising capacities. The political violence we associate with fascism after 1918–19 overwhelmed and largely subsumed the more isolable forms of action already developing before 1914. The recourse to violence after 1918 bespoke a political logic, whether intended or entailed, that abrogated those political rules whose purpose was to contain the use of physical force, while organising and enabling the pluralist cohabiting of differences.

I understand fascism in the early twentieth century as the recourse to organised collective violence in the midst of an extreme polarisation of differences heading for a general crisis of society. And here is a really stark contrast. The recourse to political violence – to repressive and coercive forms of rule, to guns rather than words, to beating up your opponents rather than denouncing them from the speaker's platform – was ultimately what distinguished fascism in Germany, Italy and elsewhere from earlier forms of right-wing or conservative politics. But at the same time, violence was not exactly absent from the conduct of politics before 1914, least of all in the countless settings of labour conflict across the various countries of capitalist industrialisation. So we need to begin by drawing some distinctions.

With the exception of Britain, where labour stayed far longer inside an older liberal framework of politics, ensuring that specifically socialist politics remained far more locally contained, Europe had three distinct geographies of working-class politics before 1914:[5]

- One was what I have called the central and northern European Social Democratic core, where an emergent model of socialist parliamentarianism and associated trade unionism dominated labour movements from the 1890s. It encompassed those parties attaining more than 25 per cent of the popular vote in democratic elections before 1914.

- A second pattern described the western Mediterranean, where anarcho-syndicalism weakened the socialist parties and rendered working-class politics more volatile, devolving it onto locally based chambers of labour, where the functions of trade unions and parties were practically mixed.
- The final pattern occurred in the broad eastern border zone of Russia, the Balkans, and much of Austria-Hungary, where weak and uneven industrialisation combined with repressive political systems to impede socialist parties or force them underground.

At the level of states and their national polities, liberal constitutionalism was just as crucial as the extent of industrialisation in shaping the initial rise of socialist parties and labour movements. Where industry made little progress, so too did socialism. But industrialisation was not an infallible guide to socialism's strength: Bulgaria, East Galicia, Finland, Norway and Sweden all showed socialist parties winning major rural support, as did many localities and regions elsewhere. Legality, a functioning parliamentary constitution and a more democratic franchise could be as enabling for socialist emergence as growth of industry. Conversely, a repressive polity (e.g. Russian autocracy) held back the political expression of popular militancy, just as a discriminatory franchise in heavily industrialised Belgium successfully depressed the Belgian socialists' electoral performance. If the polity's early liberalisation could compensate for the absence of capitalist industry, then in the more industrial economies an absence of liberalisation might still hamper a labour movement's rise. The "constitutional factor" could either anticipate or impede the consequences of industrial class formation.

Any robust liberal constitutionalism required a liberal system of the rule of law. Under the European constitutional settlements of 1867–71, a functioning parliamentary constitution usually secured the classic civil freedoms, including rights of association and assembly, plus the legalising of trade unions. Unsurprisingly, the western Mediterranean pattern of weaker socialist parties was accompanied not only by a thinness of parliamentary culture but also by far greater police repression and anti-labour violence. Indeed, with its preference for direct action and community-based militancy, syndicalism directly responded to the viciousness of policing, deployment of troops and the failure of a parliamentary socialist party to bring government under constraint of law. This was precisely the Italian dialectic during 1901–03: while Giolitti walked his tightrope of legislative negotiations with parliamentary socialists, the police were killing strikers in a series of "proletarian massacres" that claimed 40 deaths between June 1901 and September 1904. Beneath this comparison of states and whole societies were examples galore of police repression, vigilantism and employer-initiated violence in central and northern Europe too – inside particular strikes, particular plants and particular communities, especially during the pan-European insurgencies of 1904–07 and

1911–13. Drawing out such locally bounded or situated dynamics is precisely the great virtue of the papers collected in this volume.

The difference between the violence of the fascists and these pre-1914 forms must be sharply marked. Violence and use of force were nothing new. The state's coercive resources were always deployed against certain kinds of opposition, whether by routine application of the law for protection of persons and property or for maintaining law and order, or by curtailment of civil liberties under pressure of national emergency, as in wartime or a general strike. Under constitutional governance between the 1860s and 1914, a wide spectrum of restrictive and authoritarian systems of public policing were embraced, whether through army, gendarmerie, citizens' militia or uniformed police as such. Coercion in that sense was an entirely typical dimension of legally constituted governing authority, whatever the political complexion. Use of force supplied predictable sanction against actions transgressing allowable boundaries of social and political dissent.

Privately organised coercion was likewise commonly found in societies undergoing capitalist economic development in the later nineteenth century: strike-breaking, vigilantism, economic paternalism and servile labour, especially in the countryside, were all entirely plentiful. The balance of public jurisdiction and such privately organised coercion, society by society, varied in extremely complex and subtle ways, including of course the forms and extent of practical collusion and fully articulated integration, whether clandestine, tacitly accepted or openly acknowledged. How this distribution of coercive tasks and practices worked to shape the boundaries of public order could be very complex: the large-scale autonomies of neo-seigneurial jurisdiction on big landed estates and the capitalist prerogatives of spatially isolated extractive industry, single-industry settlements, and company towns are only the most obvious instances of how that worked. As a number of the essays show, ships were another instance of the same kind. Nor did the incidence of privately deployed coercion necessarily correlate with strength of constitutional government or liberal systems of the rule of law. Such violence was far *more* prevalent, even endemic, in the United States before 1914 than in Germany, for example. To take a single notorious case: in the Ludlow Massacre of April 1914, a combined assault by National Guard and company enforcers massacred some two dozen people, including women and children, with aggregate death toll of nearly 200 lives during the strike. Nothing remotely like this happened during the German industrialisation before 1914.[6] In July 1917, the Phelps Dodge Corporation used cattle cars to deport 1,300 striking copper miners and supporters from the company town of Bisbee, Arizona, to the New Mexico desert 200 miles away, aided by 2,000 deputised vigilantes commanded by the county sheriff. It was preceded by a smaller deportation from the company town of Jerome.

In Germany pre-1914, such privately organised coercion was becoming ever-more visibly reined in. Armed force was gathered steadily inside the state's jurisdictional realm. Beginning in the 1860s, state-managed repression became itself ever-more strictly subject to constitutional limitations, which by the 1900s seemed more and more secure. Precisely when measured by these pre-1914 precedents, fascist violence after 1918–19 was something shockingly new. Bismarck's Anti-Socialist Law of 1878–90; the harassment, deporting and imprisonment of left-wing activists; and the unleashing of police or troops against strikers and demonstrators – all these were one thing. But *terror*, first by means of a militarist and violently confrontational style of politics (1919–23, 1928–33), then as a principle of state organisation (post-1933), was quite another.

Violence returns, 1914–23: fascism as breach

The years 1914–23 were a crucial watershed. The disaster befalling the German right in 1918 – the doubled trauma of military defeat and popular-democratic revolution – viciously radicalised its emotional and ideological temper. During the civil-war-like disorders prevailing for most of the years 1918–23, there was ample scope for the resentful militancy of the returning "front soldiers" and their civilian compatriots, simultaneously elevated and brutalised by the wartime, morally enraged by the dissolution of familiar values they saw accompanying the revolutionary circumstances of the new Republic's foundation. The paramilitary formations coalescing across Germany from the end of 1918 became the practical medium for mobilising and deploying this counter-revolutionary anger, together with the *völkisch* and anti-Semitic associations mushrooming during the same time.

Much of that momentum persisted into the Weimar Republic's years of so-called relative stability between 1923–24 and 1928–29. Its instituted forms then contributed vitally to the full-scale national-political arrival of the Nazi Party between the elections of 1928 and 1930. This passage from the counter-revolutionary confusion of 1918–23 to the growing concentration of right-wing energies around the Nazis during the Republic's demise needs far more detailed explication. But the new willingness to use political violence against one's opponents was impossible to ignore. Moreover, hatred of the left, meaning not only communists and Social Democrats but also pacifists, feminists, left liberals and any other defenders of democracy, supplied vital impetus behind this right-wing political violence.

To be blunt: *killing* socialists rather than just arguing with them, or at most legally and practically restricting their rights, was the most radical of departures. The brutality of this break cannot be overstated. Anti-socialism as such certainly defined the German right pre-1914. That earlier history embraced not only recourse to "exceptional legislation" on the model of the 1878 Anti-Socialist Law and other forms of legal harassment, but also far wider strategies aimed at suppressing socialism and other popular radicalisms, while neutralising the labour movement and generally resisting the spread of democracy, or at least regulating its encroachments and containing its effects. Those strategies encompassed many "normal" phenomena endemic to the Wilhelmine polity after the 1890s, including policing and use of the judiciary; routine discrimination via the state apparatuses; strategically conceived welfare legislation and other social reforms aimed at dividing some categories of workers from others; private systems of company-based welfare; ambitious schemes of social discipline targeting young people; and systematic propaganda offensives among the working class. This German record was entirely consistent with responses to socialism elsewhere.

But *this* anti-socialist politics occurred within normative legal and political frameworks bringing it gradually under constraint: the liberal-constitutionalist polities generalised across Europe after the 1860s, which rendered arbitrary authority increasingly accountable to elected government, parliamentary oversight, and liberal protocols of law. As the European socialist parties gained in electoral strength and parliamentary influence from the 1890s they brought repressive policing under further review and restraint. Although during the 1900s fresh polarisation could be seen gathering pace, this incremental bolstering of constitutional politics enabled political life in much of Europe to settle on the given parliamentary terrain. So, it was *this* political culture of relative civility that the massive disruption of the First World War so badly disordered. This was the practical ground of functioning pluralism that fascists wanted to tear apart.

In Germany by the early 1900s, precisely such a parliamentary stabilisation had been setting in. In the 1890s, some parts of the German right continued hankering after the chimera of a coup d'état against the 1871 Constitution, a so-called *Staatsstreich*, involving confrontation with the Reichstag, abolishing the democratic franchise, returning to monarchical authority and if necessary, the imposing of martial law. In fact, the government did attempt a number of times to replicate the former Anti-Socialist Law by severely restricting civil liberties, as in the Revolution Bill (*Umsturzvorlage*) in 1895 and a proposal to revise the Prussian Law of Association (so-called Little Anti-Socialist Law) in 1896–97. But each of those initiatives *failed*, defeated by parliamentary majorities. While *Staatsstreich* talk persisted, climaxing during spring-summer 1897, government became decisively stabilised and plans were shelved. It was only amid the right's parliamentary isolation after the disastrous 1912 elections that some circles returned to the idea of revising the Constitution, this time by killing the democratic franchise with versions of anti-democratic "corporative representation".

But from the later-1890s until this resurgence of right-wing designs against the Constitution in 1912–14, public life settled on constitutionalist ground. Politics was now conducted by rules and procedures, by argument and persuasion, by observing the practical norms of pluralist competition and orderly exchange. Socialists now fought on their own terms – namely, by leaflets and speeches, agitation and propaganda and patriotic mobilisation of one's own supporters, rather than straightforward repression. In this emergent repertoire of anti-socialist practice, in other words, the coming political violence of post-1918 had no place. Wilhelmine anti-socialism always stopped short of the violence so commonplace in the years 1918–23 and 1928–34. Reeling from shocks of defeat and revolution, sneering at the 1919 republican Constitution, enraged by apparent disrespect for property and privilege, the left's opponents in this later context turned to a new kind of extreme. But before 1914 the constitutionalist norms stayed solidly intact. So to repeat: it was this practical ground of political civility that the post-1918 right chose to desert.

Amid the polarised climate of collapsing authority and working-class insurgency, the abrupt loss of an earlier consensual framework in autumn 1918 called the fascist option to the stage. When that happened, the left's *strength* was initially the driver. The right's parliamentary weakness and unaccustomed severance from access to government opened a space for more violent alternatives. For a while – *before 1914* in the imperfect but democratically elected parliamentary arena of the Empire, *after 1918* in the full-scale parliamentary democracy of the new Republic – the polarising of options still worked potentially to the left's benefit, so long as politics stayed ordered along electoral and constitutionalist lines. Even as the original republican consensus eroded and an emergent centre-right seemed possibly on the cards in 1924–28, the Weimar Constitution's pluralist logic held steady, inside practical scenarios of compromise and negotiation. Albeit equivocally and at the cost of internal splits, the DNVP (German National People's Party) was drawn briefly into that process, joining governments first in 1924–25 and again in 1927–28, much to the rage of its intransigent anti-republican wing.

In a severe crisis, this syndrome – breadth of right-wing hostility against a polity tilted structurally to the left – could become a source of acute danger. That dynamic was indeed repeatedly the trigger for right-wing political violence. That occurred initially in 1918–23, when working-class insurgency threatened to exceed the parliamentary confines of the given revolutionary changes. It happened still more dangerously in 1930–33, when the welfare state, the defensive recalcitrance of trade unions, and the mobilised popular resources of SPD (Social Democratic Party of Germany) and (KPD) Communist Party of Germany seemed to be impeding Germany's economic and political recovery as the right had conceived it. The right proved increasingly willing to turn its back on democracy and embrace extra-parliamentary solutions once politics had reached an impasse: liberal-constitutionalist governance seemed to have exhausted any remaining capacity for stabilising a protracted societal crisis deteriorating apparently towards endless stalemate. As the most extreme version of an authoritarianism demanding to cut through the entanglements and immobilities of democracy, *fascism* could then offer a credible and appealing alternative.

Conclusion

The micro-dynamics of anti-labour violence, across multivarious workplace, plant-level and community-based settings, are always linked to larger political histories shaped by polity and state, whether we approach that connectedness via constitutional questions and forms of law or via the socio-cultural effects of structural and symbolic violence. And here, the post-1918 rupture was crucial: combined with the rise of fascism, the popular insurgencies of 1919–23 produced back-and-forth excesses of political violence, under circumstances tantamount to civil war, that overwhelmed any more isolable local forms of anti-labour violence of the kind prevalent before 1914. This occurred unevenly across Europe, but increasingly with effects that were pervasive and transcendent rather than spatially confined. In Italy it was especially intense in 1919–22. The revolutionary and counter-revolutionary tumults in Germany make it equally hard to isolate vigilantism, workplace intimidation and other forms of anti-labour violence in the manner of the pre-1914 years. After a lull in the mid-1920s, this German cycle resumed with a vengeance after 1928–29.

Pre-1914, things were much different. If, after 1918, anti-labour violence was subsumed into the fascist-inspired political violence in society at large, then before 1914 the widening political civility made anti-labour violence more isolable and subject to constraint. Here Germany is especially interesting. From the late-1890s the German right vacated its ideal program of constitutional revision and anti-socialist laws, in a pragmatics of adjustment that became strengthened after 1903–04, when an SPD electoral landslide joined major strikes in throwing big employers onto the defensive. That close repressive nexus following the Paris Commune between government and a broad propertied front of bourgeois society, at its peak in the 1880s and early-1890s, became severed. In severe crises (e.g. the 1905 Ruhr coal strike), the state backed big employers with its policing, but explicitly ruled out any new Anti-Socialist Law or equivalent exceptional legislation. When the SPD and the Catholic Centre Party raised the cry of the "The Constitution in Danger" in the 1898 elections, both government and right-wing parties hastily withdrew.

Under ensuing conditions of the right's political weakness in the early 1900s Social Democrats had to be fought on their own terms – not with police measures and martial law, but at the ballot box, on the hustings, with the propaganda leaflet and via agitational campaigns, i.e. with words and paper, rather than truncheons, bullets and swords. Biggest impetus came from the SPD's post-1890 electoral advance, the post-1895 explosion of mass unionism, and the 1896 completion of the Code of Civil Law. There followed endless guerrilla skirmishing through the courts of law, whose signs historians invariably misread. Thus, in his close analysis of trade unions and the law, in an exhaustive empirical study of court records, Klaus Saul delivered an imposing indictment of class justice, state partisanship and judicial repression during the early 1900s. But on his own evidence, judicial rulings constantly pushed government into having to devise fresh expedients of legal chicanery in order to continue harassing the unions, and these years were certainly a time when the rule of law steadily constrained the latitude for arbitrary intervention against labour and civil rights.[7]

Under all of this pressure, the biggest employers fell back onto self-help, developing an impressive repertoire of tactics, including new shop-floor discipline; black lists of militants, agitators, union-joiners and other "trouble-makers"; labour exchanges; compulsory welfare schemes; company housing; nationally centralised employers' associations; company unions. Several things stand out in this new system of company-based authority:

- It was different from the older *Herr-im-Hause* system associated with the Saar heavy industrialist Carl Ferdinand von Stumm in the Bismarckian era, or the aristocratic mining estates of the Pless family in Upper Silesia, where direct physical violence was endemic.

- The new company paternalism was only feasible under benefit of the most advanced capitalist industry, including the highest levels of monopoly concentration, supplying the necessary resources of coordination and scale.
- The new system was common across the highly concentrated sectors, regardless of political affiliations. Indeed, it was Siemens, a self-consciously liberal employer in the more dynamic electro-technical sector with strong links to left liberalism, that *pioneered* the aggressively confrontational techniques of company or "yellow" unionism in a bitterly fought battle with the SPD Free Union in 1905.
- Finally, the political complement to the self-help strategy of company unions was the drive for an anti-democratic realignment of the so-called "bourgeois parties", a goal borne most clearly by the Imperial League Against Social Democracy launched in 1904. There was little consensus over how this might unfold, however, and it was only after 1910 that a strategy cohered.

These specific modalities of isolable and contained anti-labour violence were structured by those processes of political stabilisation inside parliamentary and electoral norms, which from the late-1890s steadily ordered violence in the polity at large. One vital dimension was a new practical ground of political civility. This was never entirely settled, sufficient or finished. And 1913–14 brought renewed signs that it might be breaking down – in renewed confrontational violence in strikes and other labour disputes, in growth of street protests and disorders, in extensions of policing and armed intervention, and in the radicalising of right-wing politics towards a possible coup. But the true rupture – the violent breach from those developing norms of civility – came in 1918–19.

In *Die Geächteten* (The Outlaws), published at the outset of this crisis in 1930 as a fictionalised memoir of his anti-Bolshevik exploits as a teenager in a *Freikorps* unit in the Baltic in 1919, Ernst von Salomon captured this new fascist sensibility:

> We ran over fields of snow and stormed into the forests. We fired into surprised crowds and we raged, we shot and hunted. We chased the Latvians like rabbits over the fields, we burnt every house and destroyed every bridge and every telegraph mast. We flung the bodies into fountains and threw hand grenades on top. We slaughtered whoever fell into our hands; we burned whatever would catch fire. . . . There were no human feelings left in our hearts. . . . A giant smoke trail marked our path. We had set fire to the stake where we burnt. . . . *the bourgeois tablets, the laws and values of the civilized world.*[8]

Notes

1 Here I proceed from the succinct helpfulness of Raymond Williams, *Keywords: A Vocabulary of Culture and Society*, rev. ed. (New York: Oxford University Press, 1983), 329–31.

2 See Gyanendra Pandey, *Routine Violence: Nations, Fragments, Histories* (Stanford, CA: Stanford University Press, 2006), 5. He continues: "The routinization of violence occurs . . .

not only in the unashamed display of spectacular and brutal acts of aggression, nor yet in the mundane, banal, everyday exercise of power over women and children, politically disadvantaged communities, and the poor. It occurs also in the construction and naturalization of particular categories of thought, in history, and in politics". Ibid., 15.

3 Alf Lüdtke, *Police and State in Prussia, 1815–1850* (Cambridge: Cambridge University Press, 1989); also "The Role of State Violence in the Period of Transition to Industrial Capitalism: The Example of Prussia from 1815 to 1848," *Social History*, 4, no. 2 (1979): 175–221; "The State and Social Domination in Eighteenth and Nineteenth-Century Prussia," in *People's History and Socialist Theory*, ed. Raphael Samuel (London: Routledge, 1981), 98–105. Also, Craig Calhoun, "For the Social History of the Present: Bourdieu as Historical Sociologist," in *Bourdieu and Historical Analysis*, ed. Philip S. Gorski (Durham, NC: Duke University Press, 2013), esp. 41–8.

4 See here Michael Taussig's classic article, "Culture of Terror – Space of Death: Roger Casement's Putumayo Report and the Explanation of Torture," *Comparative Studies in Society and History* 26, no. 3 (1984): 467–97; *States of Violence*, ed. Fernando Coronil and Julie Skurski (Ann Arbor: University of Michigan Press, 2006).

5 I developed this threefold categorization in Geoff Eley, *Forging Democracy: The History of the Left in Europe, 1850–2000* (New York: Oxford University Press, 2002).

6 See Thomas G. Andrews, *Killing for Coal: America's Deadliest Labor War* (Cambridge, MA: Harvard University Press, 2008).

7 Klaus Saul, *Staat, Industrie und Arbeiterbewegiung im Kaiserreich. Zur Innen- und Sozialpolitik des Wilhelminischen Deutschland, 1903–1914* (Düsseldorf: Droste Verlag, 1974), 188–282.

8 Robert Gerwarth, "The Central European Counter-Revolution: Paramilitary Violence in Germany, Austria and Hungary after the Great War," *Past and Present*, 200 (2008): 196.

1 Introduction

Strikebreaking and industrial vigilantism as a historical problem*

Matteo Millan and Alessandro Saluppo

American historian Warren B. Catlin wrote in 1926,

> If it be true that the history of nations has been too largely taken up with warfare and the remembrance of these struggles has served to perpetuate animosity from generation to generation, doubtless the same might be said to have been the effect of the prominence given to strikes, lockouts, and boycotts in the popular discussion of labor activities.[1]

In the late nineteenth and early twentieth centuries, Europe, the United States and large areas of the globe experienced labour unrest and multiple strike waves at an unprecedented pace and intensity, some of which developed a quasi-revolutionary momentum. From the bitter conflicts of the pre-war period, through the epochal tremors of war and revolution, to the violent spasms of the 1920s and 1930s, a sense of impending cataclysm, symbiotically associated with fears of revolutionary upheaval and forebodings of social anarchy, ceaselessly haunted those who had assumed the role of guardians of the established order. While much work has been devoted to socialist parties and revolutionary organisations, the multifaceted experiences of anti-labour mobilisation and privately organised coercion have not received the same degree of scholarly attention.

As Martin Conway explains in his contribution to this volume, several reasons concur to explain this neglect. There is, first of all, a material problem due to the lack or scarcity of sources. Actors, ranging from employer associations to corporate security and commercial strikebreaking services, have tended to be very protective of their archives or have left few papers behind. This paucity of records, however, is in significant contrast to the important role these actors played in social conflicts. Many years ago, Charles Tilly invited historians to consider the plurality of actors involved in strikes: not only workers and employers, but also local and regional authorities, bystanders and civil and military powers, including "private police", since it is "the relationship of workers to other groups [that] determines the frequency and character of collective conflict".[2] Tilly's invitation has not always been taken up in the field of labour history. As it turns out, historians have generally explained the repressive strategies of both employers and governments as merely Pavlovian responses to the maturation of socialist organisations. This also implies a sort of automatic identification of those workers organised by left-wing trade unions, parties and associations with the *whole* of the working class. As a consequence, independent and company unions, non-socialist associations as well as strikebreakers and "scabs" were usually out of the general picture or, at best, received little attention.

Studies on the topic have also been limited by the fact that "the boundaries of the nation-state" often turned into "an analytical cage".[3] In spite of global interdependencies and the transferability of social-political experiences that increasingly bound the fate of industrialised and industrialising countries, research on the methods by which the business and propertied classes attempted to solve the "labour problem" has relied on accounts that have rarely broken through the permeability of national boundaries.[4] The result has often been that national singularities were taken for granted and even exalted, as in the exemplary case of the supposed authoritarian paternalism characteristic of the equally suppositious backward, feudal-like attitudes of German employers.[5] In contrast, we hope that the comparative angle adopted here may contribute to defusing such apparent national particularities and to outlining how and to what extent coordinated anti-union and anti-strike strategies constituted a common repertoire of action across different countries.

Analyses of industrial conflict have, furthermore, tended to focus on the cores of capitalist development, deemed to be comprehensive and paradigmatic examples, with the consequent marginalisation and downplaying of the structural tensions between work, technology and authority in other parts of the world besides North America and Europe. At the same time, the narrative field has too often been restricted to specific industrial sectors or individual companies. This means that, with few exceptions, little attention has been paid to the complex realities of labour disciplining in imperial and trans-imperial settings as well as in secondary markets and industries. At its worst, research has depicted the development of industrial vigilantism, commercial strikebreaking and labour espionage as a uniquely American experience. To be sure, some of the anti-labour strategies and weapons used by employers and managers in the industrial heartlands of the United States still display "archetypical features".[6] Yet, this does not presuppose that company police systems and cases of para-policing explicitly geared towards counteracting strike action did not exist in Europe and the rest of the world. It would be sufficient to consider the extent of cross-national commonalities in the lexicon applied by trade unionists to anti-labour methods and weapons to refute the postulate of American exceptionalism.[7]

In particular, one of the characterising features usually attributed to the American way of dealing with strikes, namely citizen vigilance and vigilantism, has rarely been investigated outside the United States. Apart from "yellow unionism", historiography has regularly overlooked exploration of "the labour problem" from the point of view of the public. Notably, the more or less spontaneous mobilisation of citizens with the aim of protecting the general welfare of the people from the disruptive effects of protracted labour stoppages has not received the consideration it might have deserved. This has led to a lack of reflection on the slippery relationship between visions of "patriotic or responsible citizenship" and the rhetoric of belonging and exclusion. At the same time, this interaction has lured historians into the teleological categorisation of pre-war anti-socialist and anti-union movements as precursors of fascism.[8] All these factors have converged into a broad underestimation of strikebreaking and yellow unionism. More importantly, these issues have rarely been considered as topics in their own right and, consequently, subject to very little comparison, contrast and cross-examination.

Previous investigations into strikebreaking activities on the part of both governments and employers in the period in question have generally been contained within the traditional boundaries of labour history and the history of industrial relations.[9] In mapping out the changing relationships between labour, capital and the state, researchers have seldom touched upon the issue of "yellow unionism" or, broadly speaking, those organisations of workers – normally established and subsidised by employers or groups of employers – who acted against trade union interests and endeavours. The lack of scholarly scrutiny into these formations has hampered detailed sociological and sociographic research on strikebreakers and, in turn, deflected questions over the place of gender, race and religion into the rifts of class solidarity and the morose landscapes of class antagonism.

The first goal of the following pages is to highlight the forgotten dynamics of "the other side of the revolutionary coin". By bringing together scholars with expertise across a broad geographical and chronological range, this book constitutes the first systematic attempt to understand the political, economic, social, cultural and legal dimensions of strikebreaking and repressive anti-union practices in the decades from the 1890s to the 1930s. Adopting a comparative and transnational perspective, the chapters in this volume reconstruct the diverse spectrum of right-wing patriotic leagues, paramilitaries, vigilantes and para-police corps, and the vast array of private security services that, in support of or in competition with law enforcement agencies, sought to counter the dual dangers of industrial militancy and revolutionary situations. They retrace the formation of an extensive market in corporate policing, privately contracted security services and yellow unionism, as well as processes of professionalisation in strikebreaking activities, labour espionage and surveillance. They also detail the emergence of transnational networks and international cartels of employers that aimed to fight trade unionism by creating their own security apparatuses or by delegating protection services to third parties. The book focuses on the organisation and evolution of these private bodies, which attempted to make inroads into the state monopoly of force. In this way, the volume adds a new dimension to our understanding of the processes of alteration, deformation or fragmentation of public order and labour relations in periods of severe political and social tensions. It also offers an important new perspective on the shocks and strains that marked industrial societies during their turbulent transition to mass politics.

****

The rise of working-class parties, trade unions and organisations after the 1880s tested different nation states and empires across the globe to unprecedented levels. Qualitative leaps in the organisation of labour movements and the increasing influence of Marxism were regularly accompanied by major outbreaks of social conflict, large numbers of strikes and industrial restructuring.[10] These largely novel challenges prompted a wide array of organised responses, from both state authorities and employers: the first part of this volume, therefore, is devoted to the various anti-union and strikebreaking strategies adopted by the preservers of order and property to deal with the social question.

Most autocratic regimes of Europe were not unscathed by the mobilisation and organisation of workers. In the semi-absolutist tsarist empire, as Volodymyr Kulikov and Irina Shilnikova argue in their "Policies and practices against labour movement in the late Russian empire", the state's attitudes and policies on labour were persistently shaped by intense worries over social control. Unlike their counterparts in Wilhelmine Germany and Habsburg Austria, the Russian governing classes prevented working-class organisations from gaining a foothold in political life and industry. Under these conditions, the development of collective workers' organisations, especially in the Stolypin years (1906–11), was systematically thwarted by the combined repressive action of the state and industrialists. Radicalised by the war, workers' despair found an explosive outlet in the proletarian-socialist revolution of 1917.

At the opposite end of the continent, Spain and Portugal were also experiencing deep political and economic transformations, which greatly affected the established balances. Assumpta Castillo Cañiz's chapter, "Violence against strikers in the rural peripheries of the Iberian Peninsula, 1890s–1915", explores the nature of anti-strike violence in three labour disputes that took place in rural areas of Spain and Portugal between the late nineteenth and early twentieth century. These conflicts shed light on how deep socio-economic and political transformations sparked violent new forms of conflict in the "double periphery" of the rural Iberian Peninsula. The consolidation of capitalism in rural areas brought with it a process of agricultural specialisation, the decentralisation of production and inter-regional interlinking of transport and energy infrastructures, as well as an increase in the mobility of the working population. At the same time, the countryside, in dynamic interaction with economic mutations, began to penetrate into the political space, in particular through the extension of suffrage and union rights. This dual process showed how the rural situation was not alien to the violent contradictions that had already manifested themselves in industrial urban areas. In all the cases examined, violence against striking workers was carried out by a mixture of public and private forces, which ranged from military and police forces to antiquated local private forces. The analysis raises questions about the strength of the state in both countries and the effectiveness of their coercive mechanisms to overcome new internal challenges.

In countries where labour parties and voters had grown sufficiently to exert influence on government policy and legislation, state authorities acted or, at least professed to act, as an impartial third-party arbitrator between employers and employees. On the one hand, recourse to repressive and malignant measures was justified to enforce public order, especially where the strikes involved public services or affected strategic economic sectors. On the other hand, the extension of the franchise, the development of mass party politics, the huge increase in union membership and, more generally, mass society meant that the use of repressive methods would have costly political consequences. The ability to strike a balance between defending order and production and protecting individual and collective rights became the means by which the wider population could measure the legitimacy and credibility of many liberal regimes. In France, in the years 1902–06, troops were mobilised "on a very large scale" to maintain public order during major labour stoppages, although this was always carefully planned to avoid bloodshed and disparage the "honour" of the Army.[11] In Britain, progress in the demilitarisation of public order suffered a dramatic setback when the government brought in over 58,000 troops to cope with the national railway strike of 1911.[12] In Sweden, as Erik Bengtsson demonstrates in his chapter, "The Swedish labour market c. 1870–1914: a labour market regime without repression?", the state was less forbearing towards the labour movement than historians have assumed so far. While it is highly disputable whether the liberal policy of gradual concessions to the working class lowered the potential for violent protest, legislative restrictions on trade unionism action continued. The 1899 Åkarp Law, for instance, penalised any attempt by strikers to coerce non-strikers into joining the strike or to prevent them from going to work and back. During the general strike of 1909, the government's premeditated passiveness played an important role in the disastrous defeat of the labour movement, as a consequence of which membership of the *Landsorganisation i Sverige* plunged to 80,000 by 1912. In several instances, troops were ordered out to protect strikebreakers and property. Little or no blood, however, was spilled until the Ådalen shootings in 1931. This apparently less violent nature of industrial confrontations distinguished Sweden from other continental countries.

In the recently founded German Kaiserreich, the 1878 *Sozialistengesetz* (anti-Socialist law) anaesthetised the labour movement for 12 years. When it lapsed, the growth of social-democratic organisation, fuelled by industrialisation and urbanisation, appeared to be unstoppable. The socialist union movement continued to be subject to political and administrative ostracism in several state legislatures, judicial discrimination and police harassment until 1914.[13] Nevertheless, on the eve of the Great War, the vigorous growth of the social democrats was such as to fuel projects for extra-parliamentary actions aimed at reforming the constitution.[14] In Austria-Hungary, too, the state's response to the rise of labour organisation was shaped by tensions between mere repression and the integration of the working classes into the political nation. In her chapter, "State authorities, municipal forces, and military intervention in the policing of strikes in Austria-Hungary, 1890s–1914", Claire Morelon examines the different types of state intervention during strikes in the Austrian part of the Habsburg Empire. The increased numbers of social conflicts from the 1880s onwards often pushed the overstretched local security forces to the limits. Police forces in most towns (except the larger cities) were still paid by the municipality and were answerable to the mayor. Local governors could only call the gendarmerie and ask for army intervention if the local forces were not sufficient to maintain order. Based on her examination of the different strategies adopted to quell strikes and the deployment of military unions to replace striking workers, Morelon argues that the Austrian economy and politics became increasingly militarised in the years immediately before the outbreak of the war.

Extending from the 1870s through to the post-war years, qualitative transformations in working-class organisation, ideological orientations and policies had regularly summoned proportionate (and frequently disproportionate) responses from owners and managerial elites around the industrial world.[15] As the secretary of the Italian Minister of Agriculture, Industry and Trade wrote in 1912, "the employers' organisations come from those of the workers. . . . These are two forces tied to a single life from two opposite poles, around a single fact: the class struggle".[16] The French economist Charles Gide invited French employers to organise themselves into strong associations in order to establish "armed peace" in accordance with the slogan "*si vis pacem para bellum*".[17] In his 1922 essay on organised capital in the United States, American historian F.W. Hilbert noted that "Employers' associations formed solely for the purpose of dealing collectively with labor, come into existence only after organizations of employees have become strong enough".[18] Associations, such as *the National Association of Manufacturers, the National Metal Trades Association, the National Founders Association, the National Erectors' Association and the International Association of Bridge and Structural Ironworkers*, were all formed at the end of the nineteenth century to protect the "open shop" from the assault of industrial unionism.[19] In Britain, the rise of New Unionism had similarly precipitated the formation of militant employer organisations and federations. The Shipping Federation, established in September 1890, was specifically envisioned by the large shipping companies as a "permanent battle-axe" in the fight against the rapid growth and militancy of maritime labour.[20] In Wilhelmine Germany, the development of employers' organisations accelerated only at the beginning of the twentieth century, when the rapid expansion of the trade union organisation prompted manufacturers to coalesce into the *Hauptstelle der Deutschen Arbeitgeberverbände* (Central Confederation of German Employers' Associations) and the *Verein Deutscher Arbeitgeberverbände* (Federation of German Employers' Associations). The initial aims of these counter-organisations, which later merged to become the *Vereinigung der Deutschen Arbeitgeberverbände* (Union of German Employers' Associations) were to fight trade union policies and oppose any outside interference in proprietorial prerogatives.[21]

In France, despite some early initiatives, such as the *Comité des Forges*, established as early as 1864, the small average size of enterprises probably slowed down the reaction of employers to the wave of labour protests that affected almost all regions and industries between 1900 and 1913. Certainly, initiatives such as the *Union des industries métallurgiques et minières* (1901), which involved big industrialists (most notably Eugène Schneider II), the *Comité Central des Armateurs de France* (1907) and the establishment of shop keepers' and small merchants' pressure groups were signs of a growing militancy by capital.[22] As of

1908, however, the methods of collective self-defence put in place to counteract strike action were mostly imitations of foreign models.[23]

Also in Italy where, at the beginning of the twentieth century, 59.8 per cent of the population was still employed in agriculture, industrialists had to take steps to centralise their response to trade unionism and Giovanni Giolitti's new-fangled policy of state neutrality in labour disputes. In 1910, this process culminated in the creation of the *Confederazione Italiana dell'Industria*. In rural areas, particularly the Po Valley, pre-war landowners' associations, like the *Interprovinciale* and the *Confederazione Nazionale Agraria*, ferociously opposed the Federation of agricultural labourers (*Federterra*) and proved especially successful in defeating strikes.[24]

In Catalonia, traditional cultural and technical clubs for the promotion of economic development, such as the *Fomento Nacional de Trabajo* and the *Instituto Agrícola Catalán de San Isidro*, paved the way for more antagonistic and resolutely centralised employers' associations, most notably the *Confederación Patronal Española* (1914), which coordinated the actions of several local employers' organisations and made arrangements with political and military authorities to repress strikes and the actions of the working class. Among the more resolute members of the *Patronal* were those Catalan employers, like Eusebi Güell and Claudio Lopez Bru, 2nd Marquess of Comillas, who also controlled the powerful and long-established Catalan militia, *Somatén*, which took to the streets several times both before and after WWI in support of the police and the army against strikers and rioters.[25]

In tsarist Russia, inspired by the national centralisation of employers' organisations in Germany, the *St. Petersburg and Moscow Societies of Factory Owners* were established in conjunction with the intensive unionisation following on from the 1905 revolution. The purpose of the organisation, according to its organisers, was to oppose the "unreasonable aspirations" of the workers.[26] Even in the Nordic countries, the growth of trade unionism convinced employers to join forces. In Sweden, the *Landsorganisation i Sverige* (Federation of Trade Unions), which had forged a close alliance with the *Socialdemokratiska Arbetare-Partiet* (Social Democratic Labour Party) on its inception in 1890, was confronted by powerful employer organisations like the *Sveriges verkstadsföreningen* (Swedish Manufacturers' Association), *the Svenska Arbetsgivareföreningen* (The Swedish Employers' Association) and the *Centrala arbetsgivareförbundet* (The Central Federation of Employers). In Denmark, the *Danish Employers' Confederation*, in an impressive display of capitalist solidarity, proclaimed the 1899 lockout as a veritable "declaration of war".[27] During the First World War, in neutral Scandinavian countries the main employers' federations of Sweden, Norway and Denmark drew up an agreement that established an anti-strike mutual insurance plan that allowed employers involved in strikes or lockouts to claim benefits of up to 80,000 crowns per week for a maximum of five weeks.[28] The counter-mobilisation of capital was a truly global phenomenon. In Australia, employers' federations were established or reactivated in response to the arbitration legislation of 1901.[29] In New Zealand, "the country without strikes", as it was internationally renowned, at least until 1905, the first national federation of employers was founded in 1902.[30] In Argentina, too, at the end of the nineteenth century bodies of employers began to federate to resist unionism and force the state authorities into enforcing more repressive policies.[31]

An interesting aspect of the mushrooming of employers' associations throughout the world was their transnational nature. Remarkably, this period of history marked a distinctive phase of international cooperation among anti-labour organisations. This is not so obvious, as it implied that employers were ready to set aside patriotic interests and to refrain from taking competitive advantage over their global competitors. In other words, the social enemy became an acceptable common foe to the extent that the threat of it could override conflicting national interests and foster forms of capitalist solidarity. In his chapter, "Employers of the world, unite!: the transnational mobilisation of industrialists around World War I", Pierre Eichenberger traces the origins of the International Organisation of Industrial Employers (IOIE). Faced with the formation of international coalitions of labour and socialist parties, employers' organisations had, since the early years of the twentieth century, supported consultations, partnerships and the coordination of resources to deal with the "labour problem" at home and abroad. In the convulsive post-war years these desires for international solidarity among producers gave rise to the IOIE. The scope of this body, founded in 1920, shortly after the Washington Treaty, was to represent and defend the interests of employers' organisations in the governing body and at the general conferences of the International Labour Office. The IOIE, whose early membership included the diplomatically isolated Germany and Austria, was the only organisation of its kind in the interwar period.

As a result of unique economic and logistical characteristics, transnational cooperation among employers and the coordination of strikebreaking strategies were conspicuous in the maritime sector.[32] Shipowners had long recognised the high degree of global interdependence in the maritime industry, which meant that the disruption of labour in one seaport inexorably reverberated in others. These conditions of vulnerability had been spectacularly proven by the cluster of maritime strikes that had cyclically swept through the Atlantic ports from 1889 onwards. Predictably enough, the shipowners were among the prime proponents and movers of the international employers' associations. In 1909, an international cartel of shipowners' federations, which included the *Shipping Federation*, the *Federation Maritime d'Anvers*, the *Sveriges Redareforening*, the *Dampfskibsreederei Foreningen*, the *Zentralverein Deutscher Rheder* and the *Nederlandsche Reedersvereentging*, established the *International Shipping Federation* (ISF). The principal scope of this body was to fight the trade union organisation and to break strikes, but its development was halted by the outbreak of war.[33] In the shipping industry, however, high levels of conflict were ingrained. By 1929, the great ports on the Atlantic and Gulf coasts of the United States still displayed "the same chaotic and tragic spectacle" as in the past.[34]

Institutional responses from governments, firms and business organisations formed only one facet of the opposition to rising working-class organisations.

The employers' need to maintain production, protect company property and deny the right of collective bargaining created a profitable market for commercial anti-union activities. In light of this, the second section of the volume is devoted to a multifaceted analysis of various strikebreaking tactics and practices, ranging from the recruitment of blacklegs along maritime routes to innovative forms of cooperation between state and private actors.

The huge disparity between the supply and demand of labour had given shipowners across the world considerable power in resisting union pressure to run a closed shop and enact protective legislation for seafarers. In those days of expanding global interconnectedness and transnational alliances in both capital and labour, class struggle transcended the confines of the nation state, powerfully intersecting with ethnic and religious identities. Drawing on research into the *Messageries Maritimes*, Charles Bégué Fawell demonstrated how France's shipping lines outmanoeuvred workers by taking advantage of the interstices between imperial governance and the exchange of global labour. The success of the shipowners and the preservation of harmonious labour relations at sea relied on a variety of anti-labour weapons and tactics, including the systemic turnover of the workforce and the manipulation of racial cleavages. As Prerna Agarwal shows in her chapter, "In the name of constitutionalism and Islam: the murky world of labour politics in Calcutta's docklands", such *divide et impera* strategies were common practices in imperial spaces for a long time. Agarwal's contribution describes how a powerful coalition of political, business and criminal interests was behind the formation of the "black-flag" *Calcutta Dockers' Union* (CDU). The organisation was expressly designated to countermand red propaganda in the port of Calcutta. When the *Calcutta Port and Dock Workers' Union* (CPDWU), affiliated to the Communist Party of India, was made illegal after the strike of 1934, shipping companies instantly recognised the CDU as the exclusive bargaining representative.

The maritime sector is a paradigmatic example of how strikebreaking dynamics worked. Nevertheless, as many chapters in this volume show, a basic law of strikebreaking applying to a wide array of sectors is identifiable: work replacement was more successful wherever workers could be easily replaced, namely in those sectors that required little or no skill from the workforce. Wherever unskilled workers predominated, a strike could only be won by mobilising the entire workforce and preventing the arrival of replacement workers. This posed huge challenges and required tremendous organisational efforts by union leaders. In very few situations was this possible, and it was often at a cost of rocketing tensions and extremely bitter confrontations, as clearly shown by events in the ports of Europe. Another paradigmatic case is that of the day labourers in Italy's Po Valley. There, socialist labour leaders were able to organise several thousands of unskilled workers in a vast network of unions, co-operatives and associations, as well as by exerting social pressure and employing coercive methods.[35]

It is no surprise, then, that in many trades that had originally relied on a skilled workforce, employers made significant efforts to increase productivity and tighten labour discipline by deskilling production, introducing piecework wages and other performance-based compensation schemes. The introduction of new organisational and technological systems magnified fears of displacement and unemployment, in particular among craftsmen. The establishment of temporary devices to stabilise employment by limiting the maximum output of the machines or regulating the way they were used proved unworkable in the long run. The reconfiguration of production and manufacturing processes gave employers an additional advantage against unions, as it significantly facilitated use of the "most formidable" anti-strike weapon: the recruitment of blacklegs.[36] Thanasis Betas, in his "Cairo, Athens, Salonica: strikebreaking and anti-labour practices of employers and the state in the early twentieth-century cigarette industry", shows that processes of labour casualisation and subcontracting also encompassed the peripheries of capitalist development. In the tobacco industries, the decision of Greek manufacturers to replace manual with machine production led to violent struggles not only between employers and employees, but also between skilled and unskilled female and juvenile labour. The sabotaging, breaking or disabling of casing machines or revolving steam boxes by workers was regularly met with severe police repression.

Anti-labour practices certainly benefitted from increased cross-border labour mobility and large emigration flows. Employers refusing to meet unions' demands for better wages, improved employment conditions or simply recognition could secure labour from other regions or countries. While the traditional stereotyping of foreign or immigrant workers as wage depressors or strikebreakers is misleading – labour migrants in fact played a prominent role in the worldwide surge in socialist organisation – there were numerous reported instances of employers importing large numbers of foreign strikebreakers during strikes. Portuguese workers were brought into Spanish Galicia to break a strike in the building sector in 1895,[37] while British shipowners were able to import labour from Sweden and the Netherlands in the 1893 Hull Dock Strike.[38] Thousands of Belgian workers were brought into the coal mines in the Pas-de-Calais region in the general strike of 1892.[39] Similarly, German employers regularly exploited cheap labour reservoirs in neighbouring Polish, Czech and Austrian territories.[40] In the United States, employers routinely recruited "scabs" from large reserves of cheap immigrant labour. It comes as no surprise, then, that the terminology used to define strikebreakers had obvious racist overtones. In common Italian parlance, labour replacements were referred to as "krumiri", with reference to a north African nomadic tribe. In France, they were sometimes called "bédouine", while "blacklegs" (or simply "blacks") was the term that British workers gave to those workers who had taken anti-trade union action or helped break a strike.[41] In America, deplorable ethnic slurs, such as "Wop", "Dago" or "Greaser", designated foreign-born American workers.[42]

Of course, besides transnational cooperation and cross-national labour strategies, employers devised a variety of comprehensive strikebreaking techniques. Importing strikebreakers from distant regions or even from abroad would have been insufficient. Apart from in the maritime sector, this option was subject to global conditions and usually proved costly and logistically demanding, so employers had first of all to find their own scabs locally. Nearly everywhere, employers played a direct role in hiring labour replacements in anticipation of or during strikes. In several cases, large companies decided to establish artificial unions in order to have a permanent (or insulated) reserve of labour in case of dispute and to undermine the solidarity and strength of the labour organisation. These bodies were variously known as "company unions", "household unions", "peaceful unions", "tame unions" or "yellows". However, while in the United States, the term "yellow" was largely used to describe bogus unions, in Europe it broadly included those unions that opposed socialist or class struggle principles and opportunistically promoted harmonious relations between employers and wage earners.[43] These unions of non-unionists gave employers the possibility to outsource the cumbersome tasks of recruiting, supplying and even protecting labour replacements to third parties and thus relieve themselves of costly legal liabilities. Not surprisingly, they found fertile soil in industries overfed by casual labour and chronic underemployment. In Britain, the National Free Labour Association (NFLA) first served the interests of shipowners and then, from the early twentieth century onwards, those of the railway companies. Founded in 1893 by former omnibus driver and one-time union organiser William Collison, the NFLA maintained a network of free labour exchanges, which funnelled thousands of unskilled or semi-skilled non-union workmen into British industry until the First World War. Although this strikebreaking organisation was normally involved in small-scale disputes, it wound up playing a decisive role in the events which led to the Law Lords' momentous decision in the Taff Vale case.[44]

In France, the *Jaunes*, as George Mosse emphatically wrote years ago, "may well provide the most important example of a working class movement of the Right before the first word war".[45] Under the leadership of Pierre Biétry, the *Jaunes* professed anti-Marxist and anti-socialist views, asserting the organic notion of class collaboration (rather than class conflict) as an essential condition for the realisation of a rich and robust national future.[46] Local branches of the *Jaunes* were subsidised financially and supported materially by industrialists and employer associations, who provided Biétry's men not only with money, but also with guns and other weapons. In exchange, the *Jaunes* took on the role of action squads to intimidate local union leaders and provoked violent incidents. This was the case in 1905 when Alexander Dreux, director of the *Comptoir métallurgique of Longwy*, subsidised Biétry and other *Jaunes* to intimidate the leader of the local socialist unions; Dreux also tried to supply the *Jaunes* with two cases of weapons, including war rifles and guns.[47]

In spite of the strong nationalist character of the *Jaunes*, their leadership – and their supporters – tried to establish international alliances based on common anti-socialist and anti-democratic cooperation around Europe. Relationships were established with employers and politicians in Switzerland and Germany, and from there French-inspired yellow unionism spread to Austria-Hungary.[48] In the aftermath of the revolutionary events of 1905–06, Biétry had already attempted, apparently with little success, to set up unions on the model of the *Jaunes* in Imperial Russia.[49]

The tsarist empire provided a particularly favourable environment for such coercive endeavours. In what was the most backward of the major European powers, anti-strike forces amongst Russian nationalists had mobilised in response to the appearance of mass-based labour organisations and popular protest, which spread first in the industrial cities and then in the vast countryside at the turn of the century. George Gilbert's chapter, "In Reaction to Revolution: anti-strike mentalities and practices in the Russian radical right, 1905–14", investigates the ideas, worldviews and types of action engaged in by the Union of the Russian People (URP) and the other right-wing bodies that emerged across the Empire to "actively oppose" labour protest. Far from being compliant forces created at the behest of Russian governance, they were driven mostly by their own desires to restore Russia to what they perceived as a time of order in contrast to the contemporary realities of unrest and conflict.

Besides creating complacent yellow unions, another option was to turn to professional union busters. The hostile attitude of American employers to trade unionism generated a vast market for investigative, private security and commercialised strikebreaking services. In September 1914, over 270 detective agencies were still assisting employers involved in strikes and lockouts.[50] This impetus towards delegating policing functions to private bodies and developing strikebreaking into a distinct occupation did not only concern America. In Europe, attempts at emulating the strikebreaking businesses of Pinkerton, Farley and Baldwin-Felts became a quasi-instinctive response of employers to the sudden strengthening of labour organisation. Amerigo Caruso, in his "We can kill striking workers without being prosecuted': armed bands of strikebreakers in late Imperial Germany", traces the forgotten stories of professional anti-strike organisations in Wilhelmine Germany. In response to the intensification of labour militancy, the most intransigent sectors of German capital resolved to arm strikebreakers and recruit "anti-strike gunfighters". Resort to strikebreaking provided an unanticipated pathway for professional criminals and men with violent reputations into legitimate industrial conflicts. By taking a micro-historical approach, his chapter explores the activities of Friedrich Hintze's band and the ill-famed strikebreaker agent Karl Katzmarek. Not infrequently, these gangs of armed strikebreakers benefitted from the support of conservative and right-wing nationalist politicians and the overt connivance of police forces.

Sometimes, however, employers and conservative parts of the "consuming public" did not simply rely on subcontracting to suppliers of strikebreakers and specialised agencies. They felt they needed to intervene directly in the repression of social unrest in order to defend private property and a social order they perceived as being in peril. This gave rise to a variety of forms of self-mobilisation by entrepreneurs and patriotic middle classes, which usually acquired violent overtones. These corps usually had controversial relationships with the legitimate holders of the monopoly of force. The third and last section of the volume, therefore, is devoted to examination of a few case studies which illustrate the complex hybridisation of private interventions in traditionally public domains.

In their chapter, "The wild west of employer anti-unionism: the glorification of vigilantism and individualism in the early twentieth-century United States", Vilja Hulden and Chad Pearson describe how employers' organisations drew on the practices and imaginaries of frontier vigilantism to praise those employers and workers who took the law into their own hands for the purpose of protecting individual freedom, private property and freedom of contract from trade union policies and methods. The chapter pays special attention to the organisation and media strategies, which included the publicity work of the writer of Western novels, Owen Winster, that were carried out by the Citizens' Industrial Association of America (CIAA) in its efforts to forestall any infringement of the "open shop". In southern Italy, landowners benefitted from the services of rural guards and other hybrid groups to enforce order, discipline and respect for their authority in their estates.[51] According to socialist accounts, semi-criminals and young thugs were recruited by capitalist leaseholders of the Po Valley to provoke members of socialist unions and to intimidate strikers.[52] French mining conglomerates also had recourse to illegal methods of control over workers by raising vigilante squads for labour espionage. For example, the *Bande à Patin*, a sort of private police, allowed the manager of the Blanzy mines, Léonce Chagot, to keep strict surveillance over employees, avert infiltration from left-wing unions and prevent strikes and conflicts within the premises of his company. The *Bande* collected information on the moral attitudes, political inclinations and religious beliefs of every individual employee, filling thousands of secret personal files. They also intimidated and threatened workers during local and national elections to ensure the results went in favour of the candidates supported by the company.[53]

In the midst of the processes of democratisation and its ruthless opposition, the issue of strikebreaking easily overstepped the boundaries of economic interest to erupt right at the very heart of the idea of citizenship. In 1913, the British-born American socialist writer, John Spargo, wrote in his critique on revolutionary syndicalism that "[s]o long as there exists sufficient armed force to preserve the essentials of public order, the middle class in every country has sufficient skill and power to prevent the complete paralysis of society". Spargo cited the example of upper and middle class Swedish citizens who volunteered for the *Frivilliga Skyddskåren* – the Public Security Brigade – to provide water, light, transport and sanitation services during the Great Strike of 1909.[54] The "Swedish experiment" attracted considerable attention in the United Kingdom, where even the prestigious *Times of London* advocated emulating it. After the transport strikes of 1911, "civic strikebreaking" turned into reality when a myriad of volunteer organisations rose up with the intent of assisting the authorities and securing the maintenance of indispensable services and supplies. Preeminent among these anti-labour bodies was the London-based Volunteer Police Force (VPF). In his chapter, "Vigilant citizens: the case of the Volunteer Police Force, 1911–14", Alessandro Saluppo reconstructs the origins, organisation and operations of this quasi-military organisation, whose purpose was to protect life, liberty and property from strike violence. The opposition of the Liberal government to increasing vigilante behaviours prevented the VPF from effectively carrying out its programme. The experience of the VPF serves to reveal the overt propensity of upper and middle classes to take defensive action in the years of the "Great Unrest".

In the post-war years, the spectre of a general strike and the fear of Soviet contagion spread across Europe and the wider world[55] and contributed to the rise of new, sophisticated forms of strikebreaking. The revival of private participation in policing strikes and the taking to the streets against supposed revolutionary threats was common to both defeated and victorious countries. Already during the war, the US government had invited private citizens to be vigilant, which resulted in the mushrooming of vigilante and surveillance groups. On mining company properties or in isolated estates, in particular, ultra-diligent citizens, who believed they were defending the Constitution and enforcing law and order, took up arms and contributed to the repression of social disturbance.[56] In Germany, in response to the quasi-revolutionary events of 1919, a largely spontaneous multitude of "defence organisations" and auxiliary militias emerged to repress strikes and social upheavals and to keep public services running. Groups like the *Einwohnerwehren* attracted hundreds of thousands of volunteers and soon acquired the semblance of a real paramilitary corps. Their aim was not simply to police industrial unrest but also to oppose Bolshevism, repress criminality and foster national cohesion. The main purpose of the *Technische Nothilfe* (Technical Emergency Corps), which was under the jurisdiction of the Ministry of Defence, was to keep operating essential public services during major strikes, ensure a modicum of productive continuity and to assist authorities in case of emergency, fire, storms and other natural disasters.[57] In Spain, the fear provoked by some huge strikes, especially in Catalonia, prompted brutal repression, in which criminal gangs and civilian militias, such as the *Somatén*, cooperated with military authorities and police forces. This sparked a vortex of violence and terrorism which became known as the age of *pistolerismo*.[58] In Britain, the renewal of industrial militancy and the bugbear that was the Triple Alliance of dockers, railwaymen and miners prompted the government to form an extensive strikebreaking apparatus. "An *embarrass de richesse* of volunteers" flooded the specialist committees of the Supply and Transport Organisation (STO) to lend their services and skills at each labour crisis. Notably, this body helped to break the General Strike of 1926.[59] In France, "good citizens" responded enthusiastically to government invitations to cooperate in the repression of social disturbances and strikes. The purpose of the *Unions Civiques* was to gather together civilian volunteers and, under the strict supervision and control of government authorities and prefects, keep the railways and public services running.[60] While the mobilisation of French urban middle and lower middle classes largely resulted in a patriotic, anti-revolutionary effort which strengthened the government's legitimacy, in Italy the situation took quite the opposite turn. There, the government's reliance on "loyal citizens" to defeat industrial action had never been so unambiguous as it was in the immediate post-war years. In his "From 'State Protection' to 'Private Defence': strikebreaking, civilian armed mobilisation and the rise of Italian fascism", Matteo Millan analyses how a combination of the government's efforts to foster civilian cooperation in strikebreaking and the largely spontaneous self-mobilisation of "good citizens" against the "red fear" contributed to irreparably jeopardising public order in the country. The limited legitimacy and contradictory attitudes of the Italian ruling elites opened a Pandora's box of clear anti-government attitudes and fuelled the emergence of a plethora of civilian militias and strikebreaking groups which ultimately became a favourable breeding ground for fascist mobilisation. At the same time, Millan's chapter shows how such post-war groups took inspiration and even legitimacy from much older forms of civilian mobilisation and points to significant continuities across the watershed of the Great War.

****

We started this introduction with historian W.B. Catlin, who, in 1926, urged his contemporaries to consider how not only wars and conflicts, but also "strikes, lockouts, and boycotts" contributed to perpetuating "animosity from generation to generation". In the end, we think that Catlin was right, and for various reasons.

What emerges from the cases presented here is that many of the social challenges which affected Europe and the wider world in the aftermath of the Great War had some similarities to or even found their precursors in the crucial decades between the 1880s and 1914. The relatively lengthy temporal focus of this book also allows us to map the strategies of states and employers as they sought to halt, or at least forestall, the advance of socialist movements. At times, overreaction to the "red threat" helped to escalate political and social crises and paved the way for the rise of fascist movements, which promised a "Third Way" between capital and labour. In most cases, coercive anti-labour practices gave way to strategies of corporate negotiation that minimised the risks of violence and usurpation of public authority. Certainly, this is not to underestimate the disruptive impact of war and revolution or to overstretch the search for historical continuities. However, drawing attention to the emergence and development of anti-labour militancy helps us trace the anxieties that occupied the minds of the governing classes, conservatives and business interests in a period marked by social turbulence, global wars and crises of capitalism. It is equally possible to retrace the ways in which these strategies were able to pass through the epochal watershed and were driven by long-term models based on previous experiences and shaped by enduring scripts. Many years ago, Charles Maier defined the corporatist agenda which characterised the "recasting of bourgeois Europe" after the Great War as being marked by "the growth of private power and the twilight of sovereignty".[61] From this volume's perspective, it appears that this transfer of power was a dream which already inhabited the minds of many employers during the Belle Époque. In this regard, additional research should be carried out to further investigate how industrial disputes, social conflicts and processes of social democratisation were intertwined with state collapse, revolutionary contagion and military defeat if we are to fully understand the unprecedented levels of paramilitary, political and ethnic violence which were a feature of Europe and global empires on the eve of the Great War.[62]

These are just a few examples of why we think strikebreaking is important, and not just as a minor erudite detail in traditional accounts of social and labour history. We are also aware that the volume is far from being exhaustive. Nevertheless, we hope that the chapters presented here may persuade readers of the potential of strikebreaking as a powerful tool with which to investigate broader questions. In fact, we think that study of the methods deployed by employers, state authorities and professional and amateur strikebreaking bodies to fight socialist political forces and trade unionism in the crucial decades from the 1890s to the 1930s has tremendous historiographical potential. We are happy that Martin Conway is able to illustrate some of them (along with many other things) in his conclusive remarks.

Notes

* This introduction has been discussed and devised together by the two co-editors. However, Alessandro Saluppo has realised the first part (approximately pages 1–8) while Matteo Millan worked on the last sections (approximately pages 9–16).

Research for this article received funding from the European Research Council (ERC) under the European Union's Horizon 2020 Research and Innovation program (G.A. 677199 – ERC-StG2015 "The Dark Side of the Belle Époque. Political Violence and Armed Associations in Europe before the First World War").

1 Warren Catlin, *The Labor Problem in the United States and Great Britain* (New York: Harper & Brothers, 1926), 516.

2 Charles Tilly, "Theories and Realities," in *Strikes, Wars and Revolutions in an International Perspective: Strike Waves in the Late Nineteenth and Early Twentieth Centuries*, ed. Leopold H. Haimson and Charles Tilly (Cambridge: Cambridge University Press, 1989), 11.

3 Daniel T. Rodgers, *Atlantic Crossings: Social Politics in a Progressive Age* (Cambridge, MA: Belknap Press of Harvard University Press, 1998), 2.

4 An early exception was Georgiy Georgievich Schwittau's *Die Formen des Wirtschaftlichen Kampfes (Streik, Boykott, Aussperrung u. s. w). Eine Volkswirtschaftliche Untersuchung auf dem Gebiete der Gegenwärtigen Arbeitspolitik* (Berlin: Julius Springer, 1912). Schwittau, at the time lecturer at the University of St. Petersburg, provided a general analysis of employer associations and their policies in a chapter titled "Die Organisation und die Politik der Arbeitgeber," 276–366.

5 See the classic criticism to such approach by David Blackbourn and Geoff Eley, *The Peculiarities of German History: Bourgeois Society and Politics in Nineteenth-Century Germany* (Oxford: Oxford University Press, 1984), 107–8.

6 The literature on strikebreaking in the United States is huge; see, among many others: Robert Weiss, "The Emergence and Transformation of Private Detective Industrial Policing in the United States, 1850–1940," *Crime and Social Justice*, no. 9 (1978): 35–48; Robert P. Weiss, "Private Detective Agencies and Labour Discipline in the United States, 1855–1946," *The Historical Journal* 29, no. 1 (1986): 87–107; J. L. Rosenbloom, "Strikebreaking and the Labor Market in the United States, 1881–1894," *Journal of Economic History* 58, no. 1 (1998): 183–205; Robert Michael Smith, *From Blackjacks to Briefcases: A History of Commercialized Strikebreaking and Unionbusting in the United States* (Athens, OH: Ohio University Press, 2003); Stephen H. Norwood, *Strikebreaking and Intimidation: Mercenaries and Masculinity in Twentieth-Century America* (Chapel Hill, NC: University of North Carolina Press, 2003); Christopher Joseph Nicodemus Capozzola, *Uncle Sam Wants You: World War I and the Making of the Modern American Citizen* (Oxford and New York: Oxford University Press, 2008), 117–43; Spencer J. Sadler, *Pennsylvania's Coal and Iron Police* (Charleston, SC: Arcadia Publishing, 2009); Rosemary Feurer and Chad Pearson, *Against Labor: How U.S. Employers Organized to Defeat Union Activism* (Urbana: University of Illinois Press, 2017).

7 Matteo Millan, "Strikebreaking during Europe's Belle Époque," *European History Quarterly* 49, no. 4 (2019): 553–69.
8 See, among others, Zeev Sternhell, *La Droite Révolutionnaire, 1885–1914: Les Origines Françaises du Fascisme*, 2nd ed. (Paris: Fayard, 2000).
9 See, for example, Geoffrey Alderman, "The National Free Labour Association. A Case-Study of Organised Strikebreaking in the Late Nineteenth and Early Twentieth Century," *International Review of Social History*, no. 21 (1976): 309–36. Edward J. Bristow, "The Defence of Liberty and Property in Britain, 1880–1914" (PhD thesis, Yale University, 1970), 229–59.
10 For longue durée comparative analyses of workers' collective action, see Beverly J. Silver, "Class Struggle and Kondratieff Waves, 1870 to the Present," in *New Findings in Long Wave Research*, ed. Alfred Kleinknecht, Ernest Mandel and Immanuel Wallerstein (New York: St. Martin's Press, 1992), 279–96; Research Working Group on World Labor, "Global Patterns of Labor Movements in Historical Perspective," *Review* 10, no. 1 (Summer 1986): 137–55. Limitedly to France, Germany and Great Britain, see Friedhelm Boll, "International Strike Waves: A Critical Assessment," in *The Development of Trade Unionism in Great Britain and Germany, 1880–1914*, ed. Wolfgang J. Mommsen and Hans-Gerhard Husung (London: George Allen and Unwin, 1985), 78–99.
11 Anja Johansen, "Policing and Repression: Military Involvement in the Policing of French and German Industrial Areas, 1889–1914," *European History Quarterly* 34, no. 1 (2004): 69–98.
12 Roger Geary, *Policing Industrial Disputes: 1893–1985* (Cambridge: Cambridge University Press, 1985); Jane Morgan, *Conflict and Order: The Police and Labour Disputes in England and Wales, 1900–1939* (Oxford: Clarendon, 1987); Steve Peak, *Troops in Strikes: Military Intervention in Industrial Disputes* (London: Cobden, 1984).
13 Klaus Saul, "Repression or Integration? The State, Trade Unions and Industrial Disputes in Imperial Germany," in *The Development of Trade Unionism in Great Britain and Germany, 1880–1914*, ed. Wolfgang J. Mommsen and Hans-Gerhard Husung (London: George Allen and Unwin, 1985), 338–56; James Retallack, *Red Saxony. Election Battles and the Spectre of Democracy in Germany, 1860–1918* (Oxford: Oxford University Press, 2017).
14 Jens-Uwe Guettel, "Reform, Revolution, and the 'Original Catastrophe': Political Change in Prussia and Germany on the Eve of the First World War," *The Journal of Modern History* 91, no. 2 (2019): 311–40.
15 On the importance of fears and emotional responses originated by strikes and workers' mobilisation to push European propertied classes towards class consciousness and organisation, see Matteo Millan, "The Shadows of Social Fear: Emotions, Mentalities and Practices of the Propertied Classes in Italy, Spain and France (1900–1914)," *Journal of Social History* 50, no. 2 (2016): 347–50.
16 Francesco Giannini, *Le Organizzazioni Padronali. Le Agrarie*, Vol. 1 (Roma: Officina poligrafica italiana, 1912), 9.
17 Charles Gide, "Le Droit de Grève," in *Le Droit de Grève: Leçons Professées à l'École des Hautes Études Sociales*, ed. Charles Gide (Paris: F. Alcan, 1909), 20.
18 F. W. Hilbert, "Employers' Associations in the United States," in *Studies in American Trade Unionism*, ed. Jacob H. Hollander and George E. Barnett (New York: Henry Holt and Co., 1912), 185.
19 Clarence Bonnett, *Employers' Associations in the United States* (New York: Palgrave Macmillan, 1922).
20 Arthur McIvor, "Employers' Organisation and Strikebreaking in Britain, 1880–1914," *International Review of Social History*, no. 29 (1984): 1–33; Alessandro Saluppo, "Strikebreaking and Anti-Unionism on the Waterfront: The Shipping Federation, 1890–1914," *European History Quarterly* 49, no. 4 (2019): 570–96.
21 Klaus Saul, *Staat, Industrie, Arbeiterbewegung im Kaiserreich: zur Innen- und Aussenpolitik des Wilhelminischen Deutschland 1903–1914*, (Düsseldorf: Bertelsmann

Universitätsverlag, 1974); Hans-Peter Ullmann, *Der Bund der Industriellen: Organisation, Einfluß und Politik klein- und mittelbetrieblicher Industrieller im Deutschen Kaiserreich 1895–1914* (Göttingen: V&R, 1976); Dennis Sweeney, *Work, Race, and the Emergence of Radical Right Corporatism in Imperial Germany* (Ann Arbor: University of Michigan Press, 2010).

22 Peter N. Stearns, "Against the Strike Threat: Employer Policy toward Labor Agitation in France, 1900–1914," *The Journal of Modern History* 40, no. 4 (1968): 474–500; Philip Nord, "Le Mouvement des Petits Commercants et la Politique en France de 1888 a 1914," *Le Mouvement Social*, no. 114 (1981): 35; Philip Nord, "Le Mouvement des Petits Propriéters et la Politique (Des Années 1880 à la Premiere Guerre Mondiale)," *Revue Historique* 275, no. 2 (1986): 407–33; Georges Lefranc, *Les organisations patronales en France du passé au présent*, Bibliothèque historique (Paris: Payot, 1976); Michel Offerlé, "L'action Collective Patronale en France, 19°-21° Siécle. Organisation, Répertoires et Engagements," *Vingtième Siècle. Revue d'histoire* 114, no. 2 (2012): 82–97.

23 Stearns, "Against the Strike Threat," 492.

24 Anthony L. Cardoza, *Agrarian Elites and Italian Fascism: The Province of Bologna, 1901–1926* (Princeton, NJ: Princeton University Press, 1982); Gian Carlo Jocteau, *L'armonia Perturbata: Classi Dirigenti e Percezione degli Scioperi nell'Italia Liberale* (Roma-Bari: Laterza, 1988); Guido Crainz, *Padania: Il Mondo dei Braccianti dall'Ottocento alla Fuga dalle Campagne* (Roma: Donzelli, 2007).

25 Soledad Bengoechea, *Organització Patronal i Conflictivitat Social a Catalunya: Tradició i Corporativisme Entre Finals de Segle i La Dictadura de Primo de Rivera* (Barcelona: Abadia de Montserrat, 1994); Eduardo González Calleja and Fernando Del Rey Reguillo, *La Defensa Armada Contra la Revolución: Una Historia de las Guardias Cívicas en la España del Siglo XX* (Madrid: Csic, 1995).

26 Victoria E. Bonnell, *Roots of Rebellion: Workers' Politics and Organizations in St. Petersburg and Moscow, 1900–1914* (Berkeley, CA: University of California Press, 1983), 282.

27 Gregory M. Luebbert, *Liberalism, Fascism, or Social Democracy: Social Classes and the Political Origins of Regimes in Interwar Europe* (New York: Oxford University Press, 1991).

28 *Sociala Meddelanden utgivna av K. Socialstyrelsen*. Stockholm, 1915, No. 7, 775–6.

29 Ray Markey, "Australia," in *The Formation of Labour Movements, 1870–1914: An International Perspective*, Vol. II, ed. Marcel van der Linden and Jürgen Rojahn (Leiden: Brill, 1990), 579–608; Verity Burgman, *Revolutionary Industrial Unionism. The IWW in Australia* (Cambridge: Cambridge University Press, 1996).

30 Erik, Olssen, *The Red Feds. Revolutionary Industrial Unionism and the New Zealand Federation of Labour 1908–1914* (Oxford: Oxford University Press, 1988).

31 Roberto P. Korzeniewicz, "Labor Unrest in Argentina, 1887–1907," *Latin American Research Review* 24, no. 3 (1989): 90.

32 Frank Broeze, "Militancy and Pragmatism. An International Perspective on Maritime Labour, 1870–1914," *International Review of Social History* 36 (1991): 165–200.

33 Saluppo, "Strikebreaking and Anti-Unionism," 583–84.

34 Catlin, *The Labor Problem in the United States and Great Britain*, 111.

35 Matteo Millan, "'The Public Force of the Private State' – Strikebreaking and Visions of Subversion in Liberal Italy (1880s to 1914)," *European History Quarterly* 49, no. 4 (2019): 625–49; Cardoza, *Agrarian Elites and Italian Fascism*.

36 Jack London, *War of Classes* (London: Macmillan, 1905), 111.

37 Gérard Brey, "Une tentative d'internationalisme concret: l'Union Galaïco-Portugaise (1901–1904)," in *Internationalism in the Labour Movement, 1830–1940*, Vol. II, ed. Frits L. van Holthoon and Marcel van der Linden (Leiden [etc.]: Brill, 1988), 392–409.

38 Raymond Brown, *Waterfront Organisation in Hull 1870–1900* (Hull: University of Hull, 1972).

39 Bastien Cabot, *"À bas les Belges!": l'expulsion des mineurs borains (Lens, août-septembre 1892)* (Rennes: Presses universitaires de Rennes, 2017).

40 Amerigo Caruso and Claire Morelon, "Fighting Strikes Across Borders: Social Conflicts, Labour Migration and Violence in Central Europe Before 1914," *Central European History*, forthcoming.

41 Robert Michels, *Political Parties, A Sociological Study of the Oligarchical Tendencies of Modern Democracy* (New York: Hearst's International Library Co., 1915), 282.

42 On immigration and labour in the United States from the late nineteenth century to the Johnson-Reed Immigration Act, see Edward P. Hutchinson, *Legislative History of American Immigration Policy, 1790–1965* (Philadelphia: University of Pennsylvania Press, 1981); Desmond King, *Making Americans: Immigration, Race, and the Origins of the Diverse Democracy* (Cambridge, MA: Harvard University Press, 2000); Daniel J. Tichenor, *Dividing Lines: The Politics of Immigration Control in America* (Princeton, NJ: Princeton University Press, 2002); Roger Daniels, *Guarding the Golden Door: American Immigration Policy and Immigrants since 1882* (New York: Hill and Wang, 2004); Robert F. Zeidel, *Immigrants, Progressives, and Exclusion Politics: The Dillingham Commission, 1900–1927* (DeKalb, IL: Northern Illinois University Press, 2004).

43 On Christian and Free Trade Unions in Germany, see, among others, Michael Schneider, *Die christlichen Gewerkschaften 1894–1933* (Bonn: Verlag Neue Gesellschaft, 1982); Klaus Mattheier, *Die Gelben. Nationale Arbeiter zwischen Wirtschaftsfrieden und Streik (*Düsseldorf: Pädagogischer Verlag Schwann, 1973).

44 John Saville, "Trade Unions and Free Labour: The Background to the Taff Vale Decision," in *Essays in Labour History*, ed. Asa Briggs and John Saville (London: St. Martin's Press, 1960), 317–50.

45 George L. Mosse, "The French Right and the Working Classes: Les Jaunes," *Journal of Contemporary History* 7, no. 3–4 (1972): 207. See also Sternhell, *La Droite Révolutionnaire*.

46 Pierre Biétry, *Les Jaunes de France et La Question Ouvrière* (Paris: Paul Placot, 1906), 35.

47 Romain Bonnet, "The Making of Counter-Internationalism. Political Violence, Strikebreaking and the Yellow Movement in Pre-1914 Europe," *Partecipazione e Conflitto* 13, no. 1 (2020): 757.

48 Romain Bonnet and Amerigo Caruso, "Europe Industrielle et Contre-Internationalisme: Le Mouvement Jaune Dans l'espace Franco-Allemand Avant 1914," *Histoire@Politique* 39 (2019).

49 Mosse, "The French Right and the Working Classes," 206. French yellow unionism certainly produced emulations across the Rhine. The "*Gelbe Arbeiterbewegung*" reared the ultra-patriotic *Bund Vaterländischer Arbeitervereine* Rudolf and Lebius's *Gelber Arbeitsbund*, whose announced goal was to fight the "Terrorism of Social Democracy", Rudolf Lebius, *Die gelbe Arbeiterbewegung: eine Materialsammlung* (Charlottenburg-Berlin Reformverlag "Der Bund", 1908).

50 Clive Emsley, "Police and Industrial Disputes in Britain and the United States," in *Britain and America. Studies in Comparative History 1760–1970*, ed. David Englander (New Haven and London: Yale University Press), 125. Emsley cites Commission on Industrial Relations, "List of Detectives," 1914.

51 Salvatore Lupo, *Storia della mafia dalle origini ai giorni nostri* (Roma: Donzelli, 1993); Paolo Pezzino, *Una certa reciprocità di favori : mafia e modernizzazione violenta nella Sicilia postunitaria* (Milano: F. Angeli, 1990).

52 Matteo Millan, "In Defence of Freedom? The Practices of Armed Movements in Pre-1914 Europe: Italy, Spain and France," *European History Quarterly* 46, no. 1 (2016): 48–71.

53 Roger Marchandeau, "La Bande à Patin, 1888–1899. Histoire de La Police Privée de La Compagnie Des Mines de Blanzy," *Revue de la Physiophile*, no. 95 (1981).

54 John Spargo, *Syndicalism, Industrial Unionism and Socialism* (New York: Huebsch, 1913), 128. Bernt Schiller, "Storstrejken 1909: Förhistoria Och Orsaker" (PhD thesis, University of Gothenburg, Gothenburg, 1967), 37; Reinhold Kramer and Tom Mitchell, *When the State Trembled: How A.J. Andrews and the Citizens' Committee Broke the Winnipeg General Strike* (Toronto: University of Toronto Press, 2010), 19.

55 Robert Gerwarth, "Fighting the Red Beast: Counter-Revolutionary Violence in the Defeated States of Central Europe," in *War in Peace: Paramilitary Violence in Europe after the Great War*, ed. Robert Gerwarth and John Horne (Oxford: Oxford University Press, 2012), 52–71.

56 Capozzola, *Uncle Sam Wants You*, 117–43.

57 Amerigo Caruso, "Joining Forces against 'Strike Terrorism': The Public-Private Interplay in Policing Strikes in Imperial Germany, 1890–1914," *European History Quarterly* 49, no. 4 (2019): 614–16. Michael H. Kater, "Die Technische Nothilfe im Spannungsfeld von Arbeiterunruhen, Unternehmerinteressen und Parteipolitik," *Vierteljahreshefte fur Zeitgeschichte* 27, no. 1 (1979): 30–78.

58 González Calleja and Del Rey Reguillo, *La Defensa Armada Contra La Revolución*; Eduardo González Calleja, *El máuser y el sufragio: orden público, subversión y violencia política en la crisis de la Restauración (1917–1931)* (Madrid: Consejo Superior de Investigaciones Científicas, 1999).

59 Keith Jeffery and Peter Hennessy, *States of Emergency. British Government and Strikebreaking since 1919* (London: Routledge, 1983), 40–142; R. H. Desmarais, "The British Government's Strikebreaking Organization and Black Friday," *Journal of Contemporary History* 6, no. 2 (1971): 112–27; R. Desmarais, "Lloyd George and the Development of the British Government's Strikebreaking Organization," *International Review of Social History* 20, no. 1 (1975): 1–15; Peter Dennis, "The Territorial Army in Aid of the Civil Power in Britain, 1919–1926," *Journal of Contemporary History* 16, no. 4 (1981): 705–24; Keith Jeffery, "The British Army and Internal Security 1919–1939," *The Historical Journal* 24, no. 2 (1981): 377–97.

60 John Horne, "Defending Victory. Paramilitary Politics in France 1918–1926. A Counter-Example," in *War in Peace: Paramilitary Violence in Europe after the Great War*, ed. John Horne and Robert Gerwarth (Oxford: Oxford University Press, 2012).

61 Charles S. Maier, *Recasting Bourgeois Europe: Stabilization in France, Germany, and Italy in the Decade after World War I* (Princeton, NJ: Princeton University Press, 1975), 9.

62 Robert Gerwarth and John Horne, eds., *War in Peace: Paramilitary Violence in Europe after the Great War* (Oxford: Oxford University Press, 2012); Robert Gerwarth, *The Vanquished: Why the First World War Failed to End, 1917–1923* (London: Allen Lane, 2016). See also Holly Case, *The Age of Questions or, A First Attempt at an Aggregate History of the Eastern, Social, Woman, American, Jewish, Polish, Bullion, Tuberculosis, and Many Other Questions over the Nineteenth Century, and Beyond* (Princeton, NJ and Oxford: Princeton University Press, 2018), 103–12.

Part 1

Institutional responses

2 Policies and practices against labour movement in the late Russian Empire

Volodymyr Kulikov and Irina Shilnikova

Introduction

On 3 October 1913 the chief of Saint Petersburg secret police submitted a report to the Department of Police about the political "spirit" in the city in which he sincerely acknowledged that any preventive measures against the labour movement, such as repression of trade unions, are useless. "The current labour movement is a kind of psychosis", he explained. "In some cases, the repressions may even turn to be harmful, because liquidation [of the workers' organisations] can only accelerate the explosion of the strike movement".[1] This note epitomises the ultimate result of tsarist's labour policy: it could not seize the labour movement despite increasing the power of its repressive apparatus. This chapter investigates why practices of the government and employers against the labour movement in the late Russian Empire turned to be inefficient.

The industrial boom in the Russian Empire, starting from the 1880s, brought economic growth and modernisation. At the same time, like other rapidly industrialised countries, it was accompanied by fierce labour conflicts. Employees demanded higher wages, fewer working hours, better living conditions and more respect. Employers were upset by the instability caused by labour migration, as well as by the low level of productivity and lack of discipline on behalf of their workers. Labour conflicts often burst into violence on both sides, which embroiled the third side – the government. Other actors, such as the church, radical socialists, journalists and scholars, were also involved, but it was mostly the industrialists and the government that determined the balance of power and the outcome of the labour conflicts.

Although the history of the labour movement in the Russian Empire has been researched in detail by historians, they paid less attention to the repressive policies and practices of the employers and state authorities; so, no comprehensive study has been written on the topic. Contemporaries studied the repressions against the labour movement in the context of elaborating factory legislations and tried to find the best solution for the so-called labour problem.[2]

Soviet historians approached the topic from the perspective of the class conflict.[3] They contributed to our knowledge about the repressive policy of the government, mostly presenting it in the context of the general repressive policy of tsarism against its citizens.[4] In the same period, especially in the 1950s to the

1960s, papers by several American and British scholars explained how the tsarist administration and the employers managed labour protests in Russia.[5]

After the collapse of the Soviet Union, interest in labour history significantly declined in Eastern Europe. However, a group of Russian scholars organised an extensive research project to study labour conflicts in the Russian Empire at the end of the nineteenth and in the early twentieth century. They collected materials about thousands of conflicts from 112 archives of the former Soviet Union and published it as a multivolume series entitled *Labour Movement in Russia. 1895 – February of 1917. Chronicle.*[6]

Using the materials of these publications, a group of historians created a relation database of all known cases of labour conflicts in the Russian Empire from 1895 until 1904 (7,769 records; about 4,757 strikes).[7] The results of the analysis of this database were presented in several publications.[8] This study also relies on the database, focusing on the empirical evidence on practices against the strikes. It is a combination of a quantitative analysis of practices against the labour movement with a qualitative analysis of anti-strike and anti-union policy.

This chapter describes the evolution of labour policy and practices against strikers adopted by the industrialists and the government in the late Russian Empire. The first part on policy presents an overview of the legislation about strikes, explores how the attitude of governments and industrialists towards the labour movement transformed in time. The second part describes the emergence and development of the repressive forces. The third part about practices is based on the results of a quantitative analysis of punitive actions against strikes. Overall, the chapter explains the strategy developed by industrialists and state authorities to prevent the labour movement and traces the evolvement of this strategy in the period from the 1870s until 1917.

To understand approaches against labour movement, national and regional chronicles of the labour conflicts, legislative materials and reflections regarding labour conflicts published by the contemporaries – industrialists, politicians and scholars in social sciences – were analysed. These sources were supplemented by some archival documents providing relevant case materials to illustrate the practices and to present the situation from the perspective of the strikers.

Striking movement in the Russian Empire: a brief overview

Strikes in the 1870s, such as that at the Nevsky Thread Manufacturing Co. in 1870, at Krenholm Manufacturing Co. in 1872, and at the Iuzovka Ironworks in 1875, marked the beginning of a new era in the economic and social development of Russia. From that time on strikes became the “new normality” in Russia.

Figure 2.1 presents the dynamics of strikes in the Russian Empire in the period between 1870 and 1894. During these decades, the labour movement was relatively moderate, with a few resonant conflicts and a low level of involvement of revolutionary organisations. The two peaks in 1878–79 and 1887 were because of a series of massive protests at the textile factories in Saint Petersburg, Moscow, and a few other centres of the textile industry.

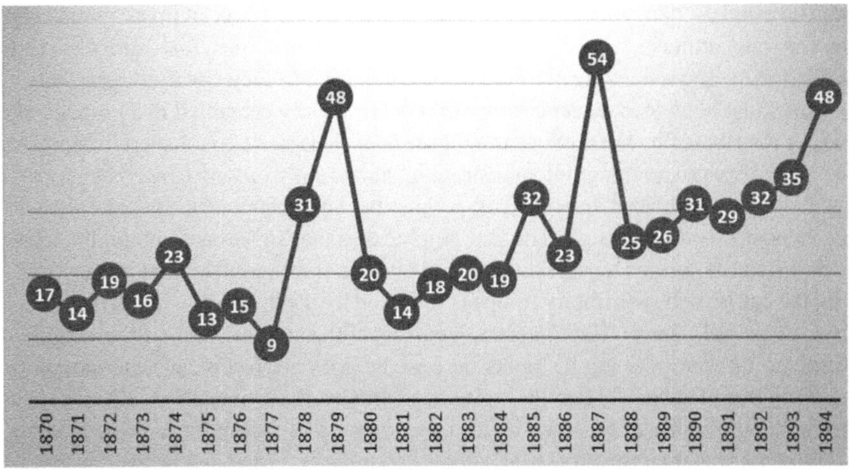

Figure 2.1 Number of strikes in the Russian Empire from 1870 to 1894

Sources: Anna M. Pankratova, *Rabochee dvizhenie v Rossii v XIX veke: Sbornik dokumentov i materialov. T. 2: 1861–1884. Ch. 1. 1861–1874* (Moscow: Gospolitizdat, 1950), 607–18.; Ibid. Vol. 2. Part 2: 1875–1884, 644–676; Moscow, 1950; Ibid. Vol. 3. Part. 1: 1885–1889, 771–802; Ibid. Vol. 3. Part. 2: 1885–1894, 620–645. Moscow, 1952.

From the mid-1890s, the labour movement transformed: strikes were no longer spontaneous but organised. The labour movement became a mass phenomenon and quickly politicalised. This was partly because of objective reasons, such as the emergence of large modern enterprises and the increasing number of professional workers, but also because of some questionable political decisions, such as the total ban of trade unions (in force until 1905). The revolutionary organisations saw the situation as an opportunity to establish themselves as the acting side in labour conflicts. They helped workers to grasp and defend their interests. On the other hand, they often encouraged workers to strike and exacerbate the conflict even if it would have been possible to avoid it through negotiations with the employers.

Daniel Brower has described a typical scenario of strike violence at the turn of the nineteenth century.[9] A series of grievances triggered the conflict. That was followed by a work stoppage and the gathering of a crowd, "unorganised but with individuals formulating complaints". The administration of the enterprise refused to negotiate until the workers got back to their working places. If there were any representatives of the authorities (a factory inspector, police force), they demanded that the strikers stopped "rioting". They explained that strikers first had to surrender unconditionally and return to their jobs, and their grievances would have been examined only afterward. They would often arrest the delegates. Workers began to attack administrative buildings and company stores. If they had got access to alcohol, it catalysed the violence. The destructive phase usually lasted a day or two. Then military troops arrived, dispersed the crowd, beat the strikers and arrested as many of them as possible. The next phase was an investigation run by the state authorities. Many of the most active strikers – the "instigators" – were imprisoned, and a few dozen of them were deported to their own villages.

The most likely consequences for strikers are vividly presented in a propaganda poster distributed by the authorities (Figure 2.2). This poster published in Moscow in 1906 displays six images demonstrating "numerous disasters caused by unjustified strikes which are harmful to all people, but primarily to the strikers, who do not wish to work honestly". The text emphasised that strikes are "no godly activity" instead, it "brings terrible distress and utter destruction". The first image showing the battle with the military troops is followed by the image of wounded workers in the hospital. The next one depicts the arrest of the strikers. In the following picture, the worker is selling his boots because he does not receive a salary anymore and run out of money. Then he is fired and finally finds himself on Khitrovka, a square in the centre of Moscow which used to be a job market for unskilled labour. This place was infamous for its unsanitary conditions, crime and overall misery.

The number of strikes in the period between 1895 and 1917, as presented in Figure 2.3, hundreds, sometimes thousands per year, indicates that the governmental propaganda must have been inefficient. In the early twentieth century, the peaks were designated by the General Strike of 1903 in Southern Russia, the Russian Revolution of 1905, and the years following the Lena massacre of 1912.

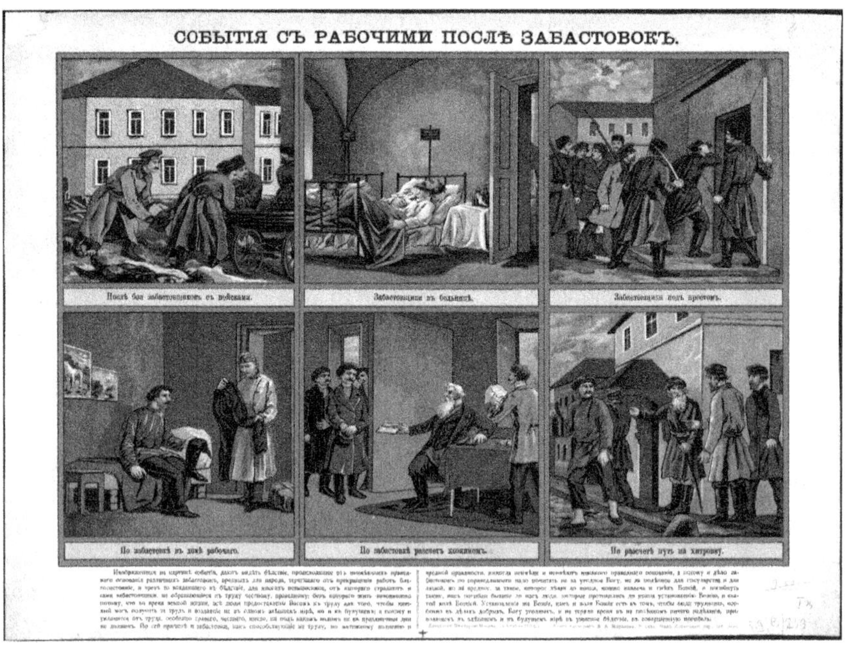

Figure 2.2 What happens to workers after the strike

Sources: "Sobytiia s rabochimi posle zabastovki," (Moscow: Tipografiia I. A. Morozova, 1906).

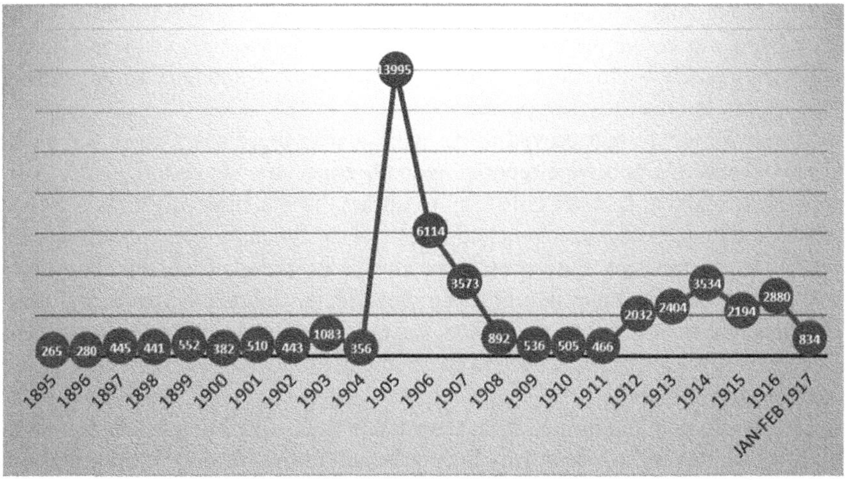

Figure 2.3 Number of strikes in the Russian Empire from 1895 to early 1917[11]

The number of strikes remained high during the First World War. There was only a short period at the beginning of the war when patriotism was skyrocketing and workers refrained from protesting.[10] Workers were ready to strike again by the autumn of 1915 because of the poor performance of the Russian army on the front and a significant decrease in their living conditions.

The rationale of tsarist labour policy

The development of the labour movement induced the government and the industrialists to develop a policy towards this phenomenon. According to the government's perception, the "patriarchal" attitude of the employers and a strict hierarchy determined the relationship between industrialists and workers. As the Minister of Finances, Sergei Witte described it in a secret circular issued on the 5 December 1895,

> The patriarchy [between master and worker] expresses itself in many cases in the concern of the factory owner for the needs of the worker and employees in his factory, in his solicitude for the preservation of harmony and agreement, in the simplicity and justice of their mutual relations.[12]

In the eyes of the government, the employer was a benevolent master who took care of the moral and material well-being of his workers. The state saw its own role as an independent agency standing above the interplay of conflicting and private interests and above partisanship.

Strike had no place in such a hierarchical model of labour relations. It was not perceived as an argument between the competing sides but as the "misbehaviour" of the subordinate side, which undermined the principle of the public order.

Theoretically, workers were offered some mechanisms to seek justice against a misbehaving employer. They were supposed to appeal to a representative of the state (who was above the employer in the hierarchy) and who could punish the violator. In practice, the enormous power of industrialists and the limited rights of workers led to many cases of power abuse.[13]

Moreover, the system proved to be inefficient in those cases when the violations of workers' rights were reported with the expectation to restore justice. This convinced workers that the only way to attract the attention of officials was to strike. In theory, both employers and employees had equal rights to receive state protection. In practice, the government always took the side of the employers and cooperated with them in repressing the strikers. Courts examined all violent conflicts, but relatively few were those cases when the administrators were punished for provoking a strike. For the government, the social order always received priority over justice.[14]

The government interpreted strikes not as a private affair but as a matter of public concern; this is the reason why the public authorities were to be informed and involved immediately in any (even potential) mass labour conflict. As Minister Sergei Witte explained, "the government cannot accept the situation that workers achieve what they wanted even if employers expressed a desire to satisfy such demands".[15] The government's approach to managing strikes was based on what economists call "collective action problem". The willingness of a company to put an end to the strike as soon as possible empowered the workers; consequently, it could harm collective entrepreneurial interests. The government presented itself as a body whose role was to balance private and collective interests for the common good and intended to regulate these through labour legislation.

In 1882, the government established a factory inspection as an institution to facilitate the implementation of factory legislation, to collect statistical information about workers and to act as a mediator between employees and employers. Factory inspectors were kept busy, preventing strikes until the end of the Russian Empire. However, many of their representatives admitted that, though this institution was very efficient in the late nineteenth and early twentieth century, after 1905 their peace-making effect and ability to negotiate significantly faded.[16]

Strikes and unions were unlawful in the Russian Empire up to 1905. Those who dared to strike risked facing "the knout, jail, or exile".[17] The first law about strikes appeared in 1845 as an amendment to the Penal Code. It was elaborated with more details and slightly changed in 1874 and 1886. According to the law, strikers were to be imprisoned for a period of two to four months, while "instigators" risked spending four to eight months in prison. In the case of aggravating circumstances, such as damaging factory property or forcing other workers to cease work, the punishment was doubled.[18] The government cancelled the criminal penalty for strikes only in 1905, and even then, with some special conditions.

The state interpreted any labour conflict as a threat to public order, even if the conflict evolved for economic reasons; this is why strikes fell inside the scope of criminal law and not of civil law. Since strikes meant a challenge to the autocratic regime, they were seen as a matter of public concern.[19] No wonder that in many official papers, strikes were called "disorder", "unrests", or "riots" (*besporiadki, bunty*).

In practice, however, it was difficult to follow the law strictly. Sometimes, strikes involved hundreds and thousands of participants, so the police could not criminalise each of them. The solution was to criminalise the group of the most active strikers, and the rest received some forms of administrative punishment. The most popular among the latter was to expel strikers to remote provinces or to the villages where they were registered.[20] Such actions were regulated by a number of secret circulars issued by the Ministry of Interior and the Ministry of Finance. The most infamous one was the circular signed on the 12 August 1897, in which the Minister of Interior Ivan Goremykin strongly recommended that the governors united the efforts of all officials and the regional police forces to stop the "disturbances among the workers". The minister demanded that the local police monitor carefully the factories and workers' houses. As a preemptive measure, he encouraged the police to arrest those individuals who were suspected to be political agitators. The circular reminded the officials that any unauthorised gathering of workers was strictly forbidden, and the organisers of such meetings were to be arrested immediately. The minister ordered his subordinates to do their best to put an end to any strike quickly and peacefully. Those workers who refused to cooperate were to be arrested and exiled.

Still, the minister acknowledged that "it is not always possible to conduct prosecution due to the lack of evidence of any crime", so his recommendation was to apply "administrative punishment on a mass scale".[21] The recommendation to punish workers who were not formally recognised guilty was unlawful; this is why the circular was disseminated secretly. Instructions like this encouraged repression rather than reconciliation and easily led to the abuse of power.

By 1905 the labour movement became so intense that it was impossible to tackle it with only repressive actions, which demonstrated the failure of the previous tsarist labour policy. The government had to liberalise the legislation. In April 1905, it cancelled the circular from the 12 August 1897. In October 1905, in the context of the revolution, the emperor issued a manifesto which granted the freedom of conscience, speech, assembly and association. The "Temporary regulations on unions and societies" issued on 4 March 1906 legalised the formation of trade unions and educational societies and, at the same time, clarified the "rules" for the workers' assemblies.

Trade unions functioned actively in 1905 and 1906, even despite the significant limitations.[22] Efforts by the unions were mostly channelled into the struggle for improving the workers' material conditions. Nevertheless even these limited activities irritated the government, which intensified the efforts to repress the unions from 1907. The slightest reason was enough to close down the existing trade unions and to obstruct the registration of new ones. The government permitted a limited restoration of the workers' assembly after the Lena massacre in April 1912, but trade unions were considered suspicious until the time when tsarism collapsed.[23]

Though those aspects of factory law which fall outside the repressive elements in labour legislation are beyond the scope of this paper, the fact itself that Russia developed its factory legislation in the period between 1882 and 1912 has a significance for the topic. More than ten acts were issued in this period regulating child and woman work, the number of daily working hours and penalties and introducing social securities. These acts improved the working conditions considerably but did not lead to a decrease in the intensity of the labour movement.

The labour policy of the industrialists

Most industrialists agreed with the government in this respect and also saw any conflict between the employer and employee as a deviation from normality, which should be hushed up by all means. Both the traditional theory of paternalism and social Darwinism, that time the two most popular social ideologies among industrialists, considered disputes and strikes as an anomaly. In terms of the paternalistic approach, strikes were a sign of a supreme ingratitude, a fight against corporate benevolence. For social Darwinism, a strike was a break in the social order: the presence of wealth and poverty was seen as a part of the "normal" order reflecting the differences among people in their abilities and efforts.

The picture of Russian workers created by industrialist was very persistent, presenting them as being backward and lazy, but amendable to the influence of socialist propaganda. Because of this image, the employers generally preferred repression to negotiation. Nikolai Avdakov, an influential member (and later chairman) of the Association of Southern Coal and Steel Producers, concluded his report in 1893 on how to secure workforce supply for coal-mining enterprises with the following words: "A rioting spirit has appeared among the miners due to the high wages and their drunkenness. Therefore, we need more police forces to maintain decorum and order among the workers".[24] Industrialists like Avdakov looked at the strikes as a zero-sum game, so power was the key to determine which side gains and which loses.

The tactic of increasing repressive forces worked on the local level but proved to be ineffective in preventing the labour movement in general. Thus, industrialists relied on the combination of stick and carrot policy. Welfare work was a recurrent topic during the discussions at the meetings of the regional associations of industrialists starting from the 1880s. From that time on, enterprises invested heavily in social infrastructure and improved the working and living conditions of their employees.[25] However, the expanding enterprises and the rapidly increasing number of workers often negated the efforts of the enterprises to improve the quality of life of its staff. Although the working and living conditions were steadily improving during the period between 1870 and 1914, many contemporaries described them even in the 1910s as inhuman and intolerable. Modern technologies and luxurious offices of the new technocracy often coexisted with primitive forms of economic coercion, debilitating physical labour and extreme poverty.[26]

The changing economic situation, the broadening and strengthening of the working class and the intensifying labour movement pushed the industrialists towards making their labour policy more flexible. Their position concerning the legalisation of worker's organisations gradually changed. Even the most conservative industrialists had to accept that the total ban of such institutions was counterproductive. The conservative chief executive of the Dnieper Company, the owner of the largest metallurgy plant in the Russian Empire, said in April 1905: "The current labour law and the law about strikes do not correspond anymore to the reality. If the law is permanently violated and the state has no power to prevent this, the law should be adjusted [to the reality]".[27] Therefore, the emperor's decision to legalise the workers' organisation in 1905 did not meet any significant opposition from the side of the industrialists.

The intensification of the labour movement also inspirited the industrialists to unite and coordinate their efforts in the face of a new threat. They started to establish their own organisations aimed to give mutual support in the struggle against strikes. These organisations were usually operating at a regional scale. The Association of Southern Coal and Steel Producers, founded in 1874, coordinated the policy and practices against the labour movement in the Dnepr-Donbas region. In Saint Petersburg, the industrialists established the St. Petersburg Society for Assistance to the Improvement and Development of Factory Industry in 1897. The society collected and analysed information about all strikes that happened in the region to adjust its labour policy. The members established a special fund for their mutual assistance in cases of lengthy strikes, and they also coordinated their actions against strikers. The Moscow entrepreneurs created the Society of Factory Owners of Moscow Industrial Region in 1907. The funding chart of this society contained articles about mutual support, including financial, consulting and legislative means. By 1908 there were 18 such societies in the Russian Empire, mostly in large cities such as Saint Petersburg, Moscow, Ekaterinoslav and Kharkov.[28]

Many Soviet historians presented the relationship between the entrepreneurs and the state as having been cooperative, aimed to repress workers: when violent conflicts arose, the industrialists and the government combined their efforts to put it down[29]. However, behind the scenes, there were many conflicting interests not only between the business and the state but also within these two groups.

The business community was characterised by local differences. Industrialists of the Moscow region retained their more traditional, patriarchal practices, firmly opposing any worker organisation. They often stated that workers are a "dark poorly-literate crowd", which can easily be manipulated by revolutionists.[30] In contrast, their peers in Saint Petersburg and the Dnepr-Donbas regions gradually shifted from oppressive towards rationalising labour policy.[31] However, there were disagreements from time to time, even within the regional groups. For example, the members of the eighteenth congress of the Association of Southern Coal and Steel Producers in December 1893 had a very heated discussion about how to tackle the labour movement. A participant of the congress, Vladimir Vagner, suggested that every ten to 15 workers elected a so-called *desiatskikh* who would represent the interests of their group and communicate it to the authorities. However, most of the industrialists present at the congress rejected the idea arguing that the workers were "backward" and not ready for such practices. Instead, they insisted on asking the government to strengthen the police forces in the region.[32]

From the perspective of the industrialists, the strengthening of the police control had several disadvantages, the most disturbing one being the police meddling in the concerns of business. The government justified police interference based on the principle of conflict prevention. To promote industrial development, the Ministry of Finance backed the interests of the industrialists. The position of the Ministry of the Interior was shaped by other influencers, such as the landowning nobility.[33] This ministry prioritised public order and the prevention of violent labour conflicts and conducted several investigations which demonstrated that many conflicts were caused by the poor working conditions and by industrialists violating the law. Thus, the ministry developed the following strategy: 1 to urge employers to improve the working conditions; 2 to prevent violent conflict through their undercover network and preventive arrests; and 3 to suppress workers' "disorders" promptly and firmly in case the preventive measures failed.[34]

Despite the previously mentioned tensions, all stakeholders agreed regarding the necessity of powerful police forces at their disposal. Police could be used either to repress the labour movement or to strengthen the employers' position during the negotiations in time of labour conflicts.

Repressive forces

The first strikes in the 1870s broke out spontaneously, and the reaction of the police was rather slow. Therefore, the industrialists had to rely on their own solutions to suppress the "rioters". The enterprises often applied the principle of *divide et impera*: they used a group of loyal workers to repress the rioting ones.[35] Factory workers could be turned against miners, skilled workers against non-skilled ones and foreign employees (who were always better paid) against the locals. Sources present some cases when companies or the local authorities armed peasants from the surrounding villages to repress the striking miners.[36]

The government found it suspicious when unofficial military groups were used, especially if it was done by foreign-managed enterprises, so it decided to enforce police presence in the factories. The government granted free access to the police into the factories, and police could inspect and arrest workers who fell under suspicion any time in the presence of a factory manager.[37] Because of the immediate interventions of the police and military forces on behalf of management, many wage conflicts tended to be characterised by the government as political.

However, the government could not provide sufficient police forces to supervise every enterprise. The presence of police was especially weak in small company towns scattered in a large geographical area. To strengthen the controlling forces, the enterprises supported the police service on their premises by establishing factory police or paying the local police department for increasing their presence at the factory. By the end of the 1890s, there were officially 572 factory policemen in Russia, mostly in the Central Industrial and South Industrial regions. Their service was costly. For example, the Aleksandrovsk South-Russian Plant of Briansk Society spent 15,900 roubles annually to support 60 policemen at the turn of the century while, in 1902, they spent 37,284 roubles on medical service and 17,282 on schools.[38] Still, the officials acknowledged that these forces were inadequate as well as distributed unequally, mostly concentrated in the large settlements.

This solution entailed an ethical problem as well: policemen receiving their pay checks from industrialists saw labour conflict through the eyes of their employer. The leadership of the police forces even acknowledged that in such cases, the police did not serve justice but acted as a servant of the entrepreneurs.[39] On the 1 February 1898, the government issued a new law enforcing police presence in the factories. The costs were divided between the taxpayers and the industrialists: the government paid the salaries while the enterprises covered the expenses of the accommodation and the utilities of the newly enforced police body.

From the 1880s, the priority tasks of the secret police in Imperial Russia, the so-called *Okhranka (Otdeleniye po Okhraneniyu Obshchestvennoy Bezopasnosti i Poryadka)*, were broadened with tackling the labour movement. This included investigating and preventing unauthorised meetings or demonstrations such as worker strikes. While the ordinary policeman, the gendarmes, were focused on formal investigations, the *Okhranka* operated through informers, spies and undercover agents.[40] From 1898 on, the *Okhranka* monitored and accumulated information about the strikes and workers' organisations all over the country. They established a system of surveillance targeting both illegal and legal worker organisations, with special focus on trade unions. A circular issued by the *Okhranka* explained that some unions "drew themselves towards extremely harmful anti-government activities and thus forced us to repress them by all possible means".[41]

Sources offer evidence that police used mercenary agents and involved street hooligans to provoke violence. A worker called Zakharkin recalled that during the 1905 revolution, the police "instigated hooligans" in looting pubs and to have a hand in Jewish pogroms. He referred to the example of Iuzovka, where there "was [the gang of] Alyoshka Sibiryak and two hundred men with him. Of course, they were connected to the police".[42]

Perhaps the most well-known enterprise of the *Okhranka* was establishing a spoiler work organisation under the control of the police at the turn of the century. Following the old principle, "if you cannot beat them, join them", the chief of the Moscow Secret Police, colonel Sergey Zubatov offered to create a legal workers' organisation under police supervision to defend their economic interests. He argued that it would allow the workers to seize the initiative from the socialist organisations and thus to have primacy in seeking for governmental support. However, his primary motivation was to have a certain degree of control over the workers' activities.[43] The police chief of Moscow, Dmitri Trepov, and the governor-general of Moscow, Grand Duke Sergei Alexandrovich, both supported the proposal of Zubatov. The minister of interior hesitated first but finally gave the green light to the project. Between 1901 and 1903, Zubatov established workers' organisations in several large cities in the European part of Russia. Zubatov's initiative faced severe opposition on behalf of the employers and in some government circles. The minister of finances, Sergei Witte, believed that the project initiated by Zubatov and Trepov "catalyzes disturbance among the workers", de facto "replaced revolutionary propaganda" and aimed "to overthrow capitalism".[44] The minister of the interior also had concerns about the project: he assumed that these legalised workers' organisations could easily be transformed into illegal and even oppositional organisations. He was afraid that workers were gaining experience in organising themselves, which they could later utilise in demonstrations, strikes and revolution.[45] The general strike of 1903 in Southern Russia was the last straw, and after that, the minister stopped the project.

In those cases, when the police forces could not stop mass violence, the government sent army troops. However, it was not infrequent that the conflict had already been over for some days by the time the army arrived. Thus, industrialists asked the government to station troops near the large enterprises in those regions where enterprises clustered. The minister of war was not very enthusiastic to comply with this request since, as he explained, stationing troops in the industrial regions to "pacify riots" obstructed proper military training.[46] Furthermore, sending military troops to repress labour violence often resulted in massacres, which attracted unwanted public attention and criticism, and ultimately contributed to the radicalisation of workers. The minister of the interior, Vyacheslav Pleve, believed that extreme mass violence threw workers to the arms of the revolutionists. Following the massacre in Zlatoust, Ufa Province, in March 1903, when local military troops killed 45 workers, he told the minister of war in private that he wished the troops would not use "such deadly bullets".[47]

Therefore, both the government and industrialists preferred to rely on the intervention of the *Cossacks*, the light cavalry force of a historically privileged social group famous for its pro-monarchist views. *Cossacks* acted violently and were very efficient in dispersing crowds, but without mass killings since they used non-lethal weapons such as *nagaika* – a thick, tightly twisted whip. However, they were inefficient against the passive resistance of workers.

Practices against strikers

Based on their rich experience in suppressing "unrests" on the factories and mines, the authorities and industrialists developed a toolbox of practices against strikers. The most popular solutions included dismissals, calling for police or military units, followed by arrests and exile, lockouts, strikebreaking and blacklisting. The following section discusses which of these were preferred by the employers and the government, and how often they were applied.

The relational database entitled "Chronicle of the labour movement" contains data about 4,757 strikes, which took place in all regions of the Russian Empire between 1895 and 1904.[48] The database allows tracing the popularity of specific repressive methods and their dynamics in this period. It also provides evidence on the efficiency of these methods to put an end to the conflict. Built on the basis of that database, Table 2.1 demonstrates that police or military troops interfered with 14 per cent of the strikes. The number of cases of police/military intrusion fluctuated from year to year, with 70 occasions on average in the period of 1895 to 1899 and 72 from 1900 through 1904. However, because of the increasing absolute number of strikes, this still means a slight relative decrease in the share of conflicts with police/military involvement, from 18 per cent to 13 per cent. The gradual decline continued after 1904 as well.

Table 2.1 Repressive practices against strikers in Russian industry in the period from 1895 to 1904

Year	*Number of strikes*	*The reaction of the authorities*				
		Police or military intervention	*Trials*	*Arrests*	*Banishment*	*Lockout or dismissal of a group of workers*
1895	265	16%	5%	9%	2%	11%
1896	280	20%	3%	18%	6%	11%
1897	445	18%	4%	15%	6%	14%
1898	441	18%	3%	13%	4%	12%
1899	552	17%	2%	15%	5%	10%
1900	382	15%	3%	12%	3%	12%
1901	510	11%	1%	11%	4%	10%
1902	443	16%	1%	10%	1%	13%
1903	1083	13%	1%	8%	1%	10%
1904	356	1%	n/a	6%	2%	7%
AVG	476	14%	2%	12%	3%	11%

There were various factors behind this phenomenon. First, though the labour moment intensified, the authorities could not develop the police forces at the same pace. Therefore, they had to be more selective about where to interfere. In the late nineteenth century, military forces were often used just to intimidate the potential rioters, as a preventive measure against labour violence. From the early twentieth century, however, the government could not afford this anymore; they sent troops only in cases of actual mass violence.

At the same time, the effect of the violent oppression of strikers has also changed. Instead of pacifying the situation, it often aroused the indignation of workers also in the neighbouring enterprises and resulted in a powerful strike movement for the sake of solidarity. The Lena massacre of 1912, which triggered an immense wave of strikes and protests in the entire empire, is a textbook example for such a process. As Michael Melancon pointed out, the Lena massacre and other similar violent episodes "delivered successive blows that cracked and then shattered the last fragile remnants of Russia's post-1905 consensus" and as a result "workers, peasants and much of the educated society turned their backs on tsarism and capitalism".[49]

In the period of the First World War, the share of "political" among all strikes were around 24 per cent in the first two years, slightly declined in 1916, then sharply increased in early 1917 to 51 per cent. The difficult situation at the front and loosening discipline on the factories and mines made the authorities put more pressure on workers. However, violence against the strikers also led to public outcry and solidarity strikes, such as the series of strikes in the Central Industrial Region of Russia in August 1915. In early June 1915, workers of the Big Linen Manufactory in Kostroma demanded an increase in housing expense reimbursement. The administration did not give them a clear answer, so the workers decided to strike. They convinced the workers of the neighbouring Belgian-owned linen factory to join them and then turned their attention to the workers of one more linen factory owned by the Zotov brothers. However, this latter company worked for the Ministry of War and was carefully controlled by the authorities. So, instead of solidary peers, the strikers were met by a police squad. The clash with the police resulted in the violent death of several strikers and the imprisonment of the organisers.[50]

A similar tragedy happened in Ivanovo-Voznesensk, another centre of the textile industry in Russia, some 100 kilometres south from Kostroma. A bloody clash between strikers and police forces left several killed and many wounded.[51] These brutal repressions caused enormous public outrage. Seven days after the Kostroma conflict, many Russian cities, including Saint Petersburg and Moscow, hosted mass strikes of solidarity. Thus, by applying brutal repression against strikers, the authorities often ended up with the opposite result: these repressions catalysed a new wave of protests.

Workers' solidarity was a serious constraining factor against the temptation to resolve all conflicts by force. The calculation presented in Table 2.1 shows that the percentage of strikes with the intervention of the police or military troops (14 per cent) is higher than the proportion of those strikes, which resulted in arrests (12 per cent), lockouts (11 per cent), or banishments (3 per cent). These numbers indicate that the appearance of the police and military troops did not necessarily lead to further repressive actions; sometimes it was enough in itself to convince the strikers to terminate their activity and to get back to work.

Table 2.1 demonstrates that lockouts or the dismissal of some workers were an instrument applied by industrialists at least since the mid-1890s. Employers relied on lockouts not only during the strikes but also as preventive measures, to get rid of pro-socialist workers.[52] During the periods of wars (the Russo-Japanese War in 1904 and 1905 and the First World War) industrialists were less keen to lock down their enterprises in case of labour conflicts. For example, in the second half of 1914, 8.5 per cent of conflicts ended up with lockouts and partial dismissal, but this number decreased to 5.1 in 1915 and 4.9 per cent in 1916.[53] During wartime, the industrialists could not afford to apply lockout because it meant that the factories ceased to operate, which could disrupt the supplies expected by the Ministry of War or the Ministry of the Navy.

Table 2.1 presents the statistics of those repressive practices that are quantifiable. However, there were practices, such as blacklisting and the cartelisation of the labour market, about which we have only anecdotal evidence. Numerous sources indicate that industrialists had practised blacklisting since, at least, from the early 1890s. Workers, whose names were in the blacklists, had difficulties in finding a job. Kliment Voroshilov, a worker in the early 1900s and later, during the Stalin era, a prominent Soviet politician, recalls in his memoirs how he struggled to find a job after being blacklisted. He was fired from a metallurgy plant in Alchevsk, a company town in the Donbas region (now Eastern Ukraine), and moved some 350 kilometres west. He hoped to find another job in one of the numerous metallurgical or metalworking enterprises of Ekaterinoslav, a large industrial city. However, Voroshilov quickly found out that he cannot get any job there either because his name was blacklisted. An informed colleague told Voroshilov that he was probably added to a list by a policeman from Alchevsk, who suspected that Voroshilov had been one of the organisers of a strike there some time ago. Voroshilov's only hope was to find temporary work at a workshop which was not covered by the blacklisting network.[54]

In the case of Voroshilov, the list was probably maintained by the police network. However, evidence indicates that the enterprises also created and distributed blacklists among themselves.[55] The practice remained popular until the collapse of the Russian Empire, especially in the industrial areas and among large employers.[56]

Industrialists cooperated to protect their interests in the labour market also by signing cartel agreements about the maximum wage limits.[57] Nikita Khrushchev, a Soviet political leader in the 1950s to the 1960s, recalled in his memoirs the practices of cartels in the labour market of the Donbas around 1908. Some groups of miners approached the owner of a mine demanding to increase their wages and threatening to strike in case their request was rejected. The answer of the owner was the following:

> I would gladly give you an increase in pay, but the mine owners have an agreement. It says that we should not have differences in wage rates. So, if all the owners of mines where there are strikes going on increase their wages, I will do the same for you. If they do not, then I am sorry, but I will not increase your wages either.

Khrushchev pointed out that when other strikers got their raises, the owner of their mine "made good on his word and increased wages, but only for men with families; the single men did not get raises".[58]

The outcome of the strikes

How did the repressive practices affect the outcome of the strikes? Table 2.2 presents the rate of successful strikes and how this relates to specific repressive practices. These data indicate that the application of repressive forces did not always mean that the workers' requirements were not satisfied. Moreover, the share of fully or partially satisfied demands is even higher in those cases when the police were involved, and various repressive means were applied compared to the overall number of the strikes.

A possible explanation might be that police and military forces were usually sent to handle those cases, which were especially difficult, threatening to outburst in mass violence (or already doing so). Such cases came under the close control of the authorities who often detected that the workers' rights had been violated.

Second, the government sent more often the police and military forces to large enterprises than to the small ones. The demands of the strikers on large factories were usually more diverse compared to those in small enterprises. Thus, the administrations of large factories had more opportunities to negotiate and to

Table 2.2 Share of the strikes resulting in total or partial satisfaction of the strikers' demands, including those which were accompanied by some repressive practices

Year	*All*	*Police or military intervention*	*Trials*	*Arrests*	*Banishment*	*Lockout or dismissal of a group of workers*
1895	22%	40%	39%	21%	50%	n/a
1896	33%	51%	25%	39%	33%	60%
1897	31%	46%	56%	37%	36%	33%
1898	29%	42%	29%	31%	33%	38%
1899	19%	29%	27%	22%	27%	40%
1900	18%	28%	50%	13%	10%	33%
1901	16%	39%	40%	21%	33%	100%
1902	12%	26%	33%	16%	33%	20%
1903	13%	37%	29%	31%	17%	33%
1904	13%	26%	n/a	38%	43%	36%
AVG	20%	36%	36%	27%	32%	44%

satisfy at least a part of the demands. The main reason to strike was the workers' dissatisfaction with their wages. Around half (in some years, more than 65 per cent)[59] of all strikes in Russia happened because of wage-related conflicts. However, the diversity of demands corresponded to the size of the enterprises. Large enterprises usually attracted many qualified workers who expected a certain level of working and living conditions. The larger an enterprise was, the more resources it had to invest in social infrastructure and to satisfy such needs. Consequently, though strikes at large enterprises were the most probable to attract repressive police intervention, still, these were the employers who were also the most open for negotiations to satisfy the workers' requests.

Industrialists were relatively open towards the workers' demands in the presence of police and military forces also because they were afraid of provoking a violent collision between strikers and the police. The arrests of strike organisers following the appearance of police often led to mass labour violence, which resulted in damaging factory property, stopping production and ultimately in financial loss.

Local state representatives also had an impact on the outcome of the strikes. In 15 per cent of conflicts, the factory inspection or another representative of the local authorities (a governor or a persecutor) interfered with the conflict and tried to resolve it. Statistics indicate that these actions tended to produce positive results: the chance to come to a compromise between the conflicting sides was higher in the presence of a state representative. However, if the state representative was inactive or aggressive with the strikers, his behaviour could provoke the explosion of violence. The strike of miners in the Central mine of Iuzovka in October 1898 was such a case. The labour conflict was peaceful until a mining engineer called Sutulov decided to intrude. The crowd of striking miners was standing around the pit head when Sutulov appeared in a state of inebriation and asked why the workers were not starting their shift. He also began to push them towards the entrance of the crate. A voice from the crowd shouted that they wanted a raise in pay. Then one of the strikers stepped forward and tried to formulate the workers' grievances. However, Sutulov interrupted the worker and ordered the foreman to take the man's name and have him fired. At that point, the entire crowd began to demand that they all be fired and hissed at Sutulov. After that, some 150 miners headed to the nearby ironworks, forced metallurgists to cease their work and knocked out all the windows in the workshop.[60]

Overall, several factors affected the outcome of a strike, including the actions of police, factory inspectors and local authorities, the behaviour of the strikers, the flexibility of the management, the efficiency of communication channels between the management and the strikers and the level of the activities of revolutionary organisations.

Conclusions

Strikes and unions were unlawful in the Russian Empire until 1905, and those who dared to participate in strikes were punished. Criminal punishment was combined with administrative measures. However, often it was the only way to attract attention to the workers' problems.

The government and the industrialists looked at strikes as a deviation from the norm and disturbance of the public order. They considered any compromise with strikers as weakness and inspiration for other workers to fight for their demands. Therefore, they gave preference to repression over negotiations. Moreover, the hierarchical relationship between the main stakeholders made the idea of strikes unacceptable. Some representatives of the state and some entrepreneurs started to change their attitude gradually to strikes and workers' organisations only from the early twentieth century. They advocated for relaxing labour law and, at the same time, for an increase in spending on welfare work.

To repress the labour movement, the government and the industrialists spent a significant amount of resources on repressive forces, including factory police and the employment of *Cossacks*. As preventive measurements, the police established a system of surveillance and spying. The secret political police were continuously searching for agitators among workers.

Employers did not have enough power to repress the labour movement and, at the same time, did not bother to establish efficient communication channels with their workers. The total ban of worker organisations which would be able to formulate and communicate the employees' demands, radicalised the labour movement and pushed the workers into the arms of revolutionaries. Any extreme violence to repress labour movement often had the opposite effect: it motivated the workers to increase solidarity and led to the outburst of mass-scale public protests.

The gradual improvement of working and living conditions from the late 1880s did not eliminate the labour movement: workers went to strikes relatively often, especially in the period from 1905 to 1907. In the period from 1895 to 1905, the government's reaction to the strikes was relatively harsh; repression peaked in

1905. Still, the labour movement during the Russian Revolution of 1905 became so overpowering that it was obviously no longer possible to repress it with police and military forces; the government had to relax the labour legislation.

When the labour movement started to decline from 1906, the authorities again returned to the old repressive methods persecuting both legal and informal worker organisations. They were able to handle local conflicts; however, they failed to confront the labour movement on a large scale. Although the labour movement was relatively weak in the period from 1907 to 1911, it sharply intensified from 1912 and in five years. The labour movement emerging as a mass phenomenon in the Russian Empire in the late nineteenth century and strengthening due to the confrontation with the authorities played an imperative role in the Revolution of 1917 and the collapse of the tsarism.

Acknowledgements

The authors thank Dóra Mérai and the editors for their comments on the draft of this chapter.

Notes

1 Zinaida I. Peregudova, *Politicheskii sysk Rossii: 1880–1917* (Moscow: ROSSPEN, 2000), 200.

2 E.g. Nikolai N. Polianskii, *Stachki rabochikh i ugolovnyi zakon* (St. Petersburg: tip. t-va Obshchestv. pol'za, 1907); Ivan Kh. Ozerov, *Politika po rabochemu voprosu v Rossii za poslednie gody: (Po neizd. dokumentam)* (Moscow: T-vo I. D. Sytina, 1906); Lev A. Tikhomirov, *Rabochii vopros (prakticheskie sposoby ego resheniia)* (Moscow: Tip. V. A. Zhdanovich, 1909).

3 See more in Evgeniia A. Vorontsova, *Predprinimatel'skie organizatsii v Rossii: istoriografiia, istochniki, istoriia* (Moscow: Eterna, 2013), 31 and further.

4 E.g. Andrei F. Vovchik, *Politika tsarizma po rabochemu voprosu v predrevoliutsionnyi period (1895–1904)* (Lvov: Izd-vo L'vov. un-ta, 1964); Vladimir Ia. Laverychev, *Tsarizm i rabochii vopros v Rossii (1861–1917 gg.)* (Moscow: Mysl', 1972); Iurii I. Kir'ianov, *Sotsial'no-politicheskii protest rabochikh Rossii v gody Pervoi mirovoi voiny, iiul' 1914 – fevral' 1917 gg.* (Moscow: In-t rossiiskoi istorii RAN, 2005).

5 E.g. Jacob Walkin, "The Attitude of the Tsarist Government Toward the Labour Problem," *American Slavic and East European Review* 13, no. 2 (1954); Gaston V. Rimlinger, "The Management of Labour Protest in Tsarist Russia: 1870–1905," *International Review of Social History* 5, no. 2 (1960); Theodore H. Von Laue, "Tsarist Labour Policy, 1895–1903," *The Journal of Modern History* 34, no. 2 (1962). These were followed by case studies on the repression of striking workers during specific conflicts, such as the Kreenholm strike in 1872, the Iuzovka cholera riot in 1892 and the Lena Goldfield massacre in 1912. See Reginald E. Zelnik, *Law and Disorder on the Narova River: The Kreenholm Strike of 1872* (Berkeley, CA: University of California Press, 1995); Theodore H. Friedgut, "Labour Violence and Regime Brutality in tsarist Russia: The Iuzovka Cholera Riots of 1892," *Slavic Review* 46, no. 2 (1987); Michael Melancon, *The Lena Goldfields Massacre and the Crisis of the Late Tsarist State* (College Station: Texas A&M University Press, 2006). While Soviet historians focused on the pieces of evidence about the cooperation between the industrialists and the government, Western scholars pointed out the controversial character of the tsarist labour policy and the conflicting interests of not only the industrialists and the government but

also within the government, between the various departments. Both Soviet scholars and their Western counterparts approached the topic from the political angle, i.e. its failure to advent the Revolution of 1917. Another limitation of these studies was that they were based on anecdotal evidence and drew their conclusions from a set of selected data.

6 Irina M. Pushkareva, Valerii I. Bovykin, and V. P. Zheltova, *Rabochee dvizhenie v Rossii. 1895 – fevral' 1917 g. Khronika. Vyp. 1–10* (Moscow: St. Petersburg, 1992–2008).

7 More about the project: Leonid I. Borodkin, Irina M. Pushkareva, and Irina V. Shilnikova, "The Structure and Dynamics of the Workers' Protest Movement at the Beginning of the 20th Century in Russia: Database Analysis," in *Striking Numbers. New Approaches to Strike Research* (Amsterdam: IISH, 2012), 74–76.

8 Irina M. Pushkareva et al., *Trudovye konflikty i rabochee dvizhenie v Rossii na rubezhe XIX – XX vekov* (St. Peretsburg: Aleteiia, 2011); Borodkin, Pushkareva, and Shilnikova, "The Structure and Dynamics of the Workers' Protest Movement at the Beginning of the 20th Century in Russia: Database Analysis"; Irina V. Shil'nikova, *Trudovye konflikty v promyshlennosti dorevoliutsionnoi Rossii: ot statistiki k mikroanalizu* (Moscow: MAKS Press, 2014).

9 Daniel R. Brower, "Labour Violence in Russia in the Late Nineteenth Century," *Slavic Review* 41, no. 3 (1982): 421.

10 Kir'ianov, *Sotsial'no-politicheskii protest rabochikh Rossii v gody Pervoi mirovoi voiny, iiul' 1914 – fevral' 1917 gg.*, 41.

11 Sources: Pushkareva, Bovykin, and Zheltova, *Rabochee dvizhenie v Rossii. 1895 – fevral' 1917 g. Khronika. Vyp. 1–10*; S. S. Atapin, *Khronika rabochego dvizheniia v Rossii s 3 iiunia 1907 g. po 31 dekabria 1910 g.* (Moscow: In-t istorii SSSR, 1981); Ministerstvo Finansov, *Svod otchetov fabrichnykh inspektorov za 1911 god* (St. Petersburg: Tip. V. F. Kirshbauma, 1912), 291; Ministerstvo Finansov, *Svod otchetov fabrichnykh inspektorov za 1912 god* (St. Petersburg: Tip. V. F. Kirshbauma, 1913), 293; Ministerstvo Finansov, *Svod otchetov fabrichnykh inspektorov za 1913 god* (Petrograd: Tip. V. F. Kirshbauma, 1914), 270; Georgii G. Kasarov, *Stachechnoe dvizhenie v Rossii v gody Pervoi mirovoi voiny. Iiul' 1914 g. – fevral' 1917 g.: Khronika* (St. Petersburg: Nestor-Istoriia, 2019), 748–49.

12 Walkin, "The Attitude of the Tsarist Government Toward the Labour Problem," 165.

13 Pushkareva et al., *Trudovye konflikty i rabochee dvizhenie v Rossii na rubezhe XIX – XX vekov*, 115 and further.

14 Polianskii, *Stachki rabochikh i ugolovnyi zakon*, 380.

15 Ibid.

16 Ministerstvo Finansov, *Svod otchetov fabrichnykh inspektorov za 1905 g.* (St. Petersburg: Tip. V. F. Kirshbauma, 1908), XVI.

17 Stephen A. Smith, *Red Petrograd: Revolution in the factories, 1917–1918* (Cambridge: Cambridge University Press, 1985), 38.

18 Polianskii, *Stachki rabochikh i ugolovnyi zakon*, 365.

19 Rimlinger, "The Management of Labour Protest in Tsarist Russia: 1870–1905," 235.

20 Sergei R. Glazunov, "Fabrichnoe zakonodatel'stvo i mekhanizmy ego realizatsii. 1882–1914 gg," *Ekonomicheskaia istoriia* 14, no. 2 (2018): 340.

21 Ivan L. Goremykin, *Sekretnyi tsirkuliar ministra vnutrennikh del ot 12 avgusta 1897 goda [o bor'be s revoliutsionnym dvizheniem sredi rabochikh]* (St. Petersburg: Gruppa rabochikh revoliutsionerov, 1897).

22 The "economic" strikes (i.e. wage and working day related) were decriminalised in 1905. In practice the authorities often categorised such strikes as "political" if they were accompanied by tensions with the police (including verbal abuse). Strikes covering workers of several enterprises were another exception. The authorities suspected that such strikes were coordinated by socialist organisations and therefore considered them as "political", i.e. unlawful.

23 Victoria E. Bonnell, "Radical Politics and Organized Labour in Pre-Revolutionary Moscow, 1905–1914," *Journal of Social History* 12, no. 2 (1978): 288.

24 Nikolai S. Avdakov, "O merakh k obespecheniiu gornykh promyslov rabochimi rukami i ob uregulirovanii prodazhi vodki v raione gornykh promyslov," in *Trudy XVIII s"ezda gornopromyshlennikov Iuga Rossii* (Kharkov: Tip. Zil'bel'berga, 1894), 356–57.
25 Leonid I. Borodkin et al., *«Ne rublem edinym»: Trudovye stimuly rabochikh-tekstil'shchikov dorevoliutsionnoi Rossii* (Moscow: ROSSPEN, 2010).
26 Volodymyr Kulikov, *Pidpryjemstva j suspil'stvo v zavods'kyh i shahtars'kyh poselennjah Donbasu ta Prydniprov'ja v 1870–1917 rr.* (Kharkiv: Vyd-vo Harkivs'kogo universytetu, 2019); Volodymyr Kulikov, "Necessity or Luxury? Welfare Work in the Company Towns of the Russian Empire," *Jahrbuch für Wirtschaftsgeschichte/Economic History Yearbook* 60, no. 2 (2019).
27 Ignatii I. Iasiukovich, *Zapiska po rabochemu voprosu v Rossii* (St. Petersburg, 1905), 3.
28 Vladimir Ia. Laverychev, "Antirabochie soiuzy kapitalistov v 1917 godu," *Vestnik Moskovskogo universiteta. Seriia 9. Istoriia*, no. 5 (1960).
29 Laverychev, *Tsarizm i rabochii vopros v Rossii (1861–1917 gg.)*.
30 Vladimir I. Shtein, *Zubatovshchina: Stranichka iz istorii rabochego voprosa v Rossii* (Moscow: tip. t-va I. D. Sytina, 1913), 103.
31 Susan P. McCaffray, "Origins of Labour Policy in the Russian Coal and Steel Industry, 1874–1900," *The Journal of Economic History* 47, no. 4 (1987): 951.
32 S"ezd gornopromyshlennikov Iuga Rossii, *Trudy XVIII S"ezda gornopromyshlennikov Iuga Rossii, byvshego v g. Khar'kove s 1 po 14 dekabria 1893 goda. Otchety, protokoly i doklady* (Kharov: Tip. Zil'bel'berga, 1894), 334.
33 Walkin, "The Attitude of the Tsarist Government Toward the Labour Problem," 177–78.
34 Edward H. Judge, *Plehve: Repression and Reform in Imperial Russia, 1902–1904* (Syracuse: Syracuse University Press, 1983), 126.
35 For example during the first labour conflict in Iuzovka in 1874, the company organised a group of some 40 skilled workers (probably many of British nationality) who dispersed the crowd of striking miners and beat up some of them. They did the same in 1887: armed a group of skilled metallurgists who imprisoned some 50 individuals among striking miners and later handed them to the police representatives. During this conflict, three strikers were killed, and 15 were wounded. Source: State Archive of the Russian Federation, Moscow. F. 7952. Op. 6. Doc. 119. P. 6, 10–11, 46.
36 Lev A. Liberman, *V strane chernogo zolota: Ocherk razvitiia zarabotnoi platy i revoliutsionnogo dvizheniia gornorabochikh Donbassa* (Moscow and Leningrad: Gos. izd-vo, 1926), 62–63; Theodore H. Friedgut, *Iuzovka and Revolution, Vol. I: Life and Work in Russia's Donbass, 1869–1924* (Princeton, NJ: Princeton University Press, 1994), 207.
37 Polianskii, *Stachki rabochikh i ugolovnyi zakon*, 368.
38 Ozerov, *Politika po rabochemu voprosu v Rossii za poslednie gody: (Po neizd. dokumentam)*, 160.
39 Ibid., 98.
40 Judge, *Plehve: Repression and Reform in Imperial Russia, 1902–1904*, 130.
41 Peregudova, *Politicheskii sysk Rossii: 1880–1917*, 193.
42 State Archive of the Russian Federation, Moscow. F. 7952. Op. 6. Doc. 120. P. 31.
43 Judge, *Plehve: Repression and Reform in Imperial Russia, 1902–1904*, 142.
44 Shtein, *Zubatovshchina: Stranichka iz istorii rabochego voprosa v Rossii*, 146.
45 Judge, *Plehve: Repression and Reform in Imperial Russia, 1902–1904*, 142.
46 Ozerov, *Politika po rabochemu voprosu v Rossii za poslednie gody: (Po neizd. dokumentam)*, 157; Laverychev, *Tsarizm i rabochii vopros v Rossii (1861–1917 gg.)*, 120.
47 Judge, *Plehve: Repression and Reform in Imperial Russia, 1902–1904*, 127.
48 About the database and its sources see Borodkin, Pushkareva and Shilnikova, "The structure and dynamics of the workers' protest movement at the beginning of the 20th century in Russia: Database analysis".
49 Michael Melancon, "The Ninth Circle: The Lena goldfield workers and the massacre of 4 April 1912," *Slavic Review* 53, no. 3 (1994): 793–95.

50 State Archive of the Russian Federation, Moscow. F. DP 4 d-vo. 1915. Doc. 30. Part 2. P. 12–12back, 15.
51 Vladimir Ia. Laverychev, *Rabochee dvizhenie v Ivanovo-Voznesenske v gody pervoi mirovoi voiny (1914 – fevral' 1917 gg.)* (Moscow: Izd-vo Mosk. un-ta, 1957), 112–17.
52 Irina M. Pushkareva, *Rabochee dvizhenie v Rossii v period reaktsii, 1907–1910 gg.* (Moscow: Nauka, 1989), 54.
53 Calculated based on: Kasarov, *Stachechnoe dvizhenie v Rossii v gody Pervoi mirovoi voiny. Iiul' 1914 g. – fevral' 1917 g.: Khronika.*
54 Kliment E. Voroshilov, *Rasskazy o zhizni (Vospominaniia). Kniga pervaia* (Moscow: Politizdat, 1968), 103.
55 Ozerov, *Politika po rabochemu voprosu v Rossii za poslednie gody: (Po neizd. dokumentam)*, 92–93.
56 Pushkareva, *Rabochee dvizhenie v Rossii v period reaktsii, 1907–1910 gg.*, 25.
57 For examples, see Ozerov, *Politika po rabochemu voprosu v Rossii za poslednie gody: (Po neizd. dokumentam)*, 92; Pushkareva, *Rabochee dvizhenie v Rossii v period reaktsii, 1907–1910 gg.*, 39.
58 Nikita S. Khrushchev, *Khrushchev Remembers. The Glasnost Tapes* (Boston, MA: Little Brown & Co, 1990), 7–9.
59 Calculated based on Kasarov, *Stachechnoe dvizhenie v Rossii v gody Pervoi mirovoi voiny. Iiul' 1914 g. – fevral' 1917 g.: Khronika.*
60 State Archive of the Russian Federation, Moscow. F. 7952. Op. 6. Doc. 1. P. 60.

3 Violence against strikers in the rural peripheries of the Iberian Peninsula, 1890–1915*

Assumpta Castillo Cañiz

New repertoires of protest in a changing rural space

In October 1903, the Spanish conservative newspaper *La Época* noted the alarm created by the "large number of workers" in the mining area of Bizkaia who were participating in the so-called Bilbao strike. According to the newspaper, this type of protest made a greater impression in Spain than in other countries where the higher level of industrial development meant that strikes were more widespread and frequent, and that therefore the authorities and society there were somehow more used to them.[1] In fact, *La Época* was right to be concerned, as strikes were on the rise in Spain, especially in contexts and sectors other than the traditional industrial ones. The same went for Portugal. Even though neither Spain nor Portugal were paradigmatic cases of social conflict during this period (the number of strikes remained comparatively low in both countries), we can see a relative upward trend in the use of strike action as an effective tactic in the collective struggle, a pattern that becomes very evident from 1909 onwards.[2] Furthermore, the levels of intensity of these strikes, measured by the number of participants and the degree of confrontation with public forces, were, on the whole, significantly high.[3] In both countries, the numerical weight of the strikes was concentrated in the main cities and their surroundings: Barcelona and Madrid, in Spain; Lisbon and Porto, in Portugal.[4] Nonetheless, in both cases the data show a gradual territorial extension of strikes. In Spain at the beginning of the twentieth century, the number of strikers began to rise even higher in other provinces where there was significant industrial activity, particularly in the mining and public works sectors.[5] In Portugal, we see Lisbon and Porto beginning to be overtaken in terms of the number of strikes by other centres where economic activities were closely linked to the primary sector, whose workers were particularly active in the years around the turn of the century.[6] In Spain, according to the fragmentary available data, the sector where strikes grew most exponentially throughout the period was agriculture (particularly from 1912 onwards). Agricultural strikes would have particular importance in Portugal from the beginning of the republican regime among the workers of the Alentejo. During these years, furthermore, areas traditionally associated with agricultural work saw this activity give way to the growth of other economic activities and new strategies of struggle, as had already occurred in the mining area of Baixo Alentejo in the last decades of the nineteenth century.[7]

This chapter examines the nature of violence against strikers in three different episodes that took place in the rural peripheries of Spain and Portugal over the last decade of the nineteenth century and the years preceding WWI. First, it examines the strike movements during the last decade of the nineteenth century and, in particular, the first two decades of the twentieth in the east of the Spanish province of Huesca (Aragon), an area particularly affected by the acute agricultural crisis.[8] The protests here were led by rural workers who were seasonally engaged in the construction of public works, namely railways, roads and water supplies, and in the energy industry. Second, it examines the strikes by rural workers that took place in 1901–2 in the Spanish province of Badajoz (Extremadura). In this area of large landowners, the turn-of-the-century crisis led to a process of cereal specialisation and expansion of the traditional model of extensive agriculture. The short-term benefit of this specialisation triggered the concentration of the proletarian population in medium-sized cities. Third, it reviews the cycle of strikes that took place at the beginning of the Portuguese Republic in the region of the Alentejo (1911–15), where cereal specialisation went hand in hand with technical and social advances. Here, economic activity was gradually diversified, the capitalist agricultural model became a pole of attraction for the working population and some industrial nuclei were created.[9]

Regional differences in the socio-economic transformation were accompanied by differences in the degree and pace of politicisation. In both Spain and Portugal, the countryside gradually entered the political space, especially through the extension of suffrage and union rights. However, Spanish laws on association (1887), male suffrage (1890), agricultural unionisation (1906) and strikes (1909), and Portuguese laws on agricultural unionisation (1894), association without previous authorisation (1907) and strikes (December 1910) had limited impact on the countryside and did not change the authorities' attitude to a fully implemented democratisation. In fact, these measures went hand in hand with the reinforcement of repressive mechanisms. As in other European countries, exceptional laws were enacted in the last decade of the nineteenth century (in Spain the repressive laws on terrorism, 1894, 1896; in Portugal the law on the repression of anarchism, 1896). However, what was most instrumental in unleashing the repressive potential of both states, particularly in the case of Spain and increasingly in the case of Portugal (especially from the beginning of the Republican regime in 1910), was their view that socio-labour conflicts, and even the rise of workers' associations, were challenges to public order that had to be occasionally repressed.[10] In all three cases, the repression of strikers was delegated to four different forces: the army, as the ultimate guarantor of so-called "public order"; the gendarmeries of each country, the Spanish Civil Guard (*Guardia Civil*) and the recently created Portuguese Republican National Guard (*Guarda Nacional Republicana*); local security forces, clearly insufficient in view of the scale and nature of these conflicts; and private forces or civilian volunteer corps, which in both countries played an important role in defending the interests of property.

The strengthening of private mechanisms for the preservation of order went hand in hand with an upward trend in employer associationism. Although this coincided with a radicalisation of positions, it was based on habitual practices of private control in areas where the political costs of repression had traditionally been lower. The exercising of the right to strike aroused new fears, even more so when, as was often the case, it was related to the penetration of new political tendencies.

Although historiography has delved into the nature of repression and police deployment in both Spain and Portugal,[11] work remains to be done, especially with regard to the interplay between the centre and the rural periphery, and between the public and private spheres in the policing of protests. The same goes for the specific practice of strikebreaking, which provides a lens through which we can shed new light on the use of violence during this period and how the elites and the state managed the challenges posed by the new mass politics.[12] In the three cases discussed in this chapter, the emergence and the nature of these strikes and how and by whom they were repressed are issues that must be assessed under the prism of belonging to a "double periphery": with respect to the most dynamic spaces of capitalism at the global level, and with respect to the decision-making centres within their respective territories.[13] These are also defining issues for many other regions and areas worldwide, hence the significance of the present contribution in this collective volume.

Tension in public order mechanisms

In 1890, the Spanish Prime Minister, Antonio Cánovas del Castillo, stated that the army was a "robust support for social order and an invincible dam against the illegal attempts of the proletariat".[14] Definitive consolidation of the process of militarisation of the public order system in Spain can be found a little more than a decade earlier with the enactment of the law constituting the army (1878). It stated that the task of the body was to act against the enemies of the fatherland, both external and "internal". In Portugal, too, the army was the main police force throughout the period, a role anticipated in the mid-nineteenth century. Although the control of public order was militarised to a far lesser degree than in Spain, this began to change with the inception of the Republican regime.[15] In 1911, the National Republican Guard was created in Portugal, which until then had been the only continental country without a gendarmerie.[16] The Spanish Civil Guard and the Portuguese National Republican Guard together with the army were the cornerstone of the repression of strikes in both countries. However, behind the territorial deployment of both bodies was not only the need to preserve or restore public order, but also the latent idea of a social upheaval following any kind of collective demonstration and certainly a work stoppage.[17] Although these episodes were usually of brief duration or the conflict was resolved through mediation between workers, authorities and employers or construction managers, the threat of force as a deterrent was on the table from the beginning.

In both Spain and Portugal, the public order model had been strengthened and adapted to meet new needs, but there were some elements that occasionally, and increasingly frequently, put pressure on both systems: the growing supra-local nature of conflicts, their actual or potential territorial extension, and their increasing simultaneity. Although these were not entirely new elements, their interaction with a more politicised context significantly changed how they were perceived and experienced.

The misgivings of the Portuguese and Spanish elites and authorities multiplied in the face of an increasingly recurrent scenario: the concentration of workers in particular areas of both countries, especially where public works were being constructed and where public or private economic activity generated a significant need for labour. In some areas, workers were gathered in their hundreds, often outside the cities, as was the case at the turn of the century during construction of the Canal of Aragon and Catalonia in the east of the province of Huesca and in the Catalan province of Lleida. In 1897, shortly after the state took over construction of the infrastructure, there were increasing concentrations of labourers demanding work on sites that were progressing only intermittently and not absorbing the anticipated workforce. Up to 3,000 workers were making such demands in towns of not even a thousand inhabitants. This was the case in San Esteban de Litera, where in mid-March a partial strike was declared. April saw a concentration of workers not only from the town itself, but also from the region's capital, Tamarite, and other neighbouring towns.[18] The supra-local nature of the protest was revealed as being of paramount importance. This is made explicit, for example, in the increasingly frequent communications between the Guardia Civil commands of the Canal construction zone in Huesca and the Ministry of War in dealing with the strikes of 1901 and 1903 in the towns of the Canal area, conflicts which would worsen in the following two years.[19] In Extremadura, the general strike of agricultural workers and stockbreeders, as well as domestic servants called by the workers' association of the city of Badajoz in May 1901 was taken up by neighbouring towns, a situation that would be repeated in 1902 with a new general strike of agricultural workers throughout the province.[20] In the Portuguese region of the Alentejo, the number of municipalities in which rural workers went on strike during the summer of 1911, mainly in the district of Évora and some areas of Portalegre and Beja, rose to 27 in just one and a half months.[21] The provincial city was the driving force and at the same time the recipient of a large number of these demands for work, sometimes with a dynamic that some called "invasion of the city". In March 1912, the Portuguese government took steps to investigate the events that had taken place during the two waves of strikes by the Alentejo's rural workers, in the summer of 1911 and in January 1912, whose epicentre was the city of Évora. As some owners told the government's delegated commission, in January "herds of people [*magotes de povo*] from the countryside" had begun to enter the city. Some newspapers would also describe this episode as an "assault on the city", an expression not far removed from the one the governor himself would use, pointing out that, despite the efforts made, the workers "gradually invaded the city".[22] Some local newspapers spoke of more than 15,000 strikers, of whom more than 10,000 would have come along the Reguengos de Monsaraz road, which became the most heavily guarded thoroughfare during this second phase of strikes, with the 5th Cavalry Regiment being sent there.[23]

Along with this, a second key element was gaining importance: the extension of the protest to new territories and involving workers from various company branches or other production areas. This was the case with the numerous works that were being carried out in the Pyrenees and Pre-Pyrenees in Catalonia and Aragon at the beginning of the century for the construction of hydroelectric power stations. It was not unusual for groups of workers to travel seasonally from one centre to another in search of work, despite belonging to different companies, as they were not very far from each other. In June 1913, more than 2,000 workers left their jobs at the *Energía Eléctrica de Cataluña*'s construction site in Capdella in the Catalan region of Pallars on the border with Aragon.[24] In December of the same year, the construction workers of another hydroelectric company, *Barcelona Traction Light and Power*, better known as "La Canadenca", had done the same in Aitona, another border town, when the company refused to approve the workers' demands.[25] In May 1914, 350 workers at the *Compañía Catalana de Gas y Electricidad*'s construction sites of the Seira and El Run hydroelectric power plants in the Ribagorza region of Huesca also determined to demand a pay raise.[26] In the context of a broader articulation of the labour movement, this extension of the protest was manifested in another way: a call for solidarity strikes. After the repression of the Évora rural workers' strike in January 1912, which resulted in one death and several serious injuries, a general strike was declared and was widely supported in several parts of Portugal, including the capital. The strikes in the mining area of Baixo Alentejo were also part of this dynamic of general protest. In Lisbon, a state of siege was declared and the city was handed over to the military authorities, an unprecedented event.[27] Previously practically isolated nuclei being drawn into cycles of conflict that affected the whole country was a new threat, something that the Spanish authorities could not fail to notice in cases such as Badajoz in 1902. Underlying this extension of the protest was another element that particularly concerned the authorities: political and union propaganda. In the province of Badajoz, territorial articulation of the labour movement became very evident when, after the initial strike episodes in 1901, the first regional workers' meetings began taking place. At the end of April 1902, the first workers' congress was held in the town of Torre de Miguel Sesmero, some 30 kilometres from Badajoz, and was attended by delegates from 21 towns representing more than 14,000 workers. Two months later, the convening power of provincial trade unionism became very clear in a new general strike.[28] In Aragon, the main concern of the central and military authorities was the proximity to Catalonia and the fear of possible "contagion". The correspondence between the military captain general's office and the Ministry of War during the celebrations of 1 May 1891 had already contained references to the "agents of Catalonia". In 1905, this concern for cross-border transfer embraced the "revolutionary work" of almost a thousand Republican elements, in the face of which the general of the 5th Army Corps informed the Minister of War that he would try to stifle movement with "the few elements" at his disposal. A year later, the authorities again became suspicious that behind the canal workers' riots and strikes were "political issues and reckless propaganda".[29] In the Portuguese region of the Alentejo, where dozens of rural workers' unions had arisen out of the strikes themselves, the National Federation of Rural Workers was created in August 1912, coinciding with a propaganda "tournée".[30] One of the questions several workers were asked as part of the enquiries of the previously mentioned delegate commission regarded the exact nature of the relationship between the rural associations of the Évora district and the Lisbon workers.

A third important element was the co-occurrence of several conflicts. It is worth mentioning that, aside from the simultaneous strike episodes that took place over a short period of time in areas such as Spain's Badajoz province and Portugal's Alentejo region, there were other waves of protest occurring at the same time but making claims of a different nature. At the beginning of 1905, nearly a thousand workers from France and Catalonia went to the mayor of Tamarite de Litera and demanded to be allowed to work on the Canal of Aragon and Catalonia. At the same time, in neighbouring towns such as Benabarre or Albelda there were tax riots and workers rioting against the wealthy of the town assuming they were responsible for them, the workers, not being admitted to the canal works. In Ballobar, the Civil Guards of five adjacent posts were brought together to counter a collective attack on private property, a protest believed to be "aggravated by recent speeches". In April, approximately 500 workers on the Tamarite section threatened to go on strike. In Zaidín, several hundred people demonstrated in front of the town hall demanding work on the site. In August, the Tamarite workers rioted and members of the Civil Guard were once again concentrated in the vicinity.[31]

Faced with this state of things, both states redoubled their coercive capacities. In Spain, the number of Civil Guard staff and posts was increased, particularly after 1899 and between 1909 and 1910. In Portugal, the Republican Guard, formerly the Municipal Guard with jurisdiction in Lisbon and Porto, extended its range to the rest of the country, becoming the National Republican Guard. It was deployed for the first time in the Alentejo region.[32] There are, however, several elements that show that there were important gaps in the apparent territorial coverage of the gendarmeries and armies of both countries, especially as the episodes of conflict multiplied. The correspondence between the Spanish Ministry of War and the regional commands of the Civil Guard and the general captains of the different military regions contains references to the excessive travelling times incurred by forces that were supposed to suppress or prevent the outbreak of conflicts. This was a major problem in areas where the railway infrastructure was scarce, such as in Extremadura, or where the railway service was highly unreliable, a frequent grievance in the east of the province of Huesca. During the 1902 strikes in the province of Badajoz, the correspondence between the forces and the central authorities pointed to the "remoteness" of some places (including some regional capitals, such as Olivenza), which brought with it some risk. As a result of simultaneous strikes and conflicts in various parts of the province, several Civil Guard commands warned that as the forces were concentrated in the capital there were none available for other areas, so requests were made to the Ministry of War to move several army units.[33] In Portugal, the Alentejo was the scene of this early deployment of the National Republican Guard. However, it was after, not before, the first wave of strikes in the summer of 1911 that the force was installed in the district of Évora, which saw the headquarters of the third battalion established there only in early November. It was not until September that there were posts in all the municipalities of the Alentejo.[34] Army intervention continued to be necessary, but it was also fully mobilised alongside the National Republican Guard in the industrial zone south of Lisbon, including units based in districts of the Alentejo, such as the 5th cavalry, mobilised in August in the Setúbal area.[35] To this must be added the frequent threats of alleged monarchical conspiracies and incursions into the north, which saw a very large number of troops mobilised between July and October 1911 and during the summer of 1912. It is certainly revealing that in the official inquiry into the strike episodes of May-July 1911 and January 1912 that opened in March 1912, the owners declared that "thanks to the deployment of the NRG" the character and especially the duration of the January strike had been markedly different. In November 1911, the civil government received repeated requests for a needed increase in the number of National Republican Guard posts. In February 1912, as several Alentejo deputies were expressing their joy at having "finally" had their properties guaranteed and defended, the civil governor of Évora warned the owners in the district of the need to reach agreements with the rural workers in the face of a probable new strike and the possibility that the resources they had at their disposal would not be sufficient to repress it.[36]

These insufficiencies could have two possible consequences: either the state's capacity to repress certain episodes of conflict would be reduced, or the lack of personnel would be particularly lethal where the conflict could not be properly managed. In 1902, a confidential note on public order from the Spanish Ministry of the Interior warned that in most cases of public disorder, a shortage of personnel meant that civilian governors were forced to entrust the military authorities with restoring calm, often resulting in "bloody scenes".[37] This is indeed what happened in the city of Badajoz on 1 June 1902, when guards seriously injured dozens of strikers, killed a day labourer and arrested 130 people. That same afternoon, a state of war was declared in the city.[38] At the beginning of March 1906 five day labourers were killed by the police in Fraga, in the Spanish province of Huesca. The stoppage at the Canal works close to the town led to protests and the calling of a general strike in the town. It was not until seven o'clock the next morning that a company from the infantry regiment arrived in the town. Three days after the event the force concentrated in the city numbered 150 men, while a company of 70 stayed for two months.[39] In Évora, the military and the National Republican Guard violently evicted demonstrators who had gathered on 23 January for the new strike that had begun on 13 January. The result was dozens of arrests, one dead and several seriously injured. However, in this case it is more difficult to talk about a shortage of forces, since they arrived from all over the country in what seemed to be a real military occupation of the city. The strike had by then spread throughout the district of Évora and to some towns in the Beja, Santarém and Setúbal areas. In fact, it seemed to be an open choice to suppress the conflict *manu militari*: in the words of the governor, when the strike had been underway for 11 days, "I decided to attack it directly on the 24th".[40]

New repressive mechanisms parallel to the state: private action

The need for repressive action in the more remote areas, something that needed not only to be done quickly but also to be maintained, spurred the involvement of the private sphere. The shortage of forces, the distance from the major cities, the empowerment of workers ensuing from their organisation and militancy, and the proliferation of simultaneous protest episodes meant that state repression was often not enough. Private citizens were therefore pushed into taking an active part in repressive tasks. The organisational boom in the workforce had its counterpart in the acceleration of the processes by which owners and employers formed associations. These platforms, however, sought not only to become economic lobbies, but also to increase their management capacities on various fronts, including policing.[41] This section outlines five strategies of private sphere intervention in the management of public order in parallel with – and often with the acquiescence of – state institutions.

The first strategy for dealing with the workers' increasing mobilisation in the context of a weak state presence was negotiation. The records of the *Instituto de Reformas Sociales* contain accounts of many episodes of strikes in Spain that were settled by "direct management between employers and workers". Sometimes this negotiation took the form of opening subscriptions and distributing coupons, as was done on many occasions in 1906 in the villages in the Canal of Aragon and Catalonia construction area in response to concerns about the increase in episodes of protest. However, this failed to meet the workers' aspirations. On other occasions, the productive calendar or mediation by the authorities were the main reasons for committing to a negotiated solution. This is what occurred at the beginning of June 1911 in Évora, where a meeting was held between employers and workers at which the latter greatly outnumbered the former. The agreements reached at this meeting represented a partial victory for the rural workers, but they were later ignored by the employers, which led to a second wave of strikes. Appearing before the commission delegated to clarify the facts, several owners declared that they had signed the agreement out of fear of reprisals and that at the time they would have signed anything the strikers wanted. Several of them also added that the forces of law and order had not been present at the meeting.[42]

The second strategy was the systematic use of law enforcement for private purposes. The difficulties that both gendarmeries had in establishing a presence throughout the entire territory were solved in innumerable cases with the active participation of owners, patrons and private companies. Companies such as the *Energía Eléctrica de Cataluña* in Capdella or the *Empresa Catalana de Gas y Electricidad* in Seira rented buildings to convert them into barracks for the Civil Guard in view of the arrival of substantial numbers of workers once work began on the plants in 1912.[43] In both countries, the central institutions warned of the abuse this practice constituted. In 1901 the Spanish Ministry of the Interior drew attention to the frequency with which the Civil Guard were concentrated in provincial capitals and other major towns "without a really justified reason". A year later, a letter sent to all the governors mentioned that the municipalities and especially individuals were making "excessive" requests. The Portuguese Ministry of War had already noted in 1887 the "repeated and excessive requests for armed force".[44] However, it is revealing that over time these requests did not diminish, but the central authorities' discouragements did, and ultimately they chose instead to approve of this private subsidy. In a circular to the district administrators in November 1911, the civil governor of Évora made it clear that it would be impossible to increase local allocations of the National Republican Guard. Aware that many employers had already tried to remedy the situation through their own means, he legally established that they would be responsible for the costs of the additional places. The employers' union of each locality was to make a request to the Ministry of the Interior to this effect. The need was "urgent", according to the governor.[45] This was not, however, a radically new practice: as early as 1908, in the last years of the monarchy and coinciding with a period of marked social agitation due to the concentration of numerous groups of workers protesting against unemployment, some "citizens' commissions" offered to pay the salaries of civil police, who were then used as private night watchmen in different towns.[46]

Closely related to this last strategy is the third: delegation of law enforcement powers by the government to groups of individuals. In Spain, the "Rural Police Law" allowed landowners' organisations to become Farmers' Associations (*Comunidades de Labradores*) or Rural Police Unions. Under this law, passed in July 1898, the public order powers previously granted to the municipality were transferred to local landowners. The vast province of Badajoz would have the largest number of these associations and police unions.[47] In 1902, after the second strike of rural workers in several areas of the province of Badajoz and at a time when there were signs of a stable workers' association, a confidential letter from the Ministry of the Interior to the civil governor of the province stressed the need for more preventive work, which was to be complemented by the active participation of the owners: "Even more important will be to bring to the minds of individuals the essential need to combine their efforts and proceed to protect their interests by forming associations in the localities", measures considered "extremely necessary" in the broad terms of the province's municipalities.[48] Although the Rural Police Law was intended to be applied particularly in areas where the *latifundia* system was prevalent, other localities operating under different systems would form their own "farmer's associations". This was the case in some of the towns involved in the Canal of Aragon and Catalonia protests, such as Barbastro, where one of these associations had already been created in 1904, very early compared with the others that would be established throughout the country, including several in the province of Badajoz. Thereafter, questions of public order disappeared completely from the municipal records.[49] Although the construction of the Canal of Aragon and Catalonia had passed into state hands in 1896, the local elites maintained a high degree of involvement in the works, mainly because they were the ones who ended up building the secondary sections of the canal. From 1894, a corps of labourer-watchmen (*peones-vigilantes*) were engaged on the work, but in the years of greatest strike agitation, an organisation was set up to defend the interests of the Canal. That same year saw towns or sections of the Canal beginning to form Associations of Irrigators (*Comunidades de Regantes*) of the canal area. Each association had a steering board composed of owners, who had police jurisdiction over their area, and a first instance jury (as did the Farmer's Associations).[50] In Portugal, however, alongside the aforementioned establishment of commissions for the private use of the police force, there appears to have been greater recourse to individual legitimate defence. Since the beginning of the republic, there had been a very noticeable increase in the number of arms licences granted to owners and traders. This was because of, among other things, the greater territorial deployment of the state and greater control over the circulation of previously unlicensed weapons. However, it also confirms an earlier trend, already noticeable from 1908 in the district of Évora. Even then, the large number of weapons, both shotguns and revolvers, declared as weapons "for self-defence" (which included defence of person and property) was noteworthy.[51]

Along with the delegation, a fourth one was the permissiveness in the constitution of private police. Significantly, this was the strategy adopted by some of the companies established mainly through foreign initiative and with foreign capital, particularly those involved in mining. Subordination to foreign capital, together with the desire to maintain good relations with these companies, ended up generating strong relationships of dependence and the ceding of important spaces of sovereignty to them.[52] This was also evident in the area of policing. Private police forces paid by company directors had become widespread since the beginning of the twentieth century in the large mines of the southern Alentejo region of Portugal owned by firms such as the British *Mason & Barry* or the Belgian *Société Anonyme Belge des Mines de Aljustrel*. The miners of the Baixo Alentejo staged several strikes in 1879, 1905, 1907 and 1912. The 1912 strike came after the constitution of the mining union and was part of the cycle of protests that took place throughout the country following the events in Évora. The companies' private police were actively involved in the repression of these strikes.[53] The same was true on the other side of the border, in the mining areas around the basins of the southern Alentejo. The Rio Tinto Company Limited, the British firm that had won the contract for the deposits in the Riotinto mining basin in the Spanish province of Huelva, Andalusia, also had its own police force, the so-called *guardiña*. The members of these corps were tasked with surveillance of both the facilities and the workers and exercised the functions of a kind of political police. Surveillance was reinforced during the strike preparations, when the numbers of *guardiña* were increased or new positions were created within the body, as happened in 1913 in Riotinto with the creation of the position of "house guard".[54] However, the large number of workers concentrated in these districts meant that these forces were insufficient to maintain public order in the event of open conflict, so the assistance of the state's repressive forces continued to be necessary. Fearing a strike, requests continued to made for units of infantry and cavalry. In Riotinto, the massacre that had taken place during a first strike in 1888 was at the hands of the private police forces, the Civil Guard and the army and was one of the bloodiest episodes of the period of Spanish Restoration. There was, furthermore, close cooperation between the company's police and the Civil Guard forces.[55]

The final strategy is of "civic defence of order". That the emergence and proliferation of patriotic leagues, civilian shooting groups and militias and the increases in their membership coincided with the main episodes of strike and social conflict is indicative. This was the case in the province of Badajoz, where the National Shooting Federation (*Tiro Nacional*), the delegation of the civil shooting federation, was especially active from 1902.[56] In 1911, the members of some municipal governing bodies of towns in the Portuguese Alentejo region, such as Reguengos de Monsaraz and Estremoz, were keen to build shootings ranges and join the so-called National Shooting Crusade (*Cruzada Tiro Nacional*).[57] The so-called battalions of Republican volunteers were involved in the strike called by the railway workers of the *Companhia dos Caminhos de Ferro do Sul e Sueste* that took place in January 1911 with demonstrations in several municipalities of the Alentejo. The Republican volunteers had emerged in the heat of the civic mobilisation that accompanied the revolution and were, according to the governor of Lisbon, the "best assistant for maintaining order" given a police force that was "not sufficiently republicanised".[58] The members of these battalions replaced striking workers and were involved in strike repression, which included arresting workers from several Alentejo towns, conduct that was later imitated in the industrial zone south of Lisbon and in the capital itself. That same month, the battalions were also instrumental in extinguishing a rural workers' strike in Estremoz.[59] In mid-August 1911, the governor of Évora in a letter to the commander of the fourth military division referred to the existence of "non-official" battalions. The word "legal" in the draft version was changed to "official" in the final version.[60] Later on, in a formal declaration to the government commission, a volunteer proudly pointed out that even before the establishment of the Republic, he had been a member of the *Carbonária* secret society. During the summer strikes he was in charge of surveillance of the rural workers and anyone else who was in the movement. He added that this type of "careful vigilance" was exercised "continuously and rigorously" by militant Republicans. A little later, in 1913, in the era of the government of Republican Democratic Party leader, Afonso Costa, the group *Formiga Branca* (the termite) was created and was supported and promoted by the institutions themselves, particularly the civil government of Lisbon. Its members were granted special police status and were authorised to carry weapons; the police could not interfere with their activities. In January 1914, alongside the National Republican Guard, they were involved in breaking the railwaymen's strike in the capital. Their role seems to have been to restrain the advance and extension of the protest, since they seem to have been involved in repressive activities in other parts of the country, signs of which could be seen in the south of Alentejo during the mining protests of 1915 and in Évora, where they allegedly supported the Republican National Guard in suppressing a demonstration and imprisoning more than 30 trade unionists in January 1916.[61]

Conclusions

The evidence presented here show a convergence of interests and a confluence of strategies on the part of the state, the employers and the wealthy classes of both countries regarding the maintenance of public order in the context of a gradual consolidation of modern capitalism. In both Spain and Portugal, we see a significant change in the methods for dealing with the rise of strikes, often caused by difficulties in implementing this capitalist modernisation. All the same, institutional permissiveness with regard to the creation of parallel forces, or even the delegation of these powers to private entities, cannot be attributed solely to a certain inability on the part of the state to cover the territory effectively in situations of conflict. In both cases, it was within the very framework of the process of strengthening the state and increasing its repressive capacity that these efforts were redoubled. On the other hand, there is no doubt that these methods reached a greater degree of complexity in regard to activities where the weight of the private sector was stronger. However, at no time did the public institutions, owners and those companies with national or foreign capital abandon the use of public force as the main element of both repression and deterrence. One of the reasons for this was undoubtedly the clearly military nature of repression exercised by the gendarmeries in the two countries, the Spanish Civil Guard and the Portuguese National Republican Guard, and by the army, which was particularly aggressive.

Nonetheless, in the case of both Spain and Portugal, the state's repressive actions were often reinforced by the active participation of the private sector. It is useful to consider this coalition as a convenient solution to the problem of covering a rural periphery in a gradual process of change. This did not exclude a certain fear that control over the maintenance of public order would be dispersed. However, this suspicion was mitigated in both countries by a confidence in the convergence of the interests of central institutions, elites and the bourgeoisie. How this process evolved depended not only on the economic situation and cycles of protest, but also on the differing political actions of both governments. Although it is difficult to establish a clear line of development or to talk about real planning in this combination of forces, we can draw up an approximate chronology covering these two and a half decades. In this, we can distinguish three periods delineated by distinct political crises and regime changes, and clear changes in the patterns of social protest or even significant transformations in repressive attitudes and strategies.

The first period covers the last decade of the nineteenth century and was marked by a notable increase in social conflicts and strikes, exceptional measures in terms of public order and the beginning of the mobilisation of the private sector. Along with this was the end-of-the-century crisis and a timid modernisation, a process that proved to have high social costs. In addition, the political crises following colonial losses by both countries resulted in a toughening of political-social measures and a certain abandonment of the maintenance of public order outside the major regional capitals. Militarisation was very evident in Spain, especially in the wake of the colonial crisis, while in Portugal exceptional measures were eased after 1897, although the army remained the main police force. The rise of property-owners' associations led to requests from individuals for greater powers in upholding public order, a dynamic that was accompanied by an increase in the use of available forces for private purposes. These years were also marked by an increase in patriotic leagues and a strengthening of the discourse on civic defence of the fatherland and order.

The second period covers the first decade of the twentieth century and was characterised by a growing fear of social overflow, the entrenchment of tough policies and the state sanction of private activities. The turn-of-the century years were particularly marked by the threat of a general strike in Spain and by a strike boom in Portugal. The aforementioned dynamics of protest were reinforced, and this coincided with a greater structuring of the labour movement and the republican alternatives. The attempted state intervention in social matters and the timid democratic opening were combined with an iron-fisted policy when it came to managing the rise of protest. While in Portugal this softened after the 1908 regicide, in Spain the process was particularly marked by the military's desire for autonomy and became more starkly evident from 1909. Moreover, with this policy repression had a lower political cost because of the radicalisation of sectors of the elite and the bourgeoisie. Aside from this, the trend towards private control of public order mechanisms continued, particularly in the rural peripheries, and was now backed by state legislation that sanctioned this private violence on a delegated basis. In addition, the use of private police increased in some industrial sectors, particularly by foreign-owned companies.

The third period covers the second decade of the twentieth century up to the beginning of the First World War and was marked by limitations to the process of democratic opening, the definitive consolidation of militarisation and the emergence of a new vigilantism. At the same time the rise of workers' associations led to a further increase in the number of strikes. However, the implementation of arbitration measures was combined with a harsh repressive policy in both countries, resulting in definitive consolidation of the militarisation of public order. In the case of Portugal, the new republican regime's quest for stability together with the conversion of the elites into new political clients was a setback for the very openness these measures announced. In contrast, there was a gradual strengthening of the model of citizen surveillance in the form of volunteer battalions and citizens' militias, which, in the midst of a formal democratisation process, was occasionally encouraged or even outrightly permitted by the institutions, and therefore circumvented certain legal constraints. At that time, in Spain, citizen militias would occasionally take to the streets in the role of anti-worker militias, as the *Somatén* did in Catalonia; this was a model that would spread to the *latifundia*, especially in the interwar years (and very particularly during the so-called Bolshevik Trienium, 1918–20). Some scattered youth militias also began to settle in provincial capitals, such as Badajoz and Huesca, leading to some incidents in the latter city.[62]

The deployment of such a plurality of practices was part of a dynamic in which the centre-periphery dialogue was a major component. This partial convergence of interests between the state, the upper-middle classes and other institutions, such as the army and the church, in relation to socio-labour conflicts would lead to new political cultures becoming more clearly defined and the pre-configuration of elements that in both Spain and Portugal would contribute to the future consolidation of authoritarian regimes.

Notes

* Research for this article received funding from the European Research Council (ERC) under the European Union's Horizon 2020 Research and Innovation program (G.A. 677199 – ERC-StG2015 "The Dark Side of the Belle Époque. Political Violence and Armed Associations in Europe before the First World War").

1 "La huelga," *La Época*, October 28, 1903, 1.

2 In Spain, during the period 1905–14 there was an average of 211 strikes per year, being higher or much higher in the years 1910–14, with a peak in 1911 (311 strikes). In Portugal where official statistics at the time are almost non-existent, the data indicate an average of 65 strikes per year for the period 1887–1908. From 1909 this record is much higher, reaching 535 strikes in 1910 and 419 strikes in 1911. Always bear in mind that the available data are fragmentary. See the reports of the Institute of Social Reforms for this period, published between 1906 and 1917 and available online in "Repositorio Documental," Ministerio de Trabajo, Migraciones y Seguridad Social. Gobierno de España, and also Javier Silvestre, "Los determinantes de la protesta obrera en España 1905–1935: ciclo económico, marco político y organización sindical," *Revista de Historia Industrial*, no. 24 (2003): 75–76. For the case of Portugal, see José Tengarrinha, "As greves em Portugal: uma perspectiva histórica do seculo XVIII a 1920," *Análise Social* 17, no. 67–68 (1981).

3 This was particularly true in Spain, as noted in Manuel Pérez Ledesma, *Estabilidad y conflicto social. España, de los iberos al 14-D* (Madrid: Nerea, 1990), 188. However police and vigilante violence reached its peak in Portugal from 1911 onwards and particularly from 1913, to the point that PM Afonso Costa was nicknamed the "*racha sindicalistas*" (unionist-breaker).

4 According to the aforementioned sources, in Spain strikes in Madrid and Barcelona represented between 30 and 50 per cent of the total between 1905 and 1914, being more than half of them in the years 1909 and 1910. In Portugal, of the 725 strikes of which we have this information between 1875–1900, 510 (70 per cent) are concentrated in Lisbon and Porto. During the turn of the century secondary industrial centres such as Setúbal and Faro gained importance, followed by other Portuguese districts in the twentieth century.

5 In Instituto de Reformas Sociales, *Memoria Estadística de las huelgas (1904–1905)* (Madrid: Imprenta de la Sucesora de M. Minuesa de los Ríos, 1906).

6 Tengarrinha, "As greves," 587.

7 Paulo Eduardo Guimarães, "O motim e a greve," in *Indústria e conflito no meio rural: Os mineiros alentejanos (1858–1938)* (Évora: Publicações do Cidehus, 2001).

8 A synthetic overview in Carlos Forcadell Álvarez, "El sector agrario aragonés en la crisis de finales del siglo XIX," in *Historia de Aragón* (Zaragoza: Institución Fernando el Católico, 1996).

9 The alleged socio-economic stagnation of these years in both Extremadura and the Alentejo has been qualified in some works. See Martin Baumeister, *Campesinos sin tierra. Supervivencia y resistencia en Extremadura (1880–1923)* (Madrid: Ministerio de Agricultura, 1997), 42–62; Helder Adegar Fonseca, "Élites agrárias e crescimento económico na periferia portuguesa do século XIX: o exemplo do Alentejo na era liberal," *Análise Social* 33, no. 146–147 (1998): 497–98; Paulo Guimarães, "O comportamento estratégico das elites económicas alentejanas face à actividade industrial: algumas evidências a partir da região de Évora (1880–1926)," *Ayer* no. 48 (2002).

10 For Spain see Demetrio Castro Alfín, "Agitación y orden en la Restauración. ¿Fin de ciclo revolucionario?" *Historia Social*, no. 5 (1989): 37–49, and Eduardo González Calleja, "La política de orden público en la Restauración," *Espacio, tiempo y forma*, no. 20 (2008): 93–127. For the case of Portugal, see Diego Palacios Cerezales, "Técnica, política e o dilema da orden pública no Portugal contemporáneo (1851–1974)," in *Lei e Ordem. Justiça Penal, Criminalidade e Polícia. Séculos XIX-XX*, ed. Pedro Tavares de

Almeida and Tiago Pires Marques (Lisbon: Livros Horizonte, 2006), 147–72, and from the same author "Estado, régimen y orden público en el Portugal contemporáneo" (PhD diss., Universidad Complutense de Madrid, 2008).

11 Eduardo González Calleja, *La razón de la fuerza. Orden público, subversión y violencia política en la España de la Restauración (1875–1917)* (Madrid: Consejo Superior de Investigaciones Científicas, 1998). For Portugal see the aforementioned works by Diego Palacios Cerezales and Gonçalo Rocha Gonçalves, "O aparelho policial e a construção do Estado em Portugal, c. 1870–1900," *Análise Social*, no. 216 (2015): 471–93.

12 On this, see Matteo Millan, "Introduction: Strikebreaking During Europe's Belle Époque," *European History Quarterly* 49, no. 4 (2019): 553–69.

13 I deliberately use the term "double periphery" despite the valuable critical contributions that have been made to the concepts of "periphery" and "centre". See, for example, Anne Radeff, "Centres et périphéries ou centralités et décentralités?" in *Per vie di terra. Movimenti di uomini e di cose nelle società di antico regime* (Milan: Franco Angeli, 2007), and Christian De Vito, "History without Scale: The Micro-Spatial Perspective," *Past and Present* 242 (2019). By using it I intend to point out not only the inclusion of Spain and Portugal in an area where the development of capitalist modernization was particularly late and costly in social and political terms, but also to note that this worked as a self-representation as well: in both countries there was a widespread idea about being "peripheral", particularly in some areas. On the one hand, in both cases there was a recurrent discourse on the need for a "Europeanization" of the country at all levels; on the other hand, there was a repeated criticism of those who felt excluded from decision-making spaces, both socially and territorially.

14 Quoted in Victor Lucea Ayala, *El pueblo en movimiento. La protesta socialen Aragón (1885–1917)* (Zaragoza: Prensas Universitarias de Zaragoza, 2009), 100.

15 See Palacios, "Estado, regimen," 3. The numbers of the Civil Guard force in Spain in González Calleja, *La razón*, 47.

16 Diego Palacios Cerezales, "Weak State and Civic Culture in Liberal Portugal (1851–1926)," in *The Making of Modern Portugal*, ed. Luís Trindade (Newcastle: Cambridge Scholars Publishing, 2013). On the extension of the gendarmerie model during the nineteenth century throughout Europe, see Clive Emsley, *Gendarmeries and the State in Nineteenth-Century Europe* (Oxford: Oxford University Press, 1999).

17 The tentacular deployment of the Spanish Civil Guard responded to the same logic of the dam, becoming, together with the army, a real force of "military occupation of the territory" as stated in González Calleja, *La Razón*, 51. In Portugal the first territorial deployment of the National Republican Guard in 1911 was in the Alentejo region, the epicentre of the strike movement outside the capital during the first moments of the Republic. When some deputies from the north of the country, which was being the main focus of monarchical incursions, complained of their lack of protection, they were told that they instead had to wait, since there "strikes were not so frequent", quoted in Palacios, "Estado, regimen", 338.

18 *El Liberal*, March 20, 1897, 1; "La crisis obrera," *El Imparcial*, April 20, 1897, 1; "El Canal de Tamarite," *La Correspondencia de España*, April 28, 1897, 1.

19 Archivo General Militar de Madrid (hereafter, AGMM), "Huelga en en Canal de Aragón," sig. 5854.61; "Huelga de obreros del canal de Aragón y Cataluña," sig. 5855.51.

20 Fernando Sánchez Marroyo, "Los Congresos Obreros de Torre de Miguel Sesmero. El surgimiento del movimiento asociativo de los trabajadores rurales en Extremadura a comienzos del siglo XX," in *Congresos obreros en Torre de Miguel Sesmero*, ed. Francisco Joaquín Pérez González (Badajoz: Diputación Provincial de Badajoz, 2003); AGMM, "Huelgas agrícolas en la provincia de Badajoz en 1902," sig. 5855.16.

21 Jesús Ángel Redondo Cardeñoso, "Democracia y conflictos rurales en Portugal: la instauración de la I República en el Alentejo (1908–1912)," in *La Historia, lost in translation? Actas del XIII Congreso de la Asociación de Historia Contemporánea*, ed.

Damían A. González Madrid et al. (Cuenca: Ediciones de la Universidad de Castilla-La Mancha, 2017), 1327. See also José Pacheco Pereira, *Conflictos sociais nos campos do sul de Portugal* (Lisbon: Publicações Europa-América, 1982).

22 Arquivo do Ministério do Interior – Arquivo Nacional Torre do Tombo (AMI-ANTT), Mç. 38, no. 141. Letter from the civil governor to the Ministry of Interior January 27, 1912.

23 *Notícias de Évora*, June 2, 1911 and June 6, 1911; *O Eco de Reguengos*, June 8, 1911.

24 Martí Boneta Carrera, "Las construcciones hidroeléctricas de la Vall Fosca, de Energía Eléctrica de Cataluña (1911–1940)," in *Capitalismo e historia de la electrificación, 1890–1930: capital, técnica y organización del negocio eléctrico en España y México*, ed. Horacio Capel Sáez and Vicente Casals Costa (Barcelona: Serbal, 2013), 109–20.

25 "Movimiento obrero. La huelga de albañiles de 'La Canadiense'," *Heraldo de Aragón*, December 12, 1913, 2.

26 "Huelga en el Run," *Diario de Huesca*, May 17, 1914, 1.

27 Palacios, "Estado, régimen," 349–50; Álvaro Arranja, *A República e os operários. A Greve Geral de 1912 na imprensa da época* (Setúbal: Centro de Estudos Bocageanos, 2017).

28 Sánchez Marroyo, "Los Congresos," 20.

29 Lucea, *El pueblo*, 445. During the interwar years this area began to stand out, together with Zaragoza, because of the rooting of anarcho-syndicalism.

30 António Ventura, *O sindicalismo no Alentejo. A "tournée" de propaganda de 1912* (Lisbon: Seara Nova, 1977), 32.

31 Lucea, *El Pueblo*, 182–84.

32 González Calleja, *La razón*, 47; Palacios, "Estado, régimen," 337.

33 AGMM, "Huelgas Agrícolas 1902 Badajoz," sig. 5855.16.

34 Arquivo Histórico da Guarda Nacional Republicana, GNR 3rd Battalion Order Book. From 3 July 1911 to 11 November 1912; Palacios, "Estado, régimen," 336.

35 Arquivo Histórico Militar, 1ª Divisão, Secção 34, Cx. 1, "1ª República (1ª fase). Revoltas e incursoes monárquicas (1910–1914)". Letter from the command of the 3rd Military Division to the Ministry of War, 20 July 1911.

36 AMI-ANTT, Mç. 38, no. 141. Statements by owners and circular letter from the civil governor of 12 February 1912. The satisfaction expressed by several Alentejo deputies in Palacios, "Estado, régimen," 336.

37 Archivo Histórico Nacional (AHN), Ministerio de Gobernación serie A, Legajo 44(3), Expediente 22. Confidential note on the maintenance of public order (1902).

38 The arrests in Archivo General Militar de Segovia (AGMSg), "Recompensas. Relativo a Orden Público," Sección 2ª, División 12, legajo 152.

39 AGMM, "Motín en Fraga (Huesca) en 1906," sig. 5868.1.

40 AMI-ANTT, Mç. 38, no. 141. Letter from the civil governor of Évora to the Minister of the Interior, 27 January 1912.

41 On the activities of these employers' organisations beyond their role as economic lobbyists and in the field of violent organisational responses to the action and demands of trade unions and working-class parties, see the comparative study by Matteo Millan, "The Shadows of Social Fear: Emotions, Mentalities and Practices of the Propertied Classes in Italy, Spain and France (1900–1914)," *Journal of Social History* 50, no. 2 (2016): 336–61.

42 AMI-ANTT, Mç. 38, no. 141.

43 José Antonio Cubero y Carlos Bravo, *La aventura hidroeléctrica en el Valle del Ésera 1912–2012* (Huesca: Diputación Provincial de Huesca, 2012); Boneta, "Las construcciones," 118.

44 AHN, Serie A, Leg. 39, Exp. 1. Arquivo Distrital de Évora (ADE), Fundo Governo Civil, H/F Policia e criminalidade, Cx. 266. Letter from the Ministry of the Interior to civil governors, dated 25 August 1887.

45 ADE, Fundo Governo Civil, E/C Instrumentos de recuperação de correspondência, Cx. 270, pç. 153. Governor's circular of November 1911.

46 ADE, Fundo Governo Civil, H/F Policia e criminalidade, Cx. 144 "Guarda Nocturna e Policia Rural".

47 The law is critically discussed in José Llagaria Ballester, *Policía rural (ley de julio de 1898). Comunidades de Labradores* (Valencia: García y Suay, 1903).

48 AHN, Serie A, Leg. 5, Exp. 1. Ministry of the Interior. Under-Secretary of Public Order. Confidential report of April 1902.

49 Archivo Municipal de Barbastro, A472–04, Libro de Actas 1904, 63. For the dates of the creation of the associations, a guide in a late work: *Censo estadístico de Sindicatos Agrícolas y Comunidades de Labradores*, Ministerio de Agricultura, 1934, 397–402.

50 *La Época*, October 20, 1902, 2; *El Liberal*, October 24, 1904, 1. More information in Antonio Ibarz Ibarz, *El Canal d'Aragó i Catalunya: cent anys d'esperança i de progrés* (Huesca: Institut d'Estudis del Baix Cinca, 2005), 73, 77, 96. Brief information available about the watchmen's corps, in Archivo Histórico Provincial de Huesca (AHPH), Fondo de Obras Públicas, OP. 381.

51 ADE, Fundo Governo Civil, H/C Licenciamentos, CX-7.

52 In the case of Portugal, there was another aspiration: the acceptance and recognition of the new regime by foreign powers. Interestingly, in other countries, other cases of private companies under purely capitalist management show this same relationship between a strong sovereignty of private capital, strong links of dependence between the workers and the company and the creation of private police forces aimed at the harsh repression of the labour movement, particularly in cases of strike. See for example Matteo Millan, "'The Public Force of the Private State' – Strikebreaking and Visions of Subversion in Liberal Italy (1880s to 1914)," *European History Quarterly* 9, no. 4 (2019): 625–49. In the same issue, and in relation to private mining companies in the Ruhr area and the activities of the *Zechenwehren* auxiliary corps, see Amerigo Caruso, "Joining Forces against 'Strike Terrorism': The Public-Private Interplay in Policing Strikes in Imperial Germany, 1890–1914," *European History Quarterly* 49, no. 4 (2019): 597–624.

53 Paulo Guimarães, "Indústria e conflito no meio rural," in *Indústria e conflito no meio rural: Os mineiros alentejanos (1858–1938)* (Évora: Publicações do Cidehus, 2001).

54 José Juan De Paz Sánchez, "Félix Lunar y el movimiento obrero en Huelva (1908–1920)," in *A cielo abierto. De Riotinto a Norteamérica*, ed. Félix Lunar (México: Imprenta Manuel León Sánchez, 1956), 64.

55 Also noted in Miguel Collado Aguilar, "La Guerra Civil y la represión franquista en la Cuenca Minera de Riotinto" (PhD diss., Universidad de Huelva, 2018), 22. Collado Aguilar also points out that the railway service during the 1913 strike was maintained for ten days by the *guardiña* (297). On the 1888 massacre there are very different estimates of the number of deaths. In a recent study Gérard Chastagnaret puts the figure at 200, taking into account concealments of dead workers, the subsequent deaths of those seriously injured and the deaths of unregistered migrant workers, in Gérard Chastagnaret, *Humos y sangre. Protestas en la cuenca de las piritas y masacre de Riotinto (1877–1890)* (Alacant: Publicacions de la Universitat d'Alacant, 2017). However, this figure is much higher than that stated by other authors and even than the figures offered by militants of workers' organisations, for example the socialist Juan José Morato, who based on the workers' press noted 30 deaths and 150 injured; in Juan José Morato, *Pablo Iglesias. Educador de muchedumbres* (Barcelona: Ariel, 1977 [1931]). It seems plausible to contemplate the figures provided by David Avery, confirmed by subsequent local investigations and an internal report by the company itself, according to which the deaths could have reached 40 (with the authors pointing out that there could have been many more): see David Avery, *Not on Queen Victoria's Birthday: The Story of the Rio Tinto Mines* (London: Collins, 1974), and María Dolores Ferrero Blanco, "Los sucesos

de Riotinto de 1888 según los directores de la *Rio Tinto Company Limited,*" *Revista de Historia Industrial*, no. 14 (1998).

56 AGMSg, "Campos de instrucción y tiro 1883–1915," Sección 2ª, División 8ª, legajo 193. Also in the correspondence with the spaces of sociability of the owner class, in Archivo de la Real Sociedad Económica de Amigos del País de Badajoz, Caja 4, 1B.1.6.

57 Arquivo Municipal de Reguengos de Monsaraz, C-1/001/00025 [1908–1911], "Registo da correspondencia official espedida a differentes auctoridades, funcionarios, corporações, etc., 81B. Letter from the Municipal Chamber to the president of the "Cruzada Tiro Nacional," ADE, Fundo Governo Civil, E/C Instrumentos de recuperação de correspondencia, cx. 270, pç. 44. From a communication by the civil government of Évora to the municipal chamber of Estremoz on 27 October 27 1911.

58 Palacios, "Estado, régimen," 354.

59 Vasco Pulido Valente, "A República e as classes trabalhadoras (Outubro de 1910–Agosto de 1911)," *Análise Social* 9, no. 34 (1972): 311–12.

60 ADE, Fundo Governo Civil, E/C Instrumentos de recuperação de correspondencia, Cx. 270, pç. 153. Letter from the civilian governor of Évora to the commander of the 4th military division, 19 August 1911.

61 *Diário do Senado da República* of January 19, 1 and 8 May 1914, quoted in Palacios, "Estado, régimen," 353–55. *A Questao Social*, 30 January 1916, quoted in Paulo Guimarães, "Os mineiros na República: aspirações e derrotas," in *Indústria e conflito no meio rural: Os mineiros alentejanos (1858–1938)* (Évora: Publicações do Cidehus, 2001).

62 AHPH, Provincial Court of Huesca. Book of criminal sentences 1913, J2575.

4 The Swedish labour market c. 1870–1914

A labour market regime without repression?

Erik Bengtsson♣

Introduction: a peaceful labour market?

From discussion on anti-labour violence and the general repression of trade unionism and strikes pre-World War I, Sweden would appear – at least from the domestic literature – to be an exceptional case. We know that peaceful industrial relations developed in the 1930s, symbolised by the famous Saltsjöbaden Agreement between unions and employers in 1938. But several scholars assert that even in the final third of the nineteenth century, there was very little repression of unionism and strikes in this country.[1] Against the view that a cooperative Swedish model emerged under Social Democratic auspices in the 1930s, the revisionists see the "bourgeois roots of the Swedish model".[2]

This essay interrogates this narrative of Swedish exceptionalism in the context of the labour market. I have indicated elsewhere that analyses of Swedish exceptionalism in terms of early democratisation and social egalitarianism tend to be overestimated.[3] This chapter starts with two research questions: was the Swedish labour market regime c. 1870–1914 uniquely liberal and labour-friendly and, if so, which social forces were behind this exceptionalism – the strength of farmers, the liberalism of the bourgeoisie or something else? The chapter does not in the main build on original archival research, but rather on a synthesis of the existing literature, combined with analysis of parliamentary materials. As parliament, the *Riksdag*, was the decision maker on labour market regulation, the essay focuses mainly on parliamentary politics. To trace social inputs on policy, extra-parliamentary forces and movements will also be discussed. The relations between workers, unions and employers, and important phenomena such as strikebreaking will also be discussed.

The conventional view and its contradictions

The conventional view of a peaceful Swedish labour market goes back to the political scientist Jörgen Westerståhl's classic 1945 study of the development of the Swedish trade union movement.[4] His analysis begins with the 1846 and 1864 liberal reforms of enterprises. Previously, the state had regulated access to professions and the setting of wages. It fined those who increased the wages of journeymen and workers, doubling the fine if the demand for higher wages had been made collectively. Collective action was seen as a form of rebellion and punished under criminal law.[5] The 1864 law abolished the requirement of guild membership and stated allegiance to "free work" (*arbetets frihet*), but still stipulated, in patriarchal spirit, that employers were the masters (*husbonde*) and should inculcate the fear of god, orderliness and sobriety in their employees. The Master and Servant Law (*Tjänstehjonsstadgan*) prevailed, together with the law of obligatory service, which allowed any landless person without lawful employment to be sentenced to forced labour.

Westerståhl argued that the 1864 reform ushered in a liberal labour market regime; apart from the "unclear" law of obligatory service, workers had "achieved a judicially completely independent standing".[6] This, he argues, was remarkable: "most other" countries implemented laws against unions and collective action. The Swedish union movement that emerged in the 1880s, Westerståhl maintained, had no specific legal barriers to surmount, and interventions by authorities were "comparatively rare".[7] Without explaining Sweden's uniquely liberal regime, he dated its advent to 1864, generally among Swedish political historians considered a liberal watershed.[8]

The journalist and political scientist Svante Nycander follows Westerståhl in arguing, in a 2008 general history of the Swedish labour market, that, after the 1864 reform, Swedish labour was organised in a climate of relative freedom, while in other countries, unions and strikes suffered direct oppression.[9] The Master and Servant Law, Nycander says, persisted in Britain, without mentioning that Sweden retained it until 1926. Generally, Sweden's treatment of unions was relatively lenient; Nycander dismisses accounts of oppressed labour activists in Sweden[10] as narratives of "martyrs", replacing them with a description of "collective laissez faire" from the government's side, which allowed and encouraged organisation of workers and employers. This, argues Nycander, provides the historical roots of the famous Saltsjöbaden Agreement of 1938.[11]

For Nycander, himself a politically organised liberal and longtime leader writer for the liberal daily *Dagens Nyheter*, Sweden owed its non-interventionist model fundamentally to the strength of social liberalism. "The main political conflict line wasn't between bourgeoisie and the labour movement, but between the left and the right", the left at this time being the Social Democrats as well as the Liberals, who won roughly 30 per cent in elections until around 1930. "Liberals prevented anti-union laws and made the decisive difference in moulding opinion for the right to organize".[12]

Another theory attributes Swedish labour market exceptionalism not to liberal reforms of the 1840s or 1860s, or to left-wing liberals, but to the farmers. Some contend that farmers had exceptional influence in Swedish politics, standing for a proto-Social Democratic line. In this vein Mary Hilson argues that it was the farmer-dominated second chamber that led Sweden to be relatively benign towards labour.[13] This version of the peaceful labour market thesis has not been very much developed but refers to a wider discussion of Swedish exceptionalism where farmers are assumed to carry a democratic and egalitarian tradition from the early modern period and into industrial society.[14]

Why question the conventional view?

Advocates of Swedish (or Scandinavian) exceptionalism educe several, presumably related societal traits: economic equality, equal political influences and peaceful relations between the classes. As one recent contribution to the genre comments: "Scandinavia is unique in Western Europe in that there has been no real class war".[15] However, both in terms of economic inequality and political democracy, the exceptionalism narratives exaggerate. In the 1890s, Sweden was one of the least democratic countries in Western Europe, in terms of suffrage laws, and one of the most unequal in terms of the distribution of incomes and wealth.[16]

From this point of view, it is interesting to revisit the idea that Sweden had unusually peaceful relations between the classes and less oppression of the labour movement. While a more conflict-oriented, and often Marxist-inflected history writing dominated in the 1970s and 1980s when the field of labour history experienced an upswing, today the history writing of the early industrial Swedish labour market is dominated by the consensus perspective. This is indicated by the fact that both textbooks on Swedish labour market history, Nycander's *Makten över arbetsmarknaden* and Lundh's *Spelets regler*, propose this perspective.[17]

The state, workers and the labour movement, c. 1870–1910

In studying the Swedish labour market in this period, we should first consider agricultural workers and servants, the major groups left out of the conventional accounts of developing industrial relations. In 1870, 72 per cent of workers were in agriculture; in 1910, 51 per cent.[18] The importance of the Master and Servant Law has been dismissed by saying that it was used mostly in sectors – agriculture – where unions did not operate,[19] but this is of course the wrong way around: the presence of the law in itself contributed to the lack of unions. From 1896 on, Social Democrats and Liberals in parliament fought for a repeal but succeeded only in 1926, which indicates the persistence of patriarchalism in Swedish society.

A recent economic study argues that this enduring law increased the exploitation of agricultural workers and reduced their chance to escape to other work.[20] Like servant-girls, who proliferated between the wars, farm workers also long continued non-unionised. Attempts to organise were stifled by the employers in the early 1890s, then in 1904–05, with a liberal use of strikebreakers, and again in 1909; they did not become a part of the union movement mainstream until the 1930s.[21]

Violence

Sweden can claim a relative lack of bloodshed in industrial relations in the period. The 1931 Ådalen shootings, when five unarmed demonstrators were killed by the army protecting strikebreakers, are legendary in Swedish labour history, but largely for their uniqueness. Compared to for example the United States, there was less bloodshed in Swedish labour market relations.[22]

The official political élite registered the arrival of a labour movement challenge in the 1870s. The use of the military to suppress a strike at a major iron mine (Persberg) in 1870 was taken in parliament to show the usefulness of a standing army, as opposed to a conscript force of soldiers who might be susceptible to radical agitation.[23] General Lars Tingsten, Minister of Defence in the early 1900s, recalls in his memoirs how as a young officer in 1879 his regiment was sent to Sundsvall to control the massive strike in its sawmills. In his account however, the army did nothing more militant than guarding strikebreakers and shepherding striking workers to speeches by the anti-union county governor, Curry Treffenberg.[24]

Letters in 1892 between Christian Lundeberg, industry leader and later leader of the Conservative party, and Patric Reuterswärd, an iron-works owner, court marshal and leading Conservative in the first chamber, tell much about the comfort of the élite. At the 1892 parliament (*Riksdag*), Liberals as they always did, proposed a wider suffrage, which was once again opposed by a rock-solid right-wing majority in the first chamber and the second (more fluctuating) chamber. Lundeberg argued in his letter that the first chamber should make no fuss over the growing extra-parliamentary suffrage movement, and Reuterswärd agreed: they must "make a strong union, to sternly stick to the *status quo*. If the first chamber should tremble, then the country is lost, and if a rebellion comes, then the sooner the better, while our military is still untainted".[25] The conservatives trusted the army to contain any outbreaks of labour militancy – as in Persberg in 1870 or the Sundsvall sawmills in 1879 – but there was never any immediate socialist threat.

This moderation cannot be explained by a relatively democratic state, because Sweden was not relatively democratic, nor by narrower class differences in incomes and wealth, because Sweden's inequality could by 1900 rival that of any capitalist country.[26] Rather, I believe that the explanation must be sought in the field of political culture and repertoires of action in politics – Sweden's élite was not more democratic or equal, but it was less violent. I return to this in the concluding section, after discussing the forms of repression that were used.

The lack of violence does not signify that the Swedish state apparatus was politically neutral versus the left and the right. In March 1920, two police detectives were in the audience for a lecture by the Social Democratic leader Hjalmar Branting, enthusiastically taking notes and waiting to hear something illegal.[27] Nothing unusual, perhaps, about such surveillance of a socialist event – except that Branting was the current prime minister! This indicates how far the socialists were from being legitimate bearers of power until the prolonged parliamentary struggles of the 1920s. Suspicion still lingered that this was an insurrectionary movement. But while the police watched everything the labour movement did, they relatively seldom intervened or stopped meetings. Eventually, the policemen became familiar to the activists, with whom reciprocal acceptance developed.[28] Thus relations between the state and the labour movement may not have been harmonious or friendly, but they rarely became violent.

Restrictions of free speech, from the 1880s to the 1900s

The Swedish Social Democratic Party was constituted in April 1889. King Oscar II immediately called Örbom, the minister of Justice – the government was then King's advisers – to the castle and recommended that the 1887 law against agitation should be sharpened. This law, called the "little socialist law" with reference to the stronger anti-socialist laws in place in Germany, outlawed incitement to crimes (rebellion, treason etc.) and was directed against socialist and radical agitation. Explicitly, this law made it illegal to incite violence (very broadly understood) against a person or property. During the 1888 "prosecution frenzy" (*åtalsraseriet*) several Social Democratic agitators had been imprisoned under these rules. By 1889, all Social Democratic newspaper editors, including the informal party leader Branting, were in prison on account of anti-religious or otherwise inflammatory statements.[29]

But in 1889 Örbom agreed with the king that the rules must be strengthened to prevent "violence and excess", to protect workers against "ruthless agitators" and to protect society from the "spiritual disease" of socialism. The law seeks to prevent verbal incitement to actions "which amount to threats against the social order or danger for its duration".[30] The Riksdag accepted Örbom's proposed revision with some amendments. The law came to be used, among other things, in several instances against leaders of mobs who had fought the police: a riot in Stockholm during the 1902 general strike in favour of universal suffrage; strikebreakers in the west coast stone industry in 1904; and rioters against a prison in 1906. More simply political cases all concerned Social Democrats: when leading party agitator and journalist Axel Danielsson on 1 May 1891 apparently encouraged the use of violence against the police, when party leader Branting on 1 May 1895 discussed the secession of Norway from the Norwegian-Swedish union and how drafted militaries should use their weapons (not against the Norwegians), and when two anarchist-leaning agitators in 1906 got 10 and three months in prison respectively for encouraging resistance to conscription.[31] The 1889 law quickly became known as the "muzzle law".

What were the social forces behind the 1887 and 1889 laws? The king was clearly one of the actors behind the 1889 law, acting from his conviction that socialism was a threat to the existing social order. Minister of Justice Axel Örbom was a lawyer and a bureaucrat of conservative bent, serving in a government, led by Baron Gillis Bildt, considered at the time to be moderately conservative. Of the ten ministers, four were noble, and Baron Bildt, a court marshal and personal friend of the king, was an estate owner. When the farmer leader Liss Olof Larsson was discussed as potential government minister, to appoint a farmer as minister was considered too brave. Bildt was court marshal and friends with the king. In sum, the government was as *ancien regime* as it gets.[32]

The 1889 "muzzle law" was voted through by a 83–25 majority in the first chamber, and 109–102 in the second.[33] Albert Lilienberg, a lawyer and member of the free-trading Centre Party, thought that the proposal was too vague, giving judges too much discretion, and with reference to the 1887 law, not necessary. In the first chamber, the criticism levelled at the reform was also that it was inefficient and/or unnecessary. There were a few more principled criticisms as well. Hans Andersson, a farmer on the liberal wing of the Country Party, fought against the law on principled grounds, arguing that it would limit the right to assembly and could lead to political trials where people would be sentenced just for arguing for reforms. One of the most prominent Liberals of the Riksdag, S.A. Hedlund, spoke of the reform as a "politics of oppression". The prominent Free Church leader Waldenström warned that this anti-socialist law might in the future be used against dissenting churches.

In the case of the 1887 law, the initiative came from the Minister of Justice von Steyern. Three farmers and one schoolteacher spoke out against the decision. Around 60 second chamber MPs voted against the law; in the first chamber, only one.

On the whole then, we might say that with a weaker first chamber and weaker royal power, repressive laws such as the "little socialist law" and the "muzzle law" would have been harder difficult to pass. The evidence here does not support the idea of liberal influence guaranteeing civil rights from the farmers. In both 1887 and 1889 farmers were quite evenly split, with more liberal free traders rejecting the repressive measures, and more conservative protectionists approving. The Liberal intelligentsia played a role through representatives including S.A. Hedin who was the most fierce and feared opponent of the conservative governments of the late 1880s and early 1890s. The king and the government were afraid of Hedin's oratory and mobilising powers, and this may to some extent have restrained their conservatism: to tack too far to the right could have sparked a revolt led by agitators such as Hedin.[34]

The restrictions of free speech continued into the twentieth century. In 1906, the liberal government of Karl Staaff outlawed anti-military propaganda. That the reformist liberal Staaff put through this reform has caused consternation among historians; it may have been a (failed) attempt to endear himself to the conservatives and make them more amenable to suffrage reform.[35] However, Staaff himself in the intemperate second chamber debate claimed that the socialists had worsened since 1889 by spawning the monster of militant anarchism. The Staaff Laws were especially directed against anti-militarist propaganda but were also used in labour market conflicts, which makes them interesting here. For example, in 1908 Carl Lind was sentenced to two months' imprisonment for encouraging a general strike, direct action and economic destruction. Hjalmar Gustafsson was sentenced to two months' penal labour for having encouraged railroad workers to join the strike at a strike meeting of 15,000 people in Stockholm in August 1909; this was illegal since they were state employees. The chairman of the miners' union in Norberg served 11 months' penal labour for a strike meeting in August 1909 where he referred to strikebreakers as traitors and encouraged a riot to free striking workers from the local jail. To sum up the Staaff Laws were indeed used to hamper strikes.[36]

What then were the social forces behind the law? As referred to earlier, they may have been political tactics to appease the conservatives. When the proposal was presented to the Riksdag's Law Committee, three members spoke against it altogether or in parts. The liberal Theodor Zetterstrand wanted to remove "praise of criminal acts" as a punishable action, while two Social Democrats opposed the entire law. The first chamber accepted it without debate, whereas the second chamber debate was intense, ending with approval by 164 votes to 51 for its main proposals.[37] There were only 13 Social Democratic MPs at the time, so quite a few liberals must have defected from Staaff's line and voted against.

Defending strikebreaking

After the union movement's breakthrough in the 1880s, it became more and more obvious to the ruling élite that unions and strikes were a significant factor in the Swedish labour market. In 1894 the new labour conflict statistics included 44 strikes and in the three years that followed the numbers grew to 65, 109 and 144.[38] At the 1892 Riksdag, J. Eliasson, a farmer, proposed a law to prevent obstacles to strikebreaking. Eliasson urged the measure by describing several "threatening phenomena, which threaten the social calm". He wanted a new law against anyone who with "cunning, temptations, threats or force" hindered anyone from working, and he argued that prosecutors must be able to prosecute such crimes without any initiative from the victims themselves. The strikebreakers, Eliasson argued, were too afraid of vengeance and therefore would not themselves attempt counter-prosecution. "It cannot be denied that several work cancellations look like and degenerate into rebellion. One has often seen that military or increased police presence has been necessary to conserve social peace".[39]

The legal technicalities of Eliasson's proposal complicated the Riksdag debate and it was once re-referred to the parliamentary Law Committee, but thereafter the motion was passed by 99 votes to 65 in the second chamber, and with little debate in the first. The only people who vigorously opposed it on principle were the urban radical liberals. S.A. Hedin, in a long tirade cited horror stories of employers' maltreatment of their workers and accused Eliasson of a biased view of justice in the labour market: no punishment for employers who dismissed workers for joining a union, yet punishment for workers who organised. Interestingly, Hedin in a way defended the farmer hypothesis of Swedish liberalism, arguing that Eliasson belonged to "a class, a stratum of society, which for centuries has been oppressed by the nobility and royal bureaucracy", and that Eliasson should see its similarity to the working class of the 1890s. Julius Mankell[40] reinforced Hedin's rejection by referring to the story of a worker who was imprisoned for eight months for having touched a strikebreaker's arm. A farmer Jonsson argued that the proposal was one-sided, limiting the union's actions but not the employer's, and that it could awaken a sleeping bear, i.e. provoke the labour movement to greater activity. But most MPs supported the proposal, and it was passed in its revised version.

Defending strikebreakers was a recurrent aim in Swedish parliamentary politics at this time. In 1897 and 1898, the conservative estate owner C.J. Jakobson of the (protectionist, conservative) New Country Party proposed that strikers should be sentenced to forced labour.[41] He warned of the "strike disease" and of "modern tyrants called trade union leaders". Thirty MPs from the same party joined in, showing again the farmers' conservative voice. Against the proposal, the liberal farmer Daniel Persson believed that the road to harmony between employers and workers would not go through the prison. Liberals and conservative farmers split over this issue, while city representatives were much more negative.[42] After the Law Committee's revisions, the first chamber passed the proposal, but the second rejected it.

In 1899, Jakobson's proposal was taken up by a Country party colleague, and this time the second chamber passed it by 118 votes to 93. This U-turn since the 1898 parliament related to growing intensity of the labour market issue. In 1898, the first Swedish trade union confederation LO (Landsorganisationen) constituted itself with the aim to organise workers in all sectors. And during the year, there was a wave of strikes, including some major ones, in the southernmost Malmöhus County, which was well represented in the second chamber. Relations between (political) farmers and workers were deteriorating.

In 1899, the farmer Pehr Persson from Åkarp, a village in southern Sweden, proposed criminalising not only successful but also failed attempts to incite strikes. The first chamber passed it without debate, but the second chamber gave it a narrow majority – 108 to 93. Conservative and moderately conservative farmers were the keenest to back it[43] and only one city dweller, a moderately liberal lieutenant expressed support. Some urban right-wing notables opposed it: the Free Church leader Waldenström and von Krusenstjerna – and the radicals naturally dismissed it as expressing "egoistic class interest" on Persson's part. All its opponents in the second chamber, bar the jurist Husberg, whose opposition was technical-legal, were liberals or radicals.[44]

This pattern further undermines the farmer hypothesis of Swedish exceptionalism and supports the bourgeois intelligentsia hypothesis. The élites of the first chamber – estate owners, capitalists and the like – favoured labour repression, farmers were rather evenly split (but increasingly Conservative over the 1890s) and urban liberals fought it.[45]

The evolution of employer attitudes and the use of strikebreakers

This chapter mainly concerns the stance of the state vis-à-vis the unions, but to understand the state's action, it is worth looking at the employers, who also carried much political weight. In the final third of the nineteenth century, employer attitudes were marked by patriarchalism. John Bernström, CEO of the important engineering company Separator in Stockholm, is typical. He was a Christian patriarch whose lifelong worldview was coloured by the Lutheran *Haustafel*. Even in 1904 he advocated that the employers should aim to defend the "rights of the master of the house in the country's industry" (*häfda husbonderätten inom landets industri*).[46]

Swedish labour history on the late 1800s is replete with depictions of anti-union activity. The iron processing companies of rural central Sweden, so dominant in their localities, shut organisers out by evicting them from company land (which was most land around the works where the workers were), or, when the organisers and agitators had found public ground to use, by measures such as commending the employees' brass band to play loudly to drench out the agitation, or commending agricultural workers on the company land to beat their milk jugs with clappers for the same purpose. As one dissertation found, most of the ironworks investigated fired the workers who joined the first union.[47]

The Separator company responded to the 1902 three-day strike in favour of universal suffrage with a lockout and by firing all the striking workers, whom they refused to reinstate unless they left the trade union.[48] The CEO Bernström would refuse to hire any organised worker and would dismiss anyone who joined a union. In practice the freedom to organise was rather limited. Bernström gradually started to accept unions after 1903, after a protracted war of attrition between unions and employers in the engineering industry, but always believed that socialist influence in the union movement should be crushed.

At the first labour conflict of the Cementaktiebolaget of southern Sweden, in 1886, the company dismissed about 40 strikers. R.F. Berg, its CEO at the end of the 1890s still spoke of Social Democracy as "hating christianity and often threatening with illegal actions and violence".[49] From 1902 on, Berg was in contact with the bourgeois reformists of the CSA – the Swedish equivalent of the Fabians or the *Kathedersozialisten* – and his anti-union attitudes mellowed; by 1906 he had embraced collective agreements. In 1908, advising on the ongoing conflict in the harbour of Norrköping, he said: "the use of strike-breakers is a very dangerous method, which we here in Scania no longer dare to use". Liberal ideas, acquired in discussions with prominent reformist intellectuals, and his Free Church experience of consorting with lower-class people were surely important to Berg's reformism after 1906, but the impression remains that it was also simply his adjustment to the attrition battle of strikes and lockouts in the 1899–1906 period.

The right of workers to organise was indeed issue of a protracted struggle between workers and employers. In the 1906 "December Compromise" between SAF, the employers' confederation, and LO, the union confederation, union organising was accepted in principle. In exchange, SAF got a guarantee from LO for the exclusive say in hiring and firing. The issue of strikebreaking was left unresolved. However, with this compromise, the employers turned away from rejecting collective agreements and used them in their own favour, to control competition over labour,[50] thus helping to usher in a new era of Swedish industrial relations. But the road to 1906 had been rocky, and conflicts continued.

The use of strikebreaking paralleled more generally the evolving employer attitudes. Before the 1890s it was easy for employers to punish strikers and win conflicts by combined strikebreaking and dismissal. Afterwards, with developing organisation in Social Democratic unions, it was harder to find spontaneous strikebreakers. At first employers resorted to importing strikebreakers – from

England, in the case of harbours – but after a violent conflict in 1908, they ceased. Next they either recruited for this purpose strikebreakers from organisations, or from other social classes, notably, military officers.[51] Some tried to form a Yellow union movement, in the shape of the Swedish Workers' Union (*Svenska Arbetareförbundet*); however, this never became very important, though it furnished strikebreakers in 1905–07.[52] In the first decade of the twentieth century, strikebreakers were still used in 20–30 per cent of all strikes, and the use flared up again in the militant interwar era during the years 1925–36, but declined after that.

The study of German employers by Paster offers a comparative perspective on employer attitudes.[53] In Paster's account, German employers after the 1890s sporadically moved from a conservative, completely anti-union "master in my house" position to a reluctant acceptance of unionism under the revolutionary threat of the First World War. The "master in my house" metaphor is of course precisely what Bernström and other Swedish employers used (Sw. *husbonde*). After 1900 some employers – fewer in heavy industry, more in industries with stronger unions – chose to negotiate rather than trying to crush the unions, Paster says. The timing is then not completely different from Sweden's. While proponents of Swedish exceptionalism imply that no employers in other countries accepted unions, this seems to overstate the degree of opposition elsewhere and the uniqueness of the Swedish experience.[54]

Why strikebreaking didn't take a stronger hold in Sweden is an interesting in a comparative European context,[55] but is difficult to answer based on the research which currently exists. That it became difficult for employers to recruit strikebreakers from the ranks of the workers themselves can be explained by the rather exceptional spread of Social Democratic class consciousness from the 1910s on – Swedish workers were to an internationally exceptional degree organised in trade unions, the Social Democratic party, and various other social and political organisations of a Social Democratic bent, such as workers' libraries, study groups and social organisations.[56] But the decline of imported and middle-class strikebreakers is less well explained, and indeed an important topic for further research.

The general strike of 1909 should be brought up here. The employers' successful use of strikebreakers in 1909 became well-known all across Europe, as is highlighted by Pierre Eichenberger's chapter in this book. But it must be said that the strike itself, while massive in its extension and very important in the short run as it depleted the unions' strike funds and caused a massive exodus of members, in the long run was less important than we would perhaps expect of a general strike. The fundamental factors leading to the conflict were, as Schiller showed in his brilliant dissertation,[57] trivial and very mundane for the time – unions' opposition to employers' demands for wage-cutting in a recession. The binding together, during the years 1907–09, of such conflicts from various sectors, led to a breaking point. Schiller shows that after the three-day general strike for universal suffrage in 1902, the issue of a general strike had been debated several times within the LO. The reason why a general strike was decided in 1909 was rather an issue of the transformation of quantity into quality – the long-standing, simmering conflicts over wage-cutting finally boiling over – rather than the result of something unique and interesting occurring in 1909. The LO leadership were tired of the recurrent demands for lowering wages and worried about how the internal left opposition could exploit rank and file dissent if the LO stood for a conciliatory policy vis-à-vis the employers too many times. The resulting win for the employers was not surprising, but not very long-lasting either: after a very drastic drop in trade union affiliation as workers could not afford the union dues or became disgruntled, the unions started growing very rapidly again, and actually grew stronger than ever before, as their political allies in the Social Democratic party grew into a party of government and as the revolutionary threat during World War I strengthened the workers' hand at the bargaining table.[58]

The growth of liberal reformism within the state apparatus

We may wonder how the liberal reformist intelligentsia responded to increasing labour unrest. Research has shown that placing social liberals in the state apparatus could indeed decisively ameliorate class conflict.[59]

In Sweden, Ernst Beckman, a leading left liberal, proposed in 1892 and 1893 in the second chamber that the state must collect official statistics on labour conflicts. Science was needed to solve the "worker question", Beckman maintained.[60] After Beckman's proposals fell, the liberal suffrage movement leader David Bergström proposed the same in 1895.[61] Interestingly, Beckman's proposal fell in the second chamber owing to fierce opposition from the leader of the New Country Party, A.P. Danielsson. Danielsson, who was the wealthiest farmer in the second chamber and involved in various companies outside of the farm sector, was staunchly conservative. This divide between urban bourgeois liberals of the social liberal type and wealthy, conservative farmers is telling.

Liberals did reach influence at the Swedish National Board of Trade (*Kommerskollegium*) where around 1903, a group of liberal-minded social reformists gathered in the labour market section, led by Henning Elmquist.[62] In this regard, as well as in employer organisations, Swedish labour market relations took a conciliatory turn around 1905.

At this time, despite the Staaff Laws, some evidence shows increased support for a more conciliatory industrial relations model among the liberal policy intelligentsia and large employers. In 1906 this tendency became policy when the Liberal government led by Karl Staaff proposed the creation of a state mediation institute to get to grips with labour market conflicts. The very serious strikes and lockouts in the previous years, especially in the engineering industry, make a substantial background to this proposal. A recent study finds that mediation, which started in 1907, had a significant effect on the outcomes of conflict, increasing the share of compromises,[63] but the important underlying question is how the mediators came to exist in the first place.

Here we can trace the influence of the liberal urban intelligentsia. During the formative period 1904–06, proposals were also going in a very different direction. Conservative MPs in 1904 and 1905, inspired by the Taff Vale case in Britain, wrote several proposals to parliament that unions should be financially responsible for any costs to employers from strikes.[64] However, in 1905, when suffrage had been extended by wage growth and inflation that pushed workers and lower-middle-class people over the income limit for the right to vote, the Liberals and the Social Democrats won a majority in the second chamber. The Liberals in 1906 could secure what Beckman and Bergström had proposed in 1892–95. The conservatives and representatives of industry in parliament though opposing state mediation, could not prevent it.

Conclusion

This paper started from two research questions. One, was the Swedish labour market regime c. 1870–1914 uniquely liberal and labour-friendly? Two, if so, which were the social forces behind this exceptionalism – the strength of farmers, the liberalism of the bourgeoisie, or something else?

The first has no easy answer. Swedish labour relations were certainly less violent in this period than in the US, France or Spain. However, it is not obvious that British labour relations were as oppressive as proponents of Swedish exceptionalism have argued. The reforms in the 1870s which ended complete repression of unions under criminal law accords rather well with the 1864 reform in Sweden.[65] While British unions were not completely immune from civil prosecution until 1906, Acts of 1871 and 1875 limited the practical impact on unions, and "fear of the courts had little effect on union organisation or industrial conflict during the 1890s".[66] The difference between Britain and Sweden is possibly not as great as might be supposed. Indeed, the phrase "collective laissez-faire" which proponents of Swedish exceptionalism use to describe the Swedish system, was invented by Otto Kahn-Freund to describe the British industrial relations system.

While bloodshed was not the rule, however, the Swedish regime was not particularly labour-friendly or union friendly. Restrictions on agricultural labourers and servants, together with the pauperism regulations, served to discipline much of the labour force. That unions were not outlawed is true, but the freedom of speech restrictions represented by the 1887 "little socialist law", 1889 "muzzle law" and 1906 Staaff Laws did restrain unions' freedom of action, as did the anti-strike measures of 1892 and 1899. It seems that employers in the tumultuous years around 1902–09 gradually thawed towards the existence of trade unions, even socialist ones. The 1907 mediation law seems to have been successful; labour market conflict declined somewhat in frequency and also shifted qualitatively, as fundamental issues of the right to organise became less common as ground for conflict, and a larger share of conflicts were about more pragmatic issues of wages and working conditions. Thus, while labour market conflict intensified in the 1920s, the conflicts were by then more within the existing system, than about (re-)shaping the industrial relations system wholesale.

On question two, it seems clear that the political representation of farmers was no guarantee of workers' civil rights. By the late nineteenth century, under the very restrictive income and wealth qualifications for the right to vote, farmer MPs were always wealthy farmers elected by other wealthy farmers who, as employers, had material interests in anti-union policies.[67] This erodes the old idea of farmers as liberal-democratic guarantors in Swedish politics or the driving force behind early social reforms.[68] I have found that urban liberals such as Hedin and Mankell were the most consistent proponents of workers' rights, but this in a sense is pleonastic, for I define this group not only by their urban residence and bourgeois class, but also by from their ideology. Other bourgeois MPs had much less interest in workers' rights, and the capital-owners in the first chamber were on the other side of the debate; the élites of the first chamber at least until the mid-1890s acted as modernisers in economic policy, but without any interest in democratisation.[69] However, the influence of social liberal policy élites in Swedish labour market relations in this period is interesting for further research.

What seems to me unique, however, about the Swedish regulation of class relations c. 1870–1914 is not that there was any consensus around liberal rights – indeed, the class divide seems to have been much the same as in any other industrialising country. Class differences in wealth and incomes around 1900 were as wide in Sweden as in other industrial countries. However, the country's means for handling class conflict were different. The exclusion of the working class from politics was as absolute as in any other country and the ruling élite contained few or no modern liberals. But workers were repressed less violently than in many countries. The thesis of Swedish exceptionalism seems overblown and reached by overestimating the degree of labour repression in other European countries, ignoring agriculture and downplaying restrictions on free speech and union action. But there may still be something special about the relative bloodlessness of the Swedish case. Tentatively, I would like to hypothesise that this has very little to do with evidence of egalitarianism or democracy – Sweden offers little of either – but comes rather from its political culture, and more specifically from its repertoire of collective action from its own history. Tilly's concept of "repertoires of contention", modes of collective action which persist over time through some kind of path dependency, is typically used to analyse popular politics, but I believe that the concept may be useful for élite politics too.[70] As Tilly argues, "contention accumulated its own history of shared beliefs, memories, models, precedents, and social ties". This could be true also for Swedish élite political action: even though the economy was severely unequal, it could have involved a relatively light repertoire of repression. Repression, at least until the suffrage reforms of 1909 and 1919, was especially carried out through the exclusiveness of the political system.

Notes

♣ Acknowledgements. Work on this chapter has been financed by the Riksbankens Jubileumsfond grant "Dynamic peasants? Agency and inequality in Swedish modernization", P16–0412:1. The paper has been presented at Lund University BAS seminar and at the workshop "Industrial vigilantism, strikebreaking and patterns of anti-labour violence, 1890s–1930s. A comparative and transnational perspective," Oxford, 23–24 October 2018; thanks to all participants for discussion and comments. Thanks to the editors Matteo Millan and Alessandro Saluppo for further comments and suggestions.

1 Jörgen Westerståhl, *Svensk fackföreningsrörelse: Organisationsproblem, verksamhetsformer, förhållande till staten* (Stockholm: Tiden, 1945); Svante Nycander, *Makten över arbetsmarknaden: ett perspektiv på Sveriges 1900-tal* (Stockholm: SNS, 2008).
2 Labour movement-oriented: Walter Korpi, *The Democratic Class Struggle* (London: Routledge, 1983). Revisionists: Svante Nycander, "Svenska modellens borgerliga rötter," *Statsvetenskaplig Tidskrift* 120, no. 1 (2018): 5–31.
3 Erik Bengtsson, "The Swedish Sonderweg in Question: Democratization and Inequality in Comparative Perspective, c. 1750–1920," *Past & Present* 244, no. 1 (2019): 123–61.
4 Westerståhl, *Svensk fackföreningsrörelse*.
5 Susanne Fransson, "Freedom of Contract, Parity and Collective Regulation: Collective Labour Law in Sweden," in *The Rise and Development of Collective Labour Law*, ed. Marcel Van der Linden and Richard Price (Berlin: Peter Lang, 2000), 227–64.
6 Westerståhl, *Svensk fackföreningsrörelse*, 12; cf. 235. On the regulations of the mid-nineteenth century see also Christer Lundh, *Spelets regler*, 2nd ed. (Stockholm: SNS, 2010), 50–61.
7 Westerståhl, *Svensk fackföreningsrörelse*, 13.
8 For example Per T. Ohlsson, *Svensk politik* (Lund: Historiska media, 2014).
9 Nycander, *Makten över arbetsmarknaden*, 17–18, 82–99. The reference for other countries is Marcel van der Linden and Richard Price, eds., *The Rise and Development of Collective Labour Law* (Berlin: Lang, 2000). Nycander's study of the United States also colours his analysis; in comparison with the US, Sweden, like any other state, seems labour-friendly. The comparison with the US is Svante Nycander, *Kriget mot fackföreningarna: en studie av den amerikanska modellen* (Stockholm: SNS, 1998). Robin Archer's comparison of labour movements and repression against them in the United States and Australia highlights how extreme the US case is. As Hilson points out, our choice of comparison countries will inevitably colour our analysis of our first country. Robin Archer, *Why Is There No Labor Party in the United States?* (Princeton, NJ: Princeton University Press, 2008). Mary Hilson, *Political Change and the Rise of Labour in Comparative Perspective: Britain and Sweden 1890–1920* (Lund: Nordic Academic Press, 2000), 18–22.
10 Per Eklund, *Rätten i klasskampen* (Stockholm: Tiden, 1974); Fransson, "Freedom of Contract."
11 Nycander, *Makten över arbetsmarknaden*, 87–91. The image of non-interventionism on behalf of the state is given also in international research such as Jackson and Sisson, who use this fact to explain why employers in Sweden created a central organisation so early (1902). Peter Jackson and Keith Sisson, "Employers' Confederations in Sweden and the U.K. and the Significance of Industrial Infrastructure," *British Journal of Industrial Relations* 14, no. 3 (1976): 306–23. Marxists such as Therborn et al. also accept Westerståhl's description of a liberal, lenient state after 1864. Göran Therborn, Anders Kjellberg, Staffan Marklund, and Ulf Öhlund, "Sverige före och efter socialdemokratin: en första översikt," *Arkiv för studier i arbetarrörelsens historia* (1979): 1–39. See page 8.
12 Nycander, *Makten över arbetsmarknaden*, 96, 99; Nycander, "Svenska modellens borgerliga rötter."
13 Hilson, *Political Change*, 43–44. One can question this view from the outset simply because the farmers were themselves employers, and so not necessarily interested in a liberal environment for unions and labour activism. Of course, this depends on their economic status: family farmers without hired labour might not be perturbed by trade unionism.
14 E.g. Øystein Sørensen and Bo Stråth, "Introduction," in *The Cultural Construction of Norden*, ed. Sørensen and Stråth (Oslo: Scandinavian University Press, 1997), 1–24. See Bengtsson, "The Swedish Sonderweg," for discussion.

15 Synnøve Bendixsen, Mary Bente Bringslid, and Halvard Vike, "Introduction: Egalitarianism in a Scandinavian Context," in *Egalitarianism in Scandinavia: Historical and Contemporary Perspectives*, ed. Bendixsen, Bringslid and Vike (London: Palgrave Macmillan, 2017), 15.
16 See Bengtsson, "The Swedish Sonderweg," 124–26, 135–38.
17 Nycander, *Makten över arbetsmarknaden*; Lundh, *Spelets regler*. However Lundh has a more critical perspective, see 65–78. But he also says that "The state at the time of the union movement's emergence followed a non-intervention line" (114). For discussion see also Erik Bengtsson and Tobias Karlsson, "What We Know and What We Don't Know about Swedish Labor Market History: Reflections on Spelets Regler," *Essays in Economic & Business History* XXXV (1): 14–35.
18 Rodney Edvinsson, *Growth, Accumulation, Crisis: With New Macroeconomic Data for Sweden 1800–2000* (Stockholm: Almqvist & Wiksell, 2005), data sheet, Table O.
19 Westerståhl, *Svensk fackföreningsrörelse*.
20 Björn Tyrefors Hinnerich, Erik Lindgren, and Per Pettersson-Lidbom, "The Political Economics of Growth, Labor Control and Coercion: Evidence from a Suffrage Reform" (Unpublished paper, Stockholms universitet, Stockholm, 2019).
21 On farm workers, Pär-Erik Back, *En klass i uppbrott: Den fackliga lantarbetarrörelsens uppkomst och utveckling* (Malmö: Framtidens bokförlag, 1961), 25, 54. On maidservants, Kerstin Moberg, *Från tjänstehjon till hembiträde: En kvinnlig låglönegrupp i den fackliga kampen 1903–1946* (Stockholm: Almqvist och Wiksell, 1978).
22 Cf. Matteo Millan, "Introduction: Strikebreaking During Europe's Belle Époque," *European History Quarterly* 49, no. 4 (2019): 553–69.
23 Per Hultqvist, *Försvar och skatter: Studier i svensk riksdagspolitik från representationsreformen till kompromissen 1873* (Gothenburg: Gothenburg University, 1955), 196–201.
24 Lars Tingsten, *Hågkomster* (Stockholm: Bonniers, 1938), 42–46.
25 Torbjörn Vallinder, *I kamp för demokratin. Rösträttsrörelsen i Sverige 1866–1902* (Stockholm: Natur och Kultur, 1962), 111.
26 Jesper Roine and Daniel Waldenström, "The Evolution of Top Incomes in an Egalitarian Society: Sweden, 1903–2004," *Journal of Public Economics* 92, no. 1–2 (2008): 366–87; Erik Bengtsson, Anna Missiaia, Mats Olsson, and Patrick Svensson, "Wealth Inequality in Sweden, 1750–1900," *The Economic History Review* 71, no. 3 (2018): 772–94.
27 Katarina Alexius, *Politisk yttrandefrihet: En studie i lagstiftning och praxis under demokratins genombrottstid* (Stockholm: Nerenius & Santérus, 1997), 332.
28 Jenny Langkjaer, *Övervakning för rikets säkerhet: Svensk säkerhetspolisiär övervakning av utländska personer och inhemsk politisk aktivitet, 1885–1922* (Stockholm: Stockholms universitet, 2011).
29 On 1889 and Örbom see Per Sundberg, *Ministärerna Bildt och Åkerhielm: En studie i den svenska parlamentarismens förgårdar* (Stockholm: Stockholms högskola, 1961), 155–56. On the 1887 law see Alexius, *Politisk yttrandefrihet*, 67–73. On the editors in prison, see Olle Svenning, *Hövdingen: Hjalmar Branting, en biografi* (Stockholm: Bonniers, 2014), 114.
30 Royal Proposition 1889 No 44. https://weburn.kb.se/riks/metadata/89/19566389.html. All parliamentary papers 1867–1970 are digitalised and available at the Royal Library's website: https://riksdagstryck.kb.se/tvakammarriksdagen.html. The quote from the final law text comes from Sundberg, *Ministärerna Bildt och Åkerhiel*m, 157.
31 The cases are discussed in Alexius, *Politisk yttrandefrihet*, 82–94.
32 On élite politics at this time in Sweden, constitutionally conservative but economically liberal, see Torbjörn Nilsson, *Elitens svängrum: Första kammaren, staten och moderniseringen 1867–1886* (Stockholm: Stockholms universitet, 1994).
33 On this law and the politics around it, see Alexius, *Politisk yttrandefrihet*, 74–83; Sundberg *Ministärerna Bildt och Åkerhiel*m, 159–62.

34 Sundberg, *Ministärerna Bildt och Åkerhielm*, 301–3, 343–45.

35 Hans Lindblad, *Karl Staaff: Försvaret och demokratin* (Stockholm: Ekerlids förlag, 2015). On Staaff on anarchism, see Eklund, *Rätten i klasskampen*, 122–28.

36 Alexius, *Politisk yttrandefrihet*, 116–54.

37 Eklund, *Rätten i klasskampen*, 122–25; Alexius, *Politisk yttrandefrihet*, 94–110.

38 Sten Carlsson, *Lantmannapolitiken och industrialismen: partigruppering och opinionsförskjutningar i svensk politik 1890–1902* (Stockholm: Lantbruksförbundets Tidskrifts AB, 1953), 130–31.

39 Motions to the second chamber 1892, No 24, pp. 6–7. The second chamber debate on the motion was held on 16 March and is found in the eighteenth book of protocols from the ordinary (*lagtima*) 1892 Riksdag.

40 Mankell is a legend of nineteenth century radical liberalism in Sweden. Cf. Victor Lundberg, "'Den siste af de typiske 1848 års män i Sverge.' Anteckningar om Julius Mankell och den svenska demokratins förhistoria," *Historisk Tidskrift* 125, no. 3 (2005): 421–40.

41 For the proposals and debates of 1897, 1898 and 1899 and the votes see Westerståhl, *Svensk fackföreningsrörelse*, 248–51; Carlsson, *Lantmannapolitiken och industrialismen*, 289–92.

42 Of the 30 farmer MPs in favour of the law, all but three belonged to the ultra-conservative Agrarian movement. This was influenced by the German *Bund der Landwirte* and was one of the centres of the ultra-right in Swedish politics around 1900. Carlsson, *Lantmannapolitiken och industrialismen*, 162–64, 247–69, 400. The BdL plays an important role in German historical research on the right-inclined legacy of modern German politics – i.e. Hans-Jürgen Puhle, "Lords and Peasants in the Kaiserreich," in *Peasants and Lords in Modern Germany*, ed. Robert G. Moeller (Boston: George Allen and Unwin, 1986), 89–97, 81–109 – but their Swedish counterpart is under-researched except for the pioneering work of Carlsson.

43 On supporters and opponents of the proposal, see Carlsson, *Lantmannapolitiken och industrialismen*, 293–97; Westerståhl, *Svensk fackföreningsrörelse*, 244.

44 In an interesting episode, the 1899 Åkarp Law influenced the German government, which in May 1899 presented an equivalent proposal in their country. Interestingly enough, this law did not pass the German Reichstag; the historian Sten Carlsson comments that "In a country like Germany with universal suffrage and strong industrialization, such a class law could not be imposed through parliament". Carlsson, *Lantmannapolitiken och industrialismen*, 297.

45 From 1899 to 1938, 813 people were sentenced under the Åkarp law. Of these, 193 were sentenced to prison and 37 to penal labour; the rest to fines. Eklund, *Rätten i klasskampen*, 325–26.

46 Jan O. Berg, *På spaning efter en svensk modell: idéer och vägval i arbetsgivarpolitiken 1897–1909* (Enebyberg: Berg Bild Rum & Färg Förlag, 2011), 114, cf. 177.

47 Åke Lindström, *Bruksarbetarfackföreningar: Metalls avdeelning vid bruken i östra Västmanlands län före 1911* (Uppsala: Uppsala universitet, 1979), 28–36.

48 Berg, *På spaning*, Ch. 3. On the freedom to organise, see 89.

49 Berg, *På spaning*, 203. The quotation from 1908: 281.

50 Nycander, *Makten över arbetsmarknaden*, 25–27; Fransson, "Freedom of Contract," 238.

51 Ingvar Flink, *Strejkbryteriet och arbetets frihet: En studie av svensk arbetsmarknad fram till 1938* (Stockholm: Almquist & Wiksell, 1978). The figures on strikebreaking are from Flink, Table 2 and 112, 133, 137.

52 Yngve Myrman, *Maktkampen på arbetsmarknaden 1905–1907: en studie av de ickesocialistiska arbetarna som faktor i arbetsgivarpolitiken* (Stockholm: Stockholms universitet, 1973).

53 Thomas Paster, *The Role of Business in the Development of the Welfare State and Labor Markets in Germany: Containing Social Reforms* (London: Routledge, 2012), Chs. 3, 5.

54 France appears to have taken a more conflictual route around 1906. Roger Magraw, *Workers and the Bourgeois Republic* (Oxford: Blackwell, 1992), 49–52.

55 Cf. the articles on strikebreaking in the special issue of European History Quarterly, No. 4 2019 and especially Millan, "Introduction". See also the other chapters of this volume.

56 Bengtsson, "The Swedish Sonderweg."

57 Bernt Schiller, *Storstrejken 1909: Förhistoria och orsaker* (Copenhagen, Bergen, Gothenburg, Stockholm and Lund: Scandinavian University Books, 1967). On the various wage conflicts see especially pp. 171–98. On the strategic considerations of employers, pp. 198–204. On the recurring LO debates on a general strike, pp. 209–21. On why the LO finally decided for general strike in 1909, pp. 226–30.

58 On the aftermath of the strike and the bouncing back of the unions, see for example Lundh, *Spelets regler*, 104–5; Klas Åmark, *Facklig makt och fackligt medlemskap: De svenska fackförbundens medlemsutveckling 1890–1940* (Lund: Arkiv, 1986), 96–114.

59 Cf. for example Garon's study of industrial relations experts and social statisticians in the British Board of Trade. Sheldon Garon, "Social Knowledge and the State in the Industrial Relations of Japan (1882–1940) and Great Britain (1870–1914)," in *States, Social Knowledge, and the Origins of Modern Social Policies*, ed. Dietrich Rueschemeyer and Theda Skocpol (Princeton, NJ: Princeton University Press, 1996), 264–95.

60 Marika Hedin, *Ett liberalt dilemma: Ernst Beckman, Emilia Broomé, G H von Koch och den sociala frågan 1880–1930* (Stockholm and Stehag: Symposion, 2002), 92–95.

61 Westerståhl, *Svensk fackföreningsrörelse*, 254–60, 299 on the 1906 reform. On Beckman and urban liberalism see Hedin, *Ett liberalt dilemma*. On A. P. Danielsson see Erik Bengtsson and Mats Olssonm "Peasant Aristocrats? Wealth and Social Status of Swedish Farmer Parliamentarians 1769–1895," *Scandinavian Journal of History*, published online February 27, 2020.

62 Schiller, *Storstrejken 1909: förhistoria och orsaker*, 55. Elmquist later became the first head of the National Board of Health and Welfare (Socialstyrelsen) as well as Minister of Social Affairs.

63 Kerstin Enflo and Tobias Karlsson, "From Conflict to Compromise: The Importance of Mediation in Swedish Work Stoppages 1907–1927," CEPR Discussion Paper 12586 (London: Centre for Economic Policy Research, 2018).

64 Eklund, *Rätten i klasskampen*, 241.

65 Gerry R. Rubin, "The Historical Development of Collective Labour Law: The United Kingdom," in *The Rise and Development of Collective Labour Law*, ed. Marcel Van der Linden and Richard Price (Berlin: Peter Lang, 2000), 291–350. On collective laissez faire see pp. 307–8. On comparisons with Britain see also Garon, "Social Knowledge".

66 James Fulcher, "On the Explanation of Industrial Relations Diversity: Labour Movements, Employers and the State in Britain and Sweden," *British Journal of Industrial Relations* 26, no. 2 (1988): 253.

67 Bengtsson and Olsson, "Peasant Aristocrats?"

68 Francis G. Castles, "Barrington Moore's Thesis and Swedish Political Development," *Government and Opposition* 8, no. 3 (1973): 313–31. Peter Baldwin, *The Politics of Social Solidarity: Class Bases of the European Welfare State 1875–1975* (Cambridge: Cambridge University Press, 1990).

69 Nilsson, *Elitens svängrum*.

70 Charles Tilly, *Popular Contention in Great Britain 1758–1834* (Cambridge, MA: Harvard University Press, 1995), esp. pp. 37–48. The quote is from p. 367.

5 State authorities, municipal forces and military intervention in the policing of strikes in Austria-Hungary, 1890–1914*

Claire Morelon

In an interpellation in the Austrian Parliament in 1908, a Social Democratic deputy denounced the actions of the police and gendarmerie in Troppau/Opava during a masons' strike:

> The attitude of district officer Klinger and the municipality of Troppau and its police towards the strikers is absolutely improper and unlawful. Instead of acting impartially, they place themselves at the service of the master builders. This of course damages the trust of the workers and, in general, their perception of justice, and undermines the authority of the officials.[1]

In early twentieth-century Austria-Hungary, in an age of growing democratisation, the expectation that authorities would be impartial in labour disputes had far-reaching consequences. The need to maintain public order, a cornerstone of state duties, increasingly faced competing challenges. From the 1890s to 1914, the number of strikes (and of strikers involved) significantly rose in Austria-Hungary in a context of growing industrialisation.[2] Consequently, employers were putting more pressure on state authorities to intervene in the management of the strikes. At the same time, the push for democratisation (culminating in 1907 with the introduction of universal and equal suffrage in parliamentary elections) and increased calls for constitutional rights to be respected meant that workers' representatives demanded greater accountability from the Austrian government.

This chapter examines how the Austrian state managed these competing demands in the two decades before the First World War. It analyses the regulation of public order in the Habsburg monarchy by examining the interaction between the different authorities at the local level and the centres of power. The interplay between the various levels highlights the discrepancy between central decisions and local practices, as well as the regional differences across the vast Empire. We limit our focus here to the Austrian half of the Empire as the organisation of the police and gendarmerie forces in the Hungarian half was wholly separate and, hence, dissimilar.[3] The much narrower franchise and the systematic persecution of the workers' movement also created a very different context where trade unions were barely tolerated and harsh repression of strikes was consistent with the law.[4] In Cisleithania, however, the expanding public sphere and constitutional liberties made severe measures more fraught. Through the topic of strikes, this chapter explores the strength of the rule of law on the ground.[5] One of the important components of this discussion was the role of the army in the repression of strikes, both in quelling unrest and in replacing strikers as a workforce. The increased militarisation of the monarchy in the lead-up to the war also had a strong influence on the debate.[6] Detailed examination of administrative correspondence and public arguments reveals the contradictions faced by the Austrian state between demands of impartiality, lack of resources and more repressive attitudes. The examples from the various corners of Cisleithania discussed here are drawn from the archives of the Interior Ministry and Defence Ministry in Vienna as well as local archives to provide a more vivid picture of strike policing across the Empire.

Strikes and public order

As the number of strikes grew towards the end of the nineteenth century, they increasingly became a matter of public order for local authorities in the Habsburg monarchy. The police apparatus in the Austrian half of the Empire had developed progressively since the 1850s. The security forces directly answerable to regional and district authorities were the gendarmerie and the state police. District officers in rural areas and smaller towns relied on gendarmerie units, while in larger cities (such as Vienna, Graz, Prague, Brünn/Brno, Lemberg/Lwów/L'viv, Cracow and Trieste/Trst), police headquarters (*Polizeidirektionen*) supervised public safety.[7] The number of state police centres in Cisleithania rapidly increased in the last decades before 1914: new police commissariats (*Polizeikommisariate*) were established in Przemyśl (1892), Mährisch-Ostrau/Moravská Ostrava (1894), Pola/Pula (1903), Rovigno/Rovinj (1910) and Borysław/Boryslav (1913), and two new police headquarters were established in Czernowitz/Cernăuți/Chernitsvi (1905) and Laibach/Ljubljana (1913). Municipalities all over Cisleithania also employed and funded their own police forces. These municipal forces were frequently involved in the policing of strikes. In contrast to the state police, local police forces were under the authority of the mayor and only assisted the state authorities.[8]

State intervention in the policing of strikes was viewed through the prism of the state's duty to maintain public peace. Local state authorities (district officers and police chiefs) therefore tended to monitor the development of strikes and call for reinforcements when necessary, but only intervened if the strike threatened to turn violent. The mobilisation of forces was gradual: if locally stationed forces were deemed insufficient, district officers called for gendarmerie reinforcements, even if they were not immediately deployed. Some regions, however, suffered from a greater shortage of gendarmerie troops. The district officer in Pisino/Pazin (Istria), for example, explained in 1909 that there were no gendarmes available in the district to be sent to the coal mines in Carpano/Krapan for an upcoming strike, as they were all mobilised elsewhere to prevent sheep thefts.[9] The frequent "concentration" of gendarmes, moving from one district to another or even from one crownland to another, to maintain order during strikes was also expensive as the gendarmes needed to be transported and housed. For example, during the second half of 1911 alone, 1,700 gendarmes intervened in strikes in 64 locations in Bohemia. The Defence Ministry (which controlled the gendarmerie) charged the expenses incurred during such operations to the Interior Ministry.[10] Costs and available manpower were thus part of the considerations taken by local authorities when making decisions on intervention. Finally, in cases of larger demonstrations or fear of violence, authorities called for the support of army units. Use of the military was officially intended to be the "utmost and last resource to maintain and restore public peace".[11] But in practice district officers sometimes asked for army support if there were insufficient numbers of gendarmes available in the area.[12]

During strikes, one of the main causes of violence – or disturbance to public order in the official jargon – was the interaction between striking workers and "strikebreakers", either workers from the factory who continued to work or imported workers brought in by the employers to replace the strikers. An example of these confrontations can be seen during a strike in 1906 at the large wagon factory in Nesselsdorf/Kopřivnice (Moravia), which employed several thousand workers. When 30 workers decided to resume work, the strikers attempted to dissuade them from going back with insults and shaming. The district officer immediately took preventive measures and commented: "The entire location in its full extent had to be occupied by gendarmes to protect the few willing workers".[13] During the following weeks, gendarmes accompanied the strikebreakers to and from the factory. As the strike continued and the number of strikebreakers grew, several small incidents occurred. On one day, the strikers blocked the road to a nearby town to stop 12 new workers on their way home. When these workers took the train instead, a crowd of 500 people came to meet them at the station, swinging sticks and shouting insults and threats. Other incidents included rotten eggs or excrement being thrown at individuals in the street or outside the factory. Some windows of private homes were broken.[14] The shaming rituals aimed at coercing non-striking workers into compliance with the strike and the frequent verbal threats and insults sometimes turned physical.[15] The tactics against strikebreakers recalled traditional forms of popular justice, such as charivaris, and can be traced back to the rural background of most of the workers at the time.[16] From the employers' point of view, police protection of "willing workers" at all times was essential to maintain their activity: the intention was to reassure the workers and encourage them to come back. In some cases, employers even armed the "willing" workers with revolvers to ensure they could protect themselves. During a lockout in Vienna in 1911, the *Arbeiter-Zeitung* mocked the "little performance" of the factory owner leading his new, armed workers outside the factory.[17]

Employers regularly complained of the insufficient protection offered by the police forces to willing workers. In a letter to his district officer, a silk factory owner in Mährisch Trübau/Moravská Třebová (Moravia) outlined his expectations:

> [we ask for] the authorities' protection against the threatening attacks of striking workers, which is due to us as citizens and taxpaying industrialists. . . . We believe we are entitled to the authorities' support in restarting the factory's

> activity with work-willing elements. [This support should consist in] preventive measures to avoid trouble, especially attacks against the work-willing. . . . Without the provision of armed police forces the work-willing could never bring themselves to enter the workplace during the strike.[18]

Furthermore, many employers wanted the state to outright eliminate any attempt by the workers to persuade others to join the strike. They thought that the legal restrictions on picketing did not go far enough. The 1870 law regulating the right of coalition did not ban individuals from standing near the establishment on strike or from giving out information; it merely specified that "intimidation" or violence could not be used for this purpose. In the early 1900s, as employers became more organised through professional associations, a movement emerged to push for reform of the current legislation. A memorandum sent to the Interior Ministry by the Union of Employers in Austria in 1906 asked for picket lines to be forbidden and for better protection of employers from the "terrorism" of striking workers. Numerous letters from employers all over Austria recounting their own experiences of strikes were sent to the Interior Ministry in support of the initiative. A company in Littai/Litija (Carnolia) described a strike in their factory in the previous year where an "ever smaller group of workers terrorised the workers", and demanded that the ministry "remove this unlawful terrorism".[19] A few years later, the employers' mouthpiece still actively campaigned for tougher legislation on picketing in line with English and American laws and blamed the "backward mores and revolutionary excesses" during strikes on "the weakness and timidity of successive governments".[20]

The debate on picketing firmly revolved around the appropriate level of intervention by state authorities. Social Democrat leaders complained of overzealous policing, which prevented workers from simply gathering or protesting outside factories. For example, seven people were arrested by the Trieste/Trst police for "bothering work-willing workers" during a strike of warehousemen in 1907. The Social Democratic newspaper *Il Lavoratore* criticised the behaviour of the police:

> when the strikers spotted a strikebreaker, they would whistle loudly at him, sneer at him and throw his betrayal in his face, then the [police] guards would move nervously, start performing ridiculous and useless "manoeuvres" and the mounted guards would press forward almost at a trot against the groups of warehousemen. . . . And whistling – there are judgments from the court of appeal – is not criminal![21]

Faced with recriminations from both sides, the government often stepped in to defend policing decisions made at the local level. The government's official position, as articulated in a speech by the interior minister in 1908, was to give some leeway to local officials in determining the extent and degree of the "intimidation". While acknowledging the strikers' right to walk about and give out information near the factory, the guidelines nevertheless underlined that pickets were not always "peaceful and harmless", which often prompted intervention from the police forces. Authorities were entitled to intervene accordingly to maintain public order. Replying to complaints about police action against pickets in Vienna, the minister insisted that they had not substantially deviated from these principles and that only in a few isolated cases had the chief of police needed to remind his men of the general instructions.[22]

By the early twentieth century, police intervention during strikes was a highly political subject and authorities were called to account by both sides. Social Democrats defended the workers' right to strike and to demonstrate based on constitutional freedoms, while employers lobbied for protection of "those workers willing to work" (*Arbeitswillige*). Contesting the very concept of strikebreaking, employers claimed they supported the freedom to choose to work, which should be guaranteed by the state.[23] Discussions and efforts to change the law at the central level constituted only one of the means used to influence policing practices. Another was to exert influence on local officials, whose responses varied greatly throughout the Empire.

The state as umpire? Central principles and local practices

As legislative change was slow and difficult to achieve, employers also attempted to put direct pressure on police forces. Complaints about the partiality of the local police surfaced in many towns throughout Cisleithania, the motives varying according to the political leanings of the municipal council. In Troppau/Opava (Silesia), Czech-speakers deplored the passive attitude of the municipal police against German youth violence.[24] In Pola/Pula (Istria) policemen affiliated with the Italian liberals were accused of mistreating Croatian-speakers and political adversaries. After one such episode, the loyalist newspaper *Omnibus* ran the title: "Down with the municipal guards! Send them all away!"[25] In the case of labour disputes, Social Democrats frequently denounced the collusion between employers and municipal policemen, who, being directly answerable to the mayor, were considered to be more biased than gendarmes or soldiers. During a masons' strike in Neutitschein/Nový Jičín (Moravia), a leaflet published by the strike committee accused the employers of "relying on the help of strikebreakers protected by the local police, whose leader is said to be a relative of the master-builder Blum".[26] Similarly, during the strike at the Witkowitz/Vítkovice steelworks in the Ostrava mining region in 1906, the workers saw the local police as acting on the orders of the management and referred to them as the "cossacks of the Vítkovice Czar".[27] Local policemen were also suspected of taking bribes or being pressured to act as guards for the employers.[28] The *Arbeiter-Zeitung* commented on the case of a policeman who arrested striking laundresses for no reason in the suburbs of Vienna following the threat of an official complaint by the employer: "the police think they are the handmaidens of the employers and execute their orders blindly".[29] The local police's independence vis-à-vis district authorities also meant that official recourse against them was not so effective. After a few incidents during a strike at a bike factory in Eger/Cheb (Bohemia) in 1912, the municipal chief of police decided to ban picket lines and to arrest any worker who tried to persuade willing workers to stop their activity. When Social Democrats complained to the district officer, the latter retorted that he had no influence over decisions taken by the autonomous police forces.[30]

The fact that the limited municipal forces could more readily defend employers' interests did not mean that employers did not resort to the state authorities or try to influence how they managed public order. The bloody repression of a large Social Democratic demonstration after the elections of 1907 in Przemyśl when the police charged into a peaceful crowd showed that a state police force was by no means a sufficient guarantee of impartiality.[31] In smaller localities, employers often directly requested the local district officer to provide gendarmerie protection or send reinforcements to areas where few men were permanently posted. In 1905, the previously quoted silk factory owner in Mährisch-Trübau/Moravská Třebová went so far as to ask the Interior Ministry to demote the district officer because he had refused to provide additional gendarmes and then call for the army to protect the willing workers. In his letter to the Moravian governor, the owner asked that a man "with more understanding of the situation and interests of the industry be nominated". The district officer had made several attempts at negotiation, which had failed, and claimed that the protection offered was sufficient.[32] As strikes could last several weeks, the costs of maintaining troops from elsewhere weighed on officials' decisions. A letter from the Union of Industrialists to the regional authorities defended the owner of an agricultural machinery factory in the Moravian countryside and requested continued gendarmerie protection during a strike:

> It seems to us out of question that the granting of protection for the work-willing should be somehow tied up with the issue of the costs of further gendarmerie protection. The question of the protection of the work-willing is a public law issue, which cannot be made dependent on the civil law factor of its costs.[33]

The Union of Austrian industrialists created in 1897 often acted as an intermediary to relay complaints of poor public management of strikes. Another local branch of the union sent a telegram to the Moravian governor to request the banning of a worker's demonstration in Sternberg/Šternberk (Moravia).[34] The union also backed a request to the Interior Ministry from a furniture factory in Buczkowice to have gendarmes posted there in order to deter socialist agitators (before a strike broke out). The company offered to house them for free.[35] To solve the difficult question of costs, companies in sparsely populated areas were sometimes prepared to make arrangements themselves to enable the gendarmes to stay. In anticipation of an upcoming strike, a mine owner in Carpano/Krapan (Istria) had built housing for the strikebreakers as well as a separate house for the gendarmerie reinforcements.[36]

For local state authorities, therefore, the relatively swift resolution of strikes had an impact on the mobilisation and use of public forces. The authorities in many cases tried to mediate between employers and workers in order to bring an end to the strike more quickly. This approach, pioneered by Prime Minister Koerber, who sent the minister of Justice to lead the negotiations during the 1900 coal miners' strike, was a combination of pragmatism and respect for constitutional rights.[37] State officials had often noticed that army or even gendarmerie intervention exacerbated tensions and saw compromise as a more efficient method of conflict resolution. This ideal of mediation was very present in instructions from the Interior Ministry, but in practice it was often flouted in favour of force. Moreover, conceptions in Vienna ministries could clash with interests at the regional or local levels. During the 1904 strike among Borysław oil workers, the Galician governor Potocki, himself an owner of oil fields, defended the oil producers' inflexible stance despite pressure from the Vienna government to find a compromise. Potocki committed to the protection of willing workers with as many military troops as necessary.[38] Even so, employers found the number of soldiers mobilised insufficient and asked for more, promising to cover the transportation costs.[39] One of the oil companies sent a telegram to Koerber requesting additional troops and asked the English consul to also push for stronger army intervention, claiming that they feared for their own safety if soldiers did not intervene.[40]

Furthermore, the necessity for impartiality in labour disputes was perceived differently across the various regions of Cisleithania. District officers in industrial regions such as Bohemia, Moravia, Upper and Lower Austria sometimes published notices limiting picketing or sent out the police or the gendarmerie early on during strikes.[41] But, conversely, there were also complaints of officials who favoured the strikers and examples of serious attempts at mediation. For example, in Marienbad/Mariánské Lázně (Bohemia) during a masons' strike in 1903, the district officer "summoned" to negotiations the masters, who refused to comply and complained about the "improper form" of these summons in parliament.[42] During the aforementioned strike in the Nesselsdorf/Kopřivnice wagon factory in 1906 as the owners refused to recognise the workers' organisation, the district officer negotiated separately over several days with the workers' leaders and the head of the factory to come to an agreement.[43] In contrast, the local district officers' management of the massive field workers' strike in Galicia in 1902 betrays a more immediate willingness to defend the employers' position. The strike was one of the largest labour movements in the Late Habsburg Empire. It started in the early summer and lasted until September, spreading through 18 districts and in 386 towns in the Eastern part of the province.[44] The day labourers, who would usually lend their services to the nearby large estate during harvest time collectively refused to take up the work. The number of "strikers" is hard to estimate since entire villages participated in the boycott movement. To be able to proceed with the harvest, landowners recruited workers from other regions, mostly from the South or West of the province, but also from as far afield as Croatia. Violent incidents against the work-willing broke out in 121 towns. In Czernichowce/Chernikhivtsi when a crowd of around a hundred people threw stones at gendarmes bringing workers back from an estate on a cart, the two gendarmes fired their weapons and wounded one man.[45]

Local authorities often reacted to the strike by requesting army intervention. As a report from the Ministry of Commerce explained, "the authorities had to commandeer the military to enable the foreign workers to bring in the harvest".[46] Yet, the Viennese government had invited the local authorities early on to find an acceptable compromise for both parties by examining the peasants' demands "strictly impartially" and, in managing public order, to avoid any "measure which could be misinterpreted as a one-sided exertion of influence by the government in favour of one party".[47] Ruthenian politicians, however, complained of the district officials' partiality and asked for employees from the Interior Ministry to be sent instead.[48] In their complaints, they described several district officers in Galicia who put out public notices to dissuade the peasants from joining the strikes and claimed that pressing for better conditions was against the law. The army was supposedly sent to one village before the strike had started.[49] According to Deputy Andrii Kos, an army officer even reported that he had been instructed by an official from the governor's office to "not spare" the population, "to harm them materially", and he had the impression the official wanted to inflict revenge upon the striking peasants.[50] Several episodes of violent repression were also criticised. In a small town in the district of Czortków/Chortkiv a crowd came to drive out the foreign workers who had been hired on the estate. To defend them, the army charged into the crowd and the gendarmes carried out a mass arrest of 137 people, who were locked in a barn for several days before being taken to the district capital for interrogation.[51] In Jaktorów/Yaktoriv, near Lemberg/Lwów/L'viv, the cavalry attacked peasants who tried to prevent a reaping machine from being started up: five suffered light injuries, three more serious injuries, one of whom subsequently died.[52]

Overall, 444 people were arrested during the summer.[53] Local authorities in Galicia did not acknowledge the workers' right to strike and construed the strike as a national insurrection (many of the peasants in the region being Ruthenian-speaking). Some of the measures taken against strikers, such as the forced billeting of soldiers in private houses, were experienced as a punishment against politically active workers. The Galician governor's detailed report to the Interior Ministry, which attempted to deflect criticism voiced in parliament and in the press, plays down the accounts of violence but tends to confirm the officials' sympathy for the landowners.[54] In the eyes of the district officers and the governor, the peasants' claims for constitutional rights of assembly or the right to strike were perceived as fundamentally illegitimate. The governor explained that the movement could not be put on a par with the wage disputes in the Western provinces and that the field labourers had been manipulated by agitators, comments which reflected the Polish landowners' prejudices against the peasantry. He also insisted on the "moral effect" on the population of the appearance of the military. His view was that the goal of army deployment was to show the peasants "the truth" of the situation and contradict the rumours that the strike was sanctioned by the state.[55] He deemed "fairy tales" the brochures that were circulating explaining the workers' right to strike. The automatic repressive measures (unlawful mass arrests, ordering the army to attack before violence had broken out) are confirmed by the reports and contrast with the management of strikes elsewhere. It also clearly emerges that state employees did not try to remain neutral or help to mediate, but saw their duty as lying in harsh repression of the movement. The notion of labour conflicts as legitimate forms of action and of workers as equal citizens was emerging slowly in Late Habsburg Austria and was not uniformly respected. The variations reflected local arrangements or interests but also more fundamentally, sometimes, as in the case of Galicia, the local officials' lack of recognition of constitutional rights.

Military assistance

The systematic deployment of military units during the agricultural strike of 1902 led to complaints of violence and raised questions about the use of auxiliary brute force (*Brachialgewalt*) in dealing with labour unrest. In spite of its length and territorial extent, the strike resulted in few serious casualties: many peasants were injured, but only one died. However, that same summer in the province's capital, Lemberg/Lwów/L'viv, five men were killed by the army in repressing a construction workers' strike.[56] In the last decades before the First World War, the army was still frequently deployed to quell unrest (strikes or demonstrations) and many citizens still died from the weapons of their own military. Army assistance was supposed to be a means of last resort. Official regulations stipulated that it should only be used when all other possibilities for reinforcement, whether gendarmerie or police forces, had been exhausted. Indeed authorities often resisted calls for army dispatches. For example despite pressure from the population for army intervention following fears of peasant unrest in Bukovina in 1907, the governor insisted on respecting the regulations and not calling the army too quickly.[57] In contrast, local officials in Hungary called on soldiers more readily and army officers themselves deplored what they saw as a misuse of military forces for political aims in the Eastern half of the Empire.[58] Austrian parliamentary deputies also complained about the use of the Common Army to influence elections in Hungary, questioning the burden of such "assistance" on the common budget.[59] In Croatia-Slavonia, too, military reinforcements were a common means of quelling unrest, for example during the 1897 rural protests.[60]

The growing illegitimacy of sending in troops against the home population and the complaints from the Social Democrats meant that army intervention, especially when it resulted in casualties, increasingly had to be justified. In this respect, national unrest sometimes furnished a useful explanation. In the case of the stokers' strike in Trieste, where 14 people were killed by the army, the spectre of irredentist agitators justified the army's prompt and firm response, even in the eyes of the liberal *Neue Freie Presse*.[61] In fact, the strike was led by the local Social Democrats and had no connection to irredentism. Similarly, in Galicia the local administration presented the 1902 field workers' strike as the work of Ruthenian anti-Polish agitators and hence a threat to the state in order to justify harsh repression and the intervention of the army.[62] In reality, even the Ruthenian National Deputy Andrii Kos acknowledged that the strike had purely economic causes and the main demands (higher wages, access to pastures, authorisation to gather wood) clearly point to classic peasant/landowner issues.[63] The threat of an insurrection or nationalist tendencies allowed justifying *ex post* the heavy-handedness of the repression.[64]

These two examples should not mislead us into thinking that army violence only took place on the periphery or that it was only there that it was lethal. Accusations of subversion or treason as a means to suppress labour unrest had its roots in earlier measures against strikes in the 1870s and 1880s.[65] Moreover, army troops sent to deal with demonstrators led to deaths in Graz during the Badeni riots of 1897, in the Bohemian Lands in 1905 and even in Vienna itself, where four workers were killed during cost-of-living riots in 1911.[66] As Social Democrat deputy Karl Leuthner claimed in 1912, "in Austria and Hungary there is more shooting than anywhere in Europe: for every election, every larger strike, every turbulent demonstration".[67] By 1914, most large cities in the Empire had witnessed a bloody episode of army repression in the preceding 20 years.

The army, for its part, perceived the recourse to military assistance by civilian authorities as potentially damaging to its prestige. In a 1911 note, the Military Chancellery commented on the recent use of military assistance that it had lost its "imposing effect on the people" in the last few years. Instead of dampening agitation, military intervention often exacerbated it and turned the crowd against the military. When weapons were used, there were discussions in parliament as to whether it was justified or not, which were then publicised in the press. Without weapons, the soldiers might have to endure the scorn of jeering crowds for days, which "shattered the troops' standing (*Ansehen*)". The Military Chancellor criticised the use of assistance troops for "scare effect" (*zum Bangemachen*) rather than for the "restoration of public order". Frequent use of army troops inured people to the "scare effect" and they became used to the "harmlessness" of the assistance troops. The note concluded that

> if the civil servant had to be answerable for "fetching the military" to the same extent as the officer is for the use of force, . . . the mob would already scatter at the approach of the military and the number of "victims" would sink significantly.[68]

In the eyes of military leaders, the civilian authorities' overreliance on the army in case of unrest undermined both the standing of the army as an institution and the effectiveness of the assistance itself.[69] The consequences of these interventions could be unpleasant and could aggravate the relationship between the civilian population and the local garrison. In a context of general conscription, it was important to maintain the army's good standing in society. Local commanders might be tempted to mend their relationship with the town's inhabitants after the use of violence. The military command in Brüx/Most (Bohemia) was thus strictly forbidden from giving the press or the municipality "excuses or explanations" as this could be interpreted as a sign of weakness. The decree sent to all military commands acknowledged the difficult position of local officers but asked them in the name of "military dignity" to refrain from expressing their regrets.[70] Finally, assistance meant that the soldiers would be attacking not a foreign enemy, but workers, sometimes women and children, in defence of private property.[71] The soldiers perceived the task as highly unrewarding and army officers considered it an "unpleasant duty".[72]

The debate on the role of military intervention in strikes concerned not just the casualties induced by the repressive measures. Despite strong Social Democratic opposition to the practice, soldiers still sometimes took the place of strikers to ensure continuity of production. For example, during the highly publicised bricklayers' strike of 1895 in Vienna, which prompted a wider discussion in the press and parliament on army and gendarmerie intervention during strikes (in this case leading to one death) and on the harsh conditions of workers, complaints also targeted the use of soldiers as strikebreakers. The interior minister insisted that only a few men had been hired "in their free time" (even the *Arbeiter-Zeitung* considered it "insignificant"), but it was seen as compromising the government's position. The troops themselves were quickly withdrawn after the parliamentary debate.[73] Officially, posting soldiers for work purposes was condemned and could only take place by express authorisation from the emperor. Whereas in the 1870s it was still accepted in exceptional cases, especially if the food supply was threatened, as it was, for example, during bakers' strikes, a War Ministry decree of 1889 severely limited the provision of soldiers for economic assistance. The decree forbade a military command from taking such a measure without authorisation from the War Ministry and made it contingent upon approval from the imperial military chancellery, which was mostly refused.[74] In practice, however, ad-hoc arrangements and the lending of soldiers still happened, even though they were not part of a systematic policy. In Trieste in 1902, the Austro-Hungarian navy provided the private company Lloyd with stokers to replace the strikers. The Minister of Commerce justified the navy's action by the need to maintain postal traffic in the public interest, claiming that the military stokers only worked on ships also carrying mail.[75] During a citywide strike of textile workers in Reichenberg/Liberec in 1904, a tailor whose workforce was on strike received the help of a few military tailors to complete orders of army uniforms. The governor similarly insisted that the military tailors had not worked on the production of civilian clothes.[76]

Asking for soldiers to perform the work of strikers was increasingly not simply a temporary improvised expedient, but part of a double strategy to defend the national economy in the lead-up to the war, first by ensuring uninterrupted services in key sectors, and second by undermining the Social Democratic movement. The strike wave of 1905 spawned demand for the systematic deployment of soldiers in strategic industries, such as bakeries, butchers, printers, transportation facilities, communication services and gas and water works. The risk of a general strike in the wake of the Russian revolution and the movement for universal suffrage was considered enough of an emergency to call for the use of soldiers to guarantee the continuation of food and energy supplies, as well as official printing presses. The governors in Lemberg/Lwów/L'viv and Linz had turned directly to local military commanders to ask if a military workforce was available to provide help in the food industries in case a general strike broke out. The Bohemian governor explained the double goal of using the military against a general strike:

> it is on the one hand an important state interest to weaken the effect of this Social Democratic weapon, but also to counter the damage caused to the public by a disrupted food supply and forced stoppage of lighting and water works. It would be a great asset, in this respect, if the most important services could be maintained through the provision of a military workforce.[77]

The War Ministry, however, reminded regional military commanders that soldiers were prohibited from working for private businesses. This position sought to preserve military discipline and military standing and spare the men from possible insults from strikers and also avoid fragmenting forces when they might be needed to restore order. If the situation were to become serious, the ministry was prepared to furnish goods from its own bakeries and stocks rather than a workforce.[78]

The notion that several key activities were too indispensable to be disrupted and that the army should then step in to maintain them came to be further reinforced in the following years. Army troops were indeed used to guarantee continuity of service, especially in larger cities. In 1908, during a strike at the Budapest gas works, 300 soldiers from the Common Army were mobilised to work for the private company while additional troops were sent to maintain order. This massive recourse to common soldiers generated outrage among Social Democrats, who saw the official justification, that the lights could not go out in the second largest city in the Empire, as a mere excuse.[79] Similarly, in Cracow in 1913, 40 soldiers replaced striking gas workers.[80]

The demonstrations and strikes in 1905 had not led to a paralysis of the economy, but the "passive resistance" of railway workers in November of that year had demonstrated the potential damage a general stoppage would cause.[81] In nearby Hungary, the weeklong strike among railway workers in 1904 had been crushed by the Tisza government through mobilisation of the workers into the *Honvéd* (Hungarian army).[82] Faced with the possibility of another movement among railway workers in Cisleithania, the emperor gave preventive authorisation for the partial mobilisation of reservist railway workers in 1907, 1908 and again in 1911.[83] In 1907, the general inspector of railways considered that military personnel should be available as temporary helpers for the good "order of a service so essential for the defence power".[84] A project law was even drafted in 1908.[85] The Railway Ministry pushed for military intervention in the case of passive resistance, as it endangered not only the economy but also the "the fighting capacity of the Empire".[86] By 1912, the War Ministry had somewhat changed its position regarding economic assistance and considered it perfectly valid to maintain train traffic, especially since disruption could create problems for the smooth mobilisation of troops in the event of war. As its preferred solution, however, the ministry recommended passing a law to make "passive resistance" a punishable offence, as was the case in Hungary.[87] In Hungarian law, the concerted refusal to work was a crime for public workers and this provision had been used to arrest the leaders of the

1904 railway strike.[88] Social Democrats denounced the "militarisation of railway workers" entailed in the project to mobilise railway employees.[89] Following a strike among state employees (especially postal workers) in Trieste in 1911, Social Democrat deputy Pittoni questioned the legality of replacing strikers with soldiers to combat passive resistance, calling it an "anti-constitutional measure".[90]

The debate in parliament and Pittoni's interpellation led to an inter-ministerial conference in early 1914 to determine the extent to which the military could be drawn upon to replace state employees. According to the final report, the commission considered that recourse to the military in state services was not a negation of constitutional rights. If "passive resistance" in economic public establishments endangered "public safety, peace and order," then replacement with soldiers was justified. The railway sector fell in this category: it provoked as much disruption as a riot, since it threatened the common well-being through its effect on supply routes, the national economy and social life. The other sectors considered indispensable to the smooth continuation of economic life were coal production in certain cases and the postal and telegraph services. Moreover, "protection of the endangered public interest" required military forces to be drawn on not only to replace state railway employees but also employees of private railway companies in order to maintain operations.[91] These provisions, which made the increased recourse to soldiers to replace strikers acceptable, corresponded to similar measures in France and Italy at the time. They also did not stand out in the context of the increased militarisation of the Habsburg monarchy immediately before the war. The War Production Law of 1912, which laid out plans for potential military mobilisation of the economy, had already given the military substantial control over labour relations in case of war. Measures to use the military to counter strikes of state employees were a logical extension of the militarisation effort driven by preparations for war.[92]

The intervention of authorities to maintain public order during strikes offers a case study in the articulation of the different layers of power in Habsburg Austria. The concrete mechanisms of containing violence during strikes reveal the links between the state as guarantor of public safety, the municipalities and the army. The gradual deployment of police, gendarmerie and army forces left local officials with a wide margin of appreciation within the limits of the general regulations. Many complaints about biases were lodged from both the side of the employers and the side of the workers' organisations. Employers took for granted that the Austrian state would intervene to further industrial interests. An ideal of impartiality on the part of the Austrian state in labour disputes definitely existed and was promoted by the Interior Ministry, at least from the Koerber era onwards. However, state intervention could take a different form at the local level, highlighting the chasm between theory and practice. Sometimes, local officials, as in Galicia, dismissed workers' actions as automatically illegitimate and fell back on earlier methods of discrediting strikes by treating them as state subversion. The Austrian state was not blind to the effects of harsh repression on public opinion and was concerned by its potential for undermining state legitimacy. The public's attitude towards the use of soldiers as strikebreakers provides, in this sense, a benchmark for the transformations in the last decades before 1914. While the practice was increasingly disdained around the turn of the century, it gained new legitimacy from the militarisation of the economy that wartime necessitated as it was felt that a patriotic emergency trumped considerations of the rule of law. This course would only be further reinforced through the increased military control of society during the First World War.

Notes

* Research for this article received funding from the European Research Council (ERC) under the European Union's Horizon 2020 Research and Innovation program (G.A. 677199 – ERC-StG2015 "The Dark Side of the Belle Époque. Political Violence and Armed Associations in Europe before the First World War").

1 Interpellation Pospíšil and associates, 16 June 1908, Österreichisches Staatsarchiv (Austrian State Archives, ÖStA), Allgemeines Verwaltungsarchiv (General Administrative Archives, AVA), Ministerium des Innern (Interior Ministry, MdI), Präsidium (Präs), K1992, sig. 20/9, no. 6744/08.

2 Michael Mesch, *Arbeiterexistenz in der Spätgründerzeit: Gewerkschaften und Lohnentwicklung in Österreich, 1890–1914* (Vienna: Europaverlag, 1984), 72–76.

3 On the Hungarian organisation, see József Zachar, "Die Rolle der k.u.k Streitkräfte in der Sicherung der inneren Ordnung zur Zeit des Ausbruchs des ersten Weltrkiegs," in *Od Sarajeva k Velké válce: sborník příspěvků vědeckého semináře k 80. výročí vypuknutí první světové války konaného ve dnech 29.-30. června 1994 v Praze*, ed. Jan Galandauer (Prague: Historický ústav Armády České republiky, 1995), 84–104.

4 Pieter van Duin, *Central European Crossroads: Social Democracy and National Revolution in Bratislava (Pressburg), 1867–1921* (New York: Berghahn Books, 2009), 41–42.

5 On the Habsburg monarchy as a state ruled by the rule of law, see Pieter M. Judson, *The Habsburg Empire: A New History* (Cambridge, MA: Harvard University Press, 2016).

6 On militarisation, see Laurence Cole, *Military Culture and Popular Patriotism in Late Imperial Austria* (Oxford: Oxford University Press, 2014).

7 Andreas Hauer, *Ruhe, Ordnung, Sicherheit: eine Studie zu den Aufgaben der Polizei in Österreich* (Vienna: Springer, 2000), 53; see also, Helmut Gebhardt, "Die Etablierung der österreichischen Polizei und Gendarmerie im 18. und 19. Jahrhundert: Aspekte zu ihrer Rolle bei der Entwicklung von Staatsorganisation und Rechtsstaat," in *Polizei, Recht und Geschichte: Europäische Aspekte einer wechselvollen Entwicklung*, ed. Helmut Gebhardt (Graz: Grazer Univ. Verl., 2006), 30–41.

8 For example, see the published rules for the municipal police in Pola/Pula (Istria): *Regolamento del Corpo delle Guardie municipali di P.S. della città di Pola* (Pola: Tipografia Martinolic, 1895).

9 District officer in Mitterburg (Pazin/Pisino) to Governor's Office in Triest (Trieste/Trst), Archivio di Stato di Trieste (State Archives in Trieste, ASTs), I. R. Luogotenenza del Littorale (Governor's Office of the Littoral, IRLdL), Atti presidiali (AP), busta 338, no. 2074, 10/c, 29 November 1909.

10 ÖStA, AVA, MdI, Allgemeine Reihe, K2083, sig. 20, no. 25985/12, 4 March 1912.

11 Minister President to Defence Minister, 16 July 1874, ÖStA, Kriegsarchiv (War Archives, KA), Zentralstellen (Central Offices, ZSt), k. k. Ministerium für Landesverteidigung (Defence Ministry, MfLV), Politischer Teil Hauptreihe, K682, no. 9966.

12 For example, during a miners' strike in Sagor/Zagorje (Carniola) as gendarmerie forces were stretched in the area due to gangs of thieves, see report from the governor of Carniola, ÖStA, AVA, MdI, Präs, K1988, no. 7410/03, 19 October 1903.

13 Moravský zemský archiv (Moravian Regional Archives, Brno, MZA), Moravské místodrzitelství – presidium (Presidium of the Governor's Office, B13), ka 374, sig. 1, in no. 6430/06, Report from the district officer in Neutitschein/Nový Jičin, no. 3397/06, 11 May 1906.
14 MZA, B13, ka 374, sig. 1, in no. 6430/06, gendarmerie report Nesselsdorf, no. 4400/06, 31 May 1906; gendarmerie report Freiberg, no. 4529/06, 1 June 1906; gendarmerie report Nesselsdorf, no. 4796/06, 6 June 1906.
15 For an analysis of these rituals in mid-nineteenth century Britain, see Thomas Linehan, *Scabs and Traitors: Taboo, Violence and Punishment in Labour Disputes in Britain, 1760–1871* (London: Routledge, 2018).
16 On the survival of these practices much later in the twentieth century, see Ilaria Favretto, "Rough Music and Factory Protest in post-1945 Italy," *Past & Present* 228, no. 1 (2015): 207–47.
17 *Arbeiter-Zeitung*, February 28, 1909, 11; see for example this accusation in the case of a miners' strike in Tlučná (Bohemia), *Nová doba*, 1 March 1900, 6.
18 Letter from Rudolf Reichert to the district officer in Mährisch-Trübau/Moravská Třebová, 21 August 1905, MZA, B13, ka 369, sig. 1, no. 5760/05.
19 ÖStA, AVA, MdI, Präsidium (Präs), K1991, sig. 20/9, ad no. 4166/06, Letter from Schwarz Zublin & Co, 3 May 1906.
20 "Streikexcesse," *Arbeitgeber-Zeitung*, October 1, 1910, 2.
21 *Il Lavoratore*, December 18, 1907, 1 and the Daily report on events from the Police Headquarters in Trieste, ASTs, IRLdL, AP, b. 317, 1/138/07, 11/a, 18 December 1907.
22 Guidelines regarding picketing from the Interior Ministry, which refer back to a speech by the minister of interior in 1908, ÖStA, AVA, MdI, Präs, K1997, sig. 20/9, no 10379/12, 26 October 1912.
23 "Streikbruch," *Arbeitgeber-Zeitung*, September 11, 1909, 2.
24 See Interpellation in parliament by Pacák and associates, 15 May 1906, ÖStA, AVA, MdI, Präs, K2134, sig. 22, no 4345/06.
25 *Omnibus*, July 16, 1907, 1, AST, IRLdL, AP, b. 318, 11/b, no. 2145/07; on the Pola context, see Frank Wiggermann, *K.u.K. Kriegsmarine und Politik: Ein Beitrag zur Geschichte der italienischen Nationalbewegung in Istrien* (Vienna: Verlag der Österreichischen Akademie der Wissenschaften, 2004).
26 Leaflet from the "organization of bricklayers," MZA, B13, ka 377, sig. 1, no. 6551/06, 30 June 1907.
27 John Robertson, "Calamitous Methods of Compulsion: Labor, War, and Revolution in a Habsburg Industrial District, 1906–1919" (PhD diss., University of North Carolina, Chapel Hill, 2014), 82.
28 Historian Jan Havránek found cases of policemen paid for their intervention, Jan Havránek, *Hornická stávka roku 1900 v severočeském hnědouhelném revíru* (Prague: Československá akademie věd, 1953), 76, 96.
29 *Arbeiter-Zeitung*, September 8, 1912, 13.
30 Report from the Bohemian governor to the Interior Ministry, ÖStA, AVA, MdI, Präs, K1997, sig. 20/9, no. 10379/12, 18 October 1912.
31 The *Arbeiter-Zeitung* held the head of the local police as personally responsible, see *Arbeiter-Zeitung*, May 24, 1907, 4; See also, John Fahey, "Undermining a Bulwark of the Monarchy: Civil-Military Relations in Fortress Przemyśl (1871–1914)," *Austrian History Yearbook* 48 (2017): 156–57.
32 Letter from Rudolf Reichert to the Moravian governor, 31 August 1905, MZA, B13, ka 369, sig. 1, in no. 6574/05; see also in the same file, reports from the district officer in Mährisch-Trübau/Moravská Třebová, no. 4913/05, 13 July 1905 and no. 5770/05, 21 August 1905.
33 Letter from the Union of Industrialists (Brünn/Brno branch) to the Moravian governor's office, MZA, B13, ka 377, sig. 1, no. 5789/07, 6 June 1907.

34 Telegram from the Union of Austrian Industrialists (Sternberg/Šternberk branch), MZA, B13, ka 370, sig. 1, no. 9630/05, 24 November 1905.
35 Letter to the Interior Ministry from the Union of Austrian Industrialists, 1 April 1902 (including the original letter to the district officer in Biala), ÖStA, AVA, MdI, Präs, K1988, sig. 20/9, no. 3030/02.
36 Report from the district officer in Mitterburg, ASTs, IRLdL, AP, b. 338, 10/c, no. 2074/09, 26 February 1910.
37 Alexander Gerschenkron, *An Economic Spurt that Failed: Four Lectures in Austrian History* (Princeton, NJ: Princeton University Press, 1977), 31–32.
38 Alison Fleig Frank, *Oil Empire: Visions of Prosperity in Austrian Galicia* (Cambridge, MA: Harvard University Press, 2005), 156–57.
39 Ibid., 160.
40 Telegram to Prime Minister Koerber from the Anglo Galician company, ÖStA, AVA, MdI, Präs, K1989, sig. 20/9, no. 4971/04, 11 July 1904.
41 For a case in Asch/Aš (Bohemia) see Interpellation Rieger, 21 February 1905, ÖStA, AVA, MdI, Präs, K1991, sig. 20/9, no. 3493/06.
42 Interpellation by Schalk and associates, 20 March 1903, ÖStA, AVA, MdI, Präs, K1988, sig. 20/9, no. 1956/03.
43 Report from the district officer in Neutitschein/Nový Jičin, 11 June 1906, MZA, B13, ka 374, sig. 1, in no. 6430/06, no. 4830/06.
44 See the report by the governor of Galicia, ÖStA, AVA, MdI, Präs, K1989, sig. 20/9, no. 7829/02, 9 October 1902.
45 Report from the gendarmerie command no 5, ÖStA, AVA, MdI, Präs, K1989, sig. 20/9, no. 5965/02, 30 July 1902.
46 See "Exposé über die Bewegung der landwirtsch. Bevölkerung in Ostgalizien" from the Ministry of Commerce, ÖStA, AVA, MdI, Präs, K 1989, sig. 20/9, no. 8148/03, 18/23 November 1903.
47 Interior Ministry to the Governor of Galicia, ÖStA, AVA, MdI, Präs, K1989, sig. 20/9, no. 5503/02, 24 July 1902.
48 See telegram by Romanczuk to Prime Minister Koerber, ÖStA, AVA, MdI, Präs, K1989, sig. 20/9, no. 5838/02, 6 August 1902.
49 See Interpellation by Romanczuk and associates, ÖStA, AVA, MdI, Präs, K1989, sig. 20/9, no. 9277/02, 18 December 1902.
50 These accusations were denied by the official in question. See copy of the debates in parliament, 29 October 1902, and the reply from the official, ÖStA, AVA, MdI, Präs, K1989, sig. 20/9, no. 7830/02, 31 October 1902.
51 The report disputes many of the details of mistreatment described in the press (chains, poor food in captivity), but it does acknowledge the mass arrest, see report from the Galician governor to the Interior Ministry, ÖStA, AVA, MdI, Präs, K1989, sig. 20/9, no. 7351/02, 9 October 1902.
52 The incident is described in the governor's report and mentions injuries but gives no number, ÖStA, AVA, MdI, Präs, K1989, sig. 20/9, no. 7829/02, 9 October 1902; a newspaper article gives the number of injured people, *Die Zeit*, 9 August 1902, no. 6135/02, Ibid., no. 7829/02, 19 August 1902; for the report from the governor on the subsequent death, see Ibid., ad no. 7829, 25 October 1902.
53 Ministry of Justice to Interior Ministry, ÖStA, AVA, MdI, Präs, K1989, sig. 20/9, no. 7559/02, 17/21 October 1902.
54 Report from the governor of Galicia, ÖStA, AVA, MdI, Präs, K1989, sig. 20/9, no. 7829/02, 9 October 1902.
55 Ibid.
56 Interpellation Semen Wityk, Stenographisches Protokoll des Abgeordnetenhauses, 74. Sitzung der XVIII. Session, 22 May 1908, 4792–93.
57 Irina Marin, *Peasant Violence and Antisemitism in Early Twentieth-Century Eastern Europe* (Cham: Palgrave Macmillan, 2018), 196.

58 *Danzers Armee-Zeitung*, May 26, 1910, 6.
59 Interpellation Šrámek and associates, 3 June 1910, ÖStA, KA, ZSt, MfLV, Präsidialbüro (Präs), K857, Faszikulatur 22, no. 2777/10.
60 See Stefano Petrungaro, *Pietre e fucile: La protesta sociale nelle campagne croate di fine Ottocento* (Roma: Viella, 2009), 107.
61 *Neue Freie Presse*, February 17, 1902, 1–2; see also, *Wiener Zeitung*, February 17, 1902, 1–2.
62 Report from the governor of Galicia, ÖStA, AVA, MdI, Präs, K1989, sig. 20/9, no. 7829/02, 9 October 1902.
63 On Kos' declarations, see copy of the debates in parliament, 29 October 1902, ÖStA, AVA, MdI, Präs, K1989, sig. 20/9, no. 7830/02, 31 October 1902; on the demands expressed during the strike, see "Exposé über die Bewegung der landwirtsch. Bevölkerung in Ostgalizien" from the Ministry of Commerce, ÖStA, AVA, MdI, Präs, K 1989, sig. 20/9, no. 8148/03, 18/23 November 1903.
64 On repression against treason see Mark Cornwall, "Treason in an Era of Regime Change: The Case of the Habsburg Monarchy," *Austrian History Yearbook* 50 (2019): 124–49.
65 Herbert Steiner, *Die Arbeiterbewegung Österreichs 1867–1889* (Vienna: Europa-Verlag, 1964).
66 See Wolfgang Maderthaner and Lutz Musner, *Unruly Masses: The Other Side of Fin-de-Siècle Vienna* (New York: Berghahn Books, 2008).
67 *Arbeiter-Zeitung*, June 5, 1912, 6.
68 Military Chancellery of His Majesty to the Minister of Defence, 7 September 1911, ÖStA, KA, ZSt, MfLV, Präs, K857, Faszikulatur 22, no. 4011/11.
69 For another critical position on military assistance from army circles, see *Danzers Armee-Zeitung*, February 20, 1902, 9.
70 Decree from the War Ministry, 9 December 1908, ÖStA, KA, ZSt, MfLV, Präs, K857, Faszikulatur 22, no. 342/09.
71 For example in the case of the 1904 Borysław strike, see Frank, *Oil Empire*, 161.
72 Günther Kronenbitter, *"Krieg im Frieden": Die Führung der k.u.k. Armee und die Großmachtpolitik Österreich-Ungarns 1906–1914* (Munich: Oldenbourg, 2003), 219.
73 *Arbeiter-Zeitung*, April 26, 1895, 2 (also quotes the interpellation in parliament); for the reply by the Minister of Interior, see *Neue Freie Presse*, April 26, 1895, 4. The strike constituted a moral victory for Social Democrats; see Peter Schöffer, *Der Wahlrechtskampf der österreichischen Sozialdemokratie 1888/89–1897* (Stuttgart: Franz Steiner Verlag), 459.
74 Gustav Otruba, "Streikbewegung, Ausstände und Militärassistenzen in der österreichischen Reichshälfte 1890 bis 1914," in *Wirtschaftskräfte und Wirtschaftswege. V: Festschrift für Hermann Kellenbenz*, ed. Jürgen Schneider (Stuttgart: Klett-Cotta, 1981), 448–49.
75 *Arbeiter Zeitung*, February 15, 1902, 10; Lawrence Sondhaus, *The Naval Policy of Austria-Hungary, 1867–1918: Navalism, Industrial Development and the Politics of Dualism* (West Lafayette: Purdue University Press, 1994), 154.
76 Report from the Bohemian Governor, ÖStA, AVA, MdI, Präs, K1989, sig. 20/9, no. 4263/04, 11 June 1904. (See also no 3237/04: Interpellation by Fresl and associates, 27 April 1904).
77 Bohemian Governor's Office to the k. u. k. 8th corps command in Prague, 8 November 1905, ÖStA, AVA, MdI, Präs, K1990, sig. 20/9, in no. 7694/05.
78 Copy of War Ministry decree Abt 5, no. 2483, 29 November 1905. See file ÖStA, AVA, MdI, K1990, sig. 20/9, no. 8292/05, 27 November 1905.
79 War Ministry to the Defence Ministry, 13 October 1908, ÖStA, KA, ZSt, MfLV, Präs, K857, Faszikulatur 22, no. 4744/08; Interpellation by Victor Adler and associates, 7 July 1908, Ibid., no. 3298/08.

80 Report from the Galician Governor's Office, 23 January 1913, ÖStA, AVA, MdI, Präs, K1998, sig. 20/9, no. 1104/13, 24–27 January 1913.
81 On the strike see Christian Koller, *Streikkultur: Performanzen und Diskurse des Arbeitskampfes im schweizerisch-österreichischen Vergleich (1860–1950)* (Vienna: Lit Verlag, 2009), 279–88.
82 Ervin Palményi, ed., *A History of Hungary* (London: Collet's, 1975), 386.
83 Defence Ministry to His Majesty, 18 May 1908 [reply 20 May 1908], ÖStA, KA, ZSt, MfLV, Präs, K857, Faszikulatur 22, no. 2533/08; Ibid., no. 672 XIV/12.
84 See, for example, the "Studie über die Aufgabe der Generalinspektion bei Arbeitseinstellungen oder passive Resistenz auf Eisenbahnen nach den vom Herrn Generalinspektor bezeichneten Gesichtspunkten," 9, ÖStA, AVA, Verkehr, Diverses, Diverse Nachlässe 8, 1907.
85 ÖStA, AVA, MdI, Präs, K1992, sig. 20/9, no. 8956/08, 17/22 September 1908.
86 Railway Ministry to Defence Ministry, 27 December 1911, ÖStA, KA, ZSt, MfLV, Präs, K857, Faszikulatur 22, no. 5898/11.
87 War Ministry to Railway Ministry, 12 February 1912, ÖStA, KA, ZSt, MfLV, Präs, K857, Faszikulatur 22, no. 774/12.
88 "Studie über die Aufgabe der Generalinspektion bei Arbeitseinstellungen," 11.
89 Interpellation by Tomschik and associates, 22 October 1912, ÖStA, KA, ZSt, MfLV, Präs, K857, Faszikulatur 22, no. 5267/12.
90 Interpellation by Valentino Pittoni and associates, Stenographisches Protokoll des Abgeordnetenhauses, 92. Sitzung der XX. Session, 8 March 1911, 1182.
91 Railway Ministry to Defence Ministry, ÖStA, KA, ZSt, MfLV, Präs, K857, Faszikulatur 22, no. 906/14, 11 February 1914.
92 On wartime military/civilian tensions, see John Deak and Jonathan Gumz, "How to Break a State: The Habsburg Monarchy's Internal War, 1914–1918," *American Historical Review* 122, no. 5 (2017): 1111–12.

6 Employers of the world, unite!

The transnational mobilisation of industrialists around World War I

Pierre Eichenberger

"The social explosiveness of capitalism increased", writes Jürgen Kocka, when "It began to expand from the sphere of circulation to the sphere of production and to reshape the world of work directly".[1] The Industrial Revolution, the rise of the factory and the dynamics of capitalist investment were global phenomena. They changed the world of work as men and women left their rural and semi-rural lives to become like cogs, semi-automatons in the production of vast amounts of manufactured goods, which in turn generated streams of cash for the factory owners. Workers, however, soon embraced internationalist agendas to advance their political rights in society and prevent wages and working conditions racing to the bottom; "Workers of the world, unite!" famously urged Karl Marx and Friedrich Engels in 1848.[2] The successive international gatherings of political parties of the left are important benchmarks in working class cooperation, from the Communist League (established in 1847), to the First (1864), Second (1889), Third (1919) and Fourth (1938) *Internationales*. Trade unions also enthusiastically welcomed internationalist agendas. Bricklayers, miners, stonemasons, transport workers and woodworkers established international federations before the end of the nineteenth century. An International Secretariat of National Trade Union Centres was created in 1901 and was transformed into the International Federation of Trade Unions (IFTU) in 1913.[3]

As a consequence, workers' uprisings and the desire to protest and strike spread across the world. Eric Hobsbawm described the "Springtime of the Peoples", in 1848, as "the first potentially global revolution"; while the 1871 Paris Commune and its bloody repression sent out a global shockwave. Even before the rulers of Austria, Germany and Russia created the Three Emperors' League in 1873 to combat the threat from workers collaborating internationally – a "capitalists' counter-International"[4] – French lawyer Léon Chotteau (1838–95) criticised the "apathy and inertia of capital" and suggested that employers' best option to prevent such social uprisings was to create an "Association Internationale des Patrons", composed of an international council made up of national and local divisions, which would spearhead ambitious plans of social reform. "So, industrialists and traders, rise!" he wrote in his brochure.[5] Chotteau's initiative failed to take wing and fly, though; only two industrialists showed up at the general gathering he organised in Paris to lay the foundations of his *Internationale*. Similarly unsuccessful was the initiative of the Paris British Chamber of Commerce in 1874–75 to create a "Chambre de Commerce Internationale" in order to provide a private international forum to debate commercial issues.[6] The idea of an *Internationale* in the employers' camp was floated again during the wave of strikes around 1900, but only in 1920 would the International Organisation of Industrial Employers (IOIE) be finally founded, with a light secretariat in Brussels, as a rallying point for employers' representation in the new (tripartite) International Labour Organisation (ILO). During one of the first meetings of the new organisation, Allan Smith (1871–1941), chairman of the British National Confederation of Employers' Organisations, told his fellow employers' delegates, who were from Belgium, Czechoslovakia, France, Italy, Sweden and Switzerland, why the foundation of the IOIE was necessary. The minutes quote:

> He laid stress on the importance of employers realising the great responsibility which rested on them in these days, when from so many quarters, even from certain Government officials, strong attacks were being made on capital and private ownership, and how they must recognise the significance of these attacks and get together and discuss all aspects of industry. He thought this could not be done satisfactorily in these days of the International Labour Organisation without the employers of labour meeting internationally and discussing their difficulties and striving to bring about uniformity of action as far as such was practicable, and thus vindicate beliefs in the duties and necessities, in the interests of the world's trade, of private employers of labour.[7]

From Paris to Brussels, via Zurich, Turin, Stockholm and Washington, this chapter tells the story of employers' transnational collaborations to unite and mobilise against labour's political, economic and social challenges. At the centre of this story are employers' associations, which specialised in addressing issues related to labour, most importantly about strikes. Created around 1900, these associations were vastly different from the older trade associations and chambers of commerce. The literature is rich with many case studies of capitalists' individual and collective actions, and investigations have been made of both trade associations and chambers of commerce (in which capitalists act as businessmen) and employers' associations (in which capitalists are represented as employers of labour). While these different bodies – and their actions – should not be regarded as separate entities, as they constitute "an integrated area of research in which market trends, technological innovations, entrepreneurial strategies, industrial relations and political concerns are all interrelated", the history of trade and employers' associations is one of separate dynamics in response to specific challenges. Numerous studies have shown that while most national trade associations were created in the last third of the nineteenth century in response to the increasing intervention of the state in the economy and the imposition of tariffs – "organized capitalism" – most employers' associations were created after 1900 specifically to combat increasing labour militancy, in workplaces and in societies, at both local and international levels. Some associations specifically formed to fight trade unionism were, however, created as early as 1890, like Britain's Shipping Federation, founded in reaction to the London dock strike of 1889, and the Arbeitgeberverband Hamburg-Altona, which mobilised employers in this stronghold of German trade unionism.[8]

Strikes "had launched a cycle of worker-employer strife whose ultimate destination no one could predict", Daniel Rodgers writes, and industrialists had the most to lose from workers' mobilisation and the new world order that internationally minded socialists wanted to create. Nations on both sides of the Atlantic around 1900 were hence haunted by the "social question", which opened up a battlefield between "a world of competing solutions". The mobilisation of employers in professional, well-founded and disciplined associations, I seek to demonstrate in this chapter, was part of this battle. The foundation of employers' associations took a good share of wind from unions' sails, reinforced the most reactionary elements among employers and conservative governments, and gave the upper hand to the employers that chose not to compromise with workers, but to confront them. In most countries, employers' self-organised defence pre-dated the first significant interventions by the state in the labour market and in social policies, which massively preempted the range of possibilities that could be implemented afterwards because it solidified a "constituted field of interests" that would prove difficult to overcome.[9] In other words, the employers got the first shots in, in many countries. This chapter argues that employers' associations were pivotal in the conservative response of industrialists to progressive ideas promoted by the labour movement; "Reactionary Avant-Gardes", wrote Hans Ulrich Jost. They were against (industrial) democracy, welfare policies and economic redistribution, and they fashioned conservatism during the Belle Époque in ways that are only now beginning to be fully understood.[10]

While most studies of employers' mobilisation have concentrated on regional or national analyses, this chapter will consider the foundation of employers' associations as a distinct transnational event, because the reasons why they were created, their respective constitutions and their actions all followed clear transnational patterns. The men – and very few women – and organisations involved in that process that would meet in the IOIE in 1920 had established powerful local, sectoral and national employers' associations around 1900 that convened internationally, learnt from one another, and built social, political and economic influence, from their local town hall to Geneva's Palais des Nations, in complex *jeux d'échelles*.[11] Because global history is "both an object of study and a particular way of looking at history", this chapter seeks to demonstrate that "what we call the 'local' is replete with elements of 'global' origins and vice versa", hence illustrating that internationalism was as important a factor in employers' collective action as it was for the representatives of labour.[12] As regards employers, however, as Philippa Hetherington and Glenda Sluga show, there was an illiberal internationalism that was locked into a continuous interaction with liberal internationalism.[13] The chapter begins by discussing the transnational contacts that framed the creation of European employers' associations before World War I, then progresses to the genesis of the IOIE, in which all of these contacts crystallised after the war ended.

The "social question" and the creation of employers' associations

In 1909, Swiss socialist leader and trade unionist Robert Grimm (1881–1958) advanced his view that the creation of employers' associations had dramatically changed the labour movement. He wrote:

> The times when trade unions could mow down one firm after the other are gone forever. Every raid on a firm is henceforth considered as a declaration of war on all employers. Immediately, the employers' federation enters the game and puts all its force to crack down on any strike and to make it ineffective.

Worried by what he called "employers' terrorism", but ready to take on this new challenge he rhetorically asked whether coalesced employers, "would succeed in preventing strikes forever and in demolishing trade unions?"[14] Just a year later, Eduard Sulzer-Ziegler (1854–1913), a major Swiss industrialist from the Sulzer company in Winterthur, warned his fellow employers about the dangers of the labour movement, as it "had declared a war on the entire social order, capitalism in general and the firm in particular". "Si vis pacem, para bellum" explained Sulzer-Ziegler: "If the employers want peace, they must unite; otherwise, if they fail to unite, if they do not get prepared for the war, then they will have the war as a matter of certainty".[15]

In Switzerland, strikes had reached their peak in around 1905–06, but this pattern of behaviour was replicated all over the industrialised world. At the turn of the century, trade unions and employers' associations both grew increasingly well organised, with each side claiming that they needed to be ready and able to face a better coordinated opposite side. "In every instance, the organization of labor is more extensive than that of the capital employing the labor", wrote the Illinois Coal Operators Association in 1901.[16] In addition, in some places, the state, although not remotely as interventionist as it would become directly after the war, and then to a greater extent in the 1930s, did not stay totally inactive. In 1902, a massive coal strike in Pennsylvania caused a coal shortage in the US that led to Theodore Roosevelt (1858–1919) intervening and imposing a mediated agreement. Laws on arbitration and extension of collective labour agreements were still in their early stages, but it was becoming clear that the fight to alter public intervention would become a much higher priority for employers. Another source of concern for employers was the fact that from 1899 – when for the first time, a socialist became part of the French government – employers started to doubt the state's resolve to take their side in the face of threats from the labour movement, a threat they perceived as existential. In fact, social policy and/or labour market regulations gained global traction around 1900, as Daniel Rodgers highlighted,[17] and all employers had to face them in one way or another.

Industrialists all over the world watched strikes erupting and the labour movement becoming better organised. Industrialists viewed this as socially, economically and politically threatening. Strikes were increasing everywhere, and qualitative changes also took place: for instance the general strike became another weapon in the unions' armoury. Swedish trade unions organised a two-day general strike to gain political rights, just like Austrian and Belgian unions did. The German Social Democrats of the SPD passed a resolution in 1905 in support of the use of general strikes to advance political rights.[18] In response, numerous publications urged industrialists to meet this challenge by the foundation of associations of defence: "*Gründet Arbeitgeberverbände*!" ("Create Employers' Associations!") wrote Wilhelm Georg Heinrich von Reiswitz (1859–1926), the secretary of the Arbeitgeberverband Hamburg-Altona in 1904.[19] Such calls to action put forward the argument that:

> The individual employer confronted with organised workers is at a disadvantage. Often, he must choose between binding to the demands that workers and their leaders dictate, or to stop his business altogether. This evil can be solved thanks to the organization of employers, so that unjustified workers' claims can be denied. But, for business activities to be safeguarded from economic damages, one should not wait that workers' said unjustified claims be formulated; the collective action must have been prepared for a long time already, and an organization must be created which is not only valid for one single case, but for all cases.[20]

Those publications reviewed foreign experiences in Britain and in Germany, in Sweden or in the USA, and adapted such models to their local context.

Large extended strikes motivated business owners to create employers' associations in a region, sector or nation. Transnational waves of activity sprang up, from Pittsburgh to the Ruhr region, from Petersburg to Turin. All over Europe, employers were confronted with similar events. Their response often varied, though, between the stick and the carrot, and syncretic plans combining strikes insurances, lockouts and the provision of strikebreakers were regularly promoted alongside plans of social reform and negotiations with trade unions.[21] Large industrial companies were the spearhead of this movement. Copenhagen's heavy industry firms had already created the *Foreningen af Fabrikanter i Jernindustrien i København* in 1885, followed by the national *Arbejdsgivere inden for Jernindustrien i Danmark* in 1902. British employers founded the Engineering Employers' Federation in 1896, French employers created the *Union des Industries Métallurgiques et Minières* in 1901, and Swedish industrial companies founded the *Svenska Arbetsgifvareföreningen SAF* in 1902 in response to the general strike. In response to the 1903–04 Crimmitschauer strike in Germany (in the textile industry), employers established the *Hauptstelle der Deutschen Arbeitgeberverbände* in 1904;[22] the National Association of Manufacturers, which had been founded in 1895 in Cincinnati, refocused its action against trade unions in 1903; and the Swiss machine industrialists created the *Arbeitgeberverband der Maschinenindustrieller* in 1905, which in turn joined with similar associations from the textile and construction industries to create a centralised association, the *Zentralverband Schweizerischer Arbeitgeber Organisationen*, in 1908.

As Grimm noted in 1909, the literature has highlighted the way that the creation of employers' associations turned the tide in industrial conflicts during the first decade of the twentieth century. Nicolas Delalande underlines the importance of the new strikes' insurances created by employers' associations,[23] and Leopold Haimson writes that these new associations offered an "increasingly ferocious resistance" to threats to managerial power, strikes in particular. With Germany in mind, Haimson highlights

> the ability and will that employers, especially those of large metal and mechanical firms, displayed individually and in concert in resorting to the use of blacklists, lockouts, as well as "yellow" unions, to stifle labor protest and to destroy the effectiveness of existing trade unions organizations.[24]

The deployment of strikebreakers became a very useful weapon of the employers with which to confront strikes, while lockouts became an effective tool for well-funded employers' associations, as they would dry up trade unions' strike insurance funds.[25] Violence was not rare, in particular in the USA, where the Pinkerton detective agency became an option for employers, but also in Britain, where the Shipping Federation used private guards to protect strikebreakers and oppose industrial democracy in ways that "explicitly called into question the state's monopoly of violence".[26] There were often "bloodless victories" won by the employers, though, whereby management exercised its power by alternative means.[27] On both sides of the Atlantic, employers' associations initiated anti-union policies, political measures aimed at the authorities and political parties and measures aimed at the discipline of their own members. Their attitude to blacklists or lockouts was that they must be rigorously implemented, with no room for ill-discipline. To achieve this those associations gathered more expensive contributions from their members to finance the strike insurances and propaganda and imposed strong discipline on their members.[28]

These associations' creation marked the changing balance of power between labour and capital. In 1905, Swedish employers started using lockouts on a large scale, with Siemens managing to destroy labour unions in its plants and usurping them with a scientific mixture of repression and targeted social policies.[29] Employers would often resort to appealing to nationalist sentiments, using unions' internationalist agenda strategically against them. Strikes, indeed, instigated diverse sorts of migrations, with international solidarity fundraising for strikers and the international exchange of strikebreakers between employers. Christian Koller argues that "strikes and strike-related transnational migration [of locked-out workers and strikebreakers] were the main causes of international cooperation between national trade unions and employer organizations".[30] In addition, strikes tended to evolve in waves that would swipe entire regions and reverberate from places to places, hence becoming increasingly European in scope and sometimes even transatlantic; this made strikes and strikers particularly vulnerable to xenophobic bashing.[31]

Men who would prove instrumental in the creation of employers' associations, like Winterthur industrialist Sulzer-Ziegler, also gathered internationally in trade associations, chambers of commerce and international conferences on social policy. From 1905 onwards, thousands of business delegates from all over the world discussed issues related to ever-increasing economic global exchanges in the International Congresses of Chambers of Commerce and Commercial and Industrial Associations, which took place every second year in a European or American town. In the preparation for the Milan gathering of 1906, a brochure described the organisation of chambers of commerce in 31 separate countries, the explicit aim being to promote the exchange of practices and mutual understanding among businesspeople from whatever part of the world they came from.[32]

For the unions and social reformists, after the first international conference for the protection of labour took place in Berlin in 1890, social policy debates gained an increasingly explicit international dimension too. Up to World War I, many international conferences – initiated by social reformists and trade unionists – promoted the idea of developing an international set of labour standards and social protection measures. A significant result of this was the creation of the International Association for Labor Legislation (IALL), which was founded in 1900 with headquarters in Basel and was considered as a frontrunner for the ILO in 1919. Not all employers frontally opposed international labour regulations, as levelling the playing field might appeal to some of them. Sulzer-Ziegler, for instance, was a delegate in the IALL. In this domain, he followed a tradition pioneered by Welsh progressive industrialist Robert Owen (1771–1858) and Frenchman Daniel Legrand (1783–1859).[33]

Strikes and the international organisation of the labour movement provided another reason for employers to build international collaborations. Following strikes running across borders (like in 1904–05 throughout Germany and Switzerland), employers took international trips to see how their foreign counterparts dealt with such actions, and how they fought back. Key actors of employers' movements in different countries thus had sustained exchanges; Sulzer-Ziegler and Alexander Tille (1866–1912), an important organiser of German employers, deputy secretary of the *Centralverband Deutscher Industrieller* and social Darwinist philosopher, knew each other well.[34] Another Swiss machine industrialist, Gustave Naville (1848–1929), who was a key figure in the 1905 foundation of the *Arbeitgeberverband schweiz. Maschinenindustrieller*, went to Munich, Berlin and Nuremberg to study how his German colleagues operated before laying down the plans of the future Swiss organisation. In this last city, Naville met with the director of the *Maschinenfabriken Augsburg-Nürnberg AG (MAN)*, Anton Johann von Rieppel (1852–1926). In 1905, Rieppel was president of the *Verband Bayer Metallindustrieller* and had just dealt with an important strike, which concerned the labour unions' demand to sign a collective agreement, a demand that German and Swiss employers rejected. In those days, German employers were among the most advanced in their ability to counter labour unions, and Naville came back with a clear idea of what needed to be done in Switzerland. Back from his trip, he remarked that "Everywhere, the necessity to create stronger organizations, with a permanent secretariat and sufficient means at their disposable, is shared".[35] It is an interesting point that at that time, MAN was one of the main competitors of some of the key Swiss machinery industry firms, like *Escher Wyss*, the firm in which Naville had made his career. Normal business competition between firms was therefore no barrier to preventing key industrialists from helping one another to deal with major waves of strike action. In the same way, the 1908 establishment of the Swiss *Zentralverband Schweizerischer Arbeitgeber Organisationen* was majorly influenced by Germany.[36]

Indices of employers' new organisational efficiency can be found in the full-blown victory for Swedish employers in the 1909 general strike; this incited major interest in Europe, and not only because European trade unions massively helped with funds to strike in solidarity with their Swedish comrades.[37] The *Svenska Arbetsgifvareföreningen* actually initiated the hostilities through lockouts. Its director, Hjalmar von Sydow (1862–1932), who was in charge on the employers' side, received visits of Europeans eager to learn from his experiences – for instance the secretary of the German employers' federation, Fritz Tänzler (1869–1944), and von Sydow toured Europe to explain his techniques afterwards. Interestingly he himself had visited Germany in 1904 to learn how German employers had taken control over labour exchanges (*Arbeitsnachweis*).[38] After his success in Sweden, he went to at least Austria, Germany and Switzerland – but most certainly to other countries as well – and paid a visit to the Krupp plant in Essen. Tänzler, as well as his Swiss colleague Otto Steinmann (1876–1961), the secretary of the *Zentralverband*, held conferences and wrote brochures describing the events and victories in Sweden; they expounded at length on the lessons that German and Swiss employers could draw from these events. There was a great deal of interest in Steinmann's analyses and his publications shaped employers' responses to the 1918 general strike in Switzerland.[39] Further information was circulated to employers in 1910, with the publication of a brochure by Steinmann; the prime conclusions were republished when the threat of a general strike loomed in the fall of 1918. Steinmann wrote that a general strike "did not represent such a great risk for society and for employers as one might think". Based on the Swedish experience, he argued that "If harsh measures are taken to maintain public order and security, if citizens, courageous and fearless, fulfil essential tasks, and, finally, if employers hold together and maintain solidarity among themselves, the failure of the general strike is unavoidable".[40] When military provocations forced trade unions to declare a general strike in November 1918 (a few weeks after Steinmann published his article), employers were ready, remained in close contact with the army and had already advanced plans to create private militias: all lessons learnt from Sweden. In three days, trade unions had to surrender.

Such informal encounters among employers reinforced already existing contacts in sectoral international associations. The International Federation of Master Cotton Spinners' and Manufacturers' Associations, founded in 1904, had goals such as the regulation of prices or the provision of commercial arbitration services.[41] Others were created to battle trade unions, like the International Shipping Federation, founded in 1909. Under British leadership and despite fierce competition, shipowners and port employers cooperated internationally, including through transnational exchanges of strikebreakers.[42] Through these international bonds, employers sought to echo the workers' international collaborations with organisations of their own that were of equal strength. Some trade unions signed agreements facilitating the mobility of their respective members: for instance, enabling migrant workers not to have to pay union fees in every country, but just in one. The mutual support that those agreements provided varied significantly. Most mentioned, for instance, that members would refuse to work as strikebreakers. Others used international congresses and conferences to meet with each other, enabling practices and information to be shared across countries. The most advanced form of international cooperation between trade unions was the foundation of international secretariats or international trade unions. As a case in point, an International Metallurgists' Bureau of Information was established as early as 1893 by trade unions of six European countries, which paved the way for the foundation of the International Metalworkers' Federation in 1904. By 1900, there were as many as 17 of these international trade union secretariats; by 1914, the number had risen to 28.[43] An International Secretariat of National Trade Union Centres was created in 1901 and was transformed into the International Federation of Trade Unions (IFTU) in 1913. However, only four international unions (in the textile, lithography, fur and bricklaying sectors) had an international strike fund at the time of World War I. Others gave their financial support to unions in other countries when they could, on a case-by-case basis. Overall German unions played a leading role, if not the prime role, in most of these international unions, until World War I at least.[44] National employers' associations in different countries combatted this by also signing agreements. The Swiss *Zentralverband*, for instance had such an agreement with Austrian and German employers, the main objectives of which consisted of preventing the migration of striking and locked-out workers. As early as 1907, employers' associations from Denmark, Finland and Sweden met regularly and introduced some level of coordination, even on the rates of wages.[45] Those formal and informal transnational contacts would become the roots of the IOIE, the employers' *Internationale*.

The genesis of the International Organisation of Industrial Employers

In 1911, the Italian lawyer Gino Olivetti (1880–1942), the founder of the *Lega Torinese degli Industriali* in 1906 and of the *Federazione Industriale Piemontese* in 1908, and by then the secretary of the 1910-founded *Confederazione Generale dell'Industria Italiana*, the central Italian employers' association, invited European employers in Turin to the first "*Congrès International des Organisations Patronales de l'Industrie et de l'Agriculture*" (28–30 September and 1 October). Olivetti contended in his invitation letter that

> In all countries, the employers' class finds itself confronted by the same problems, born from the same causes: the universal effects of economic laws, the rise of social reform policies in all countries, the existence in all industrial

> centres of a labour movement which offers everywhere the same fundamental characteristics and uses of the same methods.

"As a consequence", Olivetti continued, an obligation has risen "for employers to organize the defence of their interests against the charges of new regulations by the state on the one hand, and against the actions of the labour movement on the other hand". Olivetti suggested three themes for the conferences: comparing the organisation and strategies of employers in different countries, their stance on the labour movement and also over social policies, while he also suggested that "a great good" might come from employers debating "the results of their experiences and the teachings of their actions".[46]

In addition to numerous Italian employers, the congress's honorary committee comprised presidents of sectoral and national employers' associations and chambers of commerce: one British, one Austrian, one Swedish (von Sydow), one Belgian and 12 Frenchmen. Although little is known about the Congress itself its final resolution is well documented. It called for the strengthening of employers' associations in every way, testifying of the common will that employers expressed in Turin. The congress gave a special mission to two Belgian congressmen – Jules Lecocq (1878–1961), a lawyer, and Jules Carlier (1851–1930), a former Belgian MP, commissioner of the Belgian delegation to the Universal Exhibitions of 1889 and 1903. Lecocq and Carlier were respectively secretary and president of the *Comité central industriel de Belgique*. The congress commissioned them to plan an organisation that would become a permanent international employers' association; hence this represents a decisive moment in the history of employers' international cooperation. Lecocq and Carlier became "pilgrims", touring Europe to spread this idea to employers' associations on the continent.[47] In 1912, they went to Paris to meet with the *Comité des Forges*. They went to London and Manchester the same year and to Berlin and Vienna in 1913, with Lecocq then drafting statutes for an international organisation of employers. A meeting was organised in May 1914 in Paris between Austrian, Belgian, British, French, German and Italian employers. If one is to trust the account Lecocq gave of the event, the birth of the International Association of Employers was greeted by a toast from each delegation. Had World War I not brought these internationalist projects to a brutal stop, an employers' *Internationale* would have been founded during that summer of 1914. The idea of such an *Internationale* in the employers' camp, which had failed after the Paris Commune in 1871, was now ready to be implemented. While chambers of commerce had only started to meet internationally in 1905, several years after their establishment, employers' associations convened very soon after they were founded. Launched in Turin in 1911, celebrated in Paris in 1914, the employers' *Internationale* came back in force after World War I.[48]

The aftermath of World War I was marked by the creation of the League of Nations and the ILO, two paramount examples of the new politics of the time; these types of initiatives were now happening on a global scale.[49] Employers found themselves on the defensive while massive strike waves ran all over the Atlantic world and beyond at the end of the war; centuries-old Central European empires crumbled and social revolution proliferated all over Europe. From employers' points of view, "recasting bourgeois Europe" turned out to be a tricky task after the earthquake of the *Grande Guerre*.[50] International trade unions had long been advocating for an international regulation of labour and had a clear upper hand when work to establish the ILO started. Among other things, the tripartite structure of the ILO – where states, trade unions and employers met at all levels of the organisation – was a victory for labour.[51] The IFTU resumed its activities in the summer of 1919[52] and it was Emile Vandervelde (1866–1938), the leader of the Second *Internationale* since 1900, who gave the main speech at the Versailles Conference in April 1919 about the creation of the future ILO. As a member of the Commission on International Labor Legislation, whose task was to prepare the foundation of the future international organisation, he was a key figure in the shaping of its structure. In Versailles, he spoke of the ILO as "a work of transition between the absolutism of the employers that was the regime of yesterday, and the sovereignty of labor, that . . . would be the regime of tomorrow".[53] Such ideas directly challenged employers' power and were interpreted as such, as the ILO offered international unions the opportunity to implement their long proposed agenda for an international regulation of labour. Employers had been less influential in the preparation of the First International Labor Conference in Washington, D.C., held in October and November 1919, and their delegates had no clear strategy during the conference. Labour representatives, in contrast, had organised an office in Washington before the conference and were very well prepared. As a result, they managed to get most of their delegates elected.[54] Furthermore, the Labor Conference adopted the first internal labour convention that limited working time to eight hours a day, the single most important international claim made by the labour movement since the middle of the nineteenth century. Even if some employers supported it, that decision substantiated for most of them the danger of the ILO's new global labour politics.[55]

This was all it took for employers' representatives in Washington to create the IOIE. After several preparatory meetings on 22 March 1920, in London, and on 7 June 1920, in Genoa, statutes were adopted on 1 and 2 October 1920, in Brussels. The IOIE's Brussels office opened in 1920 with a staff of only three people: Jules Lecocq, who had toured Europe between 1911 and 1914, was chosen as the secretary for the IOIE, and he could count a few years later on the help of an assistant and a stenographer. The first president of the IOIE was Jules Carlier, the other "pilgrim" of the pre-World War I times. Other members of the first elected executive committee were either major industrialists, typically the president of the central national employers' federations or the professional director of these federations. Some of them, like Frenchman Robert Pinot (1862–1926), the secretary of *Comité des Forges*, a key figure of the Musée social and close to Frédéric Le Play (1806–82),[56] the Briton Allan Smith mentioned earlier or the Swedish mechanical engineering industrialist Sigfrid Edström (1870–1964), were major figures of industrial circles in their country and internationally.

IOIE's statutes made it clear that the association's aim revolved around the ILO, but they also underlined that the association would collect members' opinions on all subjects relevant to employers, plus they would collect data and distribute information.[57] The ILO, however, would remain at the very centre of IOIE's preoccupations, and the histories of both organisations are inseparable, for instance in their joint rejection of communism, as Marieke Louis shows. From the start, the IOIE had a fairly broad membership. By June 1920, the association already counted 15 countries, mainly in Europe but also Japan and the Transvaal. A dozen others joined during the 1920s, so that almost all European countries were members of the IOIE, making the IOIE a crucial node of private internationalism in the interwar period, not least because it included delegates from countries that were not (yet) members of the League of Nations, like Germany and Austria at the beginning of the 1920s. In addition the IOIE had regular contacts with employers' associations not (yet) formally affiliated in Argentina, Australia, Canada and India. Despite the long absence of the USA from the ILO, the IOIE also kept in touch with the National Association of Manufacturers all through the interwar period.[58]

The IOIE was not the only international business organisation created in the aftermath of World War I. In 1920, delegates from the victorious countries in the war (Belgium, Britain, France, Italy and the USA) created the International Chamber of Commerce (ICC). A clear division of labour was established: while the IOIE dealt with ILO-related matters, strikes, labour relations and social policy, the ICC functioned as a trade association, representing business interests in matters of international trade, transportation and finance. The same individuals were often active in both the IOIE and the ICC, simultaneously or at different times. This was the case for the organiser of the 1911 employers' conference, Gino Olivetti, but also for many others, like the Italian rubber industrialist Alberto Pirelli (1882–1971) and Sigfrid Edström, both among the founders of the IOIE and later ICC presidents.[59]

Conclusion: employers and illiberal internationalism

"There can be no revolution without counter-revolution", wrote Arno Mayer.[60] This chapter has described the action of employers in the face of labour's mobilisation. While scholars have focused on the trade unions, a careful examination of employers' social and political mobilisation is indispensable to fully grasp the conflicts created by industrial capitalism, which involved "organised armies of Capital and Labor", as *The Economist* called them in 1928.[61]

This chapter has shown that the creation of employers' associations was a transnational phenomenon, and that once they were created, they reached out to one another. The events narrated in this chapter also suggest that transnational encounters shaped employers' strategies, stances on industrial policies and on social policy, at the very least from the first decades of the twentieth century onwards. Hence, this research provides a double contribution to the existing literature: first in studying the lesser known dimension of collective action from employers (battling trade unions and not as businessmen), and, while most studies are regional or national in scope, in revealing the transnational context in which those local events took place. Despite its importance in shaping the attitudes and action of employers' delegates in the ILO – the IOIE was "the backbone"[62] of the employers' group – the literature on the history of the ILO has until now failed to fully identify the role of the IOIE.[63] The relative neglect of the IOIE in the literature on the ILO is just one example of the general lack of attention to the historical role of employers. While new research has shown that employers' influence on social policy was highly debated and conflictual among employers,[64] there is much to discover on the transnational dynamics surrounding employers' associations: for instance the way they shaped social, political and economic conservatism. Further studies might investigate the extent to which such employers' transnational encounters contributed to a specific form of illiberal business internationalism, nurtured in opposition to workers' internationalism.[65]

Inspiration might be taken from German experts writing during World War I, who mentioned five possible motivations for employers to meet internationally: to regulate competition for workers in order to avoid wage increases; to produce in collaboration in case of strikes; to prevent locked-out workers finding employment in neighbouring countries; to prevent workers' shortages; and to organise financial support among employers facing strikes. Those forces were, however, compromised by competition between firms, while foreign competitors posed the threat of taking advantage of a strike to capture new customers instead of helping their foreign competitors to oppose strikers.[66] There were indeed clear caveats to the international collaboration of employers, which provide promising research avenues. In 1926, in the context of the British General Strike, the IOIE explicitly rejected the idea of international financial support to employers affected by big strikes. The risk, the IOIE decided, was that such a solidarity action would backfire against employers if it were to become public and would lead to more international collaboration between labour unions.[67] Hence, there was a tactical limit to international collaboration among employers.

Scholars have underestimated the transnational contacts among employers, assuming that classes were "not well organized internationally" and that "one can hardly speak of any institutionalized and permanent transnational characteristic of any class in modern society".[68] The IOIE and the ICC, among other structures, display durable international class-based collective action by enterprises' owners and managers, which are still active today, all of it awaiting proper historical investigation. Researchers might take many paths from there. What was at stake during the barely known World Congresses of Employers, held in different European capitals during the 1920s? What was the shape and reach of private diplomatic networks created by the IOIE or the ICC? How did nationally organised business communities negotiate the balance of competition and cooperation within international associations such as the IOIE?

Glenda Sluga and Patricia Clavin recently invited historians "to begin the process of recovering and re-imagining the plurality of internationalisms that fed political faith and disillusionment and the processes of historical change shaping the modern world".[69] The transnational mobilisation of employers constitutes one form of internationalism; this is a form that has barely been studied, though. This chapter has shown that the importance of transnational encounters should not be minimised in the explanation of the mobilisation of industrialists against strikes at the turn of the century, but the extent of business internationalism remains to be fully investigated in diverse contexts and periods, as employers have not finished reacting to Chotteau's urge: "So, industrialists and traders, rise!"

Notes

1 Jürgen Kocka, *Capitalism. A Short History* (Princeton, NJ and Oxford: Princenton University Press, 2016), 45. This research benefited from the support of the Swiss National Science Foundation, grant number 158916, "An International for the employers? The International Organization of Industrial Employers from the 1920s to the 1950s". For their helpful comments on earlier versions of this paper, I am grateful to Thomas David, Matthieu Leimgruber, Janick Marina Schaufelbuehl and Maiju Wuokko. I am also indebted to the conveners of the Zurich Geschichtskontor in December 2016 and to the participants to the 2018 European Business History Conference.

2 Eric Hobsbawm, *The Age of Revolution*, ed. Abacus (London: Longman, 2012 [1962]). Joshua B. Freeman, *Behemoth. A History of the Factory and the Making of the Modern World* (New York and London: W.W. Norton, 2018).

3 Nicolas Delalande, *La Lutte et l'Entraide. L'âge des solidarités ouvrières* (Paris: Editions du Seuil, 2019); Geert van Goethem, *The Amsterdam International. The World of the International Federation of Trade Unions (IFTU), 1913–1945* (Aldershot: Ashgate, 2006).

4 Eric Hobsbawm, *The Age of Capital*, ed. Abacus (London: Abacus, 2012 [1975]), 22 for the first quotation. On the Paris Commune, see pages 200–202. The second quotation is on page 201.

5 Léon Chotteau, *L'Internationale des Patrons* (Paris: Armand Le Chevalier, 1871). "So, industrialists . . ." on page 20 and "apathy and inertia . . ." on page 5.

6 See the letter from the Paris British Chamber of Commerce, signed by K. B. Murray, Director of the Paris British Chamber of Commerce, to the president of the *Association Industrielle et Commerciale Suisse*, November 16, 1874, 480.2.1.1, IB Vorort-Archiv, Archiv für Zeitgeschichte (AfZ), Zurich.

7 "Minutes of the Meeting of the Provisional Committee and Other Members," March 22, 1920, 1.03, Historical archives of the International Labour Organisation, Geneva, IOIE Archives. On Allan Smith, see Terence Rodgers, "Sir Allan Smith, the Industrial Group and the Politics of Unemployement," *Business History* 28, no. 1 (1986).

8 For a state of the art consideration of the literature, see Luca Lanzalaco, "Business Interest Associations," in *The Oxford Handbook of Business History*, ed. Geoffrey Jones and Jonathan Zeitlin (New York: Oxford University Press, 2008), quotation on page 295. See also Cathie Jo Martin and Duane Swank, *The Political Construction of Business Interests: Coordination, Growth and Equality* (New York: Cambridge University Press, 2012). On the militant anti-labour activities of the Shipping Federation see Alessandro Saluppo, "Strikebreaking and Anti-Unionism on the Waterfront: The Shipping Federation, 1890–1914," *European History Quarterly* 49, no. 4 (2019).

9 Daniel Rodgers, *Atlantic Crossings. Social Politics in a Progressive Age* (Cambridge, MA: Harvard University Press, 1998), 259–60. See page 10 for "had launched . . .", and page 20 for "a world . . ." and "State paternalism . . .".

10 Hans-Ulrich Jost, *Les avant-gardes réactionnaires. La naissance de la nouvelle droite en Suisse 1890–1914* (Lausanne: Editions d'en bas, 1992). Zeev Sternhell, *La droite révolutionnaire, 1885–1914: Les origines françaises du fascisme* (Paris: Editions du Seuil, 1978). Saluppo, "Strikebreaking and Anti-Unionism on the Waterfront: The Shipping Federation, 1890–1914."

11 Jacques Revel, "Micro-analyse et construction du social," in *Jeux d'échelles. La micro-analyse de l'expérience*, ed. Jacques Revel (Paris: Gallimard/Le Seuil, 1996).
12 In that order, Sebastian Conrad, *What is Global History?* (Princeton, NJ: Princeton University Press, 2016), 11. Pierre-Yves Saunier, *Transnational History* (Basingstoke: Palgrave Macmillan, 2013), 123. Madeleine Herren, "Von der Binnendifferenzierung zum 'Cosmopolitan Pluralism'. Neue Perspektiven für die Geschichte der internationalen Gewerkschaftsbewegung," *Traverse: Zeitschrift für Geschichte – Revue d'histoire* 7, no. 2 (2000).
13 Philippa Hetherington and Glenda Sluga, "Liberal and Illiberal Internationalisms," *Journal of World History* 31, no. 1 (2020).
14 Robert Grimm, "La lutte des fédérations patronales en Suisse contre les syndicats ouvriers," in *Comité central de la fédération suisse des ouvriers sur métaux* (Bern: Peter Lang, 1909). "Employers' terrorism" on page 16, "The times . . ." on page 57, and "would succedd . . ." on page 55.
15 Eduard Sulzer-Ziegler, "'Ueber Arbeitgeber-Verbände'," *Annual Report of the ASM* (1910): 61, 72.
16 Herman Justi, *Organization of the Employer Class* (Chicago: Illinois Coal Operators Association, 1901), 7.
17 Rodgers, *Atlantic Crossings. Social Politics in a Progressive Age*, 52–75.
18 Jesper Hamark and Christer Thörnqvist, "Docks and Defeat: The 1909 General Strike in Sweden and the Role of Port Labour," *Historical Studies in Industrial Relations* 34 (2013).
19 Wilhelm Georg Heinrich von Reiswitz, "Gründet Arbeitgeberverbände!" in *Sozialwirtschaftliche Zeitfragen*, ed. Alexander Tille (Berlin: Elsner, 1904). See also, Henry Axel Bueck, *Die Organisation der Arbeitgeber* (Berlin: Guttentag, 1904).
20 Emil Richard, *Organisation der schweizerischen Arbeitgeber* (Zürich: Zürcher Handelskammer, 1905), 10.
21 Pierre Tronel, *Essai sur l'organisation de la défense patronale* (Lyon: P. Grange & Refoubelet, 1911). Sulzer-Ziegler, "'Ueber Arbeitgeber-Verbände'." On strikebreaking see Matteo Millan, "Introduction: Strikebreaking During Europe's Belle Epoque," *European History Quarterly* 49, no. 4 (2019).
22 Achim Knips, *Deutsche Arbeitgeberverbände der Eisen- und Metallindustrie: 1888–1914* (Stuttgart: Steiner, 1996).
23 Delalande, *La Lutte et l'Entraide. L'âge des solidarités ouvrières*, 236–40.
24 Leopold H. Haimson, "Conclusion," in *Strikes, Wars, and Revolutions in an International Perspective: Strike Waves in the Late Nineteenth and Early Twentieth Centuries*, ed. Leopold H. Haimson and Charles Tilly (Cambridge and Paris: Cambridge University Press and Editions de la Maison des Sciences de l'Homme, 1989), 527.
25 Peter Swenson, *Capitalists against Markets. The Making of Labor Markets and Welfare States in the United States and Sweden* (Oxford: Oxford University Press, 2002).
26 Saluppo, "Strikebreaking and Anti-Unionism on the Waterfront: The Shipping Federation, 1890–1914," 590; Patricia Cayo Sexton, *The War on Labor and the Left. Understanding America's Unique Conservatism* (Boulder: Westview, 1991). Allan Pinkerton described communists as "a class of human hyenas worth all notice and attention". For that citation (p. 57).
27 Howell John Harris, *Bloodless Victories. The Rise and Fall of the Open Shop in the Philadelphia Metal Trades, 1890–1940* (New York: Cambridge University Press, 2000).
28 Pierre Eichenberger, *Mainmise sur l'Etat social. Mobilisation patronale et caisses de compensation en Suisse (1908–1960)* (Neuchâtel: Alphil – Presses Universitaires Suisses, 2016), 85–147.
29 Swenson, *Capitalists against Markets. The Making of Labor Markets and Welfare States in the United States and Sweden*, 79–83. On Siemens see Ilse Costas, "Management and Labor in the Siemens Plant in Berlin (1906–1920)," in *Strikes, Social Conflict and the First World War: An International Perspective*, ed. Leopold Haimson and Giulio Sapelli (Milano: Feltrinelli ed, 1992).

30 Christian Koller, "Local Strikes as Transnational Events: Migration, Donations, and Organizational Cooperation in the Context of Strikes in Switzerland (1860–1914)," *Labour History Review* 74, no. 3 (2009): 314.
31 Leopold Haimson and Charles Tilly, eds., *Strikes, Wars and Revolution in an International Perspective. Strikes Waves in the Late Nineteenth and Early Twentieth Centuries* (Cambridge and Paris: Cambridge University Press & Maison des Sciences de l'Homme, 1989).
32 Aeltesten der Kaufmannschaft von Berlin, *Die Handelskammern. Ihre Organisation und Tätigkeit. Bericht an den Internationalen Handelskammer-Kongress in Mailand 1906* (Berlin: Georg Reimer, 1906). On the congress see Clotilde Druelle-Korn, "The Great War: Matrix of the International Chamber of Commerce, a Fortunate Business League of Nations," in *The Impact of the First World War on International Business*, ed. Andrew Smith, Simon Mollan, and Kevin D. Tennent (New York and London: Routledge, 2016), 105.
33 Jasmien van Daele, "Engineering Social Peace: Networks, Ideas, and the Founding of the International Labour Organization," *International Review of Social History*, no. 3 (2005). Rodgers, *Atlantic Crossings. Social Politics in a Progressive Age*, 52–74; Delalande, *La Lutte et l'Entraide. L'âge des solidarités ouvrières*. On Sulzer-Ziegler see Arthur Straessle, *Eduard Sulzer-Ziegler 1954–1913. Von der politischen und sozialpolitischen Tätigkeit eines Winterthurer Industriellen* (Zurich: Abhandlung zur Erlangung der Doktorwürde der Philosphishen Fakultät I der Universität Zürich, 1968), 85–86.
34 Erich Gruner, "Die Arbeitgeberorganisationen – Spiegelbild oder Überbietung der Gewerkschaften?" in *Arbeiterschaft und Wirtschaft in der Schweiz 1880–1914, Band II: Gewerkschaften und Arbeitgeber auf dem Arbeitsmarkt; Streiks, Kampf ums Recht und Verhältnis zu andern Interessengruppen*, ed. Gruner Erich (Zürich: Chronos, 1988), 817.
35 VSM Vorstand N°105, 17 November 1905, p. 8, 1.2.2.1, Swissmem VSM Archives, AfZ, Zurich.
36 Jürgen Schmid, "Rieppel, Anton Johann von," in *Neue Deutsche Biographie* (Berlin: Duncker & Humblot, 2003). ASM Vorstand N°17, 15 December 1906, pp. 9–10, 1.3.2.1., Swissmem ASM Archives, AfZ.
37 On the strike, see Hamark and Thörnqvist, "Docks and Defeat: The 1909 General Strike in Sweden and the Role of Port Labour." On international solidarity Delalande, *La Lutte et l'Entraide. L'âge des solidarités ouvrières*, 240–44.
38 Desmond King and Bo Rothstein, "Institutional Choices and Labor Market Policy: A British-Swedish Comparison," *Comparative Political Studies* 26, no. 2 (1993): 151.
39 Otto Steinmann, Betrachtungen über den Schwedischen Generalstreik des Jahres 1909, *Schriften des Zentralverbandes Schweizer. Arbeitgeber-Organisationen,* N°2, 1910. See Pierre Eichenberger, "Les organisations patronales et la Grève générale de 1918," *Traverse – Zeitschrift für Geschichte* 25, no. 2 (2018).
40 Quoted in Eichenberger, "Les organisations patronales et la Grève générale de 1918," 129.
41 Jonathan E. Robins, "A Common Brotherhood for Their Mutual Benefit: Sir Charles Macara and Internationalism in the Cotton Industry, 1904–1914," *Enterprise & Society* 16, no. 4 (2015).
42 Saluppo, "Strikebreaking and Anti-Unionism on the Waterfront: The Shipping Federation, 1890–1914."
43 van Goethem, *The Amsterdam International. The World of the International Federation of Trade Unions (IFTU), 1913–1945*, 15.
44 Delalande, *La Lutte et l'Entraide. L'âge des solidarités ouvrières*. Paul Hermberg, "Die internationalen Beziehungen der deutschen Arbeitgeber-, Angestellten- und Arbeiterverbände," *Weltwirtschaftliches Archiv* 5 (1915). He indicates that on the eve of the war, out of 46 members of the *Zentralverbänden gewerblicher Arbeiter*, 41 were engaged in international agreements or organisations.
45 Swenson, *Capitalists against Markets. The Making of Labor Markets and Welfare States in the United States and Sweden*, 104.

46 Annexe 1 of the "Note de Mr. Jules Lecocq," [1950], IOIE Archives, 10.01, Origines et évolution de l'OIE, 1919–1969. On Gino Olivetti see Andrea M. Locatelli and Paolo Tedeschi, "Notes on the Genesis and Development of Business Interest Associations in Milan (19th–20th Centuries)," in *Historical and International Comparison of Business Interest Associations: 19th-20th Centuries*, ed. Danièle Fraboulet, Andrea M. Locatelli, and Paolo Tedeschi (Brussels: Peter Lang, 2013), 87.

47 "Note de Mr. Jules Lecocq," [1950], IOIE Archives, 10.01, Origines et évolution de l'OIE, 1919–1969, p. 4. On Carlier, Marieke Louis, "Building a Transnational Business Community. The International Organisation of Employers and the International Labour Organisation," August 2018, p. 8.

48 Pierre Waline, *Un patron au Bureau International du Travail, 1922–1974* (Paris: Editions France-Empire, 1976), 29–31.

49 Adam Tooze, *The Deluge. The Great War and the Remaking of Global Order, 1916–1931* (London: Allan Lane/Penguin Books, 2014), 416.

50 Charles S. Maier, *Recasting Bourgeois Europe. Stabilization in France, Germany, and Italy in the Decade after World War I*, (Princeton, NJ: Princeton University Press, [1975] 1988). On the strikes after World War I, see Leopold Haimson and Giulio Sapelli, eds., *Strikes, Social Conflict and the First World War an International Perspective* (Milano: Feltrinelli ed., 1992).

51 Sandrine Kott and Jöelle Droux, eds., *Globalizing Social Rights: The International Labour Organization and beyond* (New York: Palgrave Macmillan, 2013). Marieke Louis, *Qu'est-ce qu'une bonne représentation? L'Organisation internationale du travail de 1919 à nos jours* (Paris: Dalloz, 2016).

52 van Goethem, *The Amsterdam International. The World of the International Federation of Trade Unions (IFTU), 1913–1945*, 13–23; Edo Fimmen, *The International Federation of Trade Unions. Development and Aims*, Publications of the International Federation of Trade Unions N°1 (Published by the International Federation of Trade Unions Amsterdam, 1922).

53 Quoted in van Daele, "Engineering Social Peace: Networks, Ideas, and the Founding of the International Labour Organization," 463.

54 Reiner Tosstorff, "The International Trade-Union Movement and the Founding of the International Labour Organization," *International Review of Social History* 50, no. 3 (2005): 429–30.

55 Louis, "Building a Transnational Business Community. The International Organisation of Employers and the International Labour Organisation," 4–8.

56 Danièle Fraboulet, "Robert Pinot 1862–1926," in *Dictionaire historique du patronat français*, ed. Jean-Claude Daumas (Paris: Falammarion, 2010).

57 "Statutes adopted by the General Council held in Brussels on October 1, 1920, and modified by the General Council held in Geneva on June 14, 1924," 1.03, IOIE Archives.

58 Louis, "Building a Transnational Business Community. The International Organisation of Employers and the International Labour Organisation." On the history of the IOIE see also Isabelle Lespinet-Moret, "L'Organisation internationale des Employeurs Industriels au sein de l'OIT: l'apprentissage du tripartisme, 1919–1939?" in *Coopérer, négocier, s'affronter: les organisations patronales et leurs relations avec les autres organisations collectives* ed. Danièle Fraboulet, Cédric Humair, and Pierre Vernus (Rennes: Presses Universitaires de Rennes, 2014). And the accounts of two former IOIE executives, Jean-Jacques Oechslin, *L'Organisation Internationale des Employeurs* (Genève: Organisation Internationale des Employeurs, 2001); Waline, *Un patron au Bureau International du Travail, 1922–1974*.

59 On the ICC, see Druelle-Korn, "The Great War: Matrix of the International Chamber of Commerce, a Fortunate Business League of Nations"; Thomas David and Pierre Eichenberger, "Business and Diplomacy in the Twentieth Century: A Corporatist View," *Diplomatica* 2, no. 1 (2020).

60 Arno J. Mayer, *The Furies. Violence and Terror in the French and Russian Revolutions* (Princeton, NJ: Princeton University Press, 2000), 45.
61 "Towards Industrial Peace," *The Economist*, July 7, 1928, 3; Issue 4428.
62 "Récit de Mr. Waline à Rome le 20.11.1954," IOIE Archives, 10.01, Origines et évolution de l'OIE, 1919–1969.
63 Jasmien van Daele, "Writing ILO Histories: A State of the Art," in *ILO Histories. Essays on the International Labour Organization and its Impact on the World During the Twentieth Century*, ed. Jasmin Van Daele et al. (Bern, Berlin, Bruxelles, Frankfurt am Main, New York, Oxford and Wien: Peter Lang, 2010), 38. See, however, the work of Marieke Louis on that question.
64 Dennie Oude Nijhuis, ed., *Business Interests and the Development of the Modern Welfare State* (London: Routledge, 2019).
65 Hetherington and Sluga, "Liberal and Illiberal Internationalisms."
66 Hermberg, "Die internationalen Beziehungen der deutschen Arbeitgeber-, Angestellten- und Arbeiterverbände," 106–7. Hermberg summarises arguments made in Wilhelm Kulemann, *Vereinigte Staaten von Amerika, Kanada, Argentinien, Australien, Neuseeland, Japan, Internationale Organisation* (Berlin: L. Simion, 1913).
67 Modern Records Centre, University of Warwick MSS 200 B/3/2 C679, Letter from Jules Lecocq to Sir James Lithgow, 27 January 1926.
68 Jaap Dronkers, "Class," in *The Palgrave Dictionary of Transnational History*, ed. Pierre-Yves Saunier and Akira Iriye (Basingstoke: Palgrave Macmillan, 2009), 161.
69 Glenda Sluga and Patricia Clavin, "Rethinking the History of Internationalism," in *Internationalisms: A Twentieth-Century History*, ed. Glenda Sluga and Patricia Clavin (Cambridge: Cambridge University Press, 2016), 13.

Part 2

Strikebreaking tactics and practices

7 Anti-labour repression in the in-between spaces of empire

The *Compagnie des Messageries Maritimes* and the steamship workers of the "China Line" (1900–20)

Charles Bégué Fawell

In the lore of labour history, strikes in ports were won or lost depending on whether the ships departed. If the ships stayed in port, the workers had succeeded; if the ships set out, the bosses had prevailed. But this narrative of labour contests lacks in nuance what it possesses in drama. After all, even when the most massive strikes broke out, many ships were already at sea. On ships at sea, moreover, outbursts of labour militancy could occur without instructions from home. Perhaps unsurprisingly, then, while the historiography of late nineteenth- and early twentieth-century labour movements in France includes comprehensive accounts of battles over the docks of major port cities like Marseille or Le Havre, far less is known about how Belle Époque struggles over labour unfolded outside the dockyards of metropolitan ports; that is, at sea, in motion and beyond the oversight of metropolitan port authorities.[1]

Syndicalism in France's maritime industries began in the 1870s, but mass actions culminated in the opening decades of the twentieth century. In Marseille, France's "gateway to the Orient", the new century ushered in a wave of massive strikes; first in 1900, then again in 1902, 1907 and 1912, after which tensions were contained during the First World War, only to explode with renewed intensity as the war concluded.[2] None of these labour conflicts was put on hold when the worksite was mobile and far from home. How, then, did shipping companies combat labour militancy in transit, far from European ports, along maritime highways?

The scarcity of responses to that question reflects, in part, scholarly assumptions regarding transit and the spaces in which it occurs. Though repeated "global turns" and "mobilities" paradigms have emphasised the importance of connectedness and the mobile subject, most scholarship continues to address the transoceanic routes connecting imperial metropoles to far-off colonies in functionalist terms, with the infrastructure of maritime routes appearing as a conveyor belt that neutrally connects port to port, as if node to node.[3] By implication, maritime highways come across as depoliticised and un-peopled – quintessential *spaces*, as opposed to *places*.[4] And yet, as this chapter suggests, maritime routes were far more crowded and contested than residual assumptions suggest. Critical arenas for the struggle over labour militancy that gripped Europe in its Belle

Époque, shipping corridors were neither neutral infrastructure nor homogenous expanses. Rather, these in-between spaces of empires were shaped by competing legal regimes, shifting borders and the complex interplay of people, ship, sea and port.[5]

Foraying into the question of how shipping companies combatted labour militancy in motion, this chapter focuses on France's largest shipping company on Europe-to-Asia routes, the *Compagnie des Messageries Maritimes*, and specifically its "China Line", an intercontinental route that began in Marseille, crossed the Suez Canal and extended (despite its name) to the Japanese port of Yokohama.[6] In the early twentieth century, the *Messageries Maritimes* experimented with a range of tactics to prevent labour militancy from spreading across this bustling and geopolitically vital highway, and to quash strikes when they arose en route. The company systematically labelled strikes as "mutinies", manned ships with scab crews and mobilised consuls and police forces in foreign layover ports. Simultaneously, the *Messageries* tacked between the French agencies historically tasked with regulating the merchant marine, and the Navy, which offered ship captains and company agents the tantalising possibility of meeting labour unrest with martial justice.

The efficacy of those tactics, however, depended on whether *Messageries* bosses in Marseille, ship captains at sea and company agents stationed along the route could outmanoeuvre workers in the interstices of imperial sovereignty and the politics of transoceanic, trans-imperial transit. In such contests, I argue, workers proved surprisingly capable of foiling company plans. The *Messageries*' ensemble of tactics thus amounted to little more than a strategy of opportunism – with one important exception. In developing a global system to recruit and circulate African and Asian workers, the *Messageries* found a structural, as opposed to opportunistic, approach to thwarting labour militancy within its mobile workforce; outsourcing *avant la lettre*.[7]

To begin, it is worth reflecting on the *Messageries Maritimes'* origins and its orientation at the turn of the twentieth century.[8] Among French companies, the *Messageries* was rivalled only by the famed *Compagnie Générale Transatlantique*, which, as the name suggests, dominated France's trans-Atlantic traffic, while leaving what lay "East of Suez" in the hands of the *Messageries*. Internationally, the *Messageries* spent the latter nineteenth-century trying to keep up with its perennial rival for Europe-to-Asia traffic, the British Empire's *Peninsular & Oriental Company* (*P&O*). However, competition was stiff enough that the lines reached an early "Gentleman's Agreement", alternating their schedules and sharing the lucrative market for trans-Suez cargo and passengers.[9] Secure in its market, the *Messageries* expanded, and by 1891 the company was transporting over 120,000 passengers annually on a fleet of 62 ships (most of them built in the shipyards of La Ciotat, near Marseille).[10] After the First World War devastated its fleet, the *Messageries* struggled to withstand challenges from the subsidised shipping lines of Germany, Japan and others. Nonetheless, France's commercial proxy "beyond Suez" remained a giant of the Age of Steam, with one of the world's largest fleets and a global network of agencies and facilities.[11]

Like the British *P&O*, the *Messageries* was privately owned but intertwined with the operations of the imperial state. From 1881 on, the French state subsidised ship construction and some of the operational costs of voyages, while the company, in turn, carried mail to the far corners of the French Empire, along with soldiers, administrators and bureaucrats, diplomats and statesmen – essentially anyone and anything the state told it to transport. Those soldiers, administrators and diplomats travelled alongside tourists, migrants, convicts, entertainers, merchants, missionaries and of course, ship workers, who, on the largest of these ships, lived by the hundreds. Certain *Messageries* ships were specialised for cargo, and others for passengers, but the boundaries between freight and voyagers – and between private commerce and imperial affairs – were anything but clear. As Jules Verne famously observed in a best-selling book of the 1870s, the nineteenth-century steamship was evolving into nothing less than a "floating city".[12] What, then, could a company like the *Messageries* do when "floating cities" became labour battlegrounds?

Makeshift solutions: the mutiny accusation and "makeshift crews"

Nomenclature was the first arena in which navigation companies responded to surging labour militancy at sea. To label the intensifying contestation of maritime workers, ship captains and company officials returned to an ancient concept: mutiny. Unlike the legendary "Mutiny on the Bounty" and other precedents from the Age of Sail, though, mutiny in the era of labour militancy did not entail commandeering a ship or capturing a captain. Nor were these mutinies equivalent to the naval uprisings of the First World War and its aftermath, when state-paid sailors contested their governments en masse. Rather, aboard the large steamships of the turn-of-the-century, militancy became mutinous when it stopped traffic, throwing a wrench into the giant assembly line of global trade that had developed in the wake of steam navigation and the Suez Canal. In the eyes of pro-business diplomats and jurists, a mutiny was merely a strike in motion, and to take the ship captains of the Age of Steam at their word, the period abounded with mutinies. Indeed, the legal threshold for such a qualification was remarkably low, for as soon as multiple crewmembers refused a direct order from their captain, they were engaging in mutinous activity.[13] In choosing not to differentiate between violent and non-violent acts of resistance, captains and their sympathisers used the mutiny accusation ("revolt" was also a common label) to suggest that insubordination *was* violence. As will be seen, however, the myriad actors who were pulled into labour negotiations en route – consuls, port police and foreign jurists – were not always as quick to conflate protest and mutiny.

Beyond rhetorical framing, the *Messageries* developed a range of concrete practices of intervention. Perhaps the most obvious tool for preventing the spread of militancy to the route was to recruit a "makeshift" (i.e. scab) crew.[14] Normally, crews had to be drawn mostly from the *Inscription maritime*, or Maritime registry, a centuries-old institution that served as a state registry of professional sailors.

During strikes, the *Messageries* was sometimes allowed to forgo the registry, instead manning its ships with unscreened applicants from Marseille's streets, or even navy men (when available). This tactic offered shippers an efficient means of sidestepping strikes, but it had glaring defects, for while the *Messageries* could slip a makeshift crew across the picket line and onto a ship, once that ship was en route, all bets were off.

A 1909 voyage of the *Messageries* ship, *Calédonien*, running the China Line from Marseille to Yokohama, illustrates the potential volatility of makeshift crews. In voyage reports, the captain of the *Calédonien* noted that his makeshift crew had performed well until laying over at Port-Saïd, the chokepoint of maritime traffic at the head of the Suez Canal, where they encountered another *Messageries* ship, this one carrying a full crew of *inscrits maritimes*, or registered (i.e. professional) sailors. In front of a crowd of foreign ships, the *Calédonien* endured an extended barrage of insults and menaces from its sister ship.[15] In a vacuum, the bloodless clash might have been of little consequence, but the route and its ports were not vacuums, so much as they were international stages.[16] For the *Messageries*, which was locked in intense and increasingly mediatised competition with other nationally subsidised lines (not to mention a near-constant public relations campaign within France to maintain government subsidies), public humiliation had real consequences. Calling the incident "a demonstration of savages attended by foreign ships", the captain and his directors declared it a significant setback in their struggle with labour; not, of course, because of the injured pride of their makeshift crew, but rather because the militant sailors encountered by the *Calédonien* had used the most crowded section of the China Line to castigate the company, exposing both its internal divisions and its reliance on underqualified sailors. The public spectacle rendered the company vulnerable to reports of instability within their ranks – reports that could rattle around the press, compromise the line's appeal to wealthy passengers and shake the resolve of critical allies within the French government.[17]

In 1912, against the backdrop of Marseille's most intense strike to date, a subsequent captain of the *Calédonien* discovered that hiring makeshift crews could backfire even without an external shock. Once again exempted from the maritime registry, the *Messageries* had manned its ship with a makeshift crew, sending it out for the roughly 80-day journey to Yokohama and back. Midway, however, labour relations broke down, thefts became rampant and the *Calédonien*'s officers discovered to their horror that the crew was sabotaging their ship. To his directors, the captain complained that his makeshift crew were "veritable apaches", using a term that evoked the infamous street gangs of Belle Époque Paris.[18] To make matters worse, faced with what he termed a "revolt" and a "mutiny" from the very men who were supposed to be quashing revolts and mutinies, he found himself powerless to react. When conflict spiked en route to their layover in Singapore, for instance, he noted:

> I waited by as long as I could, and I even ceded in Singapore when they refused to serve in front of the Consul, so that the passengers could have no

> doubt that we were dealing with a crew of apaches, and because we were in foreign land, and it would have had a very poor effect to show that we were working with an undisciplined crew, recognizing no authority at all, and, on the contrary, in a state of revolt.[19]

As the incidents suggested, the company could wrangle its way into recruiting a makeshift crew to keep the China Line moving, but once in motion, there was no guarantee that the crew would obey orders.

The reproachful gaze of passengers and foreign commentators, meanwhile, constrained the company's ability to punish rebellious workers.

Cops, consuls and the interstices of imperial jurisdictions

Makeshift crews may have been, to the *Messageries*, an infuriatingly unreliable means of clearing labour militancy from the route, but other resources were available to captains and company agents. Every layover port on the China Line had a French consul, for instance, whose pro-company sympathies and direct lines to port police made them compelling allies in anti-labour operations. Again, though, voyage reports of the *Messageries* reveal the limits of calling in consuls and cops to crack down on mutinous workers.[20] Often enough, campaigns to mobilise consular networks and port police became mired in uncertainty over the jurisdictional boundaries between localities and foreign ships. Likewise, determining when a strike, or mutiny, had become disruptive enough to threaten security proved surprisingly thorny. For one of many examples in which anti-labour crackdowns idled in the interstices of imperial sovereignty, let us return to the *Calédonien*, which set out for East Asia in 1913 with a new crew and captain, only to endure another unpunished mutiny, despite the total sympathy of a French consul and the proximity of port police.

As reams of reports relate, the mutiny broke out in the Indian Ocean, shortly before the *Calédonien* reached its scheduled layover in British Colombo, Ceylon (today's Sri Lanka).[21] Tensions crystallised dramatically when, just after the decision had been made to halt work, a crewmember succumbed to typhoid fever. Instead of carrying out the burial at sea, as rules prescribed, the workers stood still, turning the rotting corpse into a sanitary time bomb and forcing the ship's officers to carry out the morbid labour themselves. After the showdown, the ship limped into Colombo's port, where officers promptly called on the French consul to avenge the insult and injury. Consular support was beyond doubt, since it turned out that France's official representative held two roles at once: consul, and general agent of the *Messageries* in Ceylon. Disgusted by the collapse of discipline aboard the ship, this consul and company man summoned the port police, only to find that they refused to board the ship out of fear of legal complications. The police, he learnt, would limit themselves to returning "deserting" sailors to the ship. Ironically, by ensuring that no one abandoned the action, this measure reinforced the strikers' cohesion.

As authorities searched for a silver bullet, Colombo's press began to criticise the company over its idling ship. Increasingly hot under the gaze of the press and ships of foreign competitors, and lacking means of repression, one officer summarised the situation simply: "We were completely disarmed". In what the consul would describe as a total "abdication of the principle of authority", the officers conceded to crew demands, crippling the case they could subsequently bring against the sailors. The ship carried on until it reached the next layover, in the French colonial port of Saigon, where an inquiry was conducted. Having tightened ranks during the week's journey between Colombo and Saigon, however, the crew refused to identify ringleaders.[22] Mobility and immobility alike had played to the workers' favour as they successfully navigated maritime borderlands.

While the *Messageries* and its sympathisers may have been disheartened by the lack of support from British authorities in Colombo, it should have come as no surprise. Trans-Suez routes were full of layovers at British ports, and this geopolitical predicament placed the *Messageries* at the mercy of a government which, again and again, refused to clarify its policy regarding intervention onboard foreign vessels. Seven years before the *Calédonien*'s officers were forced into their humiliating "abdication of the principle of authority" in Colombo, for instance, a Russian ship laying over in the South Asian port met a similar fate, sparking a legal debate among British authorities that exposed the ambiguities of mutiny in the age of labour militancy, and sovereignty in the in-between spaces of empires.

In spring of 1906, the *Grigory Moerch* pulled into Colombo's harbour with a cargo of petroleum for what appeared to be a routine layover on the ship's long voyage to Vladivostok. A desperate cable to the Russian consul shattered the illusion of mundanity. The crew, it warned, "was mutinous and the Captain's life was in danger".[23] As it turned out, the Russian consul was not Russian at all, for the position had been recently delegated to the French Consul. A French consul negotiating with British colonial officials over the fate of a Russian crew may sound exceptionally complicated, but it was not even the only international knot tying up the China Line at that moment; at the exact same moment in Naples, for instance, a few layovers westward, British, Italian and Chinese state officials were negotiating the fate of a British ship and its mutinous Chinese crew.[24] In Colombo, the French-turned-Russian consul promptly requested that police board the ship, "strictly", he insisted, "to protect the Captain from violence". The crew, however, wisely refrained from provoking the police guard, and when the consul and captain sought a mass arrest of the crew, they were denied by Ceylon's attorney general. Faced with a peaceful mutiny, the police guard withdrew. As he explained to superiors in London, the attorney general would not authorise a crackdown unless the harbour's security was threatened or violence occurred on board, and while he suspected there had been threats of violence, he had to admit, "But here we have no threat, only a strike, and with that we cannot interfere on a Foreign ship".[25] His colleague was less circumspect: "The Consul is anxious to force the crew . . . ashore, but this is no business of ours".[26]

Floating in Colombo's harbour, the *Grigory Moerch*'s engine remained silent and the sailors refused to budge. Inside Colombo, meanwhile the ship's officers and consul continued to lobby for repression, after which the captain planned to replace his rebellious countrymen with a "native crew". Eventually, they procured a warrant to arrest the entire crew, only to watch the attorney general revoke it at the last moment. With internal divisions growing and the local press speculating on the standoff, port authorities hatched a plan to tow the petroleum ship outside of Colombo's harbour and abandon its crew to their fate. At last, just before the operation launched, an offer of back pay and safe passage to Russia reached the crew, who accepted, coming ashore and ending the strike.

If the facts of the episode were straightforward enough, its legal implications were practically indecipherable. Embarrassed by the confusion that had reigned throughout the standoff, British authorities in Ceylon wrote to London requesting legal precedents to answer two seemingly simple questions: did a colonial government have "legal power to interfere by coercive action in the event of a difficulty, not involving a breach of the peace, arising between the Master and crew of a foreign ship lying in harbour", and if so, how far would they be "authorized in arresting mutineers on board a foreign ship when requested to do so by a Captain of the ship and the Consul of the State to which the ship belongs?"[27] Unfortunately for them, historical precedent merely multiplied the questions. The last Russian ship to run into labour disputes in British waters, for instance, was thought to have been boarded forcibly by the police, yet there existed no administrative record of the invasion whatsoever, raising the troubling spectre of extra-legal operations.[28] As the legal debate climbed to the Foreign Office, moreover, it became tangled in a web of complicating factors. Binational treaties seemed to clash with municipal codes, while scholars of international law disagreed over whether local law and ship law were concurrent or mutually exclusive. Commentators contradicted each other over whether crimes committed by crewmembers at sea became null once in harbour, while others cautioned that cases against crewmembers would crumble if crimes were tried on land after being tried at sea. Different rules applied to a merchant vessel and a "man-of-war", yet few could say with clarity what to do when a merchant vessel was carrying military materiel or had been contracted by a foreign state. Having "searched in vain for a decided case", Ceylon's attorney general threw up his hands.[29]

Their questions answered with a cacophony of interpretations and precedents, British authorities settled on a policy of ambiguity. Physical crackdowns would be authorised only when the British port in question was threatened, or violence was occurring on-board a foreign ship. Shrewdly, though, no one supplied a basic definition of what constituted a threat to port security, or when violence "breached the peace". China Line shippers, then, faced a dilemma: the worker "mutinies" occurring along the route were sufficiently severe to force a state-backed company to the table, yet insufficiently bloody to trigger intervention by foreign port police. On the China Line, "foreign" almost invariably meant British, and the British government was far from confident that intervening in labour disputes aboard foreign ships was lawful, or in its interest. Asked to choose between their right to monopolise violence on British territory and their responsibility to act as the unpaid muscle for any foreign ship that steamed into port with a mutinous crew, British authorities declined to choose at all.

Sovereigns of the route

Faced with the reality that even the most sympathetic French consul could not guarantee a police response to labour militancy along the route, *Messageries* bosses might simply have steered ship captains to French ports, where police were unburdened by fears of sovereign violations. While the British were hegemons "East of Suez", French captains belonged to an empire with a host of territories around the Indian Ocean and South China Sea, many possessing ports that could serve as bases for coordinating anti-labour reprisals: Djibouti, on the Red Sea; Madagascar, Réunion and a constellation of smaller Indian Ocean islands; coastal enclaves in India and China; and most importantly, Indochina, whose ports were becoming critical nodes of the empire's Indian and Pacific Ocean traffic. Yet, from the company's perspective, even French territory provided a shaky foundation for exerting authority over militant labour. After all, while company agents could call French police, their workers could appeal to the aged and complex institution of the *Inscription maritime* (Maritime registry).

Founded in the late seventeenth century, the *Inscription maritime* emerged to replace press gangs with a registered maritime workforce that could sustain trade routes and fill the ranks of the royal navy in times of crisis. Despite its royal pedigree, the institution survived the revolution, but its reaffirmation in revolutionary law came with a crucial caveat transferring the power to punish sailors from captains and admiralty courts to common law tribunes. This principle of equality under the law was undermined by reforms of the Second Empire (1852–70), which reasserted a special legal regime for sailors of the *Inscription* and re-empowered captains to act as judge and jury. In 1896, however, captains were again stripped of some of these coercive powers, and the disciplinary code for sailors was again open to debate and interpretation.[30] Among the 100,000-plus workers who populated France's *Inscription* in 1900, few could say with certainty where the institution would place its weight in the coming struggles over labour rights. On the one hand, the *Inscription* tied sailors to a special penal code in which they might be hurled in prison for work infractions or accused of desertion if they abandoned their worksite at the wrong moment. On the other hand, the *Inscription* existed to ensure that France would always have a body of professional sailors available in times of crisis, meaning that it was less concerned with the profits and pride of shipping magnates than with preventing sailors from fleeing their line of work. Whether merchant mariners could count on an institutional champion in the state, at the very least they would have an arbiter.[31]

By 1900, as Marseille's era of massive strikes began, this spectre of state arbitration horrified ship captains, who believed that their authority was under siege and that only new allies in the French state could save them. As one captain put it in 1900, "The situation has become all too clear. 1) They have made sure to disarm the Captains totally. 2) Punishment by disembarkment is illusory today. 3) By order, the Consuls are disarmed".[32] His despair was understandable. Having faced a rebellious crew for weeks, he had failed to punish them in the Japanese port of Yokohama, the terminus of the China Line, where an attempt to dissuade striking sailors with a combination of consular orders and police interventions had totally missed the mark (like their British counterparts, it seems Japanese authorities preferred sending labour disputes down the line over clogging their courts with the problems of foreigners). Then, during a homebound layover in French Saigon, the captain appealed to the *Inscription*, only to watch its magistrate grant the accused sailors the right to a trial on metropolitan soil in their homeport of Marseille, a month's journey away. As a result, the sailors who had contested this captain's sovereignty were able to, as he put it, "rejoice in the most perfect impunity for six weeks" – ample time to craft a legal defence, jump ship or foment anger among fellow workers.[33] To company directors, the captain named the last weapon in his arsenal, writing, "What remains are the warships – in the future, when punishments are called for, and there will be no shortage of that, I am going to address myself solely to the warships and that will do it".[34]

Writing nine years later, after multiple strikes had rocked the maritime sector, another captain from the China Line drew a similar picture. This time, however, he called not only for the *Messageries* to rely on Navy justice, but to *deploy* the Navy in an institutional attack against the *Inscription*. Thanks to the pervasive influence of "strike-spreaders [*gréviculteurs*], saboteurs and others", who had entered the ranks, he explained in correspondence with company headquarters:

> we are henceforth dealing with personnel who, while they don't have very well-formulated ideas about their duties, are on the other hand extremely up to date on their rights. On voyages where the layovers are numerous, we can hardly shift a straw. . . . To remediate this disaster, it will be necessary for anyone having anything to do with the Navy to ceaselessly battle the long-outdated regime of the *Inscription maritime*.[35]

And indeed, faced with militancy in motion, many *Messageries* captains adopted this strategy. Taking advantage of the statutory liminality of sailors and the gaping loophole available to any captain who could claim a threat to the security of navigation, they simply avoided ports altogether, pouncing instead on French warships along the route, and preventing the *Inscription* from fanning the fire of labour militancy.[36]

As China Line captains reacted to labour unrest by blocking the *Inscription* from acting in its capacity as an arbiter, they simultaneously leaned more heavily than ever on that very same *Inscription* to handle a host of other cases occurring outside French ports. Indeed, the company may have been attacking the institution on two fronts: starving it of influence over labour conflicts, while flooding it with petty administrative burdens. This, at least, was the fear of A. Jaquemart, the man who headed the *Inscription* in Saigon for much of the early twentieth century. In correspondence with Indochina's governor general, Jaquemart accused the consular network "East of Suez" of being squarely in the pocket of the *Messageries*. As he explained to the governor general, the unholy alliance between company agents and French consuls along the China Line may not have been enough to guarantee mass arrests of mutinous crews, but consuls were compensating captains by empowering them to disembark individual troublemakers in

Saigon. Conveniently for the company, the *Inscription* footed the bill of legal proceedings, imprisonment and repatriation. What they could not solve in foreign ports and navy courts, in other words, *Messageries* captains brought to the French government in Saigon. As a result, Saigon's *Inscription* was ballooning into what Jaquemart described as the unmanageable "headquarters of a maritime arrondissement stretching from Suez to Yokohama".[37] Offloading dissident individuals and petty offenders onto the *Inscription* when large-scale crackdowns were made impossible by foreign law codes, *Messageries* captains and agents continued exploiting the benefits of access to navy ships – and navy justice – whenever they could claim a "threat to security of navigation". Here was an anti-labour recipe composed of opportunism, expert navigation of state agencies and a cynical appraisal of the vagaries of maritime law.

But was this approach to combatting labour militancy systematic, merely opportunistic or, in a sense, a strategy built around maximising opportunism? After all, navy vessels were not always available, since their locations were contingent upon international relations and shrouded in secrecy. As for using the *Inscription* as a dumping ground for lesser offenders (or sailors who had wisely offended outside of French ports), eventually an angry administrator like Jaquemart could push back against the company. And indeed, for two decades, Jaquemart did just that, tirelessly working to expose the company's abuse of state resources and legal loopholes.[38]

Colonial subjects and maritime labour

For companies like the *Messageries*, perhaps the one truly systemic approach to combatting labour militancy arose from a system of hiring and rotating Asian and African workers, most of them subjects of the French and British Empires. The practice of manning Europe-to-Asia ships with Asian and African crews dated to the earliest trade routes; indeed, the very incident that inspired Grotius to theorise the "Free Sea" in the seventeenth century involved two European ships manned largely by inhabitants of the Indian Ocean littoral.[39] In France, however, the practice had been disputed since the 1790s, when revolutionary law mandated that any flag-bearing ship have a crew of which 75 per cent were French nationals; for officers, the requirement rose to 100 per cent. Over the next century, steamship companies formed powerful political lobbies and chipped away at the requirements. By 1900, French citizens on flag-bearing ships operating in the Red Sea and Indian Ocean could legally constitute as little as 50 per cent of a crew. Unsurprisingly, the French-citizen workforce in Marseille detested the hiring of colonial subjects, and demands to abolish the practice, often framed in viscerally racist terms, were central planks of syndicalism from its origins.[40]

Like its British counterpart, the *P&O*, the *Messageries* handled these criticisms adeptly. On *its* lines, directors made clear, the flow of traffic beyond Suez could be guaranteed only with contingents of African and Asian workers. Specifically, *Messageries* negotiators insisted that if Europeans worked in scorching-hot engine rooms during the Red Sea passage, they would die in droves. While maritime unions and their allies argued that employing "indigenous" sailors was unpatriotic and unsafe (their imputed cowardice and inability to communicate being posited as hazards during shipwrecks), even unionists accepted the premise that certain occupational hazards of maritime labour could only be resolved by hiring non-European workers.[41] In a series of legal contortions, the most servile jobs aboard steamships were gradually bundled into this logic over the latter nineteenth century, so that Asians and Africans were overrepresented not only in brutally hot engine rooms, but also among deckhands and service "boys". Simultaneously, the *Messageries* and *P&O* endorsed laws restricting non-European sailors from working above certain latitudes. The stance was less counterintuitive than it appears, since by selectively ratifying the critique of non-European workers as untrustworthy safety hazards, these shipping giants of the Indian and Pacific Oceans effectively cut off competitors in the Atlantic and Mediterranean from the gold mine of low-wage workers recruited in colonial territories.[42]

The commercial advantages of hiring subject-workers cannot be overestimated. Compared to Europeans, they were paid less, lodged in smaller spaces and ate in kitchens with less equipment. Perhaps most importantly, they had no unions and little recourse to consuls and colonial branches of the *Inscription*. Thanks to the ease with which subject-workers could be recruited at layover ports along the route, moreover, captains frequently menaced mutinous sailors with replacement. Citizen sailors, who, in the case of the *Messageries*, came largely from Corsica and Provence, might enter the *Inscription*'s database as early as 15 years old, and would contribute to a pension fund when they began work a few years later. By contrast, "indigenous" sailors were recruited in a far more informal manner, through "Serangs": brokers, translators and team leaders who coordinated relations between "indigenous" workers and the ship's officers. Subject-workers could be recruited at essentially any port of layover on the China Line, but for the *Messageries*, Aden and Hong Kong were particularly prominent hubs for recruiting Somali engine-room teams and Cantonese service workers ("boys" in colonial colloquialism).[43] As captains occasionally admitted, recruiting workers with dubious papers and only the fuzziest of official identities gave the *Messageries* wide latitude in disembarking subject-workers, as well as how and, critically, *where* to handle their complaints. Captains could, for example, choose to disembark or punish a Somali sailor of the Red Sea in French Djibouti or British Aden, depending on what suited them best, by turning a blind eye to shoddy papers or casting doubt on legitimate ones.[44] When the captain of the *Messageries* ship *Cordillère* became frustrated with his Indian engine-room team, meanwhile, he needed only a quick missive to contacts in the British government, and with a signature and a stamp, Indian subjects of the British Empire were transformed into subjects – for legal and punitive purposes at least – of a floating parcel of French land.[45]

Through the China Line ships of companies like the *Messageries* and *P&O*, a pan-imperial procession of subject-workers flowed, leaving behind a shadowy presence in company records. Usually recorded with catchall categories (Arab, Malay, Chinese, Indian/Lascar, black, etc.), individuals' names generally went undisclosed in voyage reports and administrative reviews, unless they had died, deserted or been implicated in a controversy – a sharp contrast with European colleagues, whose names, basic biographies and employment history figured regularly in the voyage reports and administrative reviews that captains and port agents submitted to company headquarters in Europe. The superiors reading those reviews never scolded their subalterns for careless bookkeeping. Indeed, relegating subject-workers to the administrative shadows was unspoken company policy.[46] The sketchiness of subject-workers' administrative status was reflected in the racial tropes with which they were evaluated. Racial tropes played important roles in justifying decisions over whom to hire, fire or transfer, but these tropes, steeped in "colonial common sense", were, of course, utterly manipulable.[47] Often enough, groups of workers who had been lauded for their race's ostensible docility and adaptability were fired for their race's impudence and stubbornness, only to be replaced by a new group of racialised workers, now deemed more docile and adaptable.

As the *Messageries* rode the wave of French imperial expansion, what began as a legal allowance to hire a few "indigenous" Red Sea workers for blistering engine rooms transformed into a sprawling network of labour recruitment, defined by a multiplicity of contracts, terms and paperwork regimes. To maintain their right to recruit imperial subjects, lines like the *Messageries* needed to argue that only subject-workers were sturdy and reliable enough for the gruelling labour of the steamship. To *expand* outsourced recruitment to a scale beyond any government's regulatory powers, however, subject-workers had to be portrayed as incompatible with stable, centralized recruitment systems; one group of subject-workers, in other words, would always have to be replaced and replenished by another.[48]

European workers, then, were not alone in fearing replacement by "natives". Those indispensable "natives" were utterly replaceable, too. Writing in 1919, after years of service, including on *Messageries* ships that spent the war dodging U-boats, the leader of an Arab engine-room team testified to the shock of that realisation. Pleading with *Messageries* bosses after learning that he and his team would be replaced by a Chinese crew, he wrote to his captain in phonetic French:

> in recompense and gratitude for our services, the company finds nothing better than to transform its crew and my command, to replace us, the Arabs, with Chinese. We are, it's true, children of the sun, but we have nonetheless a heart to love, a conscience to judge, and a spirit to appreciate, and I refuse to believe, my Captain, that your noble sentiments of humanity and equitable justice would be able to act in concert with the company for such procedures. . . .[49]

Whatever the captain's feelings regarding the heartfelt plea, bosses in Marseille remained unmoved. "Let the serang [team-leader] of the Arabs know", a superior wrote in response, "that we don't have to explain our reasons for embarking in his place a team of Chinese coalers". Indeed, not having to explain was one of the greatest luxuries afforded to the *Messageries* by its globalized labour network.

Their system of racialising the workforce and setting it into near-constant rotation afforded the *Messageries* more than just bottom-line savings and flexibility in hiring and firing. The practice also prevented meaningful relationships from developing between "European" and "Indigenous" crewmembers – relationships with the potential to transmit labour militancy between citizens and subjects. Officially, the unions castigated the employment of imperial subject-workers and denigrated those workers themselves (it took decades before the unions experimented with advocating equal pay and benefits), but there were exceptions on the ground, or rather, on the deck. At times, workers reached beyond the colour lines. In 1910, one China Line captain watched this unfold, when the leader of his Arab engine-room team issued a protest that included the line, "I lead a team of men and I don't even have the wages of a low-down European coaler who doesn't know how to do anything other than pour oil into a bucket".[50] As the captain investigated further, he found troubling implications in the reclamation, which struck him as anything but isolated. "We must never lose sight", he wrote to superiors, "of the fact that these men are in contact with the workers of the Workshops and the European coalers who, according to intelligence given to me by the mechanics, seek to catechize them and push them into militancy".[51] The company had good reason to fear sociality across racial boundaries, since their profitability relied upon racially stratified wages and working conditions. Contact between "European" and "indigenous" personnel could lead to pan-racial agitation for workplace improvements. For the *Messageries*, then, ensuring the failure of labour's "catechism" meant shuffling subject-workers as often as possible in a system of racialised substitution. The workforce was thus endowed with a permanent racial Other whose race was ever-changing.

During the First World War, as hundreds of thousands of French merchant mariners were drawn into the war effort, the *Messageries* accelerated efforts to hire Africans and Asians. For the first time, though, these subject-workers possessed the leverage to win substantial increases in wages and benefits, thanks to the scarcity of labour and the exceptional risks incurred by their wartime service. *Messageries* bosses may have feared that their fabled goose was running out of golden eggs, but with few options available to them, they stuck to their playbook of segregating and rotating the workforce by race. By the end of 1915, for instance, company directors in Marseille and Paris launched plans to replace more of the "European element" with an "Indigenous element". As the top technical advisor in the *Messageries*' Central Administration explained in a widely circulated memo, "given the difficulties created by the Unions [and] the less-and-less easy recruitment of European personnel, it would be good to take advantage of the conditions opened up by the war". To this end, European personnel would be phased out of new ships as much as possible; "Tonkinese" would be sought for the restaurants and cabin service; "Japanese, preferably", would replace the Chinese workers; and increasingly troublesome "Arab coalers" would be replaced by Indians, deemed "more intelligent than the Arabs".[52] When those Indian coalers outstayed their welcome in the *Messageries* roster, they were labelled weak and irritable, and Marseille sent its port agents instructions to replace them with Arabs, Chinese or Japanese.[53] Similar processes were playing out in British companies along the China Line.[54]

When the war ended, mass-mobilisation of organised labour led France to become the world's only country to extend eight-hour workday legislation to its maritime sector. With striking ships piling up in French ports along the China Line, a chorus of captains and company agents vented unprecedented disdain for their European personnel and called for increasing recruitment of Asians and Africans.[55] Before the rise of the maritime unions, such calls had been based on the unbearable conditions of steamship engine rooms; by the interwar, they were based on the unbearable character of the unionised sailor.

Conclusion

Maritime labour militancy extended well beyond the dockyards of major European port cities. A mobile proletariat, merchant mariners brought militancy with them to sea. To quell labour activism along its trans-Suez routes, the *Messageries* mobilised a vast network of port agents, consuls, captains, lobbyists, bureaucrats and police. In the struggles that ensued, maritime workers proved remarkably capable of outlasting their bosses and outmanoeuvring them in the interstices of imperial sovereignty. The mutinous mariners of the early 20th century took advantage of the fact that their worksite was a bundle of often-contradictory roles. After all, every steamship was a mobile coal plant for some and a floating luxury hotel for others; a profit-generating machine for private capital and an instrument of state power; a world unto itself and an emissary hopping from port to port with little regard for imperial boundaries. In such a setting, the conditions of possibility for workers were set by the politics of mobility and the peculiar nature of governance in the in-between spaces of empires. Ultimately, the ingenuity of steamship workers met its match in the company's racialisation and rotation of an informal workforce. By the mid-twentieth century, when maritime unions attempted interracial solidarity in earnest, new threats to organised labour were already appearing, not least among them automation.[56]

Notes

1 M. R. Loew, *Les Dockers de Marseille* (L'Arbresle: Économie et Humanisme, 1946); W. Sewell, "Uneven Development, the Autonomy of Politics and the Dockworkers of Nineteenth-century Marseille," *American Historical Review* 93, no. 3 (June 1988): 604–37; Pacini and Pons, *Dockers à Marseille* (Paris: Payot, 1996); B. Marnot, *Les Villes portuaires maritimes en France, XIXe-XXI siècle* (Paris: Armand Colin, 2015); J. Barzman, "Dock Labour in Le Havre 1790–1970," in *Dock Workers: International Explorations in Comparative Labour History, 1790–1970*, ed. S. Davies, C. Davis, D. de Vries, L. Heerma van Voss, L. Hesselink, and K. Weinhauer (New York: Routledge, 2017). Maritime historians have been urged to look beyond the docks more recently in M. Dusinberre and R. Wenzlhuemer, "Editorial – Being in Transit: Ships and Global Incompatibilities," *Journal of Global History* 11, no. 2 (2016): 155–62; Chaline, Knab-Delumeau, and Kowalski, "Le navire à la mer," *Revue d'histoire maritime* 25 (2019).

2 Ronan Viaud, *Le syndicalisme maritime français. Les organisations, les hommes, les luttes (1890–1950)* (Rennes: Presses universitaires de Rennes, 2015); J. Charles-Roux, "Les grèves et l'inscription maritime," *Revue des deux mondes. Tome 54* (November–December 1909): 124–46.

3 Dusinberre and Wenzlhuemer, "Editorial – Being in Transit"; J. W. Konvitz, "The Crises of Atlantic Port Cities, 1880–1920," *Comparative Studies in Society and History* 36, no. 2 (1994): 293–318; A. Vigarie, *Ports de commerce et vie littorale* (Paris: Hachette, 1979).

4 Michel Foucault, "Des espaces autres," *Empan* 54, no. 2 (2004): 12–19.

5 See R. Mawani, *Across Oceans of Law: The Komagata Maru and Jurisdiction in the Time of Empire* (Durham, NC: Duke University Press, 2018); William Walters, "Migration, Vehicles, and Politics: Three theses on Viapolitics," *European Journal of Social Theory* 18, no. 4 (2015): 469–88.

6 Via layovers in Naples, Port-Saïd, Aden or Djibouti, Bombay or Colombo, Singapore, Saigon, Hong Kong, Shanghai and Kobe.

7 Future research may uncover a second domain of strategic (as opposed to opportunistic) anti-labour practice in the *Messageries*' collaboration with the British Shipping Federation. As the co-editor of this volume, Alessandro Saluppo discovered the *Messageries* reacted to a massive seamen's strike in 1902 by writing to the federation. The founding of the *Comité Central des Armateurs Français* the next year suggests that the *Messageries* was seriously considering pooling resources with foreign firms, sharing blacklists and forming a transnational body of professional strikebreakers. See Alessandro Saluppo, "Strikebreaking and Anti-Unionism on the Waterfront: The Shipping Federation, 1890–1914," *European History Quarterly* 49, no. 4 (2019): 570–96.

8 M. Beneron-Couvenhes, *Les Messageries maritimes. L'essor d'une grande compagnie de navigation française, 1851–1894* (Paris: Presses de l'Université Paris-Sorbonne, 2007); P. Ramona, *Paquebots vers l'Orient* (Paris: Alan Sutton, 2013); P. Bois, *Le grand siècle des Messageries maritimes* (Marseille: Chambre de commerce & de l'industrie de Marseille-Provence, 1986).

9 Berneron-Couvenhes, *Les Messageries maritimes,* 406–7.

10 *Le Journal des transports: revue internationale des chemins de fer et de navigation* 14, no. 14 (1891): 417.

11 Today, the *Messageries* survives in the Marseille-headquartered container-shipping giant, CMA-CGM; the world's third largest, into which it was bundled in the 1970s. "An Entrepreneurial Adventure," CMA-CGM Group, accessed July 3, 2020, www.cmacgm-group.com/en/group/history/entrepreneurial-adventure.

12 Jules Verne, *Une ville flottante* (Paris: Hetzel, 1871).

13 For a discussion of this distinction, see Naina Manjrekar, "'Violent and Not Quite Modern?': Lascars and Everyday Resistance Across the Sail-Steam Divide," *Labour History: A Journal of Labour and Social History* 116 (2019): 29–55; see also M. H. Renaut, "L'Histoire par les Lois: Trois siècles d'évolution dans la repression des fautes disciplinaires de la marine marchande," *Revue historique de droit français et étranger* 80, no. 1 (2002): 23–56.

14 "Makeshift" conveys the French phrase, *équipage de fortune*.

15 Voyage Report of Commandant Cassanova, China Line, 1 September 1909, Messageries Maritimes (MM) 86, Dossier Voyage Reports of the Caledonien (1908–17), Chambre de Commerce & de l'industrie Marseille-Provence (CCIMP), Marseille, France.

16 Nowhere did this apply more than in the Suez Canal. See Valeska Huber, *Channeling Mobilities: Migration and Globalisation in the Suez Canal Region and Beyond, 1869–1914* (Cambridge: Cambridge University Press, 2013).

17 Ibid.

18 Voyage Report 22, China Line, Commandant Tivolle, 25 October 1912, MM 86, Dossier Calédonien Voyage Reports (1908–1917), CCIMP, Marseille, France. The term apache almost certainly derived from the North American Apache Indians; see Michelle Perrot, "Dans la France de la Belle Époque, les 'Apaches,' premières bandes de jeunes," *La Lettre de l'enfance et de l'adolescence* 67, no. 1 (2007): 71–78.

19 Voyage Report 22, China Line, Commandant Tivolle, 25 October 1912, MM 86, Dossier Calédonien Voyage Reports (1908–1917), CCIMP, Marseille, France.

20 The official police presence onboard *Messageries* ships was limited to officers (the company occasionally hired private detectives to investigate trafficking, and probably militancy as well, though I have found no record of the latter). Officers, especially the *capitaine d'armes* were entrusted with surveillance and police work, as was, to a lesser extent, the *maître d'équipage*, or boatswain. Even when acting in a police capacity officers' power to repress rebellious workers was limited by a determination not to attract unwanted attention from paying passengers and the fact that they rarely outnumbered the workers who they would be repressing (neither limit applied to port police). The thin police presence onboard such passenger steamships was reflected in remarkably frequent evasions of traveling convicts and soldiers.

21 Inquiry by Commandant Froment, 19 June 1913, MM 86, Dossier Calédonien (1908–17), "Incident à Colombo," CCIMP, Marseille, France.

22 Letter from the General Consul, 26 February 1913, MM 86, Dossier Calédonien (1908–17), "Incident à Colombo," CCIMP, Marseille, France.

23 "Legality of Action by Colonial Govt in case of mutiny tc. Arising on Foreign Ship lying in Colonial Port," March 1906, Foreign Office (FO) 372/28/59, The National Archives of the United Kingdom (TNA), London, UK.

24 "Mutiny of Chinese crew of SS Epsom at Naples and their Repatriation," March 1906, FO 369/25/32, TNA, London, UK.

25 "Attorney General to Lt. Governor," 3 March 1906, FO 372/28/59, TNA, London, UK.

26 "Ashmore to Daniels," 23 March 1906, FO 372/28/59, TNA, London, UK.

27 "Minute by Davidson," 9 March 1905, FO 372/28/59, TNA, London, UK.

28 "Lt. Governor – AMS," 27 March 1906, FO 372/28/59, p. 19, TNA, London, UK.

29 "Re. the Warrant to arrest the crew of the Russian S.S. 'Grigory Moerch'," 2 April 1906, FO 372/28/59, TNA, London, UK.

30 It would take another three decades, however, for the draconian disciplinary code to be fully overhauled. Renaut, "L'Histoire par les Lois: Trois siècles d'évolution dans la repression des fautes disciplinaires de la marine marchande," 23–56.

31 Hence for instance the pension that *Inscription* sailors received. Viaud, *Le Syndicalisme maritime français*, 13–20.

32 Voyage Report 21, Commandant Schmidt, China Line, 14 October 1900, MM 559, Dossier Yarra Voyage Reports (1893–1907), CCIMP, Marseille, France.

33 Ibid.

34 Ibid.

35 Voyage Report 19, Commandant Bruno, Madagascar Line, 14 September 1909, MM 551, Dossier Voyage Reports Yarra (1908–17), CCIMP, Marseille, France.

36 Voyage Report 8, Australia Line, Commandant Melber, April 1911, MM 86, Dossier Voyage Reports Caledonien (1908–17), CCIMP, Marseille, France; Voyage Report 22, China Line, Commandant Tivolle, 25 October 1912, MM 6, Dossier Voyage Reports Amazone (1919–20), CCIMP, Marseille, France; "Commandant Lapousse, China Line," 17 April 1920, MM 20, Dossier Andre Lebon (1919–21), CCIMP, Marseille, France; Voyage Report 11, China Line, Commandant Cousin, 19 October 1920, MM 20, Dossier Andre Lebon (1919–21), CCIMP, Marseille, France.

37 "Jaquemart (Chef du service maritime) au Gouverneur-général à Hanoi," 23 February 1910, IA/Dossier 2909, Saigon Inscription Maritime (1907–1913), National Archives of Vietnam Center 2, Ho Chi Minh City, Vietnam.

38 Jaquemart's files from the Saigon Inscription Maritime span IA/Dossiers 2909, 2808, and 27202 of the National Archives of Vietnam Center 2, Ho Chi Minh City, Vietnam.

39 Peter Borschberg, "The Seizure of the Sta. Catarina Revisited: The Portuguese Empire in Asia, VOC Politics and the Origins of the Dutch-Johor Alliance (1602–1616)," *Journal of Southeast Asian Studies* 33, no. 1 (2002): 42.

40 Viaud, *Le Syndicalisme maritime français*, 32–40.

41 Gopalan Balachandran, *Globalizing Labour? Indian Seafarers and World Shipping, c. 1870–1945* (Oxford: Oxford University Press, 2012), 122–30. A typical example of the

discourse can be found in J. Beaumont, *Ships – and People* (London: Geoffrey Bles, 1921), 20–21.

42 Berneron-Couvenhes, *Les Messageries maritimes*, 165–67, 490–92; Balachandran, *Globalizing Labour?* 126–28.

43 Paul Bonnetain and Louis Tillier, *Histoire d'un paquebot* (Paris: Quantin, 1894), 70–81.

44 The incoherence of Red Sea paperwork regimes is on vivid display in the Centre d'archives diplomatiques de Nantes' foreign consul files for Aden and Port-Saïd. See also R.I. Lawless, "Recruitment and Regulation: Migration for Employment of 'Adenese' Seamen in the Late Nineteenth and Early Twentieth Centuries," in *New Arabian Studies*, ed. R. L. Bidwell, G. Rex Smith, and J. R. Smart (Exeter: University of Exeter Press, 1994), 75–95.

45 "Note of 7 Feb. 1918". 7 February 1918, MM 152, Dossier Diverse Correspondence Cordillère (1912–20), CCIMP, Marseille, France.

46 At the time of research, voyage reports for *Messageries* ships were held by two archival centers: the Association French Lines in Le Havre and the Chambre de commerce et de l'industrie Marseille-Provence in Marseille.

47 Ann Stoler, *Along the Archival Grain: Epistemic Anxieties and Colonial Common Sense* (Princeton, NJ: Princeton University Press, 2009).

48 "La Ciotat" December 1919, MM 59, Dossier Diverse Correspondence Australien (1916–18), CCIMP, Marseille, France; see also, "Indiens, Arabes, Chinois. Amazone," 25 January 1918, MM 5, Dossier Diverse Correspondence Amazone (1912–18), CCIMP, Marseille, France.

49 "Lettre d'un surang," 12 December 1919, MM 6, Dossier Diverse Correspondance, Amazone (1919–1920), CCIMP, Marseille, France.

50 "Lettre de réclamation d'un surang Arabe," 17 March 1910, MM 165, Dossier Diverse Correspondence Djemnah (1903–1918), CCIMP, Marseille, France. See also, Voyage Report 17, 9 November 1917, MM 152, Dossier Voyage Reports Cordillère (1912–1920), CCIMP, Marseille, France.

51 "Lettre de réclamation d'un surang Arabe," 17 March 1910, MM 165, Dossier Diverse Correspondence, Djemnah 1903–1918, CCIMP, Marseille, France.

52 "Essais de l'Andre Lebon, Note sur le personnel subalterne," 5 December 1915, MM 19, Dossier Diverse Correspondence Andre Lebon, CCIMP, Marseille, France.

53 "Indiens, Arabes, Chinois. Amazone," September 1918, MM 6, Dossier Diverse Correspondence, Amazone, CCIMP, Marseille, France.

54 See, for example, TNA Ministry of Transport (MT) 23/785; TNA MT 23/621; TNA Home Office 45/13392

55 Voyage Report 10, Commandant Cochery, China Line, 31 May 1920, MM 129, "Chili" (1917–1922), Dossier "Indiens," CCIMP, Marseille, France.

56 For perspective, one of the world's largest container ships, the *Jules Verne*, belongs to the *Messageries*' successor, CMA-CGM. Longer than the Empire State Building, the vessel is operated by a mere 26 people; eight French officers and 16 Filipino crewmembers. "'Jules Verne', le plus gros porte-conteneurs du monde," *Le Parisien*, June 5, 2013.

8 In the name of constitutionalism and Islam

The murky world of labour politics in Calcutta's docklands

Prerna Agarwal

In December 1934, thousands of dockers disrupted imperial trading that passed through the Port of Calcutta.[1] They went on a strike, part of a series, for shorter working hours across the various ports in British India. Even though the demands of workers were in consonance with the recommendations of an imperial inquiry, the Royal Commission of Labour, the legitimacy of the strike as a "genuine" labour dispute dominated the official and public discourse. It being admitted only as an official afterthought (in confidential documents) that the strike was, in fact, a success from the point of view of workers.

The strike was led by a newly formed red-flag union known as Calcutta Port and Dock Workers' Union (CPDWU) with several nationalist-revolutionaries, communists and socialists in its leading body.[2] The colonial state perceived the strike as announcing the resumption of radical activity in Calcutta, in the aftermath of the Meerut Conspiracy Trial.[3] The radical leaders of CPDWU were arrested for sedition, strike pickets were violently repressed and CPDWU was declared an unlawful organisation along with several other labour and communist organisations. Such reactions reflected the deep anxieties of the colonial state faced with a militant labour movement, which was charged with revolutionary symbols and was associated with a range of self-identified revolutionaries in communist, socialist and nationalist traditions.[4] This article assesses the responses of the colonial state and how these shaped the labour movement in Calcutta's docklands.

The responses of the colonial state must be placed into the context of its dilemmas regarding the labour question as it emerged in early twentieth century India. Since the aftermath of the First World War, non-existence of labour organisations and any kind of official machinery for the resolution of labour disputes was considered to be a problem. The vacuum in the trade union field was being filled by red-flag activists in several major industries, and this was to remain the main official concern throughout the interwar period. The dock strike of 1934 was one of the first successful strikes marking the revival of militant labour politics in Calcutta's industrial neighbourhoods and proving the inadequacy of the Meerut Trial in stamping out communist activity. As the imperial authorities stepped up the repression, even the existing Trade Union Act of 1926 appeared to be too liberal as it allowed the formation of radical trade unions. The peculiar problem that the government faced was summed up by the Trade Union Registrar of the

Bengal Labour and Commerce Department thus: "I expect one day to receive an application from a union one of whose objects is to establish 'dictatorship of the proletariat', must I as a registrar, register the union?"[5]

Yet the imperial authorities were concerned that the repressive policies did not go against the "genuine" labour unions.[6] But these were hardly to be found on the ground. In the largest industry of Bengal, jute mills, the influential trade unions were of two types: red-flag unions or white unions, the latter emerging as a real threat to the existence of militant unions in a number of industries.[7] The white unions were characterised by their espousal of communal politics, which resulted in Hindu-Muslim riots multiple times.[8] In fact, the mastermind behind the formation of these unions was the rising star of Muslim communal politics in Bengal, Huseyn Shaheed Suhrawardy.[9] He would also come to hold the portfolio of Labour in the first provincial government of colonial Bengal (formed in 1937). The imperial authorities, it would seem, were cultivating conservative and communal trade unions, behind the scenes, even as they talked about the necessity of "genuine" trade unions.

The local allies of colonial rulers had different motivations for meddling in labour affairs. The emergence of labour militancy in the interwar period across industrial Calcutta threatened to unsettle the traditional authority of local clerics and politicians as well, at a time when Muslim communalist politics was gaining ground. The docklands were constituted by the poorest neighbourhoods of the city – Kidderpore, Mominpore and Watgang – also forming the largest concentration of working-class Muslims.[10] The docklands thus had fallen in the purview of Muslim politicians since the beginning of the twentieth century.[11] However, influential labour leaders among them were not always advocates of communalist politics or primarily used religion as a mobilisational tool.[12] From the mid-1930s onward, the Bengal Muslim League rose as a cohesive and formidable political party on the basis of religious nationalism. This was part of the communalisation trends in anti-colonial politics, which culminated in a frenzy of Hindu-Muslim riots in 1946–47.[13] It was in such a context that the dock neighbourhoods emerged central to popular mobilisation for communal politics, so much so that one historian even called Kidderpore as part of the "riot-zone of Calcutta".[14] The dockers, predominantly of Muslim origin[15] and migrants from UP, Bihar, particularly from the Darbhanga region,[16] and Orissa, along with the boatmen had participated in major riots as early as 1926.[17] The dockers as well as the seamen and the boatmen were thus to form an important constituency for a range of Muslim politicians looking to establish muscle power in the streets of Calcutta.

Taking a microhistory approach, this chapter focuses on the dock strike of 1934 and the modus operandi of dockers' unions. It largely relies on the intelligence documentation produced by the Special Branch of Calcutta Police, which recorded the everyday activities of radical political groups in the city's industrial districts in minute details. The records produced for the purposes of "keeping an eye" are highly abbreviated for the most part, but combined with occasional investigations which provide crucial detailing, enable us to place the accent on working-class agency, as well as reveal the murkier dimensions of labour politics.

They allow a reflection on how labouring aspirations, anxieties and militancy were finding an outlet into a bewildering mix of political causes, including varied visions of anti-colonialism. It is thus that the vantage point of the docklands discloses the antinomies of the responses of colonial authorities towards the radicalisation of politics of labour. It draws attention to the acceleration of communalisation of politics in working-class districts in the decade preceding the Partition of India, as the colonial government formed alliances with Muslim Nationalists, in an attempt to resurrect a dangerous and consequential counterweight. The research shifts the attention away from Muslim politics as played out in the legislative assemblies, municipal corporation, party offices and drawing rooms,[18] towards the streets of Calcutta's docklands, to highlight the embedding and congealing of political trends that would burst out into the open as the city was caught in between the Partition riots and waves of strikes in the post-war period.

The strike

The dock strike of 1934 had been planned for over six months and it initiated the establishment of a red-flag trade union at the Port: Calcutta Port and Dock Workers' Union (CPDWU). The dockers were employed as casual labour by stevedores through various contractors and not directly by the Calcutta Port Trust. In total, they numbered around 15,000–18,000 and were spread out in various parts of the port; a large number of them being unemployed at any given point.[19]

The strike must first be placed in a wider context. The Royal Commission of Labour had recommended limiting working hours at the docks to nine hours, with an allowance of three hours of paid overtime.[20] However, these recommendations were to be partially implemented after the strikes at all major ports. Between October 1929 and November 1937, there were several strikes of dockworkers at all the Indian Ports – Karachi, Rangoon, Madras, Bombay, Calcutta and Bombay (in that order).[21] In Calcutta, workers' demands included higher wages, shorter working hours, compensation for accidents and two days of leave in addition to government holidays. Separate demands for wages were formulated by the winchmen, the salt department and the chipping and painting department.[22]

In the winter of 1933, a few dockers of British India Steam Navigation, including the "pioneer" Mohammad Salim (a dockworker of Bombay),[23] who had known Charles Mascerenhas, an early communist and an associate of M.N. Roy;[24] a few members of the Labour Party, including one of its founders, Niharendu Dutt Mazumdar; and labour activists of M.N. Roy's newest organisation, the Indian Republican Party, decided to form a union of dockworkers and called it the Calcutta Port and Dock Workers' Union.[25] The secretary of the union was Shishir Roy, of the famous Sarishabari Bomb case, who was now a member of a "communist – cum – terrorist" group. The president of the union was another dockworker, Sher Khan, a winchman (a skilled docker) from Bombay originally from Jalandhar, who is described as a "follower" of Rajani Mukherji, leader of the Calcutta section of M.N. Roy's organisation. Rajani Mukherji was vice-president along with Md. Yusuf, also a winchman and the president of the Bengal Labour Party. Santi Ram Mondal, an ex-railway clerk, who had been prominent in organising the Lilooah Railway workshop strike of 1928 was also amongst the leadership of this union.[26] The profile of the union leadership indicates that the early communist groups attracted workers into their ranks. What's more, such workers were openly taking the risk of being associated with known communists and infamous revolutionary-terrorists. A few were even willing to travel across the country to organise other workers as was the case with Md. Salim; he was "a volunteer" of the Dock Workers' Union in Bombay and after his stint at the Calcutta docks, went to United Provinces to organise the peasants "under the instructions" of Mazumdar.

In the first meeting of the union, held in January 1934, radical speeches were made and red flags were hoisted.[27] A series of regular meetings and demonstrations followed till the end of the year. Ideas attacking the state as the '*mā-bāp*'(mother-father) of the employers and not that of workers were discussed by the activists. The police were identified as the "*fauj*" (army) of the employers. It was said that the workers must organise their own *fauj* and even a government of their own. Mazumdar even argued that workers "could not allow the government to exist if it failed to stop molestation of the workers". Union leaders constantly asserted that the workers were capable of fighting without the aid of the government or the police, which were in fact considered the enemy. In one of these meetings, Mazumdar in his characteristic grandiose manner extolled the collective power of workers, proclaiming "when the 7 ½ lakhs [750,000] workers in and around Calcutta were organised the police and the government would '*salām*' (salute) them". Continuing the reference to the army world, he argued that as the British government fortified its borders in Rangoon and Peshawar, so should the workers defend the entry points to the Port in Metiaburuz and Kidderpore during their strike. The various slogans of these meetings were "*Lāl Jhaṇḍā kī jai*" (Long live the red-flag), "*Communist International kī Jai*", "*Mazdūr Kisān Hukumat kī Jai*" (Long live the workers' and peasants' government) and "Long Live Revolution". In other words, radical ideas in the communist repertoire were discussed repeatedly, openly and rather consistently. Such ideas would have sounded very unusual to labourers who had witnessed politicians' speeches before, but rarely did any of them talk about the strength of working class, let alone about a government of workers and peasants.

This recently formed union held its annual conference in April 1934. Sher Khan "hoisted the communist flag with ceremony". A.M.A. Zaman led a "squad of volunteers wearing red sashes with inscriptions of CPDWU and the hammer and sickle emblem" and marched in front of the flag.[28] The resolutions that were passed were not only about the day-to-day problems of dockworkers. First of all, the changes in the Trade Disputes Act were criticised and the attitude of the government of India was "condemned" for renewing an act that helped continue "oppression of workers". The meeting popularised the May Day. Resolutions also warned the workers against the Municipal Corporation dominated by the Congress Party leaders. It reminded the audience that the corporation had called the police to shoot at workers during the scavengers' strike in 1928. Release of political prisoners and "labour workers" (which included the names of known communists) was also demanded. The annual conference of the union was an explicitly political affair, aiming to inform members of the important matters relating to the labour movement as well as the anti-colonial movement.

Meanwhile, as no concessions came for any of the workers' demands, the union took charge of the preparations for the strike, which included formation of a strike committee composed mainly of workers.[29] The strike, in contrast to the union, involved a large majority of workers – between 8,000 and 15,000 out of the total 18,000, according to different estimates presented in the Bengal Legislative Council, and it lasted for 20 days. Throughout the duration of the strikes, pickets were organised at the docks and at the offices of principal stevedores in charge of recruiting labour, and these often led to breakouts of violence since the police was heavily deployed in the defence of the stevedores and shipping interests.[30] Contemporary newspapers described the scenes of strikebreakers, mainly recruited among outsiders: Anglo-Indian youth, Chinese labourers and Coconada workers.[31] On the day the strike was to be discussed in the Bengal Legislative Council, around 7,000 strikers marched to the council house to present their petition.[32] Some even attended the session, leading *The Statesman* to report about the "unaccustomed visitors [the dockers]".[33] Because of the demonstrations and heavy picketing, the strike was seen as highly disruptive by contemporary observers, and as one of them observed, "the strike was a standing menace to the peace and tranquility of Calcutta not to mention the loss of trade",[34] or to put it in another perspective, it was a very visible labour dispute.

The entry of Suhrawardy and the making of a "white-union"

The strike ended in very curious circumstances still, which were reported in *The Statesman* as "Maidan Meeting Scenes". According to the newspaper, it was declared over in a meeting of at least 5,000 workers. Rajani Mukherjee announced that the union had received an assurance from the shipping agents that there will be no victimisation if workers resumed work and so, they should resume work.[35] After the strike was declared over by the activists of CPDWU, Huseyn Shaheed Suhrawardy, a member of the Bengal Legislative Council, arrived and told the workers that the shipping agents had refused to deal with the CPDWU because "it was influenced by extraneous considerations as distinct from the interests of the men" and the workers must form a new union under his leadership.[36] This was unusual; it was one thing for a member of the Legislative Council to discuss labour issues but another to actually come and give speeches to thousands of workers. In any case, a new union called the Calcutta Dockers' Union (CDU) was formed with Suhrawardy as the president and it was duly recognised by the Master Stevedores' Association (MSA) "as a *legitimate trade union* [emphasis added] formed in the interests of the workers".[37] The MSA refused to recognise unions such as CPDWU, which were "under communist or subversive influence".[38] Subsequently, the CPDWU was even declared unlawful along with a number of "communist" organisations in the city,[39] although, the stevedores remained sceptical of asking the workers to sign a document stating that they were no longer members of or had never been members of CPDWU as demanded by the shipping companies.[40] The dockers won a reduction in working hours by an hour,[41] and they were to be on board quarter of an hour before starting time (a reduction of 15 minutes from the previous starting time).[42] In addition, a strike agreement was drawn between the shipping companies, the MSA and Suhrawardy's CDU covering the major terms of employment.[43]

Suhrawardy was a deeply conservative man but with a good grasp of street politics and intimate connections with the criminal world of Kidderpore. Belonging to an elite ashrāf family, he was one of the rare Muslim politicians of the time to build links with the urban masses, which were to transform Muslim politics in Bengal in the decade leading to independence. As deputy mayor of Calcutta Corporation, he had been operating in the milieus of poor urban Muslims since the early 1920s. In one incident he enlisted the support of the Muslim butchers of Calcutta's Municipal Market through allowing the burial of their beloved *pīr* (saint) under the main drains of the meat section of the market, causing a lot of controversy amidst which the "butchers allegedly threatened bloodshed".[44] During the 1926 Hindu-Muslim riots, Suhrawardy was found with other Muslim public figures like the Ariff brothers, inciting violence from the mosques. He was also said to have connections with the city's underworld, so much so that the British government had thought of externing him from the province.[45] According to a biography penned by a family relative, he was so deeply affected by the riots of 1926 that he became one of the first to advocate the cause of Muslim communal interests[46] and championed them right through to the Partition of India. He was the organising secretary of Muslim League, held the Labour portfolio in the first provincial government, was the minister of supplies during the Second World War and the premier of Bengal in the post-war government. The man straddled the world of the streets and that of high politics.

With the opening of the possibilities of representation of Muslim maritime trade unions in the new provincial legislative assembly, a range of Muslim politicians, including Suhrawardy, had started taking systematic interest in the trade unions of the dockers and the seamen in the early 1930s.[47] By 1934, Suhrawardy had successfully engineered a split in the most influential of seamen's trade unions, Indian Seamen's Union and Indian Quarter-Masters' Union, to form the rival Indian Quarter-Masters' Union.[48] Through the establishment of CPDWU and the popular strike of 1934, dockers were developing a working-class identity; they were exploited but were capable of challenging exploitation, without the help of politicians like him. Not only did they participate in well-orchestrated strikes but (some) also in regular meetings and demonstrations, where symbols of revolutionary upturning of society such as the red flag and the hammer and sickle were openly displayed, songs of protest were sung and slogans such as "*Mazdūr rāj*" echoed. A politician like Suhrawardy was quick to realise the dangers of such self-expression of workers and assertions of working-class politics. He vehemently opposed radical ideologies like communism and fashioned himself as the great champion of anti-communism. The colonial government in Calcutta, on the other hand, had found an experienced politician as interested as them in dampening the rising radicalism of labour movements.

Suhrawardy presented a note to Sir Harry Haig of the Bengal Legislative Council on the "labour question" in January 1934. Here, he argues that "constitutional labour agitation" under the then government was "futile" and therefore, labour is being "captured by the attractiveness of Communist slogans". According to him, "Government should further broadcast anti-communist literature through newspapers and pamphlets, both vernacular and English. Today the propaganda is all one-sided and in favour of 'mazdur raj'". He added, "Persons must be trained with facts and figures, to speak and deliver lectures against Communism". He went as far as to say that since the reds have their organisers in the constitutional trade unions, the "constitutionalists" should have their men in the "red organisations" and the government can be of "great help".[49] He was helping give a practical shape to the government's drive against the communists in the labour field, placing the emphasis on conducting anti-communist propaganda, presumably to give the workers another worldview for interpreting their experiences and struggles, and providing for loyalist men to function in workers' milieu. Such functions were, in fact, better envisaged and performed under the leadership of a native politician like Suhrawardy.

The case of dockers' strike shows that the colonial state was receptive to Suhrawardy's offers, so much so that, the president of the newly formed CDU, which was recognised by the employers as soon as it was formed, was Suhrawardy himself. The shipping employers didn't need to look far, they found a "trade union leader" from within the Bengal Legislative Council, who was even to climb the ladder of colonial governmental apparatus to serve as a labour minister from 1937. The collusion between the employers, the colonial government and a section of the nationalist politicians could not have been starker. Moreover, it was commented in the official correspondence that:

> The strike was finally settled by the intervention of Mr. H.S. Suhrawardy, through whose good offices a new union working on *lawful and constitutional* [emphasis added] lines was formed. I refer to this for it shows that our action is in no ways directed against *bona-fide labour* [emphasis added] unions: we are fully satisfied that no such unions are affected by our action.[50]

In other words, a trade union which had been formed to break a popular strike was conveniently presumed to be "lawful" and "constitutional", barely a few months into its operation, never mind the criminal record of its president in successfully inciting religious violence. What follows will further shed light on the vacuity of the claim that CDU was a "lawful" trade union and explicate how in search of such "constitutional unions", the imperial authorities were aiding in the communalisation of politics in the labour world, at a time of rapid religious polarisation in Indian politics.

To start with the CDU was able to, in effect, disorganise an important strike as well as the red-flag union that emerged with the strike. The former union declared its loyalties to the colonial state as it made it clear that it would operate on "constitutional lines" at several moments. In effect, this version of "constitutionalism" only went as far as avoidance of strikes until absolutely necessary.[51]

For next couple of years, CPDWU found it very difficult to survive, as the CDU established itself under employer patronage but also that of the newly formed Bengal provincial government. Given the casual nature of work at the docks the main and most efficient strategy was the control of recruitment in the docks. In the chipping department workers were asked to present chits from Suhrawardy himself to get work. Certain *sirdars* were intimidated and told that no men will be employed under them by Suhrawardy's men, who were also known as *dalāls* (agents). Workers were told that if they attend meetings they will not be employed. They were asked to join the CDU. The stevedores themselves openly told *sirdars* "to go over the side of Suhrawardy". Many of the *sirdars* lost their work because of the strike and were not re-employed for over two years.[52] In 1937 again, 60 men were reported to be unemployed because the *dalāls* had decided so.[53] From then on, the two trade unions among the dockers would play a crucial role in securing work for coming decades. In 1949, an informant of Brocklebank Shipping line, reported, as a matter of fact, that the MSA mostly employed dockers of white union, while the dockers of red unions were employed mainly for government contracts.[54]

The second plank of mobilisation of labour adopted by the CDU was the instrumentalisation of religion among dockers who predominantly were of Muslim origin. The leadership of CDU, and Suhrawady in particular, became known for Islamic propaganda. Even though Suhrawardy himself was probably not religious, he was described by a contemporary as "totally unscrupulous, but not communal or religious. He ate ham and drank scotch and married a Russian actress".[55] Many workers perceived his politics to be deeply divisive and dangerous. For instance, Jafar Bhai remembered how Suhrawardy had suggested the Hindus and Muslims to march separately "at the foot of the monument at Dhurrumtolla" on the eve of the strike.[56] Rahim Bhai argued that the policy of Suhrawardy would lead to communal riots and all the union funds he is collecting will be used to "bury the workers who would be killed in communal strife".[57] He also noted how Suhrawardy, on behalf of the workers, had attempted to create divisions through the platform of the legislature as the labour minister. He had said: "Dear Muslims, separate yourselves. A Hindu is after all a Hindu. Why do you go and mix with them?"[58] Rahim Bhai concluded: "Thus they create divisions. All these leaders are the betrayers of the community".[59] Calcutta's red-flag activists identified the white unions as a real obstacle in the dock areas.[60] In fact, a major communal riot broke out in Titagarh jute mill town in 1938 in the aftermath of a general strike in the jute mills in 1937, as a direct result of communal propaganda.[61] The instrument of religion could also serve the purpose of mobilising to defend the empire. In May 1940, the union held a "prayer meeting" attended by 1,500 dockers for the victory of Allies in the war and proclaimed its support for Britain.[62]

The depth of impact on dockers can only be appreciated with a sense of the growing communalisation of politics around them. CDU's politics of sowing religious division was part of a wider strategy adopted by the all-India Muslim League from the mid-1930s onward under Jinnah.[63] Muslim League, a hitherto "aristocratic" party,[64] which now formed an important part of a coalition of Muslim parties in Bengal Ministry, was hyperactively building a popular base in Eastern India, including among the poor peasants and workers. The *Star of India*, the leading Muslim English daily (patronised by the British),[65] provides enough evidence to argue that the League was bidding for a mass base among the poor Muslims in the late 1930s for separatist politics. Labour issues were strikingly prominent in the *The Star*.[66] The popular discontents with Congress Ministry[67] in provinces such as Bihar and United Provinces were decried as ills of "Hindu rule" in headlines such as "Hindus blow up Muslim graveyard with dynamite".[68] The Bengal Ministry's tenancy reforms, in fact spearheaded by Krishak Praja Party (KPP),[69] were used excellently for mobilising support for the Muslim League among the peasants of Bengal and against the "Hindu" Congress.[70] As part of the same exercise, seamen, who also came from the East Bengali Muslim peasanty, formed a special focus. The *Star* published calls for help through financial donations and doctors when floods struck East Bengal[71] and a Seamen Bangia Sahajyo Samity (Seamen Flood Relief Association) was initiated.[72] Splits were engineered in the rival Indian Seamen's Union, and 45 seamen and dockers (including some members of CPDWU), along with one of the most important leaders of the Indian Seamen's Union, Aftab Ali, were implicated in a criminal case; charges included "conspiring to kill" the acting shipping master.[73] The jute mill workers, with a significant proportion of Muslims from Bihar and United Provinces, formed another important constituency for the League.[74] By the end of the decade, League propaganda was bearing fruit; it could boast of Muslim politicians, such as Suhrawardy and Fazlul Huq, being received in demonstrations of tens of thousands of workers on several occasions, in Calcutta and even in the outlying jute towns.[75] One such demonstration organised by a number of maritime unions associated with the Muslim parties was attended by 7,000, and "an address of welcome" was presented in a "silver casket" to Suhrawardy.[76]

The CDU was thus born and shaped as an employers' union under the twin patronage of shipping employers, and the Bengal Ministry, through the offices of the labour minister and Muslim League politician Suhrawardy. The colonial government aided one of the most reactionary politicians of the time to realise his vision of trade unionism; after all it was counterposed to "communist" unions. The union was one of the early ones of its kind and was to form part of a network of city-wide white unions, collectively part of the Bengal National Chamber of Labour, under the patronage of Suhrawardy.

As the subcontinent was drawn into the Second World War, and the colonial government's panic about labour reached new heights, the director of Intelligence Branch went as far as clearly stating that "white unions" are "officially sponsored".[77] The official discussions within the provincial government concluded that white union (and/or constitutional unions) men should provide relevant information to local police officers, and employers must assist in the smooth functioning of what was now known as the "White-Union system", to allow for "concerted action" between "H.M. (C.&L.)[78] – Police – Labour Commissioner – Employers – White Union".[79] The network for state repression of the labour movement could not have been more clearly laid out.

Of violence and volunteers

Even so, the CPDWU was never entirely silenced, it re-emerged as Dock Majdoor Union (DMU) to avoid illegality. As the rising prices and the uncertainties of the war added to the pressing material issues of the dockers, they contested the CDU's leadership and attempted to give the union a more militant shape. By 1941, the fragile coalition of Muslim parties in Bengal Ministry was witnessing another split and had ramifications for the balance of forces between the various Maritime trade unions, proving fortunate for the DMU to some extent.[80] Popular collective action continued to face enormous obstacles, but labour militancy was not so easily suppressed; it only found narrower and more dangerous channels.

The rivalries between the two unions intensified and, most significantly, were being imposed through armed as well as externally funded (to whatever extent) "Volunteers". Historians have noted the proliferation of Volunteer groups in interwar period in the Indian context.[81] Paramilitary groups, often armed and uniformed, were organised by political parties across the spectrum on national and regional scales to fulfil the urgent needs of defence against both the perceived internal and external enemies.[82] The term "paramilitary" has been used here to underline that such groups "sought state power or, proposed ethnic nationalism" and attempted to take on state functions in a period that became crucial in claim-making by conflicting nationalist forces.[83] Many such groups[84] became infamous for their dictatorial post-colonial visions, overt militarism and their espousal of fascist ideologies, methods and symbolisms. Nandini Gooptu has been one of the few historians to focus on the role of Volunteers among the urban poor; the interactions of Volunteers and labour politics have hardly received any attention.[85]

As early as 1934, the intelligence noted the practice of a march led by A.M.A. Zaman in the docklands, under the banners of "workers of the world unite". In fact, since the inception of the DMU, formation of a Volunteer corps was considered necessary, as Zaman argued in a speech "not for any breach of the peace but to keep order in their meetings and processions".[86] A resolution to form Jamiruddin Fauj was passed in July 1938 in the union's meeting.[87] It was named after a textile worker Jamiruddin, who had been murdered for not joining a company union.[88] In the late 1930s, Volunteer groups emerged in several industries; intelligence reports for the year 1938–39 mentioned a number of such groups mainly associated with Congress-linked Bengal Labour Association (BLA), Indian Seamen's Union and the two unions of dockers.[89] The labour Volunteers associated with the BLA disappeared from the radar by 1940.[90] In fact, Jamiruddin Fauj and the labour militia of CDU lasted for the longest duration, pointing to the strength of organised working class in the docklands as well as the higher prevalence of violence in labour relations.

Initially, such groups were set up to settle inter-union rivalries, but their field and scope of operation quickly expanded. Volunteers associated with both the dockers' unions enjoyed the patronage and functioned as part of a wider network of such groups in the city, which were in turn connected to national political parties. Jamiruddin Fauj at the docks was part of a citywide body organised by the Bengal Labour Party, whose members were often seen in public meetings "clad in red-shirts, khaki shorts and Gandhi cap".[91] They practised *lāthi*-play, held regular drills and had access to free uniforms at times. The organisers and office-bearers sometimes received pocket money. Most interesting are the links formed with two militaristic political organisations, which had found affinities with the Nazis. Bengal Labour Party actively sought alliances with Subhas Chandra Bose's[92] Forward Bloc and campaigned in favour of it among workers, and in return, Bose promised money for the party's Volunteers.[93]

Even more striking are the Bengal Labour Party leaders' ambitions of forming alliances with the Khaksar Tehreek (movement of the humble), the most militant of anti-colonial Muslim paramilitary groups in the interwar period. Khaksar leadership idealised dictatorship as a way forward for society, and its leader Allama Mashriqi (sage of the east) even claimed to have inspired the Nazis. The Khaksars carried spade on their shoulder, in a remarkable similarity to the symbols of Nazi *Reichsarbeitsdienst* (Reich Labour Service). Mashriqi advocated the domination of Islam through an organisation based on the values of militarism, obedience to the leader and unity.[94] In 1939, the intelligence mentioned that Khaksar had a strength of 3,000 in Calcutta alone, and it was the only Muslim Volunteer group that was labelled as "specially dangerous".[95] It was especially active in Kidderpore. The Khaksar uniform included khaki coats, breeches, belts, boots, putties, spades and Reza Shah Pahlavi caps.[96]

The Volunteers of the CDU, whose uniform included blue shirts, caps and *lāthis*,[97] formed part of closely associated Volunteer groups organised on religious-nationalist basis like the Muslim National Guard and the Khilafat Guards.[98] Even Khaksar men participated in some such joint activities.[99] Even though Khaksar and Khilafat volunteers had existed previously, the basis of an all-India Muslim League National Guard was laid by Jinnah in 1937. In Calcutta, the numbers of League and Khilafat Guards remained in few hundreds between 1938 and 1942.[100] They paraded during demonstrations of Bengal Ministry, or during Muslim League sessions, they attempted to police such mobilisations.[101] They protected the mosques, arranged relief measures even for events in Turkey, agitated for the Palestine question, demanded "boycott" of Congress and above all, the fight for protection of Islam was their battle cry.[102] These Volunteers had comparatively elaborate uniforms: League volunteers' uniform included green shirts, white shorts/pyjamas, green fatigue caps and half *lāthis*.[103] The Khilafat volunteers wore khaki coats and shirts, khaki round caps with a crescent and carried half *lāthis* and white badges.

In fact, Kidderpore emerged as one of centres of the activity of the Muslim League Volunteers, reflecting the close and the kind of relationship that the

Muslim League had fostered among the local habitants, a significant proportion of whom were maritime workers. For instance, one Muslim League volunteers meeting in the neighbourhood was attended by as many as 800, a number of "parties" from all over Calcutta arrived, including members of Khaksar and Khilafat. Most strikingly, some of the local ones were named as such: Kidderpore Muslim League (Boys group) under the leadership of Noor Mohammed, Hakim Liaqot Hossain's Party of Watgunge street, Abdul Latif Ostad's Party of Orphangunge Market, Kidderpore, Abdul Hakim and Bulaki's Party of Mominpore, Kidderpore, testifying to organisations constituted on a local level in the dock neighbourhood under a one-man leadership. The highlight of the meeting was "physical display", which included a stick, sword and bayonet play, and Jiu Jitsu.[104] The colonial government was strikingly tolerant of such displays of arms on the streets; these Volunteers were repeatedly labelled as "not dangerous", as opposed to the "potentially dangerous" Jamruddin Fauj and Khaksar Tehreek.[105]

Such popularity of a range of Volunteer groups in the docklands demands closer attention towards their function in the social and political life of maritime workers. An incident outside the office of a stevedore, on a payday in November 1941, exemplifies the role such groups came to play, revealing the ongoing criminalisation of labour politics, as well as the militant assertions of working-class anti-colonialism. Ziauddin Ahmed, nephew of Suhrawardy, and the secretary of the CDU, provided the following description of the incident. As the workers were being paid, a *sirdar* was pushing them to contribute towards the war fund. When a worker agreed to pay, the information was passed on to "organisers of Red-flag dressed in red shirt and cap" who were waiting outside the office. "At this the agitators became furious and assaulted Jaffar Khan as soon as he came out of the office". Ziauddin further claimed that the incident had "created a great panic in the minds of the loyal labourers", who in his view did not feel safe enough to contribute to the war fund anymore. The incident was narrativised differently in an official police inquiry. It revealed that there were clashes on the day after Badiur Rahman, a well-known worker-militant belonging to DMU, raised objections against deductions for the war fund stating that this union had a separate fund for aid to the Soviet Union. Several workers from both the unions were injured and arrested. Importantly, the intelligence didn't mention the presence of uniformed workers in contradiction with the report of Ziauddin.[106] Yet, the latter's version cannot be easily dismissed. Given that Jamruddin Fauj had been built for precisely the functions of armed defence of the red union, it is probable that the Volunteers were involved in the incident.

The main point of significance is that DMU worker-militants, whether uniformed or not, had taken up the risky and internationalist cause of opposing the war through not paying for the Allies war fund. This was not a one-off incident; small groups of workers had been agitating for the cause in the dock neighbourhoods. In one instance, eight workers of the union made a procession and one of them made a ten-minute anti-war speech. We do not have access to the full speech; the police only recorded that he had argued that workers shouldn't subscribe the war fund, since they were already paid so little, in front of a hundred workers. Dockers proclaimed, in a number of speeches, that they were collecting for the Soviet Union, making it clear that they were also contributing towards a larger issue if the rival union was collecting money to fight fascism under the slogans of "Hitler *Barbād* (destroy Hitler)".[107] They not only voiced anti-war opinions against supporting the British but felt (physically) strong enough to use violence against their opponents on an issue as ideologically charged as taking sides in the war. All this at a time when the government had an extremely repressive policy against any expressed scepticism let alone criticism of the war effort.[108] As far as we can see, this was not as a result of worker militants relying on the anti-war feelings of the wider layers of workers. It is more plausible to say that small groups of armed men, probably belonging to the Volunteers discussed earlier were imposing their power on rest of the workers. Moreover, there are indications that DMU was receiving protection from the Chief Minister Fazlul Huq[109] who was rallying the dockers against Suhrawardy at a time of a ministerial crisis. Historians like Gooptu have seen Volunteers as a crystallisation of subaltern radicalism in the face of perceived passivity of the mainstream nationalist parties.[110] This incident adds a crucial dimension by showing that such resistance was an expression of the few, such acts of resistance involved a handful of individuals, organised in disciplined and even armed groups, who relied on intimidation and violence to make their point of view publicly visible to the rest as opposed to popular actions. This was not the only incident. In the same year, the intelligence noted the high frequency with which the two rival unions clashed violently.[111]

In the same year as dockers associated with the Bengal Labour Party were showing their muscle power to publicly defend their lack of support for the British in the Second World War, an intelligence report noted that regular parades of Khaksar were being held close to seamen's lodging houses in the docklands, where they were seen wearing uniforms and *belćas* (spades). Notably, several of them even belonged to the Indian Seamen's Union,[112] which was close to DMU and Bengal Labour Party.[113] The same reports are suggestive of motivations for undertaking the risks of participating in such militant and militaristic anti-British spectacles. To start with, the reports all refer to a brief period during the war – May-June 1941, when Arab Nationalist Rashid Ali al-Gailani had just led an anti-British military coup in Iraq. Rashid Ali was seen as a comrade by the local Khaksars. The event had raised hopes that Khaksars too could play such a role in the Indian independence; an ex-sailor had even set up a shop in Kidderpore bazaar, from where he spread such ideas.[114] He was not alone, the intelligence worryingly noted that the cause of Rashid Ali, who "had been acting more in the interests of Islam than for any other power", had found favour among the local seamen, many of whom had just returned from the Middle East with a "defeatist mentality".[115]

In other words, notwithstanding the state's claims of assisting constitutional trade unionism, working-class anxieties, aspirations and militancy were finding outlet into a bewildering mix of political causes including varied visions of anticolonialism. Moreover, even the radical labour leadership, Bengal Labour Party in this case, not only advocated the defence of the Soviet Union somewhat under the protection of Bengal Ministry, it was already collaborating with Subhash Chandra Bose and was also hoping for alliances with Khaksar Tehreek. The latter was probably due to the pressures of party's seamen base. Thus, even as labour militancy was outpouring in widening visions of anti-colonialism and crystallising in red-flag trade unionism, the latter was already leaning on the forces of emergent nation(s)[116] as manifest in the Volunteer groups, to assume, impose and sustain the balance of power on its side.

The deep anxieties of colonial state vis-à-vis a rising radical labour movement made for strange bedfellows, forcing collaborations with the rising star of Bengal Muslim League – Suhrawardy, a popular, elite and conservative politician who had proven adept at instrumentalising and fanning religious fanaticism for high politics. The efforts at quelling a red-flag trade union born out of popular collective mobilisation opened the way for politics of patronage of the powerful communitarian parties, and of communalisation, abetting the building of a popular base for the Muslim League in the docklands. Notwithstanding the highly militant record and revolutionary claims throughout the period, red-flag trade unionism proved vulnerable to pressures of its political climate. Access to channels of emergent nation(s) was becoming important in running the show even for the most radical of unions. The modus operandi of Volunteer groups in the docklands exemplify such trends, pointing to the violence of the few becoming a determining factor in labour politics, even if for the time being. The post-war period saw another moment of collective mobilisation. Even so, the violent rivalries between CDU and DMU had been deeply entrenched. In the late 1940s, the former smoothly shifted its allegiances to the ruling Congress Party after independence and became an instrument in the hands of the new rulers for countering labour radicalism. Ironically enough, the CDU, which had been nurtured by the torchbearers of Muslim separatism, now found it opportune to cast DMU as belonging to "Pakistani communists".[117]

Notes

1 The chapter discuss the dockers employed through the stevedores, who provided skilled loading and unloading labour directly to the shipping companies. Another set of dockers were employed through the Bird and Company, the single largest contractor for those working at the sheds and warehouses. Their politics followed a different course and is not the subject matter of this chapter.

2 The characterisation "red-flag" or simply "red" was attributed by the employers and government officials, and in popular parlance, to a host of socialist and communist groups, and the associated organisations and unions that proliferated in this period at the port and in fact, in other industrial sites of Calcutta.

3 The most important of a series of trials in British India which attempted to nip the communist movement in the bud through charging communists with conspiring to deprive the king-emperor of sovereignty over British India. As part of the Meerut trial, the state attempted to outlaw communist ideology as such, by linking its adherents to the Soviet Union. Contrary to its purpose, the trial became key in launching communist politics across British India even as a number of prominent leftists were incarcerated. For details see Ali Raza, "Separating the Wheat from the Chaff: Meerut and the Creation of 'Official' Communism in India," *Comparative Studies of South Asia, Africa and the Middle East* 33, no. 3 (2013): 316–30.

4 It is important to note that these ideological divisions were not as clear-cut at the time. Even though the colonial government branded all those militant political groups active among labour as communists, they often held ambivalent and conflicting ideas as to the role of working-class *revolution* vis-à-vis the nationalist movement in the anti-colonial struggles.

5 West Bengal State Archive (Hereafter, WBSA), File no. 274/35, Cancellation of the certificate of registration under article 8 of Indian Trade Unions Act, 1926 – Question of amending the Act.

6 WBSA, File no. 304/35, Question in Assembly: Communist Organisations.

7 Nirban Basu, *Trade Union, Working Class Politics and Protest* (Kolkata: Progressive Publishers, 2019), 34–35. Subho Basu, *Does Class Matter? Colonial Capital and Workers' Resistance in Bengal, 1890–1937* (New Delhi and Oxford: Oxford University Press, 2004), 259–61.

8 Ibid.

9 At the outset, it is important to define communalism, a term that holds specific meanings in the Indian subcontinent.

Communalism refers to politics based on defending the interests of a religious community, as against the (perceived or real) threat of another, which often led to hatred, riots, and organised violence. Gyan Pandey shows how the politics of religion acquired the pejorative label of communalism from the 1920s, as a new vision of Indian nationalism took shape that attempted to rise above primordial divisions like religion and caste.

Gyanendra Pandey, *The Construction of Communalism in Colonial North India* (New Delhi and Oxford: Oxford University Press, 2006). For a historical and conceptual discussion of the term.

10 Janam Mukherjee, "Hungry Bengal: War, Famine, Riots and the End of the Empire, 1939–1946" (Doctoral diss., University of Michigan, 2011), 226–27.

11 Kenneth Mcpherson, "The Muslims of Calcutta, 1918 to 1935: A Study of the Society and Politics of an Urban Minority Group in India" (PhD diss., Australian National University, 1972), 56–57.

12 Nirban Basu, *The Political Parties and the Labour Politics, 1937–47* (Kolkata: Minerva, 1992), 116. For instance Mohammad Daud, an influential labour leader of the seamen, kept his distance from Muslim politicians as did Aftab Ali.

13 For instance, see Sabyasachi Bhattacharya, *The Defining Moments in Bengal: 1920–1947* (New Delhi: Oxford University Press, 2014), Ch. 6. For the rise of Hindu Communalism, in the same period, see Joya Chatterji, *Bengal Divided: Hindu Communalism and Partition, 1932–1947* (Cambridge: Cambridge University Press, 1994).

14 Suranjan Das, "The 1992 Calcutta Riot in Historical Continuum: A Relapse into 'Communal Fury'?" *Modern Asian Studies* 34, no. 2 (2000): 281–306, 294.

15 Basu, *Trade Union*, 332. According to one reference out of a total of 14,000 dockers, 9,000 were approximated to be Muslims from UP and Bihar, and 5,000 were Hindus from Orissa.

16 Royal Commission of Labour in India (hereafter, RCLI), v. pt. 2, 436.

17 Mcpherson, "Muslims of Calcutta," 166.

18 For instance, see Tazeen M. Murshid, *The Sacred and the Secular: Bengal Muslim Discourses, 1871–1977* (Oxford: Oxford University Press, 1995); Shila Sen, *Muslim Politics in Bengal, 1937–1947* (New Delhi: Impex India, 1977); Harun-or-Rashid, *The Foreshadowing of Bangladesh: Bengal Muslim League and Muslim Politics, 1906–1947* (Dhaka: The University Press, 2003).

19 RCLI, v. pt. 2, 436.

20 University of Gottingen Online Database [UGOD, hereafter], Monthly Reports of the Indian Branch Office of the International Labour Organisation, January 1933, Maritime Affairs, d) Hours of Work and Age of Employment of Dock Labourers: Efforts to elicit Opinion prior to Legislation, 70

21 UGOD, Monthly Reports, October 1929, Conditions of Labour, Dockworkers' strike Karachi, 18–19; April 1931; Conditions of Labour, Burmese Dock Labourers' Strike, Rangoon, 35–36; March, 1932, Maritime Affairs a) Dock Workers' Strike Bombay b) Dock Yard Workers' Strike, Madras, 77–79; December 1934, b) Dock Workers' Strike, Calcutta, 68–69; November 1937, Conditions of Labour, i) Bombay Dock Workers strike, 26.
22 WBSA, File no. 553, Prosecution of A.M.A, Zaman and others . . . in connection with the annual conference of Port and Dock Workers Union, Port and dockworkers Annual Conference 29 April 1934.
23 Ibid.
24 John Patrick Haithcox, *Communism and Nationalism in India: M.N. Roy and Comintern Policy, 1920–1939* (Princeton, NJ: Princeton University Press, 1971), 175.
25 All the descriptions of activists and their activity in this paragraph are based on the file (unless indicated otherwise): British Library (Hereafter, BL), Action taken under criminal law amendment Act 1908 against communist organisations, L/P&J/12/474, Note on the Calcutta Port and Dock Workers' Union, 38–41.
26 BL, L/P&J/12/474, Action taken under criminal law amendment Act 1908 against communist organisations, R.S.N. & I.G.N. Ry. Companies Labourers and Workers' Union, 64.
27 BL, L/P&J/12/474, Action taken under criminal law amendment Act 1908 against communist organisations, A note on the Calcutta Port and Dock Workers' Union, 41–51. The description of the meetings between January and December 1934 is from this document unless otherwise stated.
28 BL, L/P&J/12/474, Action taken under criminal law amendment Act 1908 against communist organisations, A note on the Calcutta Port and Dock Workers' Union, 43.
29 Ibid.
30 BL, L/P&J/12/474, Action taken under criminal law amendment Act 1908 against communist organisations, A note on the Calcutta Port and Dock Workers' Union; Bengal Legislative Council Proceedings 1934 [Hereafter, BLCP], Motion of Adjournment, 105.
31 BLCP, Motion of Adjournment,106.
32 *The Statesman*, [date unclear].
33 *The Statesman*, December 13, 1934.
34 BLCP, Motion of Adjournment, 120.
35 *The Statesman*, December 17, 1934.
36 Ibid.
37 National Maritime Museum in Greenwich, London (Hereafter, NMM), IPC/3/12, Calcutta Liners Conference, Minutes of the proceedings of a meeting of the Calcutta Liners Conference held at the Royal Exchange, 3 Clive street, Calcutta on the 1 April 1935, Calcutta Port and Dock Workers' Union.
38 Ibid.
39 BL, L/P&J/12/474, Action taken under criminal law amendment Act 1908 against communist organisations.
40 NMM, Calcutta Liners Conference, Minutes of the proceedings of a meeting of the Calcutta Liners Conference held at the Royal Exchange, 3 Clive street, Calcutta on the 1 April 1935, The Calcutta Port and Dock Workers' Union.
41 *Trade Union Record*, February 1935; KPTMA, 6612/2/II, *Calcutta Port Trust Worker*.
42 NMM, Calcutta Liners Conference, Minutes of the proceedings of a meeting of the Calcutta Liners Conference held at the Royal Exchange, 3 Clive street, Calcutta on the 13 May 1935, Stevedores Labour: Hours of work under the strike agreement.
43 NMM, IPC/3/12, Calcutta Liners Conference, Minutes of the Proceedings, reports for the year 1935.
44 McPherson, "Muslims of Calcutta," 148–49.

45 Ibid., 167, 171–72; Chatterji, *Bengal Divided*, 81.
46 Begum Shaista Suhrawardy Ikramullah, *Huseyn Shaheed Suhrawardy, A Biography* (New Delhi: Oxford University Press, 1991), 25–26.
47 Mcpherson, "Muslims of Calcutta," 249–51.
48 Ibid.
49 PC Joshi Archives of Contemporary History, JNU, New Delhi, Labour 1934/ 70, Notes on the Labour Question and the Congress Parliamentary Board by Shri H.S. Suhrawardy, M.L.C.
50 WBSA, File no. 304/35, Question in Assembly: Communist Organisers.
51 Kolkata Police Museum (Hereafter, KPM), KPM/SB/03128/05, Calcutta Dockers' Union, 1940; KPM/SB/03127/05, Calcutta Dockers' Union, 1938.
52 WBSA, File no. 105/35, Proposed prosecution of Rajani Mukheriji and Shamsul Huda for objectionable speeches under section 124 A of the Indian Penal Code.
53 WBSA, File no. 389/37, Proposed prosecution of Abdul Rahim@ Rahim Bhai.
54 Merseyside Maritime Museum, Liverpool, B/BROC/5/2/11, Report by Mr E.C. Cottingham and Mr. E.A. Newland on their visit to India and Ceylon, etc. 1948–49.
55 Chatterji, *Bengal Divided*, 84.
56 WBSA, File no. 105/35, Proposed prosecution of Rajani Mukherji and Shamsul Huda for objectionable speeches under section 124 A of the Indian Penal Code.
57 Ibid.
58 WBSA, File no. 105/35, Proposed prosecution of Rajani Mukherji and Shamsul Huda for objectionable speeches under section 124 A of the Indian Penal Code.
59 Ibid.
60 KPM/SB/00–90/05, Labour News Service; KPM/SB/00513/05, Bengal Labour Party – Trade Union Activities, Dock Mazdoor Union (BLP), August 1939.
61 Basu, *Does Class Matter*, 258–59.
62 KPM/SB/03128/05, Calcutta Dockers' Union, 1940.
63 A number of scholars have written about the rise of Muslim separatist politics from the mid-1930s onward under the leadership of Muslim League. A trend which eventually culminated in the partition of the subcontinent, in the face of Congress intransigence. Separatist politics refers to the nationalism of religion, or communalism, which increasingly came to eclipse other trends in Muslim politics. It asserted that Muslims were a separate nation on the Indian subcontinent and foregrounded the idea of a Muslim "community" as something homogenous. The other side of the coin was the rise of Hindu communalism and the hardening of religious differences within the subcontinent's population, which broke out in a number of religious riots.

    For United Provinces, see Francis Robinson, *Separatism among Indian Muslims: The Politics of the United Provinces' Muslims, 1860–1923* (Oxford India Paperbacks. New Delhi: Oxford University Press, 1993); Pandey, *The Construction of Communalism in Colonial North India*; for Bengal, Sen, *Muslim Politics in Bengal, 1937–1947*.
64 Mcpherson work is the only one of its kind that charts out the rise of Muslim politics from a marginal trend in 1918–19 to a major urban political force in Bengal politics, with a base among merchants, artisans, ratepayers and trade unionists by 1936.
65 Basu, *Does Class Matter*, 232–33.
66 See for instance, *The Star*, July 15, 1939; August 4, 1938.
67 *The Star*, July 12, 1938.
68 *The Star*, August 3, 1938.
69 Chatterji, *Bengal Divided*, 105. Krishak Praja Party (KPP), literally the Peasants and Tenants Party, was a populist rich-middle peasant party and was not an overtly communal organisation.
70 Chatterji, *Bengal Divided*, 121–22.
71 *The Star*, September 28, 1938.
72 *The Star*, September 19, 1938.
73 *Advance*, August 12, 1938; July 11, 1938. KPM/SB/00225/05, Search of 4 Puddapukur Square on 24 January 1940 (Dock Majdoor Union).

74 *The Star*, September 19, 1938; August 8, 1938; August 11, 1938; August 15, 1938.
75 Ibid.
76 KPM/SB/03127/05, Dockers' Unions.
77 KPM, SB File no. SM-572/40, Action under the defence of India Rules against Communist and Labour agitation.
78 Her Majesty (Commerce and Labour), a reference to the Labour and Commerce Department of the Bengal Ministry.
79 KPM, SB File no. SM-572/40, Action under the defence of India Rules against Communist and Labour agitation.
80 KPM/SB/03128/05, Calcutta Dockers' Union, 1940.
81 Nandini Gooptu, *The Politics of the Urban Poor in Early Twentieth-Century India* (Cambridge and New York: Cambridge University Press, 2001); Markus Daechsel, *The Politics of Self-Expression: The Urdu Middle-Class Milieu in Mid-Twentieth Century India and Pakistan* (London and New York: Routledge, 2006); Ian Talbot, "Crowds, Ceremonials and State Symbolism: The Role of the Muslim National Guards in the Pakistan Movement," in *Freedom's Cry: The Popular Dimension in the Pakistan Movement and Partition Experiences in North-West India*, ed. Ian Talbot (Karachi: Oxford University Press, 1996), 59–80; Ian Copland, "'Communalism' in Princely India: The Case of Hyderabad, 1930–1940," *Modern Asian Studies* 22, no. 4 (1988): 783–814.
82 For an account that brings an all-India perspective to the volunteer groups and places the history in that of global fascism, see Ali Raza and Franziska Roy, "Paramilitary Organisations in Interwar India," *South Asia: Journal of South Asian Studies* 38, no. 4 (2015): 671–89.
83 Ibid., 673–74.
84 A conservative estimate suggests that the total membership of all volunteer groups was 94,247 in 1940. Raza and Roy, 685.
85 Gooptu, *The Politics of the Urban Poor*.
86 WBSA, File no. 553/1934, Prosecution of A.M.A. Zaman and the others.
87 KPM/SB/00716/05, Gist of the review of the weekly "*Sathi*" dated 27 July 1938.
88 KPM/SB/00716/05, "Mazduro ke liye comrade Jamir shaheed (Comrade Jamir becomes a martyr for the cause of workers", in *Sathi*.
89 KPM/SB/02574/05, Volunteer Organisations, 1938.
90 Ibid.
91 KPM/SB/00513/05, Bengal Labour Party – Trade Union Activities.
92 Subhas Chandra Bose, a well-known nationalist leader from Bengal, was a proponent of armed struggle against the British and was a leading figure of the left-wing in Indian National Congress. During the Second World War, Bose, who had been an admirer of Mussolini, is most known for his collaboration with the Nazis and setting up the Indian National Army (INA) in South East Asia.
93 KPM/SB/00513/05, Bengal Labour Party – Trade Union Activities.
94 Raza and Roy, 680–88.
95 KPM/SB/02574/05, Volunteer Organisations, 1938.
96 Ibid.
97 Ibid.
98 KPM/SB/02423/05, Muslim League National Guard.
99 Markus Daeshsel, "Visionary of Another Politics: Inayatullah Khan 'al-Mashriqi' and Pakistan," in *Muslims against Muslim League*, ed. Ali Usman Qasmi and Megan Eaton Robb (Cambridge: Cambridge University Press, 2018). The article discusses the relationship of Khaksars with the other Muslim nationalist parties. Khaksar leadership had a vision of united Hindustan and thus, sustained a hostile relationship with the Muslim League.
100 Ibid.
101 KPM/SB/02423/05, Muslim National Guard, 1938, Extract from a note from D.C., S.B. to C.S., H.D., giving brief histories and an account of the recent activities of major volunteer organisations operating in Calcutta.

102 KPM/SB/02423/05, Muslim National Guard, 1938.
103 KPM/SB/02574/05, Volunteer Organisations, 1938.
104 KPM/SB/02423/05, Muslim National Guard, 1938, Kidderpore Muslim League.
105 KPM/SB/02574/05, Volunteer Organisations, 1938.
106 KPM/SB/03128/05, Calcutta Dockers' Union, 1940.
107 Ibid.
108 Sanjoy Bhattacharya, *Propaganda and Information in Eastern India, 1939–1945: A Necessary Weapon of War* (Richmond: Curzon, 2000), 135–39; Prerna Agarwal, "Planting the Red-flag: Early Communists and the Politics of Labour at the Port of Calcutta, 1920s-1940s" (Unpublished PhD diss., Kings College London, 2018). For accounts of state repression of meetings and processions in the wartime.
109 KPM/SB/03128/05, Calcutta Dockers' Union, 1940.
110 Gooptu, *The Politics of the Urban Poor*, 416–18.
111 KPM/SB/03128/05, Calcutta Dockers' Union, 1940, Re: Creating frictions and parties among the Dockers' labourers by the interested Stevedores.
112 KPM/SB/03123/05, Shipping Strikes, 1938, Memorandum, Central Intelligence Office, 20 June 1941.
113 KPM/SB/03123/05, Shipping Strikes; KPM/SB/03128/05, Calcutta Dockers' Union, 1940. The Dock Majdoor Union was even "merged" with the Indian Seamen's Union temporarily in 1938.
114 KPM/SB/03123/05, Seamen's Movement, 12 June 1941.
115 KPM/SB/03123/05, Seamen's Movement, 5 June 1941.
116 The terminology is used to underline that the various nationalist parties (in provincial government and outside) were assuming some state functions in the lead up to independence.
117 KPM/SB/5891/09, Calcutta Dockers' Union, 1949.

9 Cairo, Athens, Salonica: strikebreaking and the anti-labour practices of employers and the state in the early twentieth-century cigarette industry

Thanasis Betas

Strikebreaking often plays a central role in accounts of the violence that has been perpetrated in the struggles between labour and capital in history. It has been argued that violence was a popular and often successful strategy for employers in the United States prior to the federal labour legislation of the 1930s. As Joshua Rosenbloom notes, one of the most visible and contentious expressions of the increasing pressures of competition in late nineteenth-century American labour markets was the widespread use of strikebreakers. The factories seem to have had no trouble in finding "scabs" to do the work. The ability of employers to replace striking workers was one of the most potent weapons they had in their efforts to defeat the demands of organised labour for improvements to employment conditions.[1] Replacement workers were used in more than 40 per cent of late nineteenth-century strikes, and if strikebreaking was also used, then there was a great likelihood that the employer would defeat the strike. A variety of factors appear to have influenced the relative supply and hence cost of recruiting replacement workers, in particular the fact that the pool of potential replacement workers was larger in industries and occupations that did not require specialised skills.[2]

Strikers were very often exasperated by the thuggery and coercion used by entrepreneurs during the strikes that broke out in American factories in the late nineteenth century. A wide array of private and government forces were brought in to suppress the strikes. Beginning in the late nineteenth century, private detective agencies supplied guards who protected company property against strikers and would sometimes even assault them. During the early twentieth century, several firms appeared that supplied strikebreakers and guards at the request of companies, drawing on what amounted to private armies of thousands of men. The largest of these operated nationally. On many occasions the state itself intervened to break strikes. As with some of the strikebreaking firms, state militiamen deployed advanced weaponry against strikers and their sympathisers, including machine guns. Firms initiated "back to work" movements to destroy the strikers' morale and used their considerable influence with the media to propagandise in the press and on the radio.[3] Whatever the case may be, employers did not simply sit back and accept the strikes of the workers.

Instead, they staged a fightback against the unions, sometimes through lawsuits and legislation, sometimes with the use of violent thugs. As Matteo Milan has argued, "the American case is certainly a clear archetype in terms of the violent counter positions between 'capital' and 'labour'... [with] images of brutal police forces employed in the services of private interests". Yet, as he notes, the violence used against strikers was not only applied in the USA in the nineteenth century but in Europe as well.[4] Recent studies have shown that in certain sectors of British industry – shipping, for example – there was a clear tendency "to employ violent, illegal and inherently subversive means to protect the management from both the opposition of trade unions and the increasing encroachment of the state into industrial matters".[5] In analysing the practices of violence during the strikes in Habsburg Austria from the 1890s until the outbreak of the First World War, Claire Morelon argues that violent confrontations between strikers, strikebreakers and the state forces that were protecting them frequently occurred. This is further evidence that industrial vigilantism and patterns of anti-labour violence occurred not only in the USA but in Europe as well at the turn of the twentieth century.[6] These penetrating studies have undoubtedly broadened the research in the field of strikes and strikebreaking, illuminating the methods used by the state and employers in European countries to deal with them. Nevertheless, the structure of violence in the Pre-First World War period remains less explored, especially with regard to the public-private interplay in the policing of labour protests in other geographical contexts.

In this chapter I thus focus on the strikes that broke out at the beginning of the twentieth century in cigarette-making factories in three different urban and industrial environments in the South-East Mediterranean – Cairo, Athens and Salonica – which are located at the periphery of capitalist growth. What were the demands of the workers? What attitudes, practices and discourses did employers and the state adopt and express against the strikers? What were the factors involved in the strikes and how did they shape anti-labour ideologies, discourses and practices of employers and the state? What similarities and differences can be observed among the cases examined and how can they be interpreted? By utilizing a comparative approach, this chapter seeks to offer answers to those questions. Drawing on newspapers and archival records, the chapter will highlight the policies and strategies of the state and employers vis-à-vis the strikes that broke out in the cigarette-making industry in the early twentieth century.

The central question is how and for which reasons were the anti-labour ideologies, discourses and practices of employers and the state shaped. I argue that the mechanisms adopted to control the labour protests were not monolithic or inflexible and one-dimensional. Instead, they covered a wide range of possibilities, from violent suppression, to the adoption of consensual methods and paternalistic mechanisms which aimed to manipulate labour protests and weaken trade unionism. This chapter will first present a broad overview of the branch of cigarette making in three different countries of the South-East Mediterranean – the Ottoman Empire, Greece and Egypt – in the late nineteenth century, with an emphasis on the shape of the labour market and tax system and their consequences for cigarette makers. This will be followed by an analysis of the case of Cairo and the protests by cigarette makers that broke out in that city at the dawn of the twentieth century. Our attention will then turn to Athens, finally to move north to Salonica, a city that was part of the Ottoman Empire until 1913.

Labour market

In the early 1880s, the Ottoman Empire established the Tobacco Régie (*Régie co-intéressée des Tabacs de l'Empire Ottoman*) with the participation of Ottoman and foreign banks. The Tobacco Régie had a monopoly over the tobacco market, exports and sales, and its purpose was to enable the Ottoman Empire to control tobacco revenues so as to service its external debt.[7] Apart from Istanbul, in other urban areas of the empire too tobacco and cigarette production employed a great number of male and female workers in the late nineteenth and early twentieth centuries. In Izmir, Samsun and Salonica, the monopoly tobacco factories employed around 1,400 women and men in total. In Salonica, industrial tobacco processing had previously been the main "industry" of the city, both in the final era of the Ottoman Empire and in the interwar period. The headquarters of Greek, Jewish, Armenian and American companies were located in Salonica, whose work involved preparing and exporting leaves and, in a very few cases, making cigarettes.[8]

The monopoly over the market meant that the tobacco sector came to be abandoned by several Greek capitalists, who sought a friendlier investment environment in the cigarette-making sector. This they found in the neighbouring country of Egypt. Cigarette makers, specialised male technicians who made cigarettes by hand, would also go to Egypt for work opportunities, since their craft was highly sought after. In Egypt, where the tax system did not impose a monopoly, cigarette production in the late nineteenth and early twentieth centuries was performed mainly by small and medium-sized businesses – some of which later grew into large tobacco industries – in which the specialised cigarette makers were men, who were highly sought after because of their craft. This enabled them to develop a strong trade union activity and in many cases disputes with their employers evolved into open conflicts.[9]

In Greece, there was no significant pre-industrial craft industry for the manufacture of tobacco products, whether cigar or cigarette making, as was the case elsewhere. The history of the handmade cigarette-making sector in the country, even though rather brief – dating from the end of the nineteenth century to the mid-1930s – is linked to the social, cultural, political and economic conditions of the period. Handmade cigarettes were the most popular tobacco product in the early twentieth century as they were smoked by the younger population and women, resulting in the constant expansion of the market. In Greece, tobacco processing – cutting and cigarette making for sale on the domestic market, in contrast to the processing sector, where selection and packaging were carried out – had become a state monopoly by the end of the nineteenth century. An 1883 law, passed after the introduction of a tax on tobacco by the government of Harilaos Trikoupis, established 80 public tobacco factories in various towns throughout the country. As stipulated by law, tobacco-cutting could only take place in public tobacco factories and the tax paid on cut tobacco was to be paid within the factories.[10] At the same time, cut tobacco processing would also take place in these facilities and be used to make tobacco products, such as cigarettes, cigars and pipe tobacco. As a result, small family businesses, those which channelled cut tobacco and cigarettes onto the domestic market, were forced to "acquire" their own space within public tobacco-cutting facilities.

After 1892, tobacco processing – cutting and cigarette making – stopped being an exclusive privilege of the state and the operation of private tobacco factories was permitted, albeit under the supervision of directors and officials from the public tobacco factories.[11] Handmade cigarettes had to be made in public tobacco factories but by male technicians – cigarette makers – chosen exclusively by the interested manufacturers. Thus, the state personnel would work in public tobacco factories that were subject to the state, but they were paid by the businessmen to whom they were attached.[12] The introduction of cigarette-making machines and the attempt to mechanise the sector in the early twentieth century provoked severe reactions on the part of the cigarette makers and led to open conflict between them and their employers.

Cairo

To understand the position taken by the Greek tobacco industrialists and the Egyptian government against the cigarette makers, we must also consider the international economic context in which the previously mentioned events took place just as much as the characteristics of those enterprises. The upturn in economic activity and the growth in international trade in the second half of the nineteenth century – after the great depression of the years 1873 to 1895 – brought international capital to the expanding Egyptian cigarette market: first, the British American Tobacco Company (TBA) and later the Eastern Tobacco Co, which took over Maspero Freres Limited, the sole British tobacco firm in Egypt, and gradually acquired Greek tobacco firms such as S.A. des Tabacs et Cigarettes Papatheologos and S. Mavridis Ltd.

As has already been mentioned, in May 1883 the Ottoman Monopoly over the tobacco trade was taken over by the newly founded company of the *Regie Cointeresse des Tabacs de l' Empire Ottoman*, which was to constitute the largest foreign investment in the empire. The monopolistic privileges of the Regies and its dominant presence put serious pressure on the existing tobacco firms, resulting in some of the companies being priced out of the market and they instead transferred to other parts of the world, such as the USA and Germany. The main place to which they relocated, however, was Egypt, specifically Cairo and Alexandria, where the invasion of the British army in 1882 changed the economic and business landscape of this Ottoman region. Many Greek tobacco dealers and craftsmen settled in Egypt, where they became involved in the tobacco trade and in cigarette making, establishing the first cigarette workshops and factories.[13] The

Koutarellis Brothers cigarette company was established in Alexandria, Egypt, by Konstantinos, Dimitrios, and Alkiviadis Koutarellis in 1890.[14] At the beginning of the twentieth century, the company modernised its machines and buildings. In 1920, it built its own privately owned factory, installing a large number of state-of-the-art cigarette-making machines and special tobacco-cutting machines and increased the technical staff. The factory underwent a series of improvements from the 1920s onwards and by the eve of the Second World War, it covered an area of 5,000 square metres.[15]

When analysing the causes behind the choice of Egypt historian Christos Chatziiosif points to the shaping of an important and dynamic tobacco market, thanks to the presence of the British army of occupation, the European communities and the large number of travellers passing through on their way to and from the East. The addiction of these consumers, who would at some point return to their homelands, created the conditions for significant exports of cigarettes to European countries.[16] The formation of a free market without any restrictions, promising significant profits thanks to exports, attracted Greek tobacco industrialists as well as cigarette makers.[17]

By the end of the nineteenth century, many Greeks would go to Egypt to learn the art of cigarette making and then return to their home regions to practice the art there. Manolis Karathanasis, one of the founders of the tobacco company of Samos mentioned earlier, went to Egypt – it is not known for how long – to "specialize" in handmade cigarette making.[18] If we go by the advertisements placed in the Greek press by Greek tobacco companies, then Egyptian cigarettes, as well as the specialised cigarette makers who came from that country, were highly valued in the Greek market. For example, an advertisement of the I Proodos company, which belonged to the Karakitis Brothers and was established in Volos at the end of the nineteenth century, boasts that its handmade cigarettes are of the same quality as those from Cairo and Alexandria, having been prepared with the same method used by cigarette makers in Egypt.[19]

Greek-owned cigarette factories in Egypt were of various sizes and with unequal degrees of production mechanisation. Machines were used only in some early production phases, such as tobacco-cutting, while cigarette packing and rolling were done by hand until the end of the nineteenth century.[20] It was in this phase of production that Greek tobacco company owners had the greatest comparative advantage because, aside from importing Eastern tobacco, they were also able import a cheap and specialised workforce composed of Greek cigarette makers.[21] However, this advantage was not due solely to the use of specialised male cigarette makers but also to the use or, more correctly, exploitation of the broader workforce, including both women and children.

Cairo in around 1900, then, was home to an advanced handmade cigarette sector and numerous tobacco factories, strengthening the position of the cigarette makers. The Greek cigarette makers organised to vociferously demanded higher wages and better working conditions through a series of strikes that took place from 1899 to 1902. More pertinently, their primary concern was to maintain the control of the labour process. Their employers at the tobacco company, however, were more concerned to ensure this did not happen and sought to undermine the position of the skilled Greek cigarette makers by having them be accompanied or even gradually replaced by two other types of less-skilled local workers, the so-called "macaronists" and "sorters".[22]

The Greek cigarette makers of Egypt, along with their Italian and German colleagues, actively participated in these strike actions. The strikes were, however, violently suppressed by the tobacco company employers with the aid of the Egyptian police. Many Greek cigarette makers were arrested as "troublemakers" and the "more dangerous" ones were expelled from the country, as happened in Cairo in December 1901. A strike had broken out in the Greek tobacco factory owned by the Susas Bros company, with demands for wage rises and better working conditions. The Egyptian government did not remain neutral in this civil conflict that arose between the Greek entrepreneurs and the Greek cigarette makers. The cigarette makers accused the Egyptian government not only of using naked violence, arrests and expulsions, but also of protecting the Greek tobacco industrialists by providing them with native workers who would enter the factory escorted by the army.[23] The strike was characterised as a "revolt" by the factory owners. The Egyptian police violently pursued the strikers, injuring many of them and arresting 25 people. There are reports that many women and children were among the injured, a fact that demonstrates the presence of women and children in the workplace as well as their dynamic participation in the conflicts that arose in the tobacco factories.[24]

The president of the Greek cigarette makers' committee in Cairo criticised the position taken by the Greek consulate of Cairo and wrote a letter to the Greek prime minister accusing the consulate of collaborating with the Egyptian authorities over the expulsions and of not caring about the community of the Greek cigarette makers and their families. Some of those family members – women and children – were also employed in the tobacco factories, alongside a male member of their family, be it their husband, father or brother. The workforce in the tobacco factories, which was composed of Greeks, Armenians and Egyptians, is of particular interest as the employers of the Greek workers also came from their homeland of Greece. The foreign citizens of Egypt, the Greeks and the Armenians, were well-paid skilled cigarette makers, while the native population worked in subordinate posts in the factory, along with the women and the children discussed previously.

These foreign citizens of Egypt – the skilled cigarette makers – played a leading role in the growth of collective action in the tobacco industry. To confront the constantly expanding labour protests of the cigarette makers, the tobacco industrialists hired native workers as strikebreakers. During the riots, the Egyptian government strongly intervened, violently suppressing the protests and incriminating the Greek cigarette makers. By ensuring that the native workers could enter the factory, they aimed to protect the interests of the Greek tobacco industrialists. This meant that the skilled foreign workers who were employed alongside their family members were confronted with the native unskilled workforce. The confrontation thus went beyond the dichotomy of capital and labour and reverberated throughout the labour force, thus bringing into the open other controversial issues within the labour force itself, in particular ethnicity and gender.

Athens

This "incident" was part of a series of labour mobilisations and struggles that took place in Egypt at the beginning of the twentieth century. A leading role was played by Greek cigarette makers and those of other nationalities, as well as specialised male craftsmen and female workers. Maintaining the production process – alongside demands for higher wages and better working conditions – was the main issue of concern for the cigarette makers in Greece too. Although Greece lacked a significant craft industry in hand-rolled cigarettes, which would have enabled the cigarette makers to strengthen their negotiating power in the labour market, as had happened in Egypt, the presence of cigarette workers in Greece was not negligible. Nor were they deprived of militancy, as the protests and strikes that broke out in the cigarette industry in Greece in the early twentieth century attest.

It appears that the Greek cigarette makers who arrived in Greece from Egypt transferred not only their undeniable abilities in the craft of cigarette making, but also the "prowess" of protest and assertion. Having returned to Greece, they had no difficulty in being hired by the tobacco firms. On the contrary, they were in high demand, as they were guaranteed to produce the best cigarettes. This peaceful cooperation between employers and employees was, however, to be short-lived, since the contradictions between the demands of both sides soon came to the fore, even if the prime tobacco of the exquisite handmade cigarettes papered over their differences.

From as early as 1902, cigarette makers in Piraeus had been requesting a wage increase of 55 drachmas for every thousand cigarettes that they produced. Some tobacco sellers, mostly the smaller ones, accepted this compromise, as the cigarette makers presented it, but the largest adamantly refused to satisfy the cigarette makers' request.[25] For them, the need to "get rid of" this specialised professional group of cigarette makers became an increasing "obsession". They were to achieve their goal a few years later with the introduction of cigarette-making machines, of which it was said that "*they will get rid of any new demand from the cigarette makers*".[26]

The first attempt to mechanise cigarette making in Greece is attributed to a private entrepreneur, the tobacco factory owner K. Angelidis. The cigarette-making machine was used first in the State Tobacco Factory of Athens in 1885 and then in Piraeus, and it had a production capacity of about 50 kilos of cigarettes per day,[27] that is about 100,000 cigarettes for a ten-hour working day. The production capacity of a cigarette maker was 3,000 cigarettes per day. By the end of the following decade, the cigarette-making machines had become much more widespread. In 1909, new cigarette-making machine models were installed and operated in the public tobacco-cutting facilities of Athens, Piraeus and Pyrgos. By 1914, private entrepreneurs, such as K. Varkas in Athens, G. Pyrpasopoulos in Piraeus,

A. Karelias in Kalamata, V. Karavasilis in Pyrgos and N. Matsaggos in Volos had installed the first tobacco-cutting and cigarette-making machines.[28] Each cigarette-making machine appears to have "replaced" about 100 cigarette makers,[29] which led to a fierce reaction on the part of the cigarette makers themselves.

As specialised craftsmen employed in public and private tobacco-cutting facilities, the cigarette makers immediately understood that the beginning of the mechanisation of the production process would lead to their end. A professional end that threatened not only their identity as male specialised craftsmen but, first and foremost their survival, as it would push them to the margins of their industry. If for the tobacco traders the automation of cigarette making meant a shift from small craftsmanship – as it had been since the pre-industrial era – to the industrial and mass production of cigarettes, for the craftsmen cigarette makers it signified the end of their craft and their "proletarianization", pushing them out of the "transitional zone", where they could still be seen as "skilled, respectable craftsmen" positioned somewhere between the workers and the bourgeoisie.[30] Their concern as to what automation meant forced them into an open conflict with the tobacco merchants.

In May 1910, cigarette makers who worked for the tobacco merchant K. Varkas, whose factory was located in Athens, went on strike in protest at his decision to procure cigarette-making machines. The cigarette makers occupied the area outside the factory and remained there until late at night and their strike was to last for several days. The cigarette-making machines had to be transported into the tobacco factory with the help of the police, as there was a risk of reprisals from the strikers. Throughout the night, the factory was also guarded by policemen. At the peak of the strike, in late May, the cigarette makers occupied the factory and for two to three days it seemed as though the authorities had lost control of public order in Athens. The cigarette makers were described in the press as "more demanding".

This description was indeed accurate as the demands of the strikers were now not only about the machinery but had extended to cover other issues related to the workplace and labour market control. In other words, in addition to attempting to prohibit the use of the machines, they also demanded the dismissal of the supervisor entrusted by the tobacco merchant Varkas, an end to replacement hiring (or the use of non-unionised workers) and the dismissal of those who had already been hired by Varkas. In addition to their demands for higher wages, fewer working hours and to maintain control of the labour process, there were also demands for control of the labour market. The collective control of the market was needed not only because the shortage of labour would lead to wage increases, but also because it was largely a prerequisite for the achievement of every collective demand. By protesting in this way, the cigarette makers were at risk of being replaced by their employers not only temporarily during a strike but also permanently. As regards their demand for collective control of the labour market, this should not be seen exclusively as the fruition of their collective struggles but in combination with their goal of maintaining their privileges as skilled craftsmen – both material and symbolic – in the workplace.

In late May, about 500 of the cigarette makers headed for the Customs Office of Piraeus, where the cigarette-making machines were being guarded, with the aim of destroying them. As a result, the first regiment and all the police force were put on guard. The strike continued until May 31 when, through the presence of overwhelming forces that aimed to put down the strike with either the threat or the use of violence, the state restored order. The machinery, which was stored in Varkas's property, had been protected.[31] Almost a month later, most of the cigarette makers appear to have returned to work. The strike ringleaders, of whom there were 28 altogether, were indicted by the district attorney for damage to property: five were sent to the High Court and four to the Criminal Court.

The demands of the cigarette makers and their conflicts with the capitalist tobacco merchants were widely discussed in the Greek parliament in the 1910s. In 1911, in response to the events of May 1910, parliament debated the imminent submission of a bill on the use of cigarette-making machines. The opinions expressed during the debate on this bill reflect the ideas, mentalities, moral issues and social prejudices of the political world of the time as regards technological innovation, the analysis of which would require a separate study. Here we shall focus on two typical opposing opinions in order to trace the attitudes and the role of the state on this matter. The first opinion displays a modernising tendency and supports the need for and the inevitability of mechanisation, despite its social costs. This came in a speech by Nikolaos Vathris, a Member of Parliament for Corfu, who was also the proponent of the bill:

> Regarding the requests of the opposing parties . . . of course, progress cannot be hindered even if means going to march on a road covered by dead bodies. . . . Steam destroyed sailing and deprived thousands of workers of work. So did railways, electricity and every progress that happens. Finally, the Commission deemed it necessary to tax the cigarette-making machines because they bring great profits to their owners, while, on the other hand, they deprived thousands of workers of work.

The second opinion, given by Dionysios Gklavas, the Member of Parliament from Achaia, shows how the introduction of technology was perceived by some politicians as a threat for both the health of the workers and also for public health: "I fully support the rightful demands of the cigarette makers. Due to the introduction of cigarette-making machines, a decline is being felt in this country and parliament must prevent the spread of this evil".[32]

Even though it was not a central demand the cigarette makers' request for financial aid so that they could purchase the cigarette-making machine themselves reveals another dimension to these events. At the very least, it forces us to reflect upon and revisit the ways in which the workforce looked upon technological innovation. Machines were seen by the cigarette makers not merely as a threat, as the tool that would replace them, but as a means of production that had been appropriated by their employer. Recognizing the value of this means, they did not seek to destroy it but rather to appropriate it. If we also bear in mind the proposal put forth by the cigarette makers' union a few years later, in May 1918, for the concession of an area within the public tobacco factory in which they could work independently,[33] then a more nuanced picture emerges, which shows the protective nature of the cigarette makers' demands towards their work during this period while also demonstrating their belief that the state – and its institutions – is the distributor of the social product.

Their behaviour and their actions – including the destruction of or threat to destroy the cigarette-making machines – should therefore be seen as something more than simply the behaviour of workers who are thinking "traditionally" within the context of a moral economy, as a result of their fear of new technology.[34] On the contrary, these specific practices are part of their negotiation strategies to gain work within the new economic and social order ushered in by the arrival of this new technology.

We can also view the proposal for the use of machines exclusively for pipe production for cigarettes within this context. As already mentioned, this specific task was carried out by male and female workers who were considered unspecialised. Specialised cigarette makers, aware that technological development would transform the production process and render old skills such as theirs, around which power relations in the place of production were structured, useless, demanded that they be able to determine the tasks in this area themselves. They therefore approached their employers in a pliant and conciliatory manner and claimed to be willing to accept the machines on the condition that they be used in an ancillary way during the production stage. This ancillary task was to be performed by "other" unspecialised "assistant" employees, thus highlighting the now common heterogeneity, contrasts, exclusions and hierarchies that could be found among employees at production sites.

To sum up, the active mobilisations of cigarette makers in the 1910s showed their fighting spirit, which was perhaps the result of two interconnected factors. First, the strong – initially – negotiating position that they had both against their employers and against the state, as they represented the few specialised craftsmen able to produce what was a very popular product. Second, the changes in work structure and organisation brought about by technological developments presupposed their own "end" – their professional "end" – and whatever this might entail on both a practical, material level and a symbolic one. Conflicts similar to the ones discussed earlier could also be observed in other cigarette factories in Greece during this period.

Salonica

Disputes between workers and employers in the cigarette-making industry over the organisation of labour, working conditions and control of the labour market broke out in the multinational post-Ottoman city of Salonica in the early twentieth century. In 1918, male and female workers in the cigarette factories went on strike, demanding a rise in wages and for workers to be hired only through the trade union. On 10 July, in a letter to the governor general of Salonica, the heads of the city's cigarette factories notified the authorities of the goals and intentions of the cigarette makers' union. This letter "challenges" us to contemplate this incident, if only briefly, and underlines how often the "discourses" that surround an event are more interesting than the event itself.

In this letter, the managers of the tobacco factories notified the general commander of Salonica of the goals and practices of the cigarette makers' trade union, in their view. They presented the union leaders as the instigators of the strike, claiming that they aspired to moral profit and that they had enthralled the majority of the workers, particularly the more "naive" and the youngest, who lack proper judgment.[35] In demanding that workers be recruited through the union, their aim – according to the managers of the cigarette factories – was to gain management power over the workers as well as over the ways and the methods in which the work was performed. This had resulted in a situation the aim of which was to "create workers who are undisciplined, disruptive, insolent, workers who deny all respect for their superiors and employers and every obligation to the assumed work". For this reason, the managers of the factories concluded that they would not only oppose the union demand to remove the strikebreakers, but they would fight to expel from all the tobacco factories of Salonica the few "troublemaker" workers who "were and will always be at the root of all arguments, the lack of discipline and, therefore, of unreasonable and inopportune strikes" and that "honest, hard-working and diligent workers" must instead be hired in their place.[36]

The cigarette factory directors responded to the demand for wage increases by expressing an interest in male and female workers who are "naïve", as the directors called them, and who are tricked "by capitalistic, so to say, workers, i.e. those who receive high wages". For this reason they suggest that

> increases should be applied not on a sliding scale but a progressive one based on wages . . . [it should] be progressively distributed in favour of those who receive low wages, who, in this case, are blatantly wronged by their colleagues.[37]

It seems that while the strikers demanded that all wages be increased by the same rate, the employers' suggestion was that wages be increased progressively and in reverse proportion, i.e. a greater increase for low wages and a lower increase for high wages.

As can be observed, then, the target of the attacks made by the cigarette factory managers in Salonica was not all the workers in their facilities. The object of their ire was specifically the most unionised workers, particularly the union leaders who also happened to be the skilled male craftsmen, meaning that they were among the best paid but at the same time the least easy to control, in other words the "troublemakers". Not only, in the eyes of factory owners and managers, did they provoke "unreasonable" and "inopportune strikes" and cause material damage to their factories, these workers also constituted a threat to the maintenance of "order and morality" in the workplace as well as outside of it.[38]

Conclusions

Maintaining total control of the labour process, higher wages and improvement of working conditions were the main demands of cigarette makers in those regions around the south-eastern Mediterranean Sea where handmade cigarettes were produced. Control over the organisation of labour – which is linked to technological and organisational changes – in the cigarette industry in those areas that were on the fringes of capitalist growth in Europe at the dawn of the twentieth century was the common factor – notwithstanding the fixed demand for wage rises – upon which labour protests were based.

In Egypt, the competition between the small Greek tobacco firms – which could even be considered family businesses – and the large multinational tobacco industry was particularly unequal. Unable to deal with the new circumstances created by technological and organisational developments in the tobacco industry in that period or to compete with the huge international tobacco firms, the Greek tobacco industrialists of Egypt sought to maintain control over the organisation of labour in their factories and to secure their profit rates through "traditional" means connected to the intensity of the labour performed, as well as through repressive and disciplinary measures against "disobedient" workers. Lastly, it could be said that the reason the Egyptian authorities imposed law and order was to secure the public peace and ensure the smooth running of the free market.

Protests and conflicts between cigarette makers and employers became widespread in Athens at the end of the first decade of the twentieth century, when certain tobacco industry owners decided to procure cigarette-making machines. The strikes became open conflicts and hand-to-hand fighting broke out between the strikers and the strikebreakers and state forces that were brought in to crush the strikes. The state, through the army and navy, acted as strong forces of suppression in an attempt to "restore" law and order. With the aim of maintaining the social order and public peace, the state initially approached the cigarette makers with an attempt to understand their position. So long as the social peace was not disturbed, either through their words or – more often – through their actions, the cigarette makers were accepted and treated sympathetically by the authorities. In this period, then, the state appears to have played an arbitrational, consensual and "paternal" role between the two opposing parties: the world of labour and the world of capital. Acknowledging this role, both parties turned to the state, asking it to help secure agreement for their demands. However, once the struggle of the cigarette makers escalated and became radicalised, the state started to behave towards them in a very different way.

The cigarette makers of Salonica were described – and identified – as "capitalistic classes of workers" by their employers, not only because they received higher wages, but also because they engaged in a fierce battle for control over labour organisation and to define responsibilities in the production area as well as for control over the labour market. Fully aware of this situation and the risks it posed for them the employers made an overt attempt to break up the workforce and consequently to weaken its capacity for collective action, as well as to "stimulate" the feelings and the "reflexes" of the state and society.

It could be argued that the attitudes, practices and mechanisms that were adopted to control the labour protests were not uniform but very diverse. Such practices and policies were often common to and similar in the cases discussed here, but they were adopted in specific periods and contexts, under particular economic, social and cultural conditions, the further study and research of which will allow us to grasp more clearly their commonalities and differences. In any case, it could be argued that for a deeper understanding of the "vehicles", ways and mechanisms of the labour protests as well as of anti-labour practices and methods of suppression, the questions posed must go beyond the labour/capital binary and be enriched with other analytical tools, such as race, gender, the family and age.

Notes

1 Joshua Rosenbloom, "Strikebreaking and the Labour Market in the United States, 1881–1894," *The Journal of Economic History* 58, no. 1 (1998): 183–205.
2 Joshua Rosenbloom, *Looking for Work, Searching for Workers: American Labor Markets During Industrilization* (Cambridge: Cambridge University Press, 2002), 147–70.
3 On the emergence of anti-labour mercenaries, see Stephen H. Norwood, *Strikebreaking and Intimidation: Mercenaries and Masculinity in Twentieth Century America* (Chapel Hill, NC: University of North Carolina Press, 2002).
4 Matteo Milan, "Introduction: Strikebreaking During Europe's Belle Époque," *European History Quarterly* 49, no. 4 (2019): 553–69.
5 Alessandro Saluppo, "Strikebreaking and Anti-Unionism on the Waterfront: The Shipping Federation, 1890–1914," *European History Quarterly*, 49, no. 4 (2019): 570–96.
6 Claire Morelon, "Social Conflict, National Strife, or Political Battle? Violence and Strikebreaking in Late Habsburg Austria," *European History Quarterly* 49, no. 4 (2019): 650–76.
7 Halil Inalcik and Donald Quataert, *An Economic and Social History of the Ottoman Empire, Volume Two: 1600–1914*, trans. Marina Dimitriadou (Athens, OH: Alexandria, 2011), 552.
8 Donald Quataert, "Labour History and the Ottoman Empire, c.1700–1922," *International Labor and Working Class History* 60 (February 2001): 93–109; Touraj Attabaki and Bricket Gavin, "Ottoman and Republican Turkish Labour History," *International Review of Social History* 54, Special Issue (2009).
9 On the collective action of cigarette makers, see Gulhan Balsoy, "Gendering Ottoman Labor History: The Cibali Regie Factory in the Early Twentieth Century," *International Review of Social History* 54, Special Issue (2009): 45–68; Pamela Radcliff, "Elite Women Workers and Collective Action: The Cigarette Makers of Gijon, 1890–1930," *Journal of Social History* (Autumn 1993): 85–108, Lina Galvez Munoz, "Gender, Cigar and Cigarettes. Technological Change and National Patterns," Session 14, *Technology, Gender and the Division of Labour*. XIV International Economic History Congress, Helsinki, Finland (2006); Lina Galvez Munoz, "Breadwinning Patterns and Family Exogenous Factors. Workers at the Tobacco Factory of Seville during the Industrialization Process, 1887–1945," *International Review of Social History* 42 (1997): 87–128.
10 Law ARKST′ of 27 April/10 May 1883, "On the enforcement of duties on tobacco consumed".
11 Ioannis Serraios, *Peri Isagogis Monopoliou en Elladi* (Athens: State Printing, 1934), 14.
12 Euaggelos Prontzas, "The Peasant, Tobacco, and the State. The Greek Tobacco Market (1887–1939)," *Ta Istorika*, no. 17 (1992): 275–300.
13 Relli Schechter, "Selling Luxury: The Rise of the Egyptian Cigarette and the Transformation of the Egyptian Tobacco Market, 1850–1914," *International Journal of Middle East Studies* 35, no. 1 (February 2003): 51–75. On the Egyptian tobacco industry see

also Relli Schechter, *Smoking, Culture and Economy in the Middle East: The Egyptian Tobacco Market 1850–2000* (London: I.B. Tauris, 2006); Joel Beinin, *Workers and Peasants in the Modern Middle East* (Cambridge: Cambridge University Press, 2001); Joel Beinin and Zachary Lockman, *Workers on the Nile. Nationalism Communism, Islam, and the Egyptian Working Class, 1882–1954* (Princeton, NJ: Princeton University Press, 1987), 49–57; Christos Chajiiosif, *I Girea Selini. I biomixania stin elliniki ekonomia 1830–1940* (Athens, OH: Themelio, 1993), 366–68.

14 The Koutarellis brothers came from the Greek village of Drakeia Piliou. Their factory employed 2,000 people and daily production rose to 3,000 kilos of cigarettes. It was the only company that was able to compete with the Eastern Co. SAE, which gradually absorbed almost the whole of the Greek and Armenian tobacco industry of Egypt. Apostolos G. Konstantinidis, *I Piliorite* en *Egipto*, no. 1 (Alexandria: Silogos Zagoras, 1963), 60–61.

15 Journal *Kapniki Epitheorisis* no. 102. pr.1955.

16 Chajiiosif, *I Girea Selini*, 336–67.

17 Schechter, "Selling Luxury," 51–75.

18 See the "Karathanasis" Archive.

19 *Empros News,* April 2, 1906.

20 Chajiiosif, *I Girea Selini,* 368.

21 Ibid., 336–67; Alexander Kitroef, *The Greeks in Egypt, 1919–1937: Ethnicity and Class* (London: Ithaca Press, 1989), 96–111.

22 Beinin and Lockman, *Workers on the Nile*, 49–57.

23 *Empros News*, December 27, 1901.

24 Ibid.

25 *Empros News*, January 10, 1902.

26 *Empros News*, October 7, 1909.

27 Serraios, *Peri Isagogis Monopoliou,* 19.

28 Christina Agriantoni, *I Aparxes tis Exbiomixanisis stin Ellada ton 19o aiona* (Athens, OH: Historical Archives of the Commercial Bank of Greece, 1986), 197.

29 Lois Labrianidis, "Industrial Location in Capitalist Societies: The Tobacco Industry in Greece, 1880–1980" (PhD thesis, London School of Economics, 1982), 123–24.

30 Eric Hobsbawm, *The Age of Empire, 1875–1914* (New York: Vintage Books, 1989), 127.

31 The first trade unions were founded in Greece in the 1870s and were run by royal charter. They were obliged to submit an annual report of accountability to the Ministry of the Interior, which was responsible for overseeing them. The Revisory Parliament of 1911 saw the right to strike in a more favourable light, marking a shift from the period of "prohibition" to the period of "tolerance". On the institutional framework of trade union freedoms and restrictions see Antonis Liakos, *Work and Politics in Interwar Greece* (Athens, OH: Historical Archives of the Commercial Bank of Greece, 1993), 157–77.

32 *Empros News*, 18 March 191.

33 *Rizospastis News,* May 26, 1918.

34 Antonis Liakos has noted that striking cigarette makers turned against the machines, highlighting a predominant moral belief in the economy. In this way we can see how the working classes, whose influence reached as far as parliament, confronted rising capitalism: with a strong belief in the moral order which, in turn, determined their political attitudes towards the problem. Liakos, *Work and Politics in Interwar Greece,* 397–400.

35 The arguments put forward by the employers are of course not new. Such tactics were used during the carpenters' strike at the Pauling and Henfrey building contractors in Manchester in 1844. Engels writes that Pauling and Henfrey attempted to increase working hours to beyond sunset, lighting the workplace by gas. The workers went on strike as they believed that this would put downward pressure on their wages. The employers took the rebellious strikers and their ringleaders to court, accusing them

of *"having intimidated the new workers into taking part in the strike"*. According to the employers "it is about the rebellious, who spread confusion among the peaceful workers" (Engels 1975, 237–88). While Engels's report may appear an anachronism, I would argue that the incident described has many points in common with our case. The literature on labour strikes is too large to be mentioned here. See for example Marcel Van Der Linden, *Workers of the World. Essays Toward a Global Labor History* (Leiden and Boston: Brill, 2008), 137–208.

36 *Macedonia News,* July 11, 1918.

37 Ibid.

38 It is particularly interesting to note that the managers of the tobacco factories described the organised cigarette makers active in the trade union as "capitalistic classes of workers". This recalls the conflict between entrepreneurs and the "labour aristocracy" that has been observed in Western Europe and the USA in the late nineteenth century and early twentieth century. See for example Jurgen Kocka, *White Collar Workers in America 1890–1940: A Social-Political History in International Perspective* (London: SAGE Publication, 1980), Eric Hobsbawm, *Labouring Men. Studies in the History of Labour* (New York: Basic Books, INC, 1964), Peter Armstrong, *White Collar Workers, Trade Unions and Class* (London: Croom Helm, 1986), John Coatsworth, Juan Cole, Michael P. Hanagan, Peter C. Perdue, Charles Tilly, and Louise Tilly, *Global Connections, Politics, Exchange, and Social Life in World History*, Vol. 2 (Cambridge: Cambridge University Press, 2015), 229–39.

10 In reaction to revolution

Anti-strike mentalities and practices in the Russian radical right, 1905–14[1]

George Gilbert

Introduction

In thinking about the nature of the Russian right's political activism, a dramatic passage from the Union of Russian People's (URP) 1905 manifesto provides the following insight:

> The enemies of the Tsar and of the country, by means of deception, threats, and violence, cause strikes in factories and mills, stop trains, disrupt trade, inflict tremendous loss to the entire state, and deprive hundreds of thousands of poor people of work in order to force them into violence through hunger.[2]

In a few short lines, the manifesto demonstrates the populism of the URP, placing this group on the side of the Russian people against subversive enemies, and, at the same time, stating their desire to defend Russian autocracy. It presents the URP as a force for law and order in a time of chaos and unrest, and focuses on the negative energies unleashed by the strike wave in late Imperial Russia.

This chapter will investigate the ideas, mentalities and activities of Russian rightists concerning the strike movement in late Imperial Russia. It will look mainly at parties and unions that styled themselves as social movements. These have sometimes been known (and referred to themselves as) "Black Hundreds", though here the term rightists (or "right") will be used to denote clear reference to the operations of specific actors – those of the right-wing parties (*pravye partii*). The argument is that the right was a novel force that posed dilemmas not only for their opponents on the left, but also for tsarism. Rightists had an opportunity to share power with authorities, including the army and police, that was never fully grasped. Though partially because of the right's lack of organisational wherewithal and tendencies towards infighting, the more intractable reason why counter-revolutionary activism did not make further inroads is the challenge to autocracy that rightists themselves posed. To illustrate this claim, the essay explores several cases from the 1905 revolution up until the First World War, particularly focusing on examples drawn from Odessa, St. Petersburg and Ekaterinoslav, though it will contextualise such findings more broadly.

The historiography on the strike movement in the late Russian Empire is deeply developed; strikes proliferated in the late Russian Empire from the 1890s in step with increasing patterns of urbanisation, industrialisation and the development of the workers' question.[3] The revolutionary epoch of 1904–7 saw a great upsurge in the strike movement, embodied in developments such as the General Strike of October 1905, which provided a defined problem for Russia's conservatives to contend with. The year forms the point of departure in Peter Holquist's summary of the "epoch of violence" (1905–21) which spanned late Imperial Russia and the early Soviet Union. Violent hostility to strike movements was one part of a much wider pattern of state, non-state and anti-state conflict.[4] As has been well demonstrated, strikes in late Imperial Russia were often brutally suppressed by the defenders of the old regime, with anti-strike violence deployed by police, Cossacks and the army.[5] Right-wing forces opposed to strikes were just another example of the old regime's defenders, prepared to use violence if necessary; intriguingly, they were not created by the old regime, but nevertheless rose to protect it.

Historians have rarely lingered long on where the Russian radical right stood in relation to these wider patterns of anti-strike violence and activism, which is surprising given the literature on the Russian right has expanded greatly since the collapse of the Soviet Union. The intellectual elements of right-wing activism – their "ideology" – has taken precedence in most studies, alongside study of party and group formation.[6] Though the "organized right" appeared earlier, the revolution of 1905 and in particular the promulgation of the 17 October Manifesto of that year provided the impetus for a wider process of right-wing group formation. The appearance of politics, parliament and civil rights compelled the appearance of new forces on the right that wished to restore Russia to an earlier time, before developments they negatively associated with both Russian and non-Russian liberalism. The final few months of 1905 saw the formation of many significant forces on the right, such as the URP, whose manifesto has been already cited, though they were joined by many smaller and less notorious organisations.

The Russian right, it must be said, was a diverse and differentiated series of organisations, and the boundaries between different groups and parties were often remarkably porous. Activists and leaders often crossed the boundaries from one group to another before, during and after the revolution of 1905, helped by the close ideological connections between the main parties and groups, and the tendency for key individuals to be closely networked to one another. Many figures appear on the membership lists of several different groups, and it was not uncommon for those previously active in groups like the Russian Assembly to later on play a role in groups including the URP or the Union of the Archangel Mikhail, which was formed at the start of 1908. However, the names of these groups – for instance, the Party of Legal Order – illustrate a commonality: a desire to defend the existing state structure. Rightists were deeply troubled by what they saw as the disorder and chaos of the new "time of troubles" that started around 1904–5, and shared a pessimistic, even fatalistic vision of the Russian future.[7] A theme uniting disparate groups on the right was their opposition to revolutionary activity, including strikes and striking workers.

Exploring the right's anti-strike activism provides vital clues to uncover their relationship with the existing forces of law and order. Hans Rogger has shown that the Russian right was largely created autonomously from the government and supported by influential backers, some of whom could not be dismissed as lackeys of the tsarist establishment, as Soviet-era scholarship on the right tended to do.[8] They tended to emerge at their own behest and their actions were not organised by employers' associations. Furthermore, rightist desires to oppose strikers and tendencies towards violence complicate their self-image as loyal defenders of law and order, and can shed light on an important question: to what extent were such groups – particularly armed groups – accepted by the Russian state when they themselves created disorder? In summarising the pan-European impact of armed associations at a colloquium on the theme, Heinz-Gerhard Haupt noted the importance of specific "conflict structures" in accounting for the emergence of violence, and, influenced by Max Weber's reading, the problem of legitimate violence in particular. These structures included the relationship between insurgent forces and existing authorities such as the army and police, and the latter's monitoring, and, if necessary, suppression, of the potential for violence.[9]

Right-wing efforts to organise parties and groups at the local level were often piecemeal and haphazard, but their appearance posed intriguing dilemmas for the Russian state.[10] Haupt's concluding questions are appropriate: how does a state, in this case an autocratic one, deal with violence deployed outside of its public monopoly on it? To what extent were such groups integrated into the state's monopoly on violence? Counter-revolutionary violence was not new: it was seen in the pogrom wave from 1903–5. Focusing on anti-strike activism as extra-authority practice illustrates a changing, often vexed relationship between the Russian state and autonomous forces. This chapter will contribute to our knowledge of both the Russian right and political violence in the Belle Époque era by exploring the nature of this relationship, examining the shop floor culture of the right as well as their ideas, visions and practices towards strikes, revealing diverse sides of the new activist mentality, one often developing outside of the auspices of the autocracy.

The workers' question and right-wing mobilisation

The Russian right's hostility to strikes was partly a question of identity, linked to the wider development of such groups, as well as the desire to articulate and clarify a response to the "workers' question" in the late Russian Empire. This was underscored by structural transformations in the Russian Empire, most of all urbanisation and industrialisation, especially from the 1880s onwards. Thinkers on the conservative right, including the ultra-monarchist Lev Tikhomirov (formerly, a member of the revolutionary group the People's Will in the early 1880s), began to explore such issues in their writings. The Russian Assembly, a cultural organisation formed in St. Petersburg and Khar'kov, first appeared in 1901.[11] The Assembly and its leaders – who originated exclusively from the gentry estate – initially had little to say about working-class activism, and their supporters came almost wholly from the elites, mainly the Russian nobility. In contrast, a few years later new groups attempted to appeal to a broader base of social support, including from workers. The names of new groups are suggestive of this trend: the Union of Russian Workers (Kiev) and the Circles of Russian Workers (Khar'kov) were two that appeared during 1904.[12] This marked a transition whereby new parties and groups were clearly aiming to cultivate the support of workers by addressing them directly. At this stage such organisations had little to say about strikebreaking as a practice, and their calls to support the Russian autocracy did little to distinguish them from older conservative groups. Over time though the nature of their appeal began to change; publications and pamphlets began to address workers specifically, as in the case of a pamphlet addressed "to Russian workers" issued in Kiev in April 1905.[13] The "workers' question" began to preoccupy intellectuals on the right as well: early in 1905, Klavdii Paskhalov, a noted Slavophile thinker who was also active in right-wing circles after 1905, spoke of a possible "revolution from the right" as one response to challenges of mass activism and political radicalism.[14]

During the revolutionary events of that year a larger strike movement appeared, culminating in the General Strike of October 1905, a major event that urged many of the newly formed parties and groups on the right to clarify a response. The response of many was to organise, and, around the same time, many parties and groups on the right desired to attract workers to their cause. From late 1905 the right expanded massively across the empire, and the formation of their own workers' groups followed patterns of national party formation. Groups like the URP exemplified a more intransigent, radical presence developing on the right in this era, some of which styled themselves as social movements (or "unions") rather than political parties, telling of the diverse constituency they wished to attract. Even so, the URP, by far the largest and most socially variegated of right-wing groups, still drew 50 per cent of its ruling council from the gentry even after the revolution of 1905.[15]

And yet evidence shows the URP sought to recruit factory workers from the final months of 1905, some of whom were attracted by their specifically anti-revolutionary message. A group in the Putilov factory in St. Petersburg, one of the largest manufacturing plants in the Russian Empire, which boasted a total workforce of around 30,000, was led by Aleksandr Polovnev; another group in the city was in the Nevskii factory, headed by Vasili Snessarev. The URP's presence in the Putilov factory towards the end of 1905 was estimated to number around 1,500 workers.[16] The formation of a so-called "fighting brotherhood" (*druzhina*) amongst URP activists in nearby St. Petersburg demonstrated a potential for conflict. Developing a base of supporters amongst factory workers was linked to opposition to striking workers, depicted as ruinous social and political forces in an atmosphere of febrile crisis.[17] The names of some of these new groups provide clues to their intention: one was called the "Society for an Active Fight with Revolution". Police records during 1907–8 estimate that together there were 3,500–4,000 "Black Hundred workers" (*chernosotenets-rabochii*) in the St. Petersburg area when taking into account the participation of all sympathetic organisations.[18]

Some of the most concentrated areas of right-wing activity were in newly industrialised regions to the South and West of the empire, in Ukraine. These contained large manufacturing plants, an active revolutionary movement and a variety of social, political and ethnic tensions that gave ample forces for right-wing movements to react against. The presence of many of these groups is recorded by the reports of the interior ministry (police), which includes lists of membership figures of rightist workers' organisations such as the Union of Russian Workers (URW). For example, the Ekaterinoslav branch in the Briansk factory, along with activists from the Trubnoi and Shoduar factories, were together estimated to comprise possibly more than 1,500 people. The URW branch at the Zaporozh'e Kamenskii factory in Ekaterinoslav district had an even larger membership, potentially consisting of 3,000. The section at the Auerbakh factory in Bakhmutskii district, also in the Ekaterinoslav region, perhaps included around 300 people. These reports, all dated from 13 September 1907, suggest a total presence in the Ekaterinoslav area of around 4,800 activists. These reports do not present the total number of workers employed at the factories, so gauging their overall success in recruitment is impossible, but these do represent sizeable figures, especially when placed in comparative context with rightist groups elsewhere.[19] Kiev also contained active branches of the URW, estimated to be around 3,000 strong in 1905, and, according to the vice-governor of Kiev, closer to 6,500 towards the end of December 1907.[20] One could expand on this image with reference to a far greater number of towns and cities, but the general trend is clear: recruitment gathered pace from the end of 1905, continuing into 1906–7.

In addition to increasing numbers, rightists also sought to recruit different types of workers. As well as targeting skilled plant workers in large factories like the ones at Putilov and Nevskii in St. Petersburg, appeals were aimed at low-skilled and seasonal workers, including in areas of pronounced mobility and transition. The latter can be seen in the port city of Odessa, another prominent area of right-wing mobilisation. Efforts to mobilise focused on the recruitment of loader workers in the port area, which had been a hotbed of revolutionary radicalism during the preceding years, but several hundred workers were recruited to the right in Odessa during 1906–7.[21] Generally speaking, right-wing support came more from temporary and seasonal workers, as well as low-skilled labourers (*chernorabochii*), especially in Odessa and other regions to the South West where industry relied on seasonal workers for much of the work, such as in Odessa's docks. Indeed according to one police report from the region in July 1907, the term *chernorabochii* had become synonymous with members of the URP.[22] The result can be seen in the formation of artels (workers' cooperatives) amongst workers from the end of 1905 in the region, which included many of these lower-skilled seasonal labourers.

A corpus of printed texts, including manifestos, books and pamphlets, make the right's sustained effort to tailor materials to a working-class demographic abundantly clear. Many pamphlets were directed "to workers", "to working people" or alternatively to "the masses": nine of the 20 texts published by the Khar'kov branch of the URP listed in the March 1907 issue of the journal *Mirnyi trud* (*Peaceful Work*) had variations of these words in their titles.[23] The messages of such pamphlets typified the central ideological tenets of right-wing groups that had cohered into the recognisable tsarist formula of "faith, tsar and fatherland" over the past several years: indicative of the continuing commitment to a strong, centralised state, Russian Orthodox religion and Russian national identity.[24] The core ideas of the right, then, did not represent an obvious challenge to the existing order, so much so that they received some government funding, especially for their newspapers and journals. Petr Stolypin's assistant at the Ministry of the Interior S. E. Kryzhanovskii reported in his memoirs that rightists received substantial disbursements from his office for their press; the newspapers *Russkoe znamia* (*Russian Banner*) was allocated 30,000 roubles and *Zemshchina* (*Realm*) was allocated more than 10,000 roubles a month.[25]

Even so, there was a clear challenge presented by the management of a larger, voluble and – at times – more vehement right-wing presence. The state's task of managing these new parties and groups in an under-governed empire with often low densities of police and army was not an easy one.[26] Some of the right's new clusters focused on martial action, such as the "fighting brotherhoods" (*druzhiny*) of the URP. This connected to older traditions of nationalist violence such as the pogroms, and the ethnic violence practised by groups known collectively as the "Black Hundreds", labels which the URP and others borrowed to describe themselves on occasion. Much of the right's activity contained within it a more political focus in this period. Such hostility could be directed against national and ethnic enemies – most of all Russia's Jews – but also the revolutionary left, bound up in the new mindset with the current strike wave. Such identities often intersected in the minds of the activists joining the groups, as well as their leaders. What follows is an investigation into the political culture surrounding rightist hostility to the strike wave.

Anti-strike mentalities and activism

A marked feature of the right as it appeared during and after 1905, including many of the groups listed earlier, was the desire to oppose and resist strikes. This was in part a reaction to the revolutionary events of 1905 itself and a wider strike movement. We can see from the declarations of the central councils a recurrent depiction of strikes themselves as ruinous and destructive formations that needed to be opposed.[27] The newspaper *Moskovskie vedomosti* (*Moscow News*) was edited by Vladimir Gringmut, a noble of Slavophile conviction who had set up the Russian Monarchist Party (RMP) in April 1905. The paper carried an editorial opposing strikes for economic motives: as a party, their policies sought to develop and preserve Russian industry, and they made the obvious point that the strike wave would cause major economic harm.[28] In the regions too, such ideas can be clearly seen. The Tsarist Society of the Russian People appeared in the city of Kazan at the end of 1905 and included in its literature a desire to oppose strikes for "economic" reasons, as detailed in a circular passed around the Alafuzovskii factory.[29] Similar ideas circulated in the congresses of the major right-wing associations, like in the Fourth All-Russian Union of the United Russian People, which met in Moscow during 1907.[30]

An intriguing feature of rightist activity was its shop floor activism, with a number of rightists justifying their actions in economic terms, a natural corollary to their protectionist and autarkic policies.[31] Following the 1905 revolution, a range of powerful employers' associations formed, such the St. Petersburg and Moscow Societies of Factory Owners (1907). Evidence suggests rightists continued to mobilise independently, away from large employers' associations, who probably viewed their activities with suspicion. On occasion, right-wing organisations showed a clear desire to work with Russia's major ministries. In May 1907 a liberal journal reported on the murder of two railway road foreman, Ivanov and Mylov, who were responsible for overseeing operations in the Aleksandrovskii factory in Ekaterinoslav. In response, workers had been on strike in the factory, leading to its closure. In response to the closure, the main council of the URP claimed that it wished to enter into an agreement with both the Ministries of Internal Affairs and of Work and Industry to keep the factory going, showing a desire to work closely with the Russian authorities. They claimed many workers would go without food as a result of the strike, so it was vital for people to continue to work. The URP branch stated that the vast majority of workers had been led astray by a small but well-organised clique of revolutionaries and that the economic consequences of the shutdown would make ordinary Russian workers suffer.[32] Elsewhere, a petition addressed to the minister of internal affairs from the aforementioned Tsarist Society of the Russian People claimed that the closure of the Alafuzovskii plant as a result of the strikes in late 1905 would mean the loss of bread for "several thousand people, including women and children". Another feature of the same report makes the populist intentions of the right clear by attacking the factory owners who "had received enormous profits" in the preceding years.[33] Though these groups wanted to open connections with the authorities in resisting strikes, the formation as well as populist instincts of these new parties and groups represented a potential threat to order on the factory floor.

Some branches went beyond articulating a justification for resistance to strikes and disorders into a much wider tranche of activities. A branch of the Union of Russian Workers active in the Briansk factory, Ekaterinoslav, which saw itself as a working-class organisation for "truly Russian" people, claimed that its main aim was to stop the unrest seen during the revolutionary year. The reasons to resist strikes mirror those previously outlined, and the union also declared its desire to work with factory owners and foremen to stop the harmful spread of strikes and oppose revolutionary forces. No armed resistance to strikes during this period is described: violence was considered the preserve of both the Social Democrats and Socialist Revolutionaries who had been active in the factories over the preceding years. In contrast, the union was described as a peaceful group which had provided food and support to the families of poor and unemployed workers at Easter time. Its activities were described as charitable, cultural and educational, with activists involved in establishing libraries and reading rooms to educate the families of workers. This was part of a desire to show the right as on the side of the Russian people, bound up with endeavours that suggested care. In this, the desire to resist strikes, painted in wholly negative terms and associated with the political left, is also clearly expressed. This political culture was developing independently of any promotion by the state, led and guided by the leaders and activists of right-wing groups themselves.[34]

This populist vision was infused with a streak of anti-capitalism, hence the derogatory reference to factory owners in Kazan: economic growth in itself was not held to be a good thing. Though the right frequently described themselves as "apolitical" or alternatively "above politics" – two frequent tropes on the Russian right (and, indeed, the right elsewhere) in this period – what we instead see as a major motivation is pronounced hostility to the political left. In almost every instance scrutinised, an active left was necessary for a right-wing group to form: putting it in other terms, the "revolution" necessarily preceded the "counter-revolution". In the Briansk factory, the Union of Workers had appeared first out of a desire to stop the revolutionary left by a group of "patriotic" local workers.[35] In the Semiannovskii factory in St. Petersburg, a group called *Tver'* promoted an idea of resisting the left including the Social Democratic movement, if necessary by a "fight". The group was set up by leaders I. Lavrov and V. Snesarev to combat "red terror" in the factories and leant on both factory bosses and foremen for support.[36] Elsewhere in St. Petersburg, workers at Putilov mobilised out of a desire to oppose revolutionary left activity in the factory; they were in receipt of a batch of revolvers from a local organiser of the URP, Iuskevich-Kraskovskii, which were likely passed on to him from the civil authorities.[37]

A view that the 1905 revolution was not Russian often appeared in the declarations of workers' groups on the right, including those that sought to oppose strikes. Most of all this hostility was directed against Russia's Jewish citizens, highlighting the prevalence of antisemitism, but also towards a range of national and religious minorities. The April 1905 edition of the right-wing journal *Mirnyi trud* reported on the formation of "Workers' Patriotic Circles" in Odessa under the leadership of N.N. Rodzevich (who would later become active in the Odessa branch of the URP), and their desire to oppose their stated enemies in the region, namely radicals, socialists and Jews.[38] For Konovnitsyn, later leader of the URP in Odessa, a major stimulus to the group's formation was to oppose revolutionary and, in particular, Jewish workers, with the revolution itself conceived of in national and religious terms.[39] An article by an unknown author in *Moskovskie vedomosti* from February 1906 on "Workers and Revolution" listed a number of new organisations on the right that appeared in Tula, Iaroslavl and Ekaterinburg, expounding on how workers had been influenced by European and/or Jewish ideas which had encouraged them to strike.[40] Similarly, a 1906 pamphlet written by Ivan Sobolev titled *Zabastovki* (*Strikes*) provided a historical overview of the strike movement in Russia and the West, claiming Russian workers were opposed to strikes but had been manipulated by Poles and Jews.[41] Union leaders themselves were presented as exploitative: "You will get officials of a certain 'union' on the lookout for a simple man, waiting for a convenient time, and then taking his 'union' money".[42] Such appeals created a conspiratorial worldview, mixing images of harmful revolutionary politics, mendacious unions and the subversive influence of non-Russian groups, suggesting manifold threats to the core ethnos of Russian people in the empire.

Conflict and violence

The end result of this hostility could be conflict in different regions of the Russian Empire, including in its largest cities.[43] Laura Engelstein's work on conflict in Moscow explored the appearance of violent "patriotic" demonstrators appearing in response to socialist and liberal forces that had mobilised in November and December 1905. The governor-general of Moscow V. Dubasov sought to quash the large-scale insurgency of Social Democrats and other radicals by drawing on these emergent forces, organising volunteer militias with the support of a new range of groups, including the then recently established URP. These counter-revolutionary movements were active under the direction of the police.[44] Following the violent crushing of the Presnia uprising in the city centre in December 1905 by the police and army, the URP branch in Moscow declared itself to be an anti-strike force; in the rightist newspaper *Veche* (*Evening*) it was described as a society for an "active fight against revolution", which aimed towards the "destruction of rioters" (*istrebliat' kramol'nikov*).[45]

A particularly vehement URP presence was recorded in Odessa, where rightists portrayed themselves as strong resisters of leftist anti-state disorders. The interim governor-general of Odessa at the outset of 1907 P.F. Glagolev looked on them sympathetically, considering them a useful counterweight to revolutionary forces: "they have already realized the harm that comes from unrest, robberies, theft and strikes, and therefore fight against them".[46] In addition to the presence of rightists amongst dockworkers, we should note the registration of a workers' artel with links to the right in Odessa.[47] Count A.I. Konovnitsyn, who had previously been involved in the Russian Society of Shipping and Trade before becoming the head of the Odessa URP in the city, was responsible for organising an artel amongst port workers in the city. The groups under his direction were raised at a time when the radical left was mobilising and aimed to physically confront radicals and get Russia's docks working again after the disruption from strike activity seen following the October 1905 General Strike.[48]

Police surveillance reports describe the actions of the URP in the area, led by Konovnitsyn, V.I. Pelikan and A. Kakhov during 1906 and 1907. Though intriguing, the sources can be suggestive and at times lack texture. Sometimes, it is not clear from the reports what is exactly going on, as they note clashes and collisions without going into much depth about the nature of these. However, in other instances we can more clearly discern what is occurring: looking closely at police records and newspaper reports of the era together can give us an effective outline, including of instances of violence in the midst of strikes occurring in Odessa through 1906 and 1907. Groups of right-wing activists confronted striking Social Democrats and others from the revolutionary wing of Russian politics, which could result in violent confrontation. Much of this occurred in the dock areas around the port region in the city centre; the ships and unloading bays were the scenes of skirmishes between the Odessan right and its enemies, an open area in the city with much footfall that naturally attracted the attention of a variety of actors, including the local police, Social Democrats in the region, and, indeed, Jewish radicals who wished to strike back against the right.[49] This conflict between revolutionary workers, Jewish self-defence forces and right-workers from artels formed in the region served to increase tensions and disrupt the town's shipping, trade and industry – an ironic twist given how URP leaders couched the actions of the group as defending the Russian economy and state in a time of strikes and disorders.[50] Elsewhere, URP activists appeared on the campus of Odessa's major university in December 1906 in response to strikes and disorders, apparently provoked by the presence of student strikes.[51] This is representative of the wider culture of revolutionary violence and counter-violence visible across the city in the era.

The exact scale of the right-wing success in suppressing strikes is open to debate; evidently, the right's own, reflective sources in recording this activity are subjective. Recalling his organisation of the group, Konovnitsyn described the violent breaking of the strike movement and clashes between URP activists and revolutionary workers in 1906, when the URP "thwarted and finally stopped the disastrous strikes amongst steamship workers who loaded and unloaded the ships" in the Odessa docks; he continued that these clashes "brought many benefits to Russian shipping, saving it many millions from strikers".[52] If he exaggerated the scale of this, other sources corroborate his claim of success: a telegram sympathetic to the URP published in the national newspaper *Novoe vremia* (*New Time*) on 28 November 1906 commented upon their activity in Odessa as follows:

> not a word has been said about the strike that was broken by the Union of the Russian people . . . as far as we know, this is the first time in Russia, that the energy of members of the Union of the Russian People has had a destructive edge over the revolutionary workers [movement].[53]

It is worth considering why the URP could gain a foothold on Odessa and employ such action effectively. At first, the Odessa branch of the URP benefitted from a largely hands-off approach on the part of the authorities, previously seen in the testimony of Glagolev, which aided their attempts to generate violence and discord against the left. The reasons for this were structural as well as cultural: as a recent formation in an under-governed empire with low-density regular policing, they profited from a degree of organisational laxity amongst the Odessa authorities. As self-stated defenders of law, order and Russian industry, they had the advantage of appearing as a counterweight to revolutionary forces that had caused a lot of unrest in the city over the preceding several years. It is also worth considering what type of weapons URP activists had at their disposal to strike fear into their enemies. Reports suggestive of violent "clashes" but with relatively few casualties might lead one to suspect cudgels or even fists as primary weapons, but other types of arms could be distributed amongst supporters to threaten and potentially kill or injure opponents. In one instance in April 1907, 20 revolvers were distributed amongst the Odessa URP by the Russian Society of Shipping and Trade – the organisation previously headed by Konovnitsyn – for the protection of this society by members of the URP against revolutionary forces. In a letter to the mayor of Odessa, the head of the society noted the need to do this given violent attacks by revolutionaries on officials from the society in recent times, citing a "night attack on the port by revolutionaries, who bombed, shot and wounded people" and were then expelled from the port area by guards.[54] Noting the destruction wrought by revolutionaries was a straightforward and emotive way in which radical rightists could justify their actions, both to themselves and the Russian authorities.

However, this form of activism posed challenges to the authorities as well as the right's erstwhile enemies. We can clearly discern a change in the authorities' attitudes towards the URP through 1906 and 1907; in part, this was a question of changing personnel within the military and civil authorities, some who regarded the URP with suspicion, but in other areas, it was a question of the activity and temper of the groups themselves. Whilst the URP and others searched both for authority support and a wider presence, their desire to provide an armed presence against revolutionary agitators made some in authority nervous. In one instance, the acting State Controller D.A. Filosofov declined a request from Konovnitsyn to organise a series of meetings on merchant ships in the Odessa dock region; it was added in the report that Prime Minister Peter Stolypin and all cabinet members present agreed with Filosofov's actions. An article from August 1907, published in the newspaper *Tovarishch* (*Comrade*), noted that a number of revolvers and "illegal" literature from the URP activists were confiscated following a recent skirmish between these activists and their revolutionary enemies, no doubt a reference to the recent distribution of weapons to Konovnitsyn under the auspices of the Russian Society of Shipping and Trade. The report did not include a specific reason as to why Konovnitsyn was not allowed to mobilise his forces on Odessa's merchant ships, only insisting such denials came from on high.[55] Bands of right-wing activists, sometimes described as "unionists" (*soiuzniki*) in such reports, were occasionally arrested by police: one reason could be that they were in possession of weapons, including revolvers and other types of arms.[56]

Eventually, the tide began to turn against the right in Odessa. Judging from the source record, clashes between the right and the revolutionary left and strikers tailed off after 1906. Partly, this is a result of the dissipation of the 1905 revolution's major energies and the gradual restoration of authority across the Russian Empire. Another, more local reason was the changing stance of the Odessan authorities. We have seen how police began to monitor rightists more closely and, if necessary, suppress them, but Konovnitsyn also lamented a lack of financial support from the authorities that he had sought to co-opt since 1906. In his efforts to stop what he saw as his Jewish enemies, he noted the presence of "unfriendly clerks" within the state bureaucracy, and he sought the "removal" of such people.[57] This criticism of the bureaucracy was a trademark of the right, which saw them as full of enemies of different types; such a conspiratorial mindset was emblematic of Konovnitsyn's worldview and can partly explain the infighting that later split the right in Odessa. This has been identified in Jacob Langer's research, which has shown how the right in Odessa was riven by factionalism, driven in part by financial corruption. Such scandals within the URP drained the groups of much-needed resources and affected many of their activities in the region, including strikebreaking and armed resistance to the left.[58]

Union activism dropped significantly after Petr Stolypin dissolved the Second State Duma in 1907, a period which signalled the ascendancy of the government's "repression and reform" response to the 1905 revolution. Even so, unlike in some other areas of the empire, the right in Odessa was active up until the eve of the First World War. The resurgence of the strike wave in 1911 provided new opportunities for anti-strike activism. One instance was the press strike of that year: the newspaper *Odesskii pechatnik* (*Odessa Press*) cites the use of members of the Odessa URP as strikebreakers by a newspaper owner, one Abraham Finkel, though given his Jewish identity, his desire to call on them as his strikebreakers (and have them obey him) in order to halt the press strike seems implausible.[59] What is more certain is how limited toleration from the civil authorities affected the development of the right in Odessa. Konovnitsyn appeared to have an uneasy relationship with the governor-general of Odessa I.N. Tol'machev, who, unlike some of his predecessors in that office, perceived a large and voluble right-wing force as a threat. Initially Tol'machev appeared supportive towards the URP, but in later years Konovnitsyn wrote in his personal communications about Tol'machev's "frequent clashes" with both himself and the URP. In one letter, Konovnitsyn reflected on Tol'machev's role in suppressing the strike movement on 1911 in Odessa, claiming that Tol'machev deliberately allowed the strike movement to gain purchase before suppressing it himself, so that he could proclaim himself as a "saviour and suppressor of riots and unrest" in Odessa rather than credit Konovnitsyn and his followers, in order to convince those in higher office of his own moral probity.[60] Suspicion of the URP increased the further the 1905 revolution receded into the distance, exacerbated by the low density of regular police across much of the Russian Empire. It is important to note rightist activism continued for longer after this point, as demonstrated by occasional resistance to the strike wave.

The regional perspective to much of this activity could be considered, as many right-wing groups proved most enduring in the South and West of the empire. This was especially the case near or within the Pale of Settlement, which contained a large Jewish population and had a history of revolutionary activism with many of these forces proudly self-identifying as Jewish. The most famous of these was the General Jewish Workers' Union (Bund), a Social Democratic mass movement that championed universalism. This gave rightists presences to mobilise against. Kiev had been a prominent site of right-wing mobilisation from late 1905, and in a telegram from February 1912 (a year before the notorious Mendel Beilis trial of 1913 when accusations of Jewish ritual murder swept the region and beyond), the governor of the region A. F. Girs noted the presence of groups that positioned themselves "for law and order" against strikers. Whilst the source record is not always clear exactly on who these people were, most telling is the claim that these "patriotic" manifestations could count on authority support if they felt it was desired.[61]

Sources from other parts of the Russian Empire show a fragmented and disunited right, or one that was in the minority in the political and social struggles taking place in Russia's factories. In Iaroslavl' during October 1906, strikebreakers appeared after rightists led by the monk Aleksei had distributed sympathetic newspapers such as *Pochaevskii izvestiia* (*The Pochaev News*) and *Russkii narod* (*Russian People*) in the factories.[62] Other reports from the time suggest that propaganda was distributed on the part of the URP and others, but sympathisers were in the minority, with most workers in one of Iaroslavl's major factories demanding the removal of agitators who were in favour to the right.[63] Rightists were involved in physical fights on the factory floor with members of revolutionary organisations but were often on the losing end of such collisions. The main reason for this is that their revolutionary enemies often outnumbered them in clashes, even in areas with a pronounced right-wing presence like Iaroslavl. Workers sympathetic to the right could be the target of hostility from others who sought to drive them out of the factories.[64] One worker, Volodin, employed at the Wolf metallurgical plant in November 1906, was said to have outraged fellow workers with declarations sympathetic to the extreme right (described as "black hundreds" in the newspaper report), and workers demanded his dismissal by the administration, or else they would kill him themselves.[65] Though vocal, the likes of Volodin were in a clear minority in this factory, and under threat from workers who did not share their views.

Though they sought to court the authorities with promises to resist strikes and disorder, even in areas where the right had a more effective presence evidence shows that right-wing strikebreakers could attract the suspicion, if not outright hostility, of the forces of law and order. Whilst their message to free Russia from the shackles of strikers was consistent, the mixed response they received from local populations and the authorities placed rightists in a contradictory position. On the one hand, they claimed to be shoring up Russian autocracy in a time of chaos, but on the other they demonstrated a contribution to instances of localised and sporadic conflict that required extra policing. Intriguingly, what these sources together do not show is factory owners and major industrialists themselves supporting right-wing strikebreakers – at most, we have rumours of isolated instances that have dubious accuracy, such as that of Finkel. This supports the claim that rightists in this era were acting mostly at their own behest, separate from the machinations of big business as well as from the authorities.

Conclusion

To return to the dilemma outlined at the start of this essay, 1904–7 was a period of turmoil in the Russian Empire, with strikes and disorders stretching authorities to their limits and beyond. Rightist strikebreakers saw themselves as defenders of law and order, but, even so, the realities of their activism posed problems for the authorities. They claimed to be defending both Russian autocracy and a strong state power, as well as to be resisting revolutionaries. These were instincts shared by many within the state's structures, but the right's independent development led to a continuing ambivalence about how to perceive and respond to them from the Russian authorities. Most of all, violence practised outside of the tsarist state's public monopoly on it raised a question of whether such groups could be integrated within the boundaries of legitimate conflict.[66] Rightists' radical temperament, desires to resist other armed forces and tendencies for violence all posed challenges at a time when restoring law and order was most crucial. Sources provide intriguing glimpses into an emerging shop floor culture surrounding rightists operating in factory environments, and their wider activism in areas of conflict. That all of this was developing away from the state – increasingly so from around 1906 after the State Duma's appearance – was what led to suspicion, with armed supporters of autocracy representing both a tribute and a threat to the Russian state.

To break down this larger historical question one can consider wider points about social structure as well as the role of key individuals. In Odessa, rightists gained traction because of the presence of specific actors active in shaping and guiding the right (such as Konovnitsyn), and a passive if not outright supportive establishment, exemplified by governor-general Glagolev late in 1905 and early in 1906. Additionally, the demographic structure of the city, with its history of worker-activism, organisation and, more recently, violent resistance to authority provided forces to react against. The interplay between these personal and structural factors allowed the right in Odessa to gain a foothold. To draw a parallel with the pogrom wave that appeared in Odessa a little before the wider formation of the political right there, commonalities existed in terms of structural factors. Gerald Surh's research on Odessa and Ekaterinoslav during the 1905 pogroms demonstrates how the police and army dealt with localised patterns of anti-Jewish violence, and the structural conditioning that allowed the pogrom wave to gain purchase in the first place. In both cases, urbanisation, hostilities between Jews and non-Jews and tolerance of so-called patriotic demonstrators by civil and military authorities can help to explain the appearance of the pogrom phenomena in these two cities in Ukraine.[67] It also highlights that there was a legacy in terms of counter-revolutionary violence being practised outside of the state's ability to control and manage it, seen here in the wide prevalence of pogroms in 1905. In cases in which rightists provided a possible counterweight to revolutionary forces they received greater latitude from the authorities, but such a stance had the capacity to shift, as seen from the gradual hardening of approaches towards the right in Odessa from 1906 to 1907. On the other hand, rightists also had the problem of attempting to implement a message directed at "truly Russian" people in areas of the empire with high densities of non-Russians, counting on high levels of animus in the Russian sections of the population towards national and ethnic minorities to successfully spread their ideas. This was not always the case in an empire that was remarkably diverse in its social, national, ethnic and religious make-up.

Still considering structural impediments, the right's influence amongst workers and strikers brings to mind the formation of "patriotic" unions under the guidance of police chief Sergei Zubatov from 1902 to 1903. This period, known as the *Zubatovshchina* (time of Zubatov), was an experiment by the secret police to infiltrate and collaborate with the trade union movement to try and encourage working-class loyalty to the state and stop strike action. Though wary of copying his techniques too closely – and often lacking the organisational wherewithal to enforce complex strategies of infiltration and collaboration – some rightists considered that there were lessons to be learnt from this movement and sought to apply them following the 1905 revolution.[68] However, the Zubatov experiment eventually failed to achieve the authorities' aims: not only did it fail to split the Trade Union movement, it provided many workers with (often formative) experiences of a distinctively unionised identity, as well as practical experience of how to oppose government practices.[69] Therefore, the recent heritage of patriotic forces operating in close proximity to union culture was not a positive one for Russia's authorities, and this institutional memory clearly affected their practices in the following years.

An important wider point raised by this case concerns development in Russia's legal culture and, connected to this, civic rights and conceptions of political pluralism. The right's antipathy towards strikes was an integral part of its dislike of civil rights. One of the state's responses to striking and revolt had been to grant a series of concessions, culminating in the 17 October Manifesto in 1905. In fact, many rightists saw the constitutional settlement associated with the civil rights enshrined by this manifesto as illegitimate in itself. This was part of a wider view that liberal political reform was a mendacious tool of Russia's enemies located within the subversive structures of politics, parliament and bureaucracy, which had emanated from harmful "Western" (i.e., non-Russian) trends. This illustrates that the right was developing independently of the state and even – to some extent – in collision with it. A key point was the appearance of, properly speaking, politics and parliament; some on the right did engage with Russia's Duma – especially the Union of the Archangel Mikhail from 1908 – but this was less the case for groups that considered themselves to be primarily social movements, which have been the focus of this chapter.

The presence of rightists in socially mixed zones of conflict, their hostility to the new legal order and also authorities' lingering suspicions of worker activism all contributed to an ambivalence between sources of state authority and the autonomous right. This presented an important conceptual dilemma in terms of power sharing as outlined by Haupt, but we should also consider local and regional factors that together provide us with a complicated and mixed picture, reflected by the source record analysed herein. Rightists continued to venerate the semi-autocratic monarchy but appeared in an era of politics and parliament that they on the whole deeply opposed: an intractable issue, and one that they never managed to fully resolve.

Notes

1 I would like to acknowledge the leaders of the PREWArAs project for inviting me to participate in their workshop "Industrial vigilantism, strikebreaking and patterns of anti-labour violence, 1890s–1930s: A comparative and transnational perspective", held by the History Faculty at the University of Oxford in October 2018. In addition the

resulting essay has been greatly improved by comments from colleagues at my home institution's internal seminar, "Conversations about Research", held at the University of Southampton during February 2020. Particular thanks to Joan Tumblety, Mark Cornwall, Peter Waldron and Christopher Prior for their comments on earlier drafts of this piece, which made me substantively rethink the argument and pay more attention to the mechanics of writing.

2 "Programme of the Union of Russian People, 1905," in *Rossiiskiia partii, soiuzy i ligi*, ed. V. Ivanovich (St. Petersburg, 1906), 117–22, accessed March 11, 2020, https://community.dur.ac.uk/a.k.harrington/Russhist.HTML/.

3 The literature here is vast: several studies that have informed the present analysis are Laura Engelstein, *Moscow, 1905. Working-Class Organization and Political Conflict* (Stanford, CA: Stanford University Press, 1982); Victoria E. Bonnell, *Roots of Rebellion: Workers" Politics and Organizations in St. Petersburg and Moscow, 1900–1914* (Berkeley, CA: University of California Press, 1983); Heather Hogan, *Strikes, Wars, and Revolutions* (Cambridge: Cambridge University Press, 1989); Charters Wynn, *Workers, Strikes and Pogroms. The Donbass-Dnepr Bend in Late Imperial Russia, 1870–1905* (Princeton, NJ: Princeton University Press, 1992).

4 Peter Holquist, "Violent Russia, Deadly Marxism? Russia in the Epoch of Violence, 1905–21," *Kritika. Explorations in Russian and Eurasian History* 4, no. 3 (2003): 627–52.

5 For instance, Bonnell, *Roots of Rebellion*, Ch. 8; Engelstein, *Moscow, 1905*, Ch. 4.

6 On the Russian right, see in English-language scholarship, Hans Rogger, *Jewish Policies and Right-Wing Politics in Late imperial Russia* (Berkeley, CA: University of California Press, 1986); Don C. Rawson, *Russian Rightists and the Revolution of 1905* (Cambridge: Cambridge University Press, 1995), and George Gilbert, *The Radical Right in Late Imperial Russia: Dreams of a True Fatherland?* (London: Routledge, 2016). The existence of a large amount of Russian-language material on the theme should also be noted: monographs that have deeply informed the current analysis are Iu. I. Kir'ianov, *Pravye partii v Rossii, 1911–1917* (Moscow: Rosspen, 2001); I. V. Omel'ianchuk, *Chernosotennoe dvizhenie v Rossiiskoi imperii, 1901–1914* (Kiev: MAUP, 2007); S. A. Stepanov, *Chernia sotnia. Chto oni sdelali dlia velichiia Rossii* (Moscow: Iuza-press, 2013). I would also like to mention the excellent study by Zbyněk Vydra, *Život za Cara? Krajní pravice v předrevolučním Rusku* (Prague: Pavel Mervart, 2010).

7 On this point of right-wingers imagining catastrophe, see Mikhail N. Luk'ianov, "V ozhidanii katastrofy: eskhatologicheskie motivy v russkom konservatizme nakanune pervoi mirovoi voiny," *Russian History* 4, no. 31 (2004): 419–46.

8 Rogger, *Jewish Policies*, 188–89.

9 Haupt's remarks in "Tagungsbericht: Armed Associations and Political Violence in Belle Époque Europe, 12.12.2017–13.12.2017 Padova, in: H-Soz-Kult, 03.02.2018," accessed November 7, 2019, www.hsozkult.de/conferencereport/id/tagungsberichte-7532; in this reading Haupt is clearly inspired by Max Weber. See for example *Economy and Society. An Outline of Interpretive Sociology*, ed. Guenther Roth and Claus Wittich (Berkeley, CA and London: University of California Press, 1968), 31–33.

10 On local organisation see for example Rawson, *Russian Rightists*, chs. 7, 8.

11 Iu. I. Kir'ianov, *Russkoe sobranie: 1900–1917* (Moscow: Rosspen, 2003).

12 Iu. I. Kir'ianov, "Predystoriia pravomonarkhicheskikh partii v Rossii, 1902–1905 gg.," *Istoricheskii arkhiv*, no. 5 (2001): 112, 125, 126, 133–35.

13 Ibid., 134–35.

14 Klavdii N. Paskhalov, *Russkii vopros* (Moscow: Institut Russkoi tsivilazatsii, 2009), 106.

15 N. N. Novo-Aksaiskii, *Politicheskaia evoliutsiia zapadnorusskoi chernoi sotni (1865–1914 gg.)* (Minsk: V. P. Il'in, 2016), 181.

16 Figures cited in I. V. Ome'lianchuk, "Rabochii vopros v ideologii i praktike Rossiiskikh konservatorov nachala XX veka," *Voprosy istorii* 3 (2010): 22–37 (28).

17 *Soiuz russkogo naroda. Po materialam chrezvychainoi sledstvennoi komissii vremennogo pravitel'stva 1917 g.*, ed. A. Chernovskii (Moscow and Leningrad: Gosudarstvennoe izdatel'stvo, 1929), 62.
18 Figures cited in Iu. I. Kir'ianov, "Pravye i konstitutsionnye monarkhisty v Rossii v 1907–1908 gg.," *Voprosy istorii*, no. 8 (1997): 92–117 (100).
19 Figures cited in ibid., 92–117 (117).
20 Figures cited in Omelianchuk, "Rabochii vopros," 22–37 (26).
21 S. A. Stepanov, "Rabochie i chernosotennye organizatsii, 1905–1917 gg.," in *Rabochie i intelligentsiia Rossii v epokhu reform i revoliutsii, 1861-fevral' 1917 g.*, ed. S. I. Potolov et al. (St. Petersburg: BLITS, 1997), 367–78 (372–73).
22 GARF, F. 102.OO, op. 316 (1905 g.), d. 999, Ch. 39, l. A, ll. 286–286 ob: police report, Odessa, 2 July 1907. This source refers to the arrest of multiple unionists (*soiuzniki*), by which is meant members of the URP.
23 "Deiatel'nost' Khar'kovskogo Soiuza Russkogo naroda," *Mirnyi trud*, 3, 1907, 197.
24 Ibid.
25 S. E. Kryzhanovskii, *Vospominaniia* (Berlin: Petropolis, u.d.), 104; P. E. Shchegolev, ed., *Padenie tsarskogo rezhima*, Vol. 5 (Leningrad: Gosudarstvennoe izdatel'stvo, 1924–1927), 412–13.
26 Neil Weissman, "Regular Police in Tsarist Russia, 1900–1914," *Russian Review* 44, no. 1 (1985): 45–68.
27 Regional examples are in *Soiuz russkogo naroda*, 136, 239, 275, 281, 339.
28 *Moskovskie vedomosti*, 15 October 1905, 274, 1–2.
29 GARF, F. 102.OO, op. 316 (1905 g.), d. 999, ch. 39, t.1, ll. 49–50 ob.: circular from the council of the Tsarist Society of the Russian People, Kazan, 27 December 1905.
30 A report in the liberal Constitutional Democrat (Kadet) publication *Vestnik narodnoi svobody* (*Messenger of the People's Freedom*) described the common desire to oppose strikes breaking Russian industry. *Vestnik narodnoi svobody*, 24 May 1907, 20, cols. 1223–38.
31 *Moskovskie vedomosti*, 14 October 1905, 273, 1.
32 *Vestnik narodnoi svobody*, 24 May 1907, 20, col. 1232. This was the journal of the Constitutional Democrat (Kadet) party.
33 GARF, F. 102.OO, op. 316 (1905 g.), d. 999, ch. 39, t.1, ll. 55–55 ob.: petition from the council of the Tsarist Society of the Russian People in Kazan to the Minister of Internal Affairs, 4 February 1906.
34 "Ocherk deiatelnosti Soiuza Russkikh rabochikh v gorode Ekaterinoslave," *Priamoi put*, February 1911, 47–50.
35 Ibid., 47–50.
36 Chernovskii, *Soiuz russkogo naroda*, 62; Stepanov, *Chernaia sotnia*, 394.
37 Chernovskii, *Soiuz russkogo naroda*, 62.
38 *Mirnyi trud*, 4, 1905, 190–91.
39 GARF, F. 102, op. 265, d. 565, ll. 995–96: letter from Count A. I. Konovnitsyn (St. Petersburg) to I. V. Sosnovskom (Odessa), 2 April 1912.
40 *Moskovskie vedomosti*, 8 February 1906, 37, 1.
41 I. Sobolev, *Zabastovki* (Moscow: I. M. Mashistov, 1906), p. 18. This publishing house was linked to the journal *Mirnyi trud*, cited earlier.
42 Ibid., 12.
43 Chernovskii, *Soiuz russkogo naroda*, 62.
44 Engelstein, *Moscow, 1905*, 210–11.
45 Chernovskii, *Soiuz russkogo naroda*, 145.
46 Cited in Stepanov, *Chernaia sotnia*, 347.
47 Stepanov, "Rabochie i chernosotennye organizatsii," 367–78 (372–73).
48 "Perepiska i drugie dokumenty pravykh 1911 goda," *Voprosy istorii*, ed. Iu. I. Kir'ianov, no. 11–12 (1998): 119–44 (121).
49 Odessa was one of a number of areas within the Pale of Settlement with a tradition of well-organised Jewish self-defence, which had been seen from 1903–6. The

long-standing presence of Jewish self-defence groups in Odessa is mentioned briefly in Gerald D. Surh, "Jewish Self-Defence, Revolution and Pogrom Violence in 1905," in *The Russian Revolution of 1905 in Transcultural Perspective: Identities, Peripheries and the Flow of Ideas*, ed. Felicitas Fischer von Weikersthal et al. (Bloomington, IN: Slavica Publishers, 2013), 55–74 (60); Shlomo Lambroza, "Jewish Self-Defence during the Russian Pogroms of 1903–1906," *Jewish Journal of Sociology* 23 (1981): 123–34 (132).

50 GARF, F. 102.OO, op. 316 (1905 g.), d. 999, ch. 39, l. A, l. 92 ob.

51 GARF, F. 102.OO, op. 316 (1905 g.), d. 999, ch. 39, t.1, l. 343: *Rus'*, 12 December 1906.

52 GARF, F. 102, op. 265, d. 565, l. 995: letter from Count A. Konovnitsyn (St. Petersburg) [URP] to I. V. Sosnovskom (Odessa), 2 April 1912; this source is reproduced in Iu. I. Kir'ianov, "Perepiska i drugie dokumenty pravykh (1911–1913)," *Voprosy istorii*, no. 10 (1999): 94–118 (114).

53 GARF, F. 102.OO, op. 316 (1905 g.), d. 999, ch. 39, l. A, t. 1, l. 82: *Novoe vremia*, 28 November 1906.

54 GARF, F. 102.OO, op. 316 (1905 g.), d. 999, ch. 39, l. A, ll. 92 ob., 98–99 ob.: letter from the director of the Russian Society of Shipping and Trade to the Mayor of Odessa, 20 April 1907.

55 GARF, F. 102.OO, op. 316 (1905 g.), d. 999, ch. 39, l. A, l. 300: *Tovarishch*, 9 August 1907.

56 GARF, F. 102.OO, op. 316 (1905 g.), d. 999, ch. 39, l. A, l. 286: police report, Odessa, 2 July 1907.

57 Kir'ianov, "Perepiska," no. 10 (1999): 94–118 (115).

58 Jacob Langer, "Corruption and the Counterrevolution: The Rise and Fall of the Black Hundred" (PhD diss., Duke University, 2007).

59 *Odesskii pechatnik*, 20 December 1911, 8, 10–11, "Delo redaktorov 'Od. Pochty' i 'Od. Slova'". I am grateful to Felix Cowan at the University of Urbana-Chicago for not only alerting me to this source, but for supplying me with his copy of the transliteration, which I have drawn upon here.

60 Kir'ianov, "Perepiska," no. 11–12 (1998): 119–44 (126).

61 Chernovskii, *Soiuz russkogo naroda*, 380.

62 GARF, F. 102.OO, op. 316 (1905 g.), d. 999, ch. 39, t.1, l. 198: *Birzhevye vedomosti*, 7 October 1906.

63 GARF, F. 102.OO, op. 316 (1905 g.), d. 999, ch. 39, t.1, l. 176.

64 GARF, F. 102.OO, op. 316 (1905 g.), d. 999, ch. 39, t.1, ll. 224–224 ob.: police report, Iaroslavl. 17 October 1906.

65 GARF, F. 102.OO, op. 316 (1905 g.), d. 999, ch. 39, t.1, l. 286: *Novaia Gazeta*, 17 November 1906.

66 "Tagungsbericht: Armed Associations and Political Violence."

67 Gerald Surh, "The Role of Civil and Military Commanders During the 1905 Pogroms in Odessa and Kiev," *Jewish Social Studies: History, Culture, Society* 15, no. 3 (2009): 39–55.

68 Stepanov, *Chernaia sotnia*, 377.

69 Jeremiah Schneiderman, *Sergei Zubatov and Revolutionary Marxism: The Struggle for the Working Class in Tsarist Russia* (Ithaca, NY and London: Cornell University Press, 1978). I am grateful to Dr. Alexandra Medzibrodszky for alerting me to this important point.

11 "We can kill striking workers without being prosecuted": armed bands of strikebreakers in late Imperial Germany*

Amerigo Caruso

During a debate in the Reichstag in 1927, the communist member of parliament Paul Bertz looked back at the rise of professional strikebreaking before the First World War. He explicitly mentioned the "bands of strikebreakers" (*Streikbrecherbanden*) led by Karl Katzmarek and Friedrich Hintze, two notorious strikebreaking agents who organised the replacement of striking workers as well as violent intimidation and repression of the labour movement.[1] Bertz argued polemically that irregular bands of strikebreakers in Wilhelmine Germany and the paramilitary Technical Emergency Corps (*Technische Nothilfe*) in the early Weimar years served similar purposes. Indeed, the corps emerged after the November Revolution with the aim of replacing striking workers in industrial sectors considered to be of national importance.[2] Left-wing politicians accused it of being "Gustav Noske's strikebreakers' guard", alluding to the Weimar defence minister, a resolutely anti-Bolshevik member of the Social Democratic Party who deployed paramilitary *Freikorps* along with government soldiers against the revolutionary uprisings in early 1919.[3]

The unlikely analogy between the Technical Emergency Corps and armed bands of strikebreakers highlights the fact that different political systems, such as Wilhelmine Germany and the Weimar Republic, were confronted with similar challenges stemming from the process of democratisation and the rise of social movements. One of the crucial challenges facing states during the early decades of the twentieth century was how to deal with militarised citizens and privately organised coercion. In an effort to tackle "strike terrorism", both the Wilhelmine and Weimar authorities supported the creation of formally regulated organisations of civilian volunteers, such as the Colliery Auxiliary Police Corps (*Zechenwehren*) in the pre-war years and the Technical Emergency Corps after the November Revolution.[4] In addition, violent gangs of strikebreakers led by charismatic figures such as Hintze and Katzmarek were already a familiar presence in labour disputes before 1914. Paul Bertz was therefore not completely wrong in claiming that mercenary bands of strikebreakers had emerged with aims similar to those of the auxiliary corps. In the case of armed strikebreakers, counter-strike strategies consisted in extra-legal, non-regulated action.

The aim of this chapter is to shed new light on the structure of internal violence and its media representation in late Imperial Germany. In doing so, I will argue that repressive functions carried out by militarised citizens were more widespread and more readily tolerated when social conflicts and political antagonism were perceived as a major threat to the established order and when state-led repression triggered divisive discussions concerning the legitimate use of violence. Although the erosion of trust in the state and political violence reached unprecedented levels after 1918, violent confrontations between strikers and strikebreakers had already been an integral part of the social reality and public discourses before the outbreak of the war. However, while debates about legitimate repression and "class justice" were led by the Social Democratic milieu in the pre-war period, it was the radical left that redirected them against the moderate SPD after the brutal repression of the Spartacist uprising.

This chapter focuses on the violence perpetrated by armed bands of professional strikebreakers before 1914, i.e. in a period in German history of massive but largely non-violent protest and relatively few episodes of brutal repression.[5] The first section examines the structure of violence in late Imperial Germany, with particular focus on the fact that it was not only ideological antagonism but also the glamorisation and sensationalisation of violence in the modern media that played a crucial role in intensifying political polarisation, hence setting the preconditions for political violence. Section two presents the context in which violent strikebreaking tactics emerged and became part of the social reality and the media reconstruction of it. Sections three to five analyse several episodes of violence, namely eight murders carried out by armed strikebreakers in the decade before the outbreak of the First World War. The sixth section explores the repertoire of action by professional bands of armed strikebreakers, including those led by Katzmarek and Hintze. This is followed by some concluding remarks.

Violence in late Wilhelmine Germany

According to Alf Lüdtke in his studies of the history of everyday life, low-level violence against outsiders and potential revolutionaries is a widespread and routine practice in modern societies.[6] Throughout the nineteenth century European states were increasingly successful in establishing a monopoly on the legitimate use of physical force, although violence perpetrated by private citizens was far from marginalised. Private violence survived as a form of counter-violence against the state, or, in contrast, as a form of private law enforcement and support for the established order. After the emergence of a modern private security industry around 1900,[7] privately organised coercion was more frequently driven by economic than political reasons. The rise of armed strikebreaking was politically motivated in that it was a counter-strike strategy supported by the so-called loyal classes, but it was also, and probably more importantly, economically motivated by the steady growth in demand for replacement workers and for the "protection" of non-strikers in the decades before 1914.

As mentioned in the introduction, collective violence and brutal repression were relatively infrequent in Wilhelmine Germany, and it is common knowledge that the SPD and the Free Trade Unions discouraged violence as counterproductive.

The picture changes, at least in part, if we take a micro-historical approach and examine the low-level aggression and violent confrontations that became a widespread phenomenon during mass demonstrations and strikes, especially where strikebreakers and pickets were involved.[8] The armed strikebreakers' repertoire of strategies included repressive practices and mafia-like activities, such as provocation, harassment, intimidation and even murder. What makes the episodes of "strike terrorism" and the activities of armed strikebreakers remarkable is that violent confrontations during labour disputes were some of the most frequently discussed and polarising topics in German newspapers. Widespread "threat communication" made conflicts and violence more visible.[9] As noted by Ian Kershaw, the processes of enlargement of the public sphere and massification of society often led to the "glamorisation of violence".[10] Sensational media reports of "strike terrorism" had an impact not only on the political debate, but also on the popular culture and everyday life. In 1910, for example, the semi-official *Norddeutsche Allgemeine Zeitung* reported that instead of playing "cops & robbers" or "cowboys & indians", children in Berlin were playing "strikebreakers & unionised workers".[11]

The heightened media attention on violent strikebreaking reflected a social reality that emerged during the decade before the First World War, when transnationally active bands of strikebreakers spread throughout the highly industrialised regions of Central Europe. The innovative aspect of their activity was that they not only replaced striking workers, they also organised multiple services, such as transportation and supplying and housing "blacklegs". Strikebreaker agents also organised "self-defence" against "strike terrorism", and intimidation of unionised workers was an integral part of their business. They were almost always armed, mostly with revolvers, sticks and daggers. Cheap handguns could be obtained with no legal restrictions, and the wide circulation of firearms became a destabilising factor in an age of class conflict, fear of social disintegration and radical nationalism.[12] Bands of strikebreakers were therefore involved not only in the broader class struggles and political antagonism of late Imperial Germany, but also in the dynamics of violent masculinity and firearm obsession that characterised the "Browning generation", i.e. those born in the late nineteenth century with no greater desire than to buy (and use) a revolver.[13]

Strikebreaking in context

In North America, the business of providing strikebreakers and armed guards during labour conflicts had already become widespread in the late nineteenth century. Several detective agencies and private police forces were widely employed to protect "blacklegs" and intimidate striking workers.[14] At the same time, famous strikebreaking agents, such as Jack Whitehead and James Farley, the latter portrayed in Jack London's novel *Iron Heel* (1907), assembled permanent groups of replacement workers to be deployed throughout the country.[15] In Great Britain, "free labour" organisations such as the National Free Labour Association (1893) led by William Collison, self-proclaimed "king of the blacklegs", also emerged around 1900.[16] Only a few years later, however, strikebreaking became increasingly professionalised, more widespread and violent in Imperial Germany as well. The intensification of strikes and social conflicts created a new sense of urgency among employers, who were interested not only in the rapid recruitment of replacement workers, but also in private security services.

In the years leading up to World War I, the Social Democratic press in Germany complained on an almost daily basis about legal discrimination against unionised workers and the intensification of violence and intimidation perpetrated by armed bands of strikebreakers, which went largely unpunished. The SPD party newspaper, *Vorwärts*, was openly critical of the fact that violent repression against the labour movement was de facto considered a legitimate course of action, while the impunity of strikebreakers represented a major threat to the rule of law in Wilhelmine society.[17] The Social Democratic propaganda pointed out that class-based justice was the result of the general incompatibility of interests and values of the working class and the capitalist elites.[18] This emotionally charged narrative of left-wing newspapers tended to exaggerate – or even invent – episodes of anti-labour repression, while, by contrast, conservative newspapers placed greater emphasis on the violence against and intimidation of strikebreakers. With the discourse radicalised on both sides, unionised workers and strikebreakers alike were accused of "terrorism".[19] However, aside from these politically motivated overstatements, violent clashes between strikebreakers and unionised workers undoubtedly intensified around 1910. What is also remarkable is that the SPD party press and its agitationary journalism were able to use sensationalised and tendentious reports as an effective political and moral weapon in the context of emerging mass communication.[20] In doing so, Social Democratic opinion making managed to create a political culture of opposition in an era in which the SPD and the "free" trade unions were unassimilated forces in Wilhelmine society.[21]

At the opposite end of the political spectrum, the threat to national interests by "strike terrorism" and growing fears of revolution were enough in the eyes of the "parties of order" to justify violent intimidation and repression of the labour movement. The right wing saw counter-strike actions by "yellow" unions and professional strikebreakers as necessary and urgent. Rudolf Lebius, a former Social Democratic journalist who founded the Federation of Yellow Unions (*Gelber Arbeiterbund*) in 1907, described the emerging yellow movement as a "fighting force" (*Kampforganisation*) against "strike terrorism".[22] This narrative was rooted in anti-socialist discourses that spread more rapidly after the Social Democratic victories in 1903 and were supported by nationalist pressure groups such as the Imperial League against Social Democracy.[23]

As a result of partly spontaneous but partly orchestrated fears of revolution and "strike terrorism", the formation of professional groups of armed strikebreakers was seen as both economically and politically necessary. The idea of rallying anti-socialist forces together, which was typical of the so-called Bülow Bloc, resulted in strikebreakers being considered part of the loyal classes and deserving of special protection, or a sort of extended right of self-defence against supposed terrorism. Hence, when two strikebreakers killed a worker during a pub brawl in north-eastern Bavaria in 1907, *Vorwärts* polemically argued that since state authorities protected strikebreakers as "useful members of the community", the murder was therefore a state crime (*Staatsverbrechen*).[24] Karl Otto Uhlig, a Social Democratic member of the Saxon Landtag, accused bands of strikebreakers of persistent immorality and criminal acts that threatened not only the unionised workers but also the entire community, and he considered it unacceptable that the police protected them.[25] What is remarkable is that non-state armed groups, such as pirates, mercenaries and bandits, were primarily characterised by their recourse to violence without state authority or in opposition to it.[26] However, these armed groups – and professional strikebreakers clearly were – could also serve as a source of extra-legal repression and law enforcement.

"We can kill striking workers without being prosecuted"

According to *Vorwärts* and other left-wing newspapers, strikebreakers had good reason to claim that they could "kill striking workers without being prosecuted".[27] This catchphrase was attributed to a strikebreaker flaunting his impunity, and it became a widespread slogan against counter-strike action and "class justice". After being mentioned for the first time in 1906, the phrase was used and reused by many left-wing newspapers in Germany, Austria and the Swiss Confederation before 1914.[28] In the summer of 1906 when there had already been widespread debates about the impunity of violent strikebreakers, a brutal fight between unionised workers and strikebreakers took place outside the "Union" motor vehicle factory near Nuremberg in Bavaria. On the morning of 17 August, during the ongoing labour dispute, the management of the company incited the strikebreakers to intimidate the leaders of the local trade unions standing outside the factory. On the evening of the same day, a group of strikebreakers assaulted striking workers with revolvers, sticks and knives. Maurer, the director of the factory, led the attack; he drove his car into the fighting crowd and used an air pump as a weapon. *Vorwärts* and the Austrian *Arbeiter-Zeitung* reported that the police were present but did not intervene to stop the attacks.[29]

During the fight, 22-year-old strikebreaker Ernst Thiel fired three times at Melchior Fleischmann, one of the local trade union leaders, who died two days later. Claiming self-defence, Thiel went unpunished. In court, the company and the strikebreakers successfully accused the striking workers of being responsible for the escalation of violence outside the factory.[30] Thiel was not the only strikebreaker armed with a revolver; another, by the name of Fackelmeier, carried weapons and threatened unionised workers with his revolver.[31] The fact that the police ignored calls to take the weapons away from the strikebreakers provoked quite frequent violent outbursts by the crowd against strikebreakers and police forces.[32]

The court case on the 1906 riot in Nuremberg resulted in five striking workers being sentenced to prison for upwards of three months. By contrast, the armed strikebreakers Fackelmeier and Thiel (who had murdered Fleischmann) went unpunished because their actions were deemed legitimate self-defence against the provocations and attacks of unionised workers.[33] Liberal newspapers such as the *Allgemeine Zeitung* defended the plea of self-defence and blamed the unionised workers who had attacked the strikebreakers.[34] The paper confirmed that Fleischmann had been killed by Thiel, although it presented the murder in a completely different way to *Vorwärts*. The *Allgemeine Zeitung* denounced the striking workers outside the "Union" factory as violent alcoholics and published detailed reports on the trial endorsing the claim of legitimised self-defence against "strike terrorism".[35]

Murders carried out by armed strikebreakers before 1914

Although the Nuremberg riot of 1906 and the murder of Fleischmann had a huge echo in the Social Democratic press, it was only after popular protests erupted in 1910 in Moabit, an industrial suburb of Berlin, that the debate about "strike terrorism", "excessive strikes" and claims for better protection of "willing workers" spread more rapidly.[36] It reached its peak in the last years before the First World War when, after the first murder case in Nuremberg, several more workers were killed by strikebreakers, strikebreaking agents and armed employers (see Table 11.1).

It is not surprising that liberal and conservative newspapers tended to overlook episodes of anti-labour violence while left-wing newspapers overstated them. Even though the narrative of "class justice" emphasised by Social Democrats needs critical reassessment, it seems clear that the *Kaiserreich*'s judicial system took a very permissive attitude towards strikebreakers' armed self-defence.[37] The quasi-impunity of armed strikebreakers was clearly demonstrated by the Nuremberg case and many similar episodes in the following years. The most sensational of these episodes involved Paul Keiling, a well-known strikebreaking agent who had 17 prior convictions for theft, violence, robbery and other crimes.[38] In February 1914, despite being well known to the police, he was able to leave German territory and offer his strikebreaking services in Austria-Hungary, where he killed the bookbinder Johann Solinger during a strike in Silesia. Keiling was sentenced to only eight months in prison in what was one of most extensively discussed murder cases in German, Swiss and Austrian newspapers until the outbreak of war.[39]

Prior to the Keiling case, the most prominent and most important transnationally, another murder had been carried out by an armed strikebreaker in Duisburg in September 1911 during the Rhineland transport company strike. Strikebreaker and former police officer Brackhage fired his revolver and killed the dockworker Meierling.[40] Brackhage's crime was also deemed to be self-defence and this unpunished murder had a huge impact on the working class. Postcards were printed to commemorate the victim and to denounce the *Kaiserreich*'s class-based justice system.[41] A few months before Meierling's murder, another episode of violence in Lübeck outraged the left-wing newspapers. In the old city port, a group of 40 strikebreakers armed with revolvers and sticks were responsible for a night of terror as pubs and stores were plundered and many citizens injured.[42]

In September 1912, a striking worker was killed by Joseph Ruppert, a prominent strikebreaking agent, near Magdeburg. Here, too, the murderer was acquitted

Table 11.1 Workers killed by German strikebreakers, strikebreaking agents and armed employers between 1906 and 1914

Date	*Place*	*Incident*	*Court decision*
17 August 1906	Nuremberg	Strikebreaker Ernst Thiel fired at one of the local trade union leaders, Melchior Fleischmann, who died two days later	Acquitted (acting in self-defence)
1907	Wunsiedel (Bavaria)	Two strikebreakers employed by the local porcelain factory, fatally stabbed the worker Schödel	Unknown
27 September 1911	Duisburg	Strikebreaker and former police officer Brackhage killed dockworker Meierling	Acquitted (acting in self-defence)
14 September 1912	Burg (Magdeburg)	Joseph Ruppert, a professional strikebreaker, killed striking worker Karl Fritsche	Acquitted (acting in self-defence)
21 April 1912	Zurich	German strikebreaker Otto Kaiser killed Swiss worker Karl Wydler	Acquitted (acting in self-defence)
6 May 1912	Aachen	Employer Von der Hecken, armed with a revolver, killed Dutch worker Hieronymus Stroet	Sentenced to three months in prison, later reprieved
4 June 1913	Frauendorf/ Golęcino (Stettin)	Strikebreaker Brandenburg stabbed striking worker Kühl with a bread knife	Acquitted (acting in self-defence)
4 October 1913	Magdeburg	Strikebreaking agent Karl Katzmarek caused a traffic collision killing a pedestrian, retired tailor Kühne	Sentenced to one month in prison
8 February 1914	Tetschen/Děčín (Bohemia)	Strikebreaking agent Paul Keiling killed foreman Johann Solinger during a bookbinders' strike	Sentenced to eight months in prison (in Austria-Hungary)

by a German court because he was deemed to have been exercising his right of legitimate self-defence.[43] A few months before Magdeburg, there was another case of a strikebreaker shooting and killing a striking worker in Zurich. The perpetrator was the German strikebreaker Otto Kaiser and the victim the unionised worker Karl Wydler, who was shot with a revolver and died a few days later.[44] Kaiser was acquitted, this time by a Swiss tribunal, because he was deemed to be acting in self-defence. This new case of "class justice" and "terrorism" once again sparked off emotionally charged discussions in the German, Swiss and Austrian press.[45] One year after Wydler's murder, on the evening of 4 June 1913 in the port city of Stettin, a strikebreaker named Brandenburg stabbed a striking worker with a bread knife. The victim, named Kühl, died almost instantly.[46]

Alongside these cases of striking workers killed by strikebreakers, there is a very long list of workers seriously injured by armed strikebreakers. In 1913, for example, three blacklegs who were working in Kassel fired their revolvers at the striking worker Ostertag, who miraculously escaped death.[47] Although the multiple episodes of violence mentioned here involved German-speaking strikebreakers and striking workers, the conflicts between unionised workers and strikebreakers, and hence the ideological antagonism between left-wing and bourgeois newspapers, became radicalised when foreign "blacklegs" were employed. In June 1906, *Vorwärts* reported from Cologne that armed strikebreakers from "semi-civilised regions", such as the Balkans and Italy, not only threatened striking workers but terrorised the entire city with their violence and criminal activities.[48] If bands of strikebreakers used a broad repertoire of violence against labour, it is also true that exploited and vulnerable migrant workers were frequently discriminated against, insulted and attacked by striking workers. Socialist and trade union newspapers used an extremely harsh tone in speaking of strikebreakers, who were not only morally stigmatised but also physically threatened. The home addresses of notorious strikebreakers were often published in left-wing newspapers, and posters with explicit death threats were frequently printed during strikes.[49] In Basel, for example, posters with explicit death threats against strikebreakers were frequently translated into Italian.[50] Xenophobic discourses against strikebreakers also clearly emerged during transport workers' strikes in Berlin, when for instance Russian replacement workers were stigmatised as "*Pollacken*" (a disrespectful term for "Polish") or "*Müllkosaken*" (rubbish Cossacks).[51]

More than isolated cases of violence?

As early as 1904, two years before the first murder case in Nuremberg, *Vorwärts* had extensively reported on the violent clashes between armed strikebreakers and unionised workers in Berlin. The SPD party newspaper argued that at least two companies in the industrial area of Berlin (Krey and Zürn & Glienicke) systematically distributed weapons to strikebreakers. Armed with sticks, they formed an "assault column" (*Sturmkolonne*) against strike pickets.[52] The newspaper of the Federation of Yellow Unions echoed these rumours and boastfully reported on the increasing number of armed strikebreakers in, for example, Wittenau near Berlin, where they were all armed with revolvers.[53] Sometimes employers did not limit themselves to arming strikebreakers but were themselves armed and actively participated in "self-defence". This was the case with the iron industry employer, Von der Hecken, from Aachen, who not only distributed revolvers to his strikebreakers, but also armed himself and killed the Dutch worker Hieronymus Stroet during a strike in 1912.[54]

What is remarkable is that it was not only the professional and hierarchically organised groups of strikebreakers, such as those led by Hintze and Katzmarek, that were armed: the more ad hoc groups also obtained weapons. However, while armed intimidation was a fundamental aspect of the business of professional strikebreakers, who were already equipped with revolvers, unorganised strikebreakers were mostly provided with weapons by the employers. Eventually, the problem of armed strikebreakers was discussed in the Reichstag. During a debate in 1907, the Social Democratic member of parliament Paul Singer showed the assembly a photograph of armed strikebreakers in Cologne symbolically carrying their weapons to "defend" the company of the industrial magnate Kohl.[55] Another SPD parliamentarian, Theodor Bömelburg, created a huge sensation when he showed the Reichstag assembly one of the steel-reinforced sticks that had been distributed to strikebreakers in the Ruhr area.[56]

The first reports of "blackleg gunfighters" (*arbeitswillige Revolverhelden*) and employers' attempts to militarise strikebreakers had appeared already around 1900 but intensified in the decade before the war.[57] Liberal newspapers also frequently reported on armed strikebreakers. Between September 1906 and March 1907, for example, the *Allgemeine Zeitung* published three articles about strikebreakers armed with revolvers in Munich, Nuremberg and Cologne.[58] These armed strikebreakers were labelled "gunfighters" by the left-wing newspapers, a term that was broadly used to demonise gun violence and criminal gangs and hence created a semantic connection between the criminal underworld and professional strikebreakers.[59] Highly evocative notions, such as "gunfighters", or "worker's murder" (*Arbeitermord*), suggested that bands of strikebreakers serving to secure capitalist interests were similar to street gangs and that violence was an integral part of their service. Although left-wing newspapers dramatically emphasised the strikebreakers' (illegal) use of violence, the polemic against "blackleg gunfighters" did partly reflect the social reality after the turn of the century when strikebreakers began systematically to use weapons, partly in self-defence and partly with the aim of intimidating workers and offering private security services to employers. It is therefore not surprising that *Vorwärts* also explicitly compared strikebreaking agents like Friedrich Hintze with Pinkerton's National Detective Agency.[60]

Bands of strikebreakers: "Yellow Katzmarek" and "Hintze's soldiers"

In the decade up to 1914, the groups led by Friedrich Hintze in Hamburg and Karl Katzmarek in Berlin emerged as the most important strikebreaking agencies in Imperial Germany. Both bands of strikebreakers were highly professionalised and active in almost the whole of German-speaking Central Europe. They were well known for their brutality and for their use of weapons as a major part of their everyday business. Katzmarek's and Hintze's activities resulted in these leaders becoming synonymous with violent, professional strikebreaking activities. In describing the broader phenomenon of strikebreaking, left-wing newspapers used their names as negative terms for violent strikebreaking (*Katzmareks*, *Hintzegardisten* and *Hintzebrüder*).[61] Katzmarek, in particular, had a great interest in his self-representation. Nicknamed "Yellow Katzmarek", he was a member of the board of the Federation of Yellow Unions and had a personal link with Rudolf Lebius, leader of the Federation.[62] "Yellow Katzmarek" was always armed with revolvers and daggers and he owned a car, which was not at all common at the time. On the night of 4 October 1913, on his way back to Magdeburg in his car, he caused a traffic collision killing a pedestrian. Socialist newspapers reported that during the trial Katzmarek tried to defend himself with the argument that he was a prominent strikebreaking agent and therefore a useful member of the community deserving of special protection. Although he had previous convictions for violence, insults and robbery, he was sentenced to only one month in prison.[63]

In 1912, during a strike in Berlin, Katzmarek joined forces with Hintze to mobilise an armed band of strikebreakers that terrorised unionised workers.[64] According to sensationalised reports in the SPD party press, violent intimidation of both striking workers and the Social Democratic milieu was the trademark activity of Katzmarek's and Hintze's bands. In 1911, during a strike in the small city of Güstrow in Mecklenburg, Katzmarek's band arrived from Berlin and took de facto control of the town and established a "rule of violence" (*Gewaltherrschaft*).[65] The same strategy had been adopted by Hintze a year earlier during a mineworkers' strike in Finkenheerd, another small town in northern Germany. When the 15 members of "Hintze's guard" arrived in Finkenheerd, they immediately set about organising a shooting range for weapons training, sending a clear message to the striking workers.[66]

After the Moabit riot in 1910, Hintze became the most notorious German strikebreaker, ironically nicknamed "the hero of Moabit" by *Vorwärts* because of his having led the so-called patriotic forces that helped to restore order after two weeks of rioting.[67] The Moabit riot was actually a labour dispute that escalated into widespread popular protests, especially after violent clashes between striking workers and strikebreakers.[68] According to the semi-official *Norddeutsche Allgemeine Zeitung*, fighting escalated on the evening of 28 September with more than 90 injured.[69] "Hintze's soldiers" undertook two tasks during the riot: they supplied substitutes for striking workers, helping to deliver coal during the day, and at night they cooperated with the police to combat "strike terrorism". Hintze and his strikebreakers had access to a temporary prison camp for arrested striking workers, where, in collusion with the police authorities, they savagely beat the prisoners. It was not only *Vorwärts* but also the liberal *Vossische Zeitung* that reported on the quasi-paramilitary organisation of Hintze's band during the Moabit uprising.[70]

In October 1910, Hintze gave a long interview to the popular newspaper *Berliner Morgenpost*, in which he described his career as a professional strikebreaker and provided insights on how he organised his business.[71] Initially, Hintze worked for the well-known strikebreaker agent August Müller in Hamburg, but shortly after Müller's death, the 21-year-old Hintze established his own organisation. He claimed to have more than 6,000 strikebreakers whom he could mobilise in only eight days. Despite this obviously exaggerated statement, Hintze was able to organise quite large groups of armed strikebreakers with long-range mobility. In 1911 *Vorwärts* reported that hundreds of "Hintze's soldiers" had travelled from Hamburg to the East Prussian city of Königsberg, which was almost 1,000 kilometres away.[72] Berlin and Hamburg were the most important logistic centres for the distribution of strikebreakers to distant cities such as Königsberg or Basel, but they more frequently operated in the regional areas of cities such as Bremen and Kassel as well as many small towns in Mecklenburg and Brandenburg.[73]

Hintze's name became a synonym for professional strikebreaking with brutal methods. According to the SPD parliamentarian Cohn, Hintze recruited violent teenagers from the poorest districts of Berlin.[74] In his interview to the *Morgenpost*, Hintze mentioned that his agency was doing very well and that he was paid ten marks for each strikebreaker he delivered. He explicitly stated that he offered not only labour replacement but also supply services, logistics (he had three cars) and, of course, organisation of the strikebreakers' "self-defence". He was aware that the interview with the *Morgenpost* was a great opportunity for free publicity and mentioned that his strikebreakers would do any kind of job that the company would pay for, but, more importantly, they could effectively intimidate unionised workers. The agent proudly proclaimed that "with thirty men I can terrify five hundred strikers".[75] Hintze's agency was not only active during strikes, it also offered its services to private companies in the aftermath of unrest to prevent the expansion of labour unions.[76] Hintze also mentioned that he was already involved in 15 different strikes and that the most important aspect of his business was to create a military-like organisation and establish military discipline among the strikebreakers.

Bands of strikebreakers combined violence, a quasi-paramilitary organisation and street gang behaviour with a highly professionalised business. It was not only Hintze who made an effort to publicise his semi-legal strikebreaking agency: Katzmarek distributed marketing brochures informing potential employers that they were to pay his strikebreakers five marks per day and that they should also pay for transportation, food supplies and housing. Katzmarek's brochure also stated that he was able to recruit service staff and cooks and to provide cooking utensils for the strikebreakers as well as "resolute foremen" and armed guards.[77] His band of strikebreakers was hierarchically organised and well known not only in Germany but also in Austria and the Swiss Confederation. Katzmarek had a right-hand man, Gründke, and a group of foremen who oversaw the other strikebreakers.[78] After his election to the central committee of Lebius's Federation of Yellow Workers in January 1908, Katzmarek was described by Lebius as someone with a charismatic but dangerously self-overestimated personality and "gipsy blood" (*Zigeunerblut*).[79] Although Katzmarek cooperated with other notorious strikebreakers, such as Hintze, he also tried to protect his lucrative business using illegal methods against his competitors. In 1913, for example, he sent falsified letters purporting to be from private companies to other strikebreaking agents resulting in these delivering "blacklegs" to the wrong place and therefore receiving no pay.[80]

Joseph Ruppert was another professional strikebreaker who killed a worker near Magdeburg in 1912 and who, during his trial, tried to justify always carrying his revolver with the argument that "weapons are the tools of our trade".[81] He was accused by *Vorwärts* of being one of the most dangerous members of Katzmarek's band.[82] More often, Ruppert worked independently with his partner Anton Meinel, another notorious strikebreaker who was also accused of being a procurer.[83]

They were involved in several episodes of violence and intimidation not only in Magdeburg but also in Berlin, Thuringia (Zeulenroda) and Nesseldorf in the Moravian-Silesian region. The Social Democratic *Arbeiter-Zeitung* reported that Meinel threatened unionised workers during a strike in Berlin claiming: "I can do what I want, I am allowed in certain circumstances to shoot, I can even kill a man".[84] Like the other "blackleg gunfighters" mentioned in this chapter, the focus of Ruppert's and Meinel's activities was less on replacing striking workers and more on intimidating them.[85]

Conclusion

Greater protection for strikebreakers had already begun to be sought by conservative politicians and employers at the end of the nineteenth century. In 1897, the Kaiser announced a programme of "protection for the national labour of the productive classes, . . . ruthless repression of all revolutionary subversion and the heaviest penalty for anyone who dares to hinder his neighbour, who wants to work, in his freedom to work".[86] This political manifesto against organised labour formed part of the so-called *Zuchthausvorlage*, the penitentiary bill designed to penalise picketing that was presented to the Reichstag in 1899 but defeated by the parliamentary opposition.[87] However, the spirit of the *Zuchthausvorlage* remained embedded in the Prussian courts, at least from a Social Democratic standpoint, even after its defeat in the Reichstag.

The de facto impunity of armed groups of strikebreakers can be explained as an extra-legal response aimed at protecting the "productive classes" after leading conservatives recognised that the intensification of repressive authoritarian practices against the labour movement was rather unpopular and could not be legally imposed. The advent of mass politics, especially the introduction of universal male suffrage and the rise of mass-produced newspapers, set new limits on state repression and authoritarian control. At the same time, "threat communication" and the radicalisation of the debates on "strike terrorism" gave greater visibility and urgency to social conflicts. As a result, strikebreaking became more professionalised and militarised after the turn of the century. This shows that the transition to democracy and mass politics opened up new horizons for privately organised coercion and motivated the redistribution of coercive tasks to non-state actors.

The debate about "strike terrorism" reached a new peak in 1907 when some of the most influential members of the conservative party stressed the urgency for greater protection for those "patriotic and loyal workers" who opposed the "red terror".[88] During a debate in the Reichstag in 1907, Arthur von Posadowsky-Wehner, the Prussian secretary of state of the interior and vice chancellor, openly encouraged presumed victims of the "red terror" to organise themselves against the intimidation and violence inflicted on them by the labour movement. Posadowsky openly supported the formation of yellow unions and armed groups of strikebreakers and assured them that Prussian courts and police authorities would tolerate counter-strike actions.[89] This proposition was well received and was taken up by the leader of the Federation of Yellow Workers, Rudolf Lebius, as stated in his pamphlet *Gelbe Gedanken* (Yellow Thoughts), published in 1908.[90] In his articles for the federation's newspaper and for several other publications, Lebius stressed the fact that the yellow unions were born out of the right to self-defence of patriotic workers who organised themselves against terrorism: "Red terrorism is the initiator of the yellow movement".[91] The Federation of Patriotic Workers (*Bund Vaterländischer Arbeitervereine*), another anti-labour organisation, created in 1907, used the same argumentative strategy as Lebius. *Deutsche Treue*, the newspaper of the "patriotic workers", claimed that "true German men" should not wait for state protection, but had to mobilise against labour militancy and socialist propaganda.[92]

In 1910, German industrialists launched a fresh campaign for better protection of "willing workers", calling for the army's intervention and the demonstrative use of machine guns against striking mineworkers in the Ruhr area.[93] State-led repression and repressive practices on the part of extra-legal groups, such as the armed bands of strikebreakers, had something in common: they all involved "collective violence". In Charles Tilly's definition, collective violence includes a vast range of social interactions and excludes "purely individual action".[94] It is therefore grounded in complex interactions and is also closely related to the perceived urgency to defend the established order against emerging social movements and their claims. Therefore, violence carried out by armed strikebreakers was, again following Tilly's definition, not simply "individual aggression writ large" but was significantly affected by "social ties, structures and process" as well as by the political discourses and media representations in Wilhelmine Germany.[95]

Defining repressive practices carried out by armed strikebreakers as collective violence raises further, more general questions: why did strikes and mass demonstrations in the first decades of the twentieth century increasingly shift into collective violence (both in late Imperial Germany and much more dramatically in the early Weimar years)? What impact did different political regimes (semi-authoritarian before 1918, democratic after 1918) have on the levels and forms of collective violence? What impact did the glamorisation and sensationalisation of collective violence in the modern media have in different political contexts? Although further studies are needed to provide exhaustive answers, the rise of armed groups of professional strikebreakers examined in this chapter is an important yet less well-studied issue within the broader framework of authoritarian responses to social conflicts. The impunity of Katzmarek, Hintze and other notorious strikebreakers gives new insights into the privatisation of repressive strategies and the mobilisation of non-state actors in defence of the bourgeois order. In the decade up to 1914, strikebreaking agents were almost always armed and frequently used mafia-like methods to intimidate unionised workers. Along with providing labour replacement, the main aim of these "gunfighters" was to effect non-bureaucratic repression of the labour movement. The violence carried out by bands of strikebreakers demonstrates that the *Kaiserreich*'s authorities were inclined to tolerate, to a certain extent, privately organised coercion, especially where social movements, democratic institutions and the modern media were effective in thwarting legal, state-led authoritarian responses.

Notes

* This chapter is part of a broader research project on social conflicts and political violence in late Imperial Germany. A monograph on these topics will be published in spring 2021 under the title *"Blut und Eisen auch im Innern". Soziale Konflikte, Massenpolitik und Gewalt in Deutschland vor 1914* (Frankfurt: Campus).

Research for this article received funding from the European Research Council (ERC) under the European Union's Horizon 2020 Research and Innovation program (G.A. 677199 – ERC-StG2015 "The Dark Side of the Belle Époque. Political Violence and Armed Associations in Europe before the First World War").

1 *Reichstagprotokolle,* Vol. 392, March 21, 1927, 9760. The term "bands of strikebreakers" has been also used by historian Stephen H. Norwood. He has examined the spread of large mercenary bands for strikebreaking purposes in early twentieth-century America. Stephen H. Norwood, *Strikebreaking & Intimidation: Mercenaries and Masculinity in Twentieth-century America* (Chapel Hill, NC: University of North Carolina Press, 2010), 10.

2 See Michael H. Kater, "Die Technische Nothilfe im Spannungsfeld von Arbeiterunruhen, Unternehmerinteressen und Parteipolitik," *Vierteljahrshefte für Zeitgeschichte* 27, no. 1 (1979): 30–78.

3 Mark Jones, *Founding Weimar. Violence and the German Revolution of 1918–1919* (Oxford: Oxford University Press, 2016), 252–59.

4 See Amerigo Caruso, "Joining Forces against 'Strike Terrorism': The Public-Private Interplay in Policing Strikes in Imperial Germany, 1890–1914," *European History Quarterly* 49, no. 4 (2019): 597–624. On "wild strikes", counter-strike reactions and armed clashes after 1919 see Dirk Schumann, *Political Violence in the Weimar Republic, 1918–1933: Fight for the Streets and Fear of Civil War* (New York and Oxford: Berghahn Books, 2009).

5 See, for example, Anja Johansen, *Soldiers as Police: The French and Prussian Armies and the Policing of Popular Protest, 1889–1914* (Aldershot: Ashgate, 2005).

6 Thomas Lindenberger and Alf Lüdtke, "Einleitung. Physische Gewalt – eine Kontinuität der Moderne," in *Physische Gewalt. Studien zur Geschichte der Neuzeit*, ed. Thomas Lindenberger and Alf Lüdtke (Frankfurt: Suhrkamp, 1995), 7–38.

7 See, for example, Pieter Leloup, "The Private Security Industry in Antwerp (1907–1934). A Historical-criminological Analysis of its Modus Operandi and Growth," *Crime, History & Societies* 19, no. 2 (2015): 119–47.

8 Johansen, *Soldiers as Police*, 134.

9 Fabian Fechner, Tanja Granzow, Jacek Klimek, Roman Krawielicki, Beatrice von Lüpke, and Rebekka Nöcker, "'We are Gambling with Our Survival.' Bedrohungskommunikation als Indikator für bedrohte Ordnungen," in *Aufruhr – Katastrophe – Konkurrenz – Zerfall. Bedrohte Ordnungen als Thema der Kulturwissenschaften*, ed. Ewald Frie and Mischa Meier (Tübingen: Mohr Siebeck, 2014), 141–73.

10 Ian Kershaw, "War and Political Violence in Twentieth-Century Europe," *Contemporary European History* 14, no. 1 (2005): 107–23, here 111.

11 *Norddeutsche Zeitung*, September 29, 1910, 2.

12 The possession of guns was not restricted but there were limitations to the right of carrying arms in public.

13 Dagmar Ellerbrock, "Gun Violence and Control in Germany 1880–1911: Scandalizing Gun Violence and Changing Perceptions as Preconditions for Firearm Control," in *Control of Violence. Historical and International Perspectives on Violence in Modern Societies*, ed. Heinz-Gerhard Haupt (New York: Springer, 2011), 185–212.

14 Robert P. Weiss, "Private Detective Agencies and Labour Discipline in the United States, 1855–1946," *The Historical Journal* 29, no. 1 (1986): 87–107.

15 Stephen H. Norwood, "Strikebreaking," in *Encyclopedia of U.S. Labor and Working-class History*, Vol. 1, ed. Eric Arnesen (New York: Routledge, 2007), 1338–43.

16 Arthur McIvor, *Organised Capital: Employers' Associations and Industrial Relations in Northern England 1880–1939* (Cambridge: Cambridge University Press, 1996), 93.
17 *Vorwärts*, February 14, 1914, 1–2.
18 Benjamin Carter Hett, *Death in the Tiergarten. Murder and Criminal Justice in the Kaiser's Berlin* (Cambridge, MA: Harvard University Press, 2004), 1.
19 See, for example, *Arbeiterwille*, April 14, 1914, 1.
20 Alex Hall, *Scandal, Sensation and Social Democracy. The SPD Press and Wilhelmine Germany 1890–1914* (London: Cambridge University Press, 1977), 11. See also Frank Bösch, *Öffentliche Geheimnisse: Skandale, Politik und Medien in Deutschland und Großbritannien 1880–1914* (München: Oldenbourg, 2009).
21 Thomas Welskopp, "Im Bann des 19. Jahrhunderts. Die deutsche Arbeiterbewegung und ihre Zukunftsvorstellungen zu Gesellschaftspolitik und sozialer Frage," in *Das neue Jahrhundert. Europäische Zeitdiagnosen und Zukunftsentwürfe um 1900*, ed. Ute Frevert (Göttingen: Vandenhoeck & Ruprecht), 15–46.
22 Rudolf Lebius, *Die gelbe Arbeiterbewegung* (Berlin: Reformverlag Der Bund, 1908), 1. See also Lebius's article against "red terrorism" in *Der Bund*, July 1909, 1. On Lebius see also Martin Kohlrausch, "Zwischen Star-Schriftsteller und Hochstapler: Der 'Fall-May' als wilhelminischer Skandal," in *Karl May: Brückenbauer zwischen den Kulturen*, ed. Wolfram Pyta (Berlin: LIT Verlag, 2010), 197–214. On transnational connections of the "yellow" movement in France, Germany and the Swiss Confederation see Romain Bonnet and Amerigo Caruso, "Europe industrielle et contre-internationalisme: le mouvement Jaune dans l'espace franco-allemand avant 1914," *Histoire@Politique* 39 (2019).
23 The increase of Social Democratic votes after the abolition of the antisocialist-laws century was accompanied by the unprecedented intensity of labour conflicts, which reached a provisional peak in the period between 1904 and 1907.
24 *Vorwärts*, November 12, 1907, 6.
25 *Mitteilungen über die Verhandlungen des Ordentlichen Landtags im Königreiche Sachsen*, 17 Mai 1912, 3389. Uhlig referred to violent activities carried out by armed strikebreakers in Reichenau.
26 Vgl. Alejandro Colás and Bryan Mabee, "Introduction," in *Pirates, Mercenaries, Bandits and Empires. Private Violence in Historical Perspective*, ed. Alejandro Colás and Bryan Mabee (New York: Columbia University Press, 2010), 1–32.
27 *Vorwärts*, February 14, 1914, 1 (*"Wir Arbeitswillige dürfen jemand totschlagen und es passiert uns nichts"*).
28 *Vorwärts*, August 21, 1906, 3. See also *Vorwärts*, November 27, 1913, 1; *Vorwärts*, June 7, 1913, 1; *Grütlianer*, February 12, 1914, 1; *Arbeiter-Zeitung*, April 14, 1914, 3.
29 *Vorwärts*, August 21, 1906, 3; *Arbeiter-Zeitung*, August 26, 1906, 7.
30 *Vorwärts*, August 22, 1906, 4. In the following weeks *Vorwärts* reported extensively on the trial, see *Vorwärts*, September 22, 1906, 4; October 10, 1906, October 3 and 12, 1906, 13.
31 *Vorwärts*, October 13, 1906, 9.
32 See Thomas Lindenberger, *Straßenpolitik. Zur Sozialgeschichte der öffentlichen Ordnung in Berlin 1900 bis 1914* (Bonn: Dietz, 1995), 200.
33 *Vorwärts*, October 17, 1906, 2.
34 *Allgemeine Zeitung*, August 24, 1906, 7.
35 *Allgemeine Zeitung*, October 14, 1906, 6–7 and October 15, 1906, 6.
36 On Moabit, see Lindenberger, *Straßenpolitik*.
37 For a comprehensive analysis of the Kaiserreich's judicial system and the political debate on "class justice", see Uwe Wilhelm, *Das Deutsche Kaiserreich und seine Justiz: Justizkritik, politische Strafrechtsprechung, Justizpolitik* (Berlin: Duncker & Humblot, 2010), 504–10. As noted by Richard F. Wetzell criminal justice in Imperial Germany was the product of a "hybrid legal culture that combined authoritarian elements with the liberal legal principles of the rule of law". Richard F. Wetzell, "Crime and Criminal

Justice in Modern Germany," in *Crime and Criminal Justice in Modern Germany*, ed. Richard F. Wetzell (New York: Berghahn Books, 2014), 1–28.

38 *Vorwärts* journalists uncovered 17 convictions between 1895 and 1912. *Vorwärts*, January 15, 1914, 13.

39 See Amerigo Caruso and Claire Morelon, "The Threat from Within across Empires: Strikes, Labor Migration, and Violence in Central Europe, 1900–1914" (forthcoming article).

40 *Vorwärts*, February 21, 1913, 10.

41 *Vorwärts*, October 6, 1911, 4.

42 *Vorwärts*, Mai 6, 1911, 9.

43 *Vorwärts*, November 31, 1912, 3.

44 *Gewerkschaftliche Rundschau für die Schweiz*, January 5, 1912, 62.

45 Along with *Vorwärts*, a total of six Austrian and 13 Swiss newspapers reported about the murder of Wydler. For example *La lutte syndicale*, June 22, 1912, 4; *La Liberté*, Mai 7, 1912, 1; *Grütlianer*, Mai 25, 1912, 2; *Arbeiter-Zeitung*, Mai 13, 1912, 5 and *Böhmerwald Volksbote*, Mai 18, 1912, 6.

46 *Vorwärts*, June 7, 1913, 1. See also *Vorwärts*, June 29, 1913, 2.

47 *Vorwärts*, April 1, 1913, 4.

48 *Vorwärts*, June 11, 1912, 4.

49 *Grütlianer*, May 31, 1906, 1. See also *Grütlianer*, June 26, 1906, 4.

50 *Grütlianer*, June 27, 1907, 6.

51 Lindenberger, *Straßenpolitik*, 216–18.

52 *Vorwärts*, November 8, 1904, 6.

53 *Vorwärts*, February 2, 1908, 4.

54 *Arbeiter-Zeitung*, July 26, 1912, 8; *Vorwärts*, July 21, 1912, 6. See also Michael Klöcker, *Die Sozialdemokratie im Regierungsbezirk Aachen vor dem 1. Weltkrieg* (Hamburg: Einhorn-Presse Verlag, 1977), 153.

55 *Reichstagprotokolle*, Vol. 227, March 1, 1907, 159–60.

56 *Reichstagprotokolle*, Vol. 201, January 23, 1905, 3990.

57 One of the first report on "blackleg gunfighters" appeared in 1902. See *Vorwärts*, June 17, 1902, 4.

58 *Allgemeine Zeitung*, September 8, 1906, 18–20; March 2, 1907, 14 and December 20, 1907, 21.

59 On dramatisation of crime in Imperial Germany see Philipp Müller, *Auf der Suche nach dem Täter. Die öffentliche Dramatisierung von Verbrechen im Berlin des Kaiserreichs* (Frankfurt: Campus, 2005).

60 *Vorwärts*, October 22, 1910, 6.

61 For this reason it is sometimes unclear whether Hintze was directly involved, or his name was used to describe other armed groups of strikebreakers.

62 *Vorwärts*, April 25, 1911, 4. Lebius was accused of offering the same services of strikebreaking agencies; see *Vorwärts*, September 15, 1908, and March 4, 11, 1910, 4.

63 *Vorwärts*, February 6, 1914, 7. The sentence was lenient also because legislation on road accidents was still in the preparation phase and the maximum penalty, for example for *Fahrerflucht* (failing to stop after being involved in an accident) was six months in prison. See Uwe Fraunholz, *Motorphobia: anti-automobiler Protest in Kaiserreich und Weimarer Republik* (Göttingen: Vandenhoeck & Ruprecht, 2002), 213.

64 *Vorwärts*, September 11, 1912, 4.

65 *Vorwärts*, July 14, 1911, 4.

66 *Vorwärts*, February 28, 1911, 4.

67 *Vorwärts*, October 5, 1910, 1–3.

68 *Norddeutsche Zeitung*, September 25, 1910, 7.

69 *Norddeutsche Zeitung*, September 29, 1910, 2. *Vorwärts* reported about 75 seriously injured persons, see *Vorwärts*, September 30, 1910, 1–3.

70 Lindenberger, *Straßenpolitik*, 283–85.

71 *Berliner Morgenpost*, October 4, 1910, 1. Founded in 1898 with a modern and accessible format, the *Morgenpost* reported a daily circulation of 250,000 copies already in 1900. Corey Ross, *Media and the Making of Modern Germany. Mass Communication, Society, and Politics from the Empire to the Third Reich* (Oxford: Oxford University Press, 2008), 27.
72 *Vorwärts*, July 4, 1911, 4.
73 *Vorwärts*, November 28, 1911, 9.
74 *Reichstagprotokolle*, Vol. 287, February 8, 1913, 3585.
75 *Berliner Morgenpost*, October 4, 1910, 1.
76 Ibid., 2.
77 *Arbeiter-Zeitung*, June 9, 1914, 10.
78 *Salzburger Wacht*, April 8, 1913, 6. See also *Vorwärts*, April 5, 1913, 4.
79 *Der gelbe Sumpf: ein Blick hinter die Kulissen der gelben Arbeiter-Vereine durch Einsichtnahme in einige Lebius-Briefe* (Stuttgart: Steiner, 1908), 15.
80 *Vorwärts*, March 20, 1913, 4.
81 *Vorwärts*, February 13, 1914, 15.
82 *Vorwärts*, September 27, 1913, 9.
83 *Vorwärts*, February 16, 1914, 7.
84 *Arbeiter-Zeitung*, February 15, 1914, 10.
85 *Vorwärts*, April 10, 1913, 4. Following the *Vorwärts*, the police provided Ruppert and Meinel with a special firearms licence, which allowed them to bear weapons during public demonstrations, see *Vorwärts*, February 14, 1914, 1.
86 Edgar Feuchtwanger, *Imperial Germany 1850–1918* (London: Routledge, 2001), 129.
87 See Geoff Eley, "The Social Construction of Democracy in Germany, 1871–1933," in *The Social Construction of Democracy, 1870–1990*, ed. George Andrews and Herrick Chapman (New York: New York University Press, 1995), 90–117.
88 *Reichstagprotokolle*, Vol. 227, April 15, 1907, 770.
89 Ibid., 772.
90 Rudolf Lebius, *Gelbe Gedanken* (Berlin: Reformverlag Der Bund, 1908), 28.
91 "Der rote Terror ist der Vater der gelben Arbeiterbewegung," *Der Bund*, July 18, 1909, 1. See also Lebius, *Die gelbe Arbeiterbewegung*, 1; Lebius, *Gelbe Gedanken*, 28; *Der Bund*, December 4, 1906, 2.
92 *Deutsche Treue*, January 19, 1908, 42 ("Selbsthilfe und die Tätigkeit der deutschen Männer").
93 See Klaus Saul, "Repression or Integration? The State, Trade Unions and Industrial Disputes in Imperial Germany," in *The Development of Trade Unionism in Great Britain and Germany, 1880–1914*, ed. Wolfgang Mommsen and Hans-Gerhard Husung (London: George Allen and Unwin, 1985), 338–56.
94 Charles Tilly, *The Politics of Collective Violence* (Cambridge: Cambridge University Press, 2003), 4.
95 Ibid.

Part 3

Civic and industrial vigilantism

12 The wild west of employer anti-unionism

The glorification of vigilantism and individualism in the early twentieth-century United States[1]

Vilja Hulden and Chad Pearson

When employers organised to address the "labour question" in the opening years of the twentieth century, they did so as the self-proclaimed champions of "independent" (that is, non-union) workers supposedly harassed by labour unions. At a moment when unions were growing, strike activity was intensifying, and the corporate-industrial order was under severe scrutiny, organised employers countered critiques of how economic power undermined democracy by wrapping themselves in a language of fairness and equal rights, characterising virtually all standard labour union practices as coercive while portraying themselves as the true defenders of American liberty.[2]

Manufacturers took the lead, as organisations like the National Association of Manufacturers (NAM), the National Founders' Association (NFA) and the National Metal Trades Association (NMTA) rallied against what they termed the "closed shop" – the common union requirement that all workers at a unionised workplace be union members – with a movement for the "open shop", a workplace that purportedly welcomed workers without regard to union membership. Although the bulk of research on the employer counterattack has focused on the manufacturers, from the beginning the movement strove for a pan-industrial reach, which crystallised in the Citizens' Industrial Association of America (CIAA). The CIAA, established in late 1903 to serve as the umbrella organisation of local associations usually known as Citizens' Alliances, included members from manufacturing, construction, lumber, banking, retail and more. It purported to work "for the protection of the common people" against the "tyranny of labor unions" and to safeguard individual pluck and initiative against the levelling influence of union contracts.[3]

In this chapter, we show how the employer anti-union movement both boosted and intersected with the American creed of up-by-one's-bootstraps social mobility. To do so, we turn our gaze away from the manufacturing sector and towards western cattle ranches, on the one hand, and urban small-time entrepreneurship, on the other. The former helps us examine how the employer counterattack linked itself with deep national mythologies of (frontier) individualism. The latter allows us to explore a context in which social mobility – on a modest but meaningful scale – was more reachable to workers than in manufacturing, somewhat changing the calculus of solidarity versus individualism. Analysing how employers manipulated the cultural tenets and grassroots appeal of social mobility and individualism enables us to better understand what made the employer message palatable to many in the middle class as well as to some workers. At the same time, it illuminates how employers deployed a double standard that cast elite-serving collective action as civic engagement while vilifying worker self-organisation as dangerous and always at risk of tipping over into mob violence.

The first portion of our chapter examines the role of the famous author and pioneer of the Western genre of fiction writing, Owen Wister, in promoting the employer cause. In his writings, Wister – appointed in 1907 as member of the CIAA's seven-person committee on Education and Publicity – justified and even glorified vigilante violence and strikebreakers by enveloping both in a great patriotic tradition of individualism.[4] The second portion focuses on employer promotion of "non-union unions", astroturf organisations that supposedly represented the interests of workers who did not wish to join labour unions. It investigates both the publicity value that such unions had for the employer anti-union movement and the circumstances that might have prompted some workers to associate with them.

Owen Wister and the virtuous scab

Best remembered as the author of the 1902 book *The Virginian: A Horseman of the Plains*, Wister educated and entertained hundreds of thousands about individual heroism and vigilante campaigns for justice. His best-selling book, based roughly on the 1892 Johnson County War – a violent conflict that pitted the elite members of Wyoming Stock Growers Association against numerous small homesteaders – promoted the goodness of individualism, the importance of defending private property, the necessity of showing respect to one's superiors and the virtue of standing up to the so-called dangerous classes. These values were consistent with the CIAA's core mission, which included efforts to de-legitimise expressions of working-class collectivism while calling on citizens to respect the men responsible for upholding "law and order".[5] By focusing on Wister's writings, we can better comprehend the ways anti-union employers championed the activities, including vigilante actions of individual anti-unionists.

Class conflict and the question of violence in 1892

Wister started writing about labour-management conflicts a decade before publishing *The Virginian*; for instance, he wrote an article on the Pennsylvania National Guard's role in confronting the Homestead strikers in 1892, which came out in *Harper's* two years later. One of the nation's iconic labour conflicts, the protest, organised by the Amalgamated Association of Iron and Steel Workers and Tin Workers, demonstrated the workers' commitment to solidarity. Plant operator Henry Clay Frick, who had locked the men out because they refused to accept a wage cut, was quite frustrated by such solidarity. Writing to owner Andrew Carnegie on 4 July, Frick complained that "The workmen seem to be well organised, and have things, so far, very much their own way, that is to say, are guarding every avenue to the works; stopping all who may, or try, to get in the works".[6]

During the conflict, Frick employed the services of the Pinkertons, which engaged in a notorious battle with protestors that resulted in the deaths of ten: seven workers and three Pinkertons. In response, Frick asked Democratic governor Robert Pattison to send in National Guardsmen.

Wister was impressed by the 8,500 scab-protecting National Guardsmen.[7] He emphasised the visual differences between the conflicting sides, saluting the guardsmen for appearing "splendid on paper and picturesque to see", while labelling their opponents "rats".[8] Wister showed little desire to understand the reasons for the workers' grievances or their desire for a union. Instead he emphasised the dangers labourers posed to property rights. Among the accusations he levelled at the "rats" were that they distributed "incendiary pamphlets", drove "owners from their property", "established an advisory committee superior to the civil law" and violated "personal liberty".[9] Examples of striker militancy, in Wister's mind, provided justification for state repression. The workers ultimately lost this struggle, and the membership of the Amalgamated Association Iron and Steel Workers and Tin Workers fell to less than 10,000 members shortly after it.[10]

Vigilante violence from above, however, was apparently quite acceptable to Wister. He condemned the Homestead strikers but showed approval for the violence employed by the Wyoming Stock Growers Association (WSGA), an organisation consisting of the state's large landowners. These men are best known for their involvement in the 1892 Johnson County War, an infamous case of vigilantism that resulted in several killings followed by a failure of justice. Here, a combined group of roughly 50 WSGA members and their hired gunmen, seeking greater control over land and cattle, invaded northern Wyoming in April 1892. They fought under the banner of combating rustling, annoyed that the courts frequently failed to punish men for this alleged offence. Indeed, juries, seeing little evidence of wrongdoing, typically declared defendants not guilty, sparking signs of disappointment in elite circles. The WSGA vigilantes, joined by Pinkertons and hired gunmen, mobilised in early April. They murdered two men, including a labour activist. After these murders, many Johnson County residents retaliated. The invaders were forced to seek protection, which they received from the governor and President Benjamin Harrison. Community defenders were shocked to discover many deadly weapons and a 70-person kill-list after the shooting ceased. This was a rural, rather than an industrial struggle. But the class divisions were just as clear in Johnson County, Wyoming as they were in Western Pennsylvania. In both cases, the ruling class believed violence was an acceptable way to resolve their problems.

The defendants in this case – one that generated nationwide attention – got off after the court dismissed all charges against the cattlemen. Yet they lost the public relations war.[11]

The Virginian and the public relations of violence

The invaders, though wealthy, wanted society to see them as upstanding ordinary people; they did not want the public to view them as suffering from what we might today call affluenza. They faced an increasingly unfriendly political and social climate: 1892 was a year that witnessed much class conflict and the rise of left-wing political activism, which hurt the image of the nation's most privileged residents. In addition to the Homestead Strike and the Johnson County invasion, miners in northern Idaho staged an extraordinary struggle against the ruthless exploitation unleashed by several mine owners, and later in the year, workers mounted a general strike in New Orleans.[12]

The backlash against what seemed like a coordinated campaign against organised labour also found expression in political formations, including the rise of the Populist Party, which held its first meeting in Omaha on 4 July. The Populist Party's platform included goals that reflected the widespread anger felt by many of the nation's farmers and workers. The platform complained about workers' inability to organise and pointed to the unequal distribution of resources, including the large amount of "land concentrating in the hands of capitalists". The organisation's sixth resolution called for the elimination of the Pinkertons, the private security force that elites employed in Homestead, Johnson County and in Idaho's Coeur d'Alene mining districts: "we regard the maintenance of a large standing army of mercenaries, known as the Pinkerton system, as a menace to our liberties, and we demand its abolition".[13]

It was impossible not to recognise that the workplace-based conflicts that erupted in late 1880s and early 1890s were class-based. Outside observers, including journalists, lawyers and government officials acknowledged this stark reality on numerous occasions. That powerful capitalists employed private and public forces added to the drama. George W. Walts, California's Bureau of Labor Statistics commissioner, wrote in 1892, "We cannot overlook the fact that at the present time the relations subsisting between capitalists and labourers are those of war".[14]

How to win these class wars and reshape public opinion in ways favourable to the nation's elites were central concerns that occupied the emotional and intellectual energy of large sections of the business community. Anti-union forces sought to win these struggles by developing a multilayered approach, which involved fighting the so-called labour problem in the legal arena, at the point of production and in the realm of popular culture.

A decade after the extraordinary class and political eruptions of 1892, WSGA members, an assortment of businessmen's associations and the ruling class generally, received help from Wister, who shared their fundamental class interests.[15] Wister had developed relationships with elite clubmen while he was a Harvard student. Some of his classmates had moved West, where they entered the cattle business, bought land, invested in livestock and employed cowboys. Wister was not in Wyoming during the 1892 invasion, but he had acquired a general appreciation of it through his ties. During his various trips, Wister made time to visit the WSGA's clubhouse, the Cheyenne Club, which he once called "[c]omfortable, and full of departed glory".[16] Whether in eastern or midwestern cities or in western ones like Cheyenne, clubhouses were fancy settings, where an exclusive fraternity of men discussed the day's politics and their personal and business interests, including their labour-related problems. They sometimes reminisced about the past. During one visit, an invasion participant, W. C. Irvine, offered personal recollections, which Wister described thus: "We stayed till one, and he branched onto his experiences during the 'invasion' of Johnson County. The story was thrilling and picturesque". Wister was captivated, telling Irvine – an influential figure who had served as a delegate to the convention that led to the formation of Wyoming statehood in 1890 – that he wanted "a written account of all these things".[17] These tales, told by one of the state's most powerful people, provided Wister much to consider. Wister wanted to captivate audiences in the same way that the story fascinated him. Such a story, in his view, needed to be told in an unambiguous moral way, one that clearly distinguished virtuous forces from evil ones. This he did in *The Virginian.*

The Virginian helped to rehabilitate the reputations of Wyoming's agricultural elites and sold extremely well, giving tens of thousands of readers a portrayal of western society as a morality tale. Rather than depict the deeply inequal power relations that generated conflicts like the Johnson County War, *The Virginian* tells us about the triumph of good against evil. In the process, the book helped to turn killers into heroes. At the same time, Wister offered a robust defence of class divisions, which he emphasised were the inevitable outcome of a society that valued hard work and merit: "every man should thenceforth have equal liberty to find his own level". The first page of chapter 13 makes the case for a society that lets "the best man win! That is America's word. That is true democracy".[18]

The novel's central character, the thoughtful, soft-spoken and ambitious horse-riding southerner, demonstrates unwavering deference to the landholding elite, a group based on the region's wealthy cattlemen. Wister created the image of wholesome and virtuous cowboys, the personification of frontier individualism.[19] And we discover that Judge Henry, the Virginian's employer, deserves deference for his "courage and common sense". Prudent men like him had experienced many humiliations, including the bane of rustling and an unfair court system that frequently freed the criminals. The Virginian complained, "For the thieves have got hold of the juries in Johnson County".[20] As literary scholar Sara Humphreys puts it, "the ranch owner, the Judge, is the only man the Virginian wishes to please".[21]

The Virginian was the quintessential company man, someone who sought to uphold the status quo. And sometimes this meant resorting to violence. In a revealing passage, Wister emphasises that the victims needed to keep their options open. Good guys, irrespective of class position, could employ "the law or popular justice".[22] If the courts were hostile or indifferent to their interests – or if the legal system simply functioned too slowly – the righteous men could engage in gunfire, kidnappings, lynchings or any other method of punishment they believed was warranted.

What did Wister mean by "the law or popular justice?" In many cases, plain old state law seemed like a reasonable option. After all, by the late nineteenth century, the legal authorities were mostly consistent in their willingness to protect both property and managerial rights in the face of challenges from rustlers, populists and labour activists. However, the American legal system was also designed to advance the principle of due process. Those accused of crimes were supposed to enjoy the presumption of innocence and the right to a trial by a jury of peers. Sometimes, elites complained, jurors were unwilling or unable to see things from their point of view. In these cases, "popular justice" remained the best course of action. The dilemma of whether to select "the law or popular justice" was not a choice simply for the western settler elite. In *The Virginian*, the always-insightful Judge Henry announces that the "ordinary citizen" had a duty to act when confronted with cases of rustling – or when faced with any other form of lawbreaking. Such vigilantism, "so far from being a defiance of the law . . . is an assertion of it".[23]

Judge Henry drew sharp distinctions between "popular justice" in the West and white supremacist vigilantism in the South. Aware of the racist cruelties of southern lynch mobs, he explains to the Virginian's fiancé, Molly Wood, that he opposed the burning of "Southern negroes in public". But he was fully supportive of the hanging of "Wyoming cattle thieves in private".[24] The South, in the judge's view, was "semi-barbarous", while "Wyoming is determined to become civilized". The off-stage popular justice of the West was merely a means of upholding law and order, not a spectacle: "We do not invite spectators to enjoy their death agony. We put no such hideous disgrace upon the United States. We execute our criminals by the swiftest means, and in the quietest way", he explained to Wood.[25] Besides being more civilised, Judge Henry explained, this was also much wiser from a business perspective, since open displays of violence had the potential of discouraging investment.

At the book's triumphant conclusion, the hero, armed with his Winchester rifle, kills the story's chief villain, Trampas – a threatening rustler, someone "courageous with whisky" and a stand-in for the cowboys killed during the 1892 invasion.[26] Trampas was not only a threat to the property interests of the region's most powerful men; he also suffered from moral lapses. The action-packed story has been read by millions and thus has shaped our understanding of 1890s-era western conflicts. The takeaway: readers gained an appreciation of the landholding elite, a group that was determined to, in the words of Christine Bold, protect "its privilege in the name of democracy".[27]

Scabs and Heroes

The project of defending "privilege in the name of democracy" also neatly describes the employer open-shop movement, launched in earnest the very year when Wister's novel appeared. It is perhaps not surprising, then, that Wister attracted the attention of the leaders of that movement, who requested his assistance in spreading anti-union propaganda. Like the western cattle ranchers, the employers who organised to oppose unions perceived themselves as – and wished to be perceived by the public as – upholders of law and order and protectors of underdogs from the onslaught of union "tyranny". The slogan of the CIAA, "For the Protection of the Common People", emphasised this role, as well as underlined what the movement stood *for* rather than what it *opposed*. Organised employers, far from being vicious union-busters, presented themselves as upholders of deep-seated American values, such as the right of a worker to work when and where he pleased, a position captured by Harvard president Charles Eliot in calling scabs "heroes", a viewpoint the National Association of Manufacturers was happy to print.[28]

Wister, too, viewed strikebreakers as heroes, as he made clear in an essay in 1904, a couple of years before he joined the CIAA's propaganda committee. The "scab", Wister explained in a *Saturday Evening Post* article,

> stands for liberty, the right to live, the right to work, every right that we have all inherited in the land of the free. As the patriots stood against George and his Stamp Act in 1776, so in 1904 does the scab stand against Unionism and dynamite. He is the human symbol of protest against tyranny.[29]

For Wister, "the scab", stigmatised and repeatedly confronted with threats and violence, deserved as much admiration as the nation's earliest and most iconic history-makers. If scabs could sometimes be violent, no matter: the morally just visionaries who led the American Revolution, including well-known military men and nameless yeomen farmers, also achieved political freedom by mobilising troops and using violence. In that founding spirit, Wister called for renewed outbursts of patriotism and self-defence in workplaces throughout the nation against the forces that sought to take away the constitutional freedoms gained from the revolution. Violent opposition to closed or union shops was, he implied, not only justifiable, but necessary and deeply patriotic.

Thus, honest "ordinary citizens" in whatever context, had a right, even a duty, to challenge what Wister and other anti-union activists considered injustice, even if they were required to take to violent means to do so. Deferential cowboys like the Virginian, who understood the moral uprightness of the elites and the threat posed by rustlers, and strikebreakers who understood how union "rats" squeezed both the employer and the non-union worker were Owen Wister's heroes. They had, and should have, the backing of both lawmen and the industrious and patriotic men behind the open-shop movement, those fully committed to helping "the common people" resist union pressure.

Wister was a big hit with those in the leadership of anti-union organisations. National and regional employers' associations praised his books in their publications, and they invited him to speak at their conferences.[30] They realised that this literary giant had the unparalleled power to shape the views of the masses, which is something ordinary employers could not achieve.

Astroturfing support: non-union unions and open-shop employers

Around the time of the founding of the Citizens' Industrial Association of America, there appeared a spate of stories about "independent workmen" opposed to unions coming together in a spirit of mutual support and labour-capital harmony. Some such stories portrayed supposed workers' organisations expressing their appreciation of leaders of the open-shop movement, such as in a *Los Angeles Times* story about James W. Van Cleave, the president of the National Association of Manufacturers, being awarded a "handsome walking stick" in recognition of his work "in the preservation of harmony between the fair-minded worker and the fair-minded employer".[31] Other stories reported on parades by such organisations, such as in a September 1904 Associated Press story about a Labor Day parade in Cripple Creek, Colorado. The non-union parade purportedly comprised "3,000 independent workmen" carrying signs that apparently rejected union organisers with such slogans as "We Don't Hire Salaried Agitators Here".[32]

These stories were, in general, either purely fake or at least comprehensively engineered by employers and/or their agents. The Cripple Creek non-union parade probably did take place: it was reported in multiple local and national papers (although the claimed participant numbers fluctuated). It was hardly a spontaneous worker rejection of unionism, however. Cripple Creek had in 1903 and 1904 been the site of a miners' strike suppressed with extraordinary and widely publicised state and vigilante violence, culminating only the month before the Labor Day parade in deportations at gunpoint of Western Federation of Miners members and sympathisers. It must have been amply clear to remaining townsfolk that suppleness in dancing to the mine owners' tune was a key qualification for continued residence in the area. The intimidating meanings of the parade were thus well understood both locally and by unionists in general, even if the parade may also have been intended to generate positive publicity among a national middle-class audience.[33] The incident where a workers' organisation honoured Van Cleave with a special present is rather less likely to have even occurred; the only paper to report the story seems to have been the then notoriously anti-union *Los Angeles Times*, and moreover, the story reported the prize being presented by one M. M. Mulhall – better known to posterity as an undercover political operative on the NAM payroll.

Though it is impossible to trace specific stories conclusively to CIAA or NAM sources, we do know that both maintained close relationships with newspaper and magazine editors (and sometimes were editors themselves) and hired publicity bureaus to conduct campaigns, including ones involving planted news stories.[34] The main function of such news was to lend plausibility to the employers' self-appointed project of "protecting the common people" and to their claims that ordinary workers were oppressed by "tyrannical" labour unions.

But parades and prize ceremonies were one-time events, easily forgotten. What if there existed sustained worker organisations that explicitly rejected unionism and allied with employers? That would provide a much stronger boost to employers' claims of being the true allies of workers. If such organisations could get off the ground, their activities could be promoted and publicised as examples of genuine grassroots discontent with labour organisations, which of course would lend significant legitimacy to employers' claims of union tyranny as well as would demonstrate the enterprising and individualistic spirit of the American workingman.

Stories about such "non-union unions" appeared with some frequency in the early years of the twentieth century, roughly coinciding with the launch of the open-shop campaign. In early 1903, news stories reported on a new organisation, later christened the Independent Labor League of America (ILLA), guided by the former Unitarian minister turned expert in moral instruction, Edwin Milton Fairchild of Albany, New York. The stated goals of this organisation were to "protect independent workmen in their independence", "sustain higher wages by skilful, energetic cooperation with our employers" and "compel labor unions to observe the laws".[35] The ILLA workers would reject strikes and instead strive to advance themselves by "earnest co-operation with employers and legitimate business methods".[36] Fairchild, who was a strong believer in instilling values and character through education, did not deny that the organisation was instigated by employers. Rather, he made that a virtue, arguing that it showed real goodwill on the part of the employers to understand that "some kind of labor organisation is proper and within the rights of employees" and thus encourage "the more intelligent and American portion of the laboring people of Elmira" to create a union that would be "an embodiment of our national spirit" and with which employers could discuss.[37]

At almost exactly the same time an "Independent American Mechanics' Union" or "Independent Order of American Mechanics" was incorporated in Anderson, Indiana to defend against any attacks on "the inalienable right of all mankind to work for such wages as shall be mutually satisfactory to the individual workman and his employer", while by the fall, an "American League of Independent Workmen" was operating in Spokane, Washington and a "Citizens' League" affiliated with the Indiana organisation had been established in Fort Bragg.[38] The ILLA also added chapters in several cities besides the original Albany and Elmira ones, and the Indiana organisation claimed to be making "rapid strides" in cities across the Midwest.[39] Labour papers noted that such non-union unions seemed to be newly proliferating, though they were not a novelty, having existed in specific industries particularly for the purposes of "making a show of non-union labor" to intimidate workers. Labour editors predicted that whatever the present purpose of such associations was, they would quickly "degenerate . . . into strikebreaking machines".[40]

There is little doubt that these "non-union unions" were closely affiliated with and initiated by the employers involved in the open-shop movement. The timing of their rise matches precisely the open-shop movement's launch; they often arose in areas with strong employer organisations; their titles and planks are worded alike and parrot the open-shop movement's language; and they usually praised open-shop employers for their "valiant work" in assisting them and occasionally invited open-shop employers to speak at their events. Indeed, non-union organisations sometimes explicitly stated that they would not establish branches in cities that already had a Citizens' Alliance, "on account of the similarity of principles" between the two.[41] Employer support, certainly, was explicit: the NAM passed a resolution at its 1903 convention to support such organisations, and its president openly offered them financial support.[42] Moreover, there is evidence that these organisations were indeed used for strikebreaking: the National Metal Trades Association (one of the key open-shop employer organisations), for example, used the Elmira ILLA's membership to recruit strikebreakers, and it seems that these organisations often cropped up at locations where there was an ongoing strike.[43]

Quite possibly, since they generally followed British developments quite closely, American open-shop employers got the idea of "non-union unions" from Great Britain.[44] There, the National Free Labour Association (NFLA) had been active since the early 1890s. The association was founded and headed by William Collison, who explained that he, though a workingman himself and a former union member, had become disgusted with trade unions. Unionism, in his telling, had veered away from "sober discrimination and . . . the path of public sympathy" that posited no "essential antagonism between master and man"; it had given way to "faction and self-interest" and been taken over by "mob managers".[45] Having left the unions, he instead created the NFLA, which preached against "union tyranny" – and found much favour with employers both for its rhetoric and for its provision of strikebreakers, earning Collison the sobriquets "King of Blacklegs" and "Prince of Scabs". In 1906, Collison visited the CIAA's annual convention in Chicago, where he was eagerly interviewed by the leaders of the open-shop movement; upon returning home, he founded a British version of the Citizens' Industrial Association, though that association was apparently not particularly active.[46]

Like the American non-union unions, the NFLA was to a great extent the creature of employers, especially those active in the powerful Liberty and Property Defence League.[47] It depended heavily on employer support and catered to employers' demand for workers who did not mind working during a strike. It also appears that its "conventions", though well publicised, were largely faked, with "delegates" collected from among down-at-heel hang abouts and paid for their attendance. And despite Collison's version of how he was motivated by a wish to combat union "dictation" and the socialist drift of British unions, the association's origins were closely tied to employers and their strikebreaking needs: before founding his own organisation, Collison was a chairman of another Free Labour Association, this one created by the Shipping Federation keen to disguise its strikebreaking activities.[48]

At the same time, Collison did in fact come from a working-class background, and he was genuinely piqued at the New Unionism and its language of class. His NFLA was in his control and in accordance with his ideology, even if his finances came largely from employers, and even if strikebreaking was his major service.[49] The individuals associated with non-union unions might, then, have had real grievances or aspirations beyond making a quick buck; the remainder of the paper explores what we might uncover, or at least speculate, regarding those aspirations based on the available sources.[50]

The problem, of course, is that information about the individuals associated with the elusive "independent labor leagues" is scarce in the extreme. By their very nature as astroturf creations, these organisations held few meetings, left behind no documents and rarely produced publications independent of those edited and written by the employers who promoted them. Most of them were short-lived; some apparently existed only to enact the occasional publicity stunt. The non-union unions' existence was much more ephemeral than that of the company or "yellow" unions that became more prominent after World War I in the

United States and that had been growing for some time before the war, e.g. in Germany.[51] Unlike company or yellow unions, the non-union unions did not enrol large numbers of workers in a sustained way and only appear to have activated substantial numbers in the context of employer-generated strikebreaking campaigns. The non-union unions also portrayed themselves more as organisations of concerned citizens than as employee representatives, so while company unions usually provided at least some employer-controlled form of representation or benefits, the non-union unions offered at best the promise of a job and possibly an informal connection to the organisation's employer sponsors, with its potential to facilitate upward mobility.

Thus, there is little formal material to draw on. Collison's American counterparts left far fewer traces of themselves than he did, either biographically or ideologically.[52] Those few whose words we do have, though, seem to reflect Collison's sentiments quite closely. For example, in 1904, a machinist named John Galloway testified against union-sponsored legislation at a congressional hearing as the representative of a Dayton, Ohio non-union union called the Modern Order of the Bees. Though probably there at the instigation of Dayton's open-shop employers, Galloway waxed quite eloquent in recounting how the union's efforts to coerce him to join "put me on my American dignity right away" and prompted him to denounce the union's socialistic ideas.[53] Galloway illustrates that in the opposite scale from unions' proposals of solidarity and contracts were the appeal of the ideology of liberty and individualism as well as the allure of social mobility and pride in modest prosperity; Galloway, for instance, spontaneously made reference to how his hard work had gotten him "a little house in Dayton that I would not exchange for Mr. Roosevelt's place" and how his "family [was] getting along as well as anyone's family". In short, there was the promise of the "American dream", if only one adhered to the right values. To the extent that non-union unions played on these emotional strings, they may have held some appeal.

Most of the non-union unions were too ephemeral to have left even many names of members or officers behind, and the claims of "hundreds" of members are probably about as reliable as Collison's convention delegate numbers.[54] However, to the extent that it is possible to trace the men whose names appeared as spokesmen or directors, they seem often to have been involved in the building industry or in urban trades. For the one organisation that was slightly longer-lived, the American League of Independent Workmen of Spokane, Washington, this was particularly true; indeed, the league, reportedly founded by an engineer called George B. Weaver, soon boasted that it was doing "more building with non-union than union men in this city".[55] The men listed in connection with the league in news stories or city directories nearly all came from the building industry. Luther Holcomb, the man most often cited as a spokesman of the league, was listed in a 1902 Spokane city directory as a carpenter, and William H. Schleppy, sometimes listed as a president for the league, is listed in a 1901 directory as a carpenter and contractor. Similarly with others linked to the organisation: T. W. Ettershank was a painter and J. P. Earl a carpenter. Most of these men also seem to have risen in the world, at least a little bit, between 1900 and 1910: Holcomb went from being a carpenter to being a building contractor, as did Earl; Schleppy went from being a contractor to being an architect; Ettershank bought a paint and varnish store with his brother.[56]

Construction was not only a major battleground between unions and employers, but local building and contracting was squarely within what Andrew Wender Cohen has called the "craft economy" – the everyday business of baking bread, transporting goods, barbering, building and otherwise keeping a city's daily life running along. This craft economy was characterised by a mix of individualism and collective governance, agreements enforced by violence and ostracism and low barriers to setting up as an entrepreneur.[57] While Cohen discusses the fluidity of the craft economy mainly from the point of view of how it retained an emphasis on "well-governed agreements" and craft rulemaking rather than efficient corporate structures and free markets or freedom of contract, seen from another angle the urban economy also lent itself to individualistic upward mobility.[58]

The distance between workers and entrepreneurs in the urban economy remained relatively short, and both had a precarious position vis-á-vis those above them in the hierarchy. The smaller among the entrepreneurs might aspire to rise in the world through association with larger businessmen, and joining the anti-union associations could provide a handy networking opportunity. As one union president snidely but astutely observed, when a Citizens' Alliance was set up in a town, the town's small businessmen flocked to curry favour with the big shots:

> [A]ll the small fry of manufacturers, as well as storekeepers, druggists, even peanut vendors, joined the alliance. Just think of the prestige they would have when the big manufacturer, driving along in his carriage and four, would clasp the hand of the peanut vendor and say, "Brother of the Labor Bursting Brigade".[59]

In the urban economy, there were many workers who were more like "peanut vendors" than full-blown proletarians with factory jobs. In the urban crafts, an aspiration for economic security and self-respect could be expressed in striving for small entrepreneur status just as rationally as it could be manifested in staunch unionism.[60]

For a worker in the early twentieth-century urban economy, to graduate from being in another man's employ to holding a place among the "small fry" of the retail, commercial and city services entrepreneurs was a realistic aspiration, and the Spokane case seems to indicate that some of those associated with non-union unions did just that. The capital required to set up as a building contractor, a baker or a team owner was minimal; the majority of such businesses were proprietorships operating on narrow margins and led by men with limited formal education.[61] And despite academics' penchant for envisioning social mobility as rising in the world through moving from manual to white-collar occupations, most working-class folk with upward aspirations in the early twentieth century dreamed not of office jobs but of small businesses that would allow them to control their work time, accumulate a nest egg and pass something more on to their children than they had received.[62] When such aspirations combined with the realistic opportunities of the craft economy and its often quite rancorous rivalries and were bolstered by a broader culture praising individualism and entrepreneurial striving, it is perhaps not surprising that some workers opted for sidling up to anti-union employers who could easily offer the capital and the business opportunities to enable a worker amenable to the anti-union message to prosper as an entrepreneur.

***

Owen Wister's career and non-union unions illustrate both the cachet of individualism in American culture and the diligence with which anti-union employers deployed it to benefit themselves and undermine working people. An individualistic frontier mythology reverberated in the willingness of Wister's heroes to take (manly) action, at the same time as this action was softened to middle-class palatability by the deference and upwardly mobile aspirations of the novel's eponymous Virginian and the figure of the virtuous scab. Similarly, a spirit of can-do attitude and hard work infused the stories about non-union unions, where upstanding workmen willing to do a fair day's work came together to defend their American liberty against union tyranny. Lost strikes and failed boycott campaigns, the frustrations of union rules and the attractions of possible upward mobility surely sometimes got workers to wonder if individualism might not offer a better deal than union solidarity. Yet – as is perhaps best illustrated by the contrast of glorifying elite-perpetrated vigilante violence while condemning even worker efforts at rulemaking as violent "tyranny" – in the wild west of employer anti-unionism, some people were more equal than others.

Notes

1 Small portions of the first part of this essay are published in "'The Law or Popular Justice': Owen Wister and the Legitimisation of Employer-Class Violence," in *Private Security and the Modern State: Historical and Comparative Perspectives*, ed. David Churchill, Dolores Janiewski, and Pieter Leloup (Abingdon: Routledge, 2020).

2 The literature on the turn-of-the-century sense of crisis over the future of democracy in the context of great trusts, economic inequality and an increasingly visible and restive lower class is too massive to be cited here. For one standard treatment see Nell Irvin Painter, *Standing at Armageddon: United States, 1877–1919* (New York: W.W. Norton, 1987).

3 The most recent work investigating these organisations is Chad Pearson, *Reform or Repression: Organizing America's Anti-Union Movement* (Philadelphia: University of Pennsylvania Press, 2016). See also Howell John Harris, *Bloodless Victories: The Rise and Fall of the Open Shop in the Philadelphia Metal Trades, 1890–1940* (New York: Cambridge University Press, 2000); Sidney Fine, *"Without Blare of Trumpets": Walter Drew, the National Erectors' Association, and the Open Shop Movement, 1903–57* (Ann Arbor: University of Michigan Press, 1995); Sarah Lyons Watts, *Order Against Chaos: Business Culture and Labor Ideology in America, 1880–1915* (New York: Greenwood Press, 1991), 143–70.

4 "National Association Committees," *The Square Deal* 2 (February 1907): 15.

5 G. Edward White, *The Eastern Establishment and the Western Experience: The West of Frederic Remington, Theodore Roosevelt, Owen Wister* (Austin: University

of Texas Press, 1989 [1968]); Darwin Payne, *Owen Wister: Chronicler of the West, Gentleman of the East* (Dallas: Southern Methodist University Press, 1985); Richard Slotkin, *Gunfighter Nation: The Myth of the Frontier in Twentieth-Century America* (Norman: University of Oklahoma Press, 1992), 135, 175, 234; Louis Tanner, "Owen Wister: The Public Intellectual" (PhD diss., The University of New Mexico, 1999); Gary Scharnhorst, *Owen Wister and the West* (Norman: University of Oklahoma Press, 2015); Stephen J. Mexal, "'My Dear Judge': Owen Wister's Virginian, Oliver Wendell Holmes Jr., and Natural Law Conservatism," *Western American Literature* 51 (Fall 2016): 279–311.

6 Henry Clay Frick to Andrew Carnegie, July 4, 1892, University of Pittsburgh digital archives, on-line: https://digital.library.pitt.edu/islandora/object/pitt%3A31735066205083/viewer#page/1/mode/2up

7 On the strikebreaking campaign and the backlash that it sparked, see David Montgomery, *The Fall of the House of Labor: The Workplace, the State and American Labor Activism, 1865–1925* (Cambridge: Cambridge University Press, 1987), 36–43; Matthew Hild, *Greenbackers, Knights of Labor and Populists: Farmer-Labor Insurgency in the Late-Nineteenth Century South* (Athens, OH: University of Georgia Press, 2007), 157.

8 Owen Wister, "The National Guard of Pennsylvania," *Harper's Weekly*, September 1, 1894, 824. On the Pennsylvania militia in the aftermath of the 1877 strike see Robert M. Fogelson, *America's Armories: Architecture, Society, and Public Order* (Cambridge: Harvard University Press, 1989), 38–39.

9 Wister, "The National Guard of Pennsylvania," 825.

10 Michael Mark Cohen, *The Conspiracy of Capital: Law, Violence, and American Popular Radicalism in the Age of Monopoly* (Amherst: University of Massachusetts Press, 2019), 129.

11 Many have written about this invasion. See Lewis L. Gould, *Wyoming: From Territory to Statehood* (Worland, Wy: High Plains Publishing Company, Inc., 1989), 137–58; Slotkin, *Gunfighter Nation*, 169–75.

12 David R. Berman refers to these mine owners as "absentee capitalists", since they tended to reside outside of northern Idaho. See David R. Berman, *Radicalism in the Mountain West, 1890–1920* (Boulder: University of Colorado Press, 2007), 19. On New Orleans see Eric Arnesen, *Waterfront Workers of New Orleans: Race, Class, and Politics, 1863–1923* (Oxford: Oxford University Press, 1991), 114–18.

13 "The Omaha Platform: Launching the Populist Party," http://historymatters.gmu.edu/d/5361/

14 Quoted in Robert Ovetz, *When Workers Shot Back: Class Conflict from 1877 to 1921* (Leiden: Brill, 2018), 193.

15 For the relationship between Wister and these vigilantes see Edward White, *The Eastern Establishment and the Western Experience*, 127–29.

16 Owen Wister, October 4, 1892, "Diary of Western Trip No. 7", Folder 1, Box 2, Owen Wister Papers, American Heritage Center, University of Wyoming, Laramie, Wyoming.

17 Owen Wister, "Diary, Bowie, Bayard, Grant, Bisbee, Tombstone, Tucson, San Francisco, Cheyanne, May-August 1894," Folder 7, Box 2, page 23, Wister papers.

18 Owen Wister, *The Virginian: A Horseman of the Plains* (Mineola and New York: Dover Publications, Inc., 2006; 1902), 85.

19 As Mark Lause has demonstrated cowboys were far from individualistic. He refers to them as "The Dangerous Classes of the American West". See Mark Lause, *The Great Cowboy Strike: Bullets, Ballots & Class Conflicts in the American West* (London: Verso Books, 2018), 53–84.

20 Wister, *The Virginian*, 240.

21 Sara Humphreys, "'Truer 'n Hell': Lies, Capitalism, and Cultural Imperialism in Owen Wister's *The Virginian*, B. M. Bwer's *The Happy Family*, and Morning Dove's *Cogewea*," *Western American Literature* 45 (Spring 2010): 37.

22 Wister, *The Virginian*, 247.
23 Ibid., 255. On the Virginian's relationship to the judge see Humphreys, "'Truer 'n Hell," 37.
24 Wister, *The Virginian*, 253.
25 Ibid., 254.
26 Ibid., 271.
27 Christine Bold, *The Frontier Club: Popular Westerns and Cultural Power, 1880–1924* (Oxford: Oxford University Press, 2013), 1.
28 Charles J. Bonaparte, "President Eliot and the American University," *Boston Evening Transcript*, March 19, 1904, 2. Also, see the NAM publication: "President Eliot on Violence and Folly Among the Unions," *American Industries* 1 (November 15, 1902): 10.
29 Owen Wister, "The Land of the Free," *The Saturday Evening Post* 117, October 29, 1904, 7.
30 "Brief Notices of New Books," *The Exponent* 3 (May 1906): 36; "Citizens' Industrial Association of St. Louis Program," *The Exponent* 3 (August 1906): 3; "Books for Christmas Gifts," *American Industries* 6 (December 1907): 40.
31 *Los Angeles Times*, December 20, 1907, 9. (The *LA Times* was notoriously anti-union at the time.).
32 *Omaha Daily Bee*, September 6, 1904, 3; *The St. Louis Republic*, September 6, 1904, 3; *The Times Dispatch*, September 6, 1904, 7. A note on newspaper sources: most newspapers cited here come from the *Chronicling America: Historic American Newspapers* collection, http://chroniclingamerica.loc.gov/. Colorado newspapers are from the *Colorado Historic Newspapers Collection*, www.coloradohistoricnewspapers.org. A few papers, such as the Spokane papers cited later, come from the *Google News Archive*, https://news.google.com/newspapers, and some major papers (like the *LA Times*) are from the proprietary ProQuest Historical Newspapers database.
33 The *Erie News*, for example, ran an item the following year in reference, apparently, to a repeat of the 1904 parade: "How Would You Like to March in a Labor Day Parade Gotten Up By the Citizen's Alliance? That is What the Miners of Cripple Creek Will Do on September 5," *Erie News*, September 1, 1905, 8, The story of the Cripple Creek labour conflict is ably told in Elizabeth Jameson, *All That Glitters: Class, Conflict, and Community in Cripple Creek* (Urbana: University of Illinois Press, 1998).
34 Vilja Hulden, "Employers' Organization Influence and the Progressive-Era Press," *Journalism History* 38, no. 1 (Spring 2012): 43–54.
35 *The Sun* [New York], January 1, 1903, 5 (reprinted in many other papers.) There were also a few brief notices in late 1902 that a secretary of a new association of workmen hoping to secure their "right to labor where they choose" was calling for expressions of interest in the organisation and had received favourable responses both from workers and from financial supporters. This may or may not have been related to the Fairchild-sponsored organisation. The secretary was called James W. Bellinger, identified as a "clerk" with an address in New York City. *New-York Tribune*, November 12, 1902, 1; *Warren Sheaf*, November 27, 1902, 7.
36 *New-York Tribune*, March 19, 1903, 1.
37 *The Sun* [New York], March 21, 1903, 8. For more on E. M. Fairchild's career, see Allison L. Jackson, "The Character Education Work of Milton Fairchild: A Prism for Exploring the Debate Between Liberal Progressives and Conservative Progressives in the Early 20th Century" (PhD diss., Notre Dame of Maryland University, 2018). For more detail on Fairchild's views and activities with regard to labour see Pearson, *Reform or Repression*, 75–77.
38 *The Butler Weekly Times*, March 26, 1903, 3; *The Spokane Press*, October 1, 1903, 1; *The San Francisco Call*, September 2, 1903, 1.
39 Pearson, *Reform or Repression*, 77; *The Indianapolis Journal*, July 20, 1903, 2.
40 *The Labor World*, March 28, 1903, 4.

41 *Spokane Daily Chronicle*, February 17, 1905, 15.
42 *The Sun* [New York], October 25, 1903, section 2, page 3; *The Indianapolis Journal*, July 20, 1903, 2; National Association of Manufacturers, *Proceedings of the Eighth Annual Convention,* New Orleans, LA, 14–16 April 1903 (New York, 1903), 290.
43 *The St. Louis Republic,* May 18, 1903, 3; for NMTA use of strikebreakers, see *The Sun* [New York], June 21, 1903, 3 and Pearson, *Reform or Repression*, 76–77.
44 British affairs are commented upon regularly in the open-shop publications; see also Howell John Harris, "Between Convergence and Exceptionalism: Americans and the British Model of Labor Relations, c. 1867–1920," *Labor History* 48, no. 2 (2007): 141–73.
45 William Collison, *The Apostle of Free Labour: The Life Story of William Collison, Founder and General Secretary of The National Free Labour Association* (London: Hurst and Blackett Limited, 1913), 39.
46 Geoffrey Alderman, "The National Free Labour Association: A Case-Study of Organised Strike-Breaking in the Late Nineteenth and Early Twentieth Centuries," *International Review of Social History* 21, no. 3 (December 1976): 309–36; Alessandro Saluppo, "Authoritarian Reflexes: The Perspectives of British Employers on Labor Repression in the United States, 1890–1914," paper delivered at 2020 *American Historical Association* meeting, January 6, 2020 (paper in possession of authors.) See also the account of Collison's talk and the questioning of him by John Kirby and others in the reprinted CIAA proceedings in *Square Deal* 2, no. 6 (January 1907): 18–22.
47 Norbert Soldon, "Laissez-Faire as Dogma: The Liberty and Property Defence Leagues, 1882–1914," in *Essays in Anti-Labour History, ed.* K. D. Brown (London: Palgrave Macmillan, 1974), 159–82; Eric Bristow, "The Liberty and Property Defence League and Individualism, 1882–1914," *Historical Journal* 18 (1975): 761–89.
48 Alderman, "National Free Labour Association."
49 Ibid.
50 As Theda Skocpol and Vanessa Williamson have noted in a different context resisting the temptation to dismiss conservative-oriented, top-down-funded "grassroots" movements as pure publicity stunts may pay off in a more complex understanding of ordinary people's relationship to political discourse. Skocpol and Williamson argue that while the Tea Party had plenty of backing from corporate interests, the grassroots element was real enough and differed in viewpoints quite substantially from the free-market orthodoxy promoted by the Koch brothers or the right-wing media pundits it is usually associated with. Theda Skocpol and Vanessa Williamson, *The Tea Party and the Remaking of Republican Conservatism* (New York: Oxford University Press, 2012).
51 For example, Klaus Schönhoven notes that yellow unions in the German iron, electrical, and chemical industries had reached a membership of nearly 300,000 by 1914. Klaus Schönhoven, "Germany to 1945," in *European Labor Unions*, ed. Joan Campbell and John P. Windmuller (Westport, CT: Greenwood Publishing Group, 1992), 149–66. On company unions in the U.S., see Daniel Nelson, "The Company Union Movement, 1900–1937: A Reexamination," *Business History Review* 56, no. 3 (Autumn 1982): 335–57.
52 Of course, the United States had its own famous men accorded the title "King of the Strikebreakers", notably James Farley and Pearl Bergoff. However, neither claimed particular ideological or emotional conviction about unions as their motive, nor claim to head a principled organisation, nor come to the business via union membership and disillusionment, like Collison. Instead, both apparently drifted to strikebreaking more or less by accident as youthful hoodlums and started "detective agencies" to carry on the business. Robert M. Smith, *From Blackjacks to Briefcases: A History of Commercialized Strikebreaking and Unionbusting in the United States* (Athens, OH: Ohio University Press, 2003), Ch. 2.
53 Statement of Mr. John Galloway, United States House of Representatives, Committee on the Judiciary, *Anti-Injunction Bill: Complete Hearings*, January 22–March 22, 1904 (Washington, DC: GPO, 1904), 279–88.

54 Often the claim was made that it was easy to recruit disgruntled union members to these non-union unions; for one example see *The San Francisco Call*, September 2, 1903, 1.

55 *The Sun* [New York], October 25, 1903, section 2, page 3. It is not clear what kind of an engineer Weaver was (building engineer? mechanical engineer?) nor is there much unambiguous information about his background, though the story in *The Sun* states that he has been shuttling around the country creating non-union unions and is associated with the ones in Indiana as well. Also, somewhat intriguing with regard to the theme of disillusionment with popular politics is that Weaver may previously have been a Populist but switched to the Republican Party; see *Colfax Gazette*, January 26, 1900, 4.

56 In addition, there was a Richard Sharpless, a jack-of-all-trades variously listed as barber, teamster, driver and clerk. All information here comes from city directories and census records contained in the HeritageQuest database. Although there are of course multiple names that could fit the names associated with the League of Independent Workmen, especially when news stories only identify them using initials, I have cross-checked the entries using e.g. information about addresses to ensure that all entries concern the same person and, with a high degree of confidence, correspond to the people named in the news stories. Ancestry.com., *U.S. City Directories, 1822–1995* [database on-line] (Provo, UT: Ancestry.com Operations, Inc., 2011).

57 Andrew W. Cohen, *The Racketeer's Progress: Chicago and the Struggle for the Modern American Economy, 1900–1940* (New York: Cambridge University Press, 2004). On anti-union employers in construction, see Fine, *"Without Blare of Trumpets"*.

58 Cohen, *Racketeer's Progress*, 48.

59 "President Lynch's Jottings from January 15th to February 15th, 1905," *The Journal* (of the Metal Polishers', Buffers' Platers', Brass Molders' and Brass and Silver Workers' International Union), 14: 3, 9 ff.

60 Decades ago, Michael Kazin criticised efforts at labour history syntheses for paying too little attention to the reality that "workers have simultaneously articulated not one ideology but several, roughly corresponding to different spheres of their lives". Though much has changed, this still retains some resonance. Michael Kazin, "Struggling with Class Struggle: Marxism and the Search for a Synthesis of U.S. Labor History," *Labor History* 28, no. 4 (September 1, 1987): 497–514; also see Dana M. Caldemeyer, "Unfaithful Followers: Rethinking Southern Nonunionism in the Late Nineteenth Century," in *Reconsidering Southern Labor History: Race, Class, and Power*, ed. Matthew Hild and Keri Leigh Merritt (Gainesville: University of Florida Press, 2018), 112–25.

61 See e.g. Cohen, *Racketeer's Progress*, 40–43.

62 Using records from the Emigrants' Savings Bank Tyler Anbinder makes this case forcefully for Irish immigrants in New York City, arguing that though they managed to save surprising amounts of money, they cared little about "their place in some imaginary occupational hierarchy". Tyler Anbinder, "Moving beyond 'Rags to Riches': New York's Irish Famine Immigrants and Their Surprising Savings Accounts," *Journal of American History* 99, no. 3 (December 1, 2012): 741–70.

13 Vigilant citizens

The case of the Volunteer Police Force, 1911–14*

Alessandro Saluppo

In the years preceding the First World War, the threat of organised labour fuelled fears of social disintegration and high levels of insecurity among conservative ranks.[1] At the same time, increasing jingoistic nationalism along with a growing deterioration in the international situation transmuted labour unrest into an expression of domestic disloyalty. Arguments about the future survival and prosperity of Britain gradually coalesced with a quest for public discipline.[2] These visions of orderliness provided the ideological framework for the emergence of a number of patriotic leagues, citizens' patrols and parapolice corps with the intention, or at least the ostensible intention, of assisting the police in the maintenance of law and order and in performing essential public services during major industrial disputes.[3] Aside from newspaper reports, little is known about these private anti-labour associations. Questions regarding their formation and structuration, their organisational functioning and operational modes have remained for the most part unanswered or outrightly ignored. In an attempt to fill this void, this chapter retraces the case of the Volunteer Police Force (VPF). Founded on Trafalgar Day (21 October) in 1911 by picture frame dealer William Mailes Power and presided over by James Hamilton, 2nd Duke of Abercorn, the VPF may be interpreted as a paradigmatic manifestation of the propagation of vigilante behaviour in the Edwardian years. During the parliamentary debate on the 1923 Special Constables Act, the Liberal MP for Newcastle-under-Lyme, Josiah Clement Wedgwood, declared:

> I remember that it was before the War that the Citizen Defence Force (*sic*) first came into being, with his Grace the Duke of Abercorn as president and a son of Mrs. Humphrey (*sic*) Ward as one of the whippersin. They had their meeting in the Crystal Palace, and decided to break the strikes. They enrolled everyone who would come along . . . in order that when next the wicked working man rose up in his might and attempted to destroy civilization . . . they might be armed at every point to resist red revolution.[4]

His harking back to the short-lived and shadowy existence of the VPF was offered as an argument against the appointment of permanent special constabularies in peacetime and to warn parliament about the risks of fascist contagion in Britain.[5]

Wedgwood's reference to the Duke of Abercorn's organisation is not as surprising as it might seem. The foundation and conduct of the VPF had caused great alarm and clamour in the press on the eve of the First World War, and it is therefore highly plausible that its name still resonated in the memories of more than a few Labour MPs. Despite the great stir it made at the time, the story of the VPF, which took upon itself the role of protector of the social order and industrial discipline, has fallen into oblivion. The main purpose of this study, therefore, is to shed light again on this forgotten case of anti-labour mobilisation and, at the same time, to use its paradigmatic story to probe the social and political tensions that characterised Britain's pre-war years. Drawing on a vast array of archival and documentary sources, this chapter reconstructs the VPF's organisation, endowments, clientage, recruitment, governance and modes of action. It also analyses the intellectual justifications and motivations which underpinned it. In doing so, the intention is to reveal the disposition of certain social groups – from aristocratic castes to the upper middle classes – to both counter the rise of political and socio-economic deviance and lay to rest the spectre of socialism with violence. Enquiry into these pressures on the state's monopoly of the use of legitimate force serves to show the considerable support for organised self-defence lent by "respectable society" during the Great Labour Unrest (1911–14). The story of the VPF also serves to complexify the conventional assumption that the potential for organised political violence in mainland Britain was marginal or even non-existent before World War I.

Crisis of cohesion and the rise of vigilante behaviours

In 1912, journalist and science fiction writer John Twells Brex published *The Civil War of 1915*. The book, which had appeared in serial form in *The Sporting Times* prophesied the near-future uprising of working masses and Britain's descent into class war. For Twells and many of his contemporaries, the spectre of a general strike of wage-earners paralysing the whole machinery of production, culminating in social anarchy, revolution and the collectivisation of property, had been gradually transfigured into a psychological reality.[6]

Between 1910 and 1914, Britain was faced with a mass upsurge in labour militancy and strike waves. Something over 4,000 strikes involving about four million workers were recorded, while working days lost peaked to an annual total of over ten million. Over the same time span, trade union membership rose from about two million to 4.1 million.[7] Among the most striking novelties of the "Great Unrest" was its "violent, unofficial and insurgent character".[8] In the Cambrian stoppage of 1910 in South Wales, a fertile terrain for revolutionary syndicalist doctrines, violence was pervasive, as evidenced by frequent acts of sabotage on installations and equipment as well as attacks on non-union workers, the houses of mine managers and the property of magistrates. Violent clashes with the police at the Glamorgan Colliery in Llwyn-y-pia led to rioting in Tonypandy.[9]

While the Cambrian dispute was dragging on, "the great outburst of 1911" commenced with a general strike of seamen and firemen in Southampton, which rapidly spread to most of the principal ports in the United Kingdom. Dockers in peacetime and transport workers came out in solidarity with the seamen, virtually arresting the movement of cargo through the docks. The bitterness with which the strike was fought and the extent of the disruption it caused, lent plausibility to Elie Halevy's portrayal of the conflict as "nothing short of a revolutionary outbreak".[10] Fierce battles between strikers and the police, arson, destruction of property, man-hunts against foreign strikebreakers and episodes akin to popular insurrection occurred in Hull, Glasgow, Manchester and Cardiff.[11] The high level of violence, which tainted the irenic image of Britain as an orderly and law-abiding society, terrified the affluent and middle classes.[12]

At the beginning of August, while the uproar associated with the dockworkers' and seamen's strike appeared to be subsiding, transport workers in other parts of the country went on strike. About 80,000 workers brought the Port of London to a standstill. From the beginning of August onwards, labour disruptions spread to the railways leading to the first national strike in that sector. At the end of a huge demonstration in Liverpool, troops opened fire on rioters killing two, an episode which became known as Bloody Sunday.[13] A few days later, a crowd attacked a train driven by "blacklegs" in Llanelli; soldiers fired shots killing two men, and a violent explosion due to an arsonist setting fire to some trucks containing cylinders of detonators resulted in more deaths.[14] Meanwhile, anti-Jew riots erupted in some Welsh mining towns.[15]

The disturbances in the summer of 1911, and later, shook the confidence of British society. *The Times* gloomily reported that:

> we are assisting at the absolute decomposition of society into its elements, in the absence of settled principles, of sane direction, and of discipline of any shape or form. . . . There is no King in Israel and every man is a law unto himself.[16]

The contemporaneous Agadir crisis, the controversy over the powers of the Lords, the suffragettes' campaign, the mounting battle over Home Rule and the subsequent arming of Ulster made industrial disorders appear more ominous than they were.[17]

Predictably enough, fears of riots, strikes and bloodshed combined with perceived deficiencies in law enforcement resulted in the rise of vigilante attitudes and behaviours. During the 1911 London Dock Strike, the manager of Raphael's Refinery informed the Home Office that he had made

> complete preparations against any attack on this place, that our men are fully armed and we shall not sit still and watch our property being looted as did the owners of property at Newport, Tonypandy, Hull, Manchester, Cardiff and other towns.[18]

London printing firms hired private guards, mostly former constables, to protect their premises.[19] In Liverpool, in response to the transport strike in the summer of 1911, business and civil society representatives formed the Civic Service League "to assist the authorities in preserving the health, safety and well-being of the City in time of need".[20] By May 1913, about 2,500 volunteers had been trained to carry out electrical and steam engineering work, stoking, motor driving and medical services in case of an industrial emergency.[21] Although the Civic Service League vowed to protect the general public from the effects of prolonged labour stoppages as its principal goal, it was essentially a "white collar" anti-labour organisation. In the meantime, "Provision Protection Committees" were formed in many parts of the country in anticipation of disorderly outbreaks and hooliganism arising from new strikes. "In every community", controversial newspaper editor W. T. Stead wrote,

> there may have to be organized a volunteer force of men willing and ready to take the places of strikers whose abstention from work threatens the whole community with the loss of the indispensable services of public utility represented by those who supply food, drink, light, sanitation, and the transmission of raw materials.[22]

At the end of August 1911, *The Times* proposed the formation of "standing volunteer force corps" in each locality to carry on operating necessary public services in case of severe disturbances as a result of industrial disputes. Modelled on the *Frivilliga Skyddskåren*, a public security brigade which had helped break the Swedish General Strike of 1909, this national strikebreaking organisation was to assist in food supply and distribution, transport and shipping at times of serious unrest.[23] In the same period, the president of the Automobile Association and future ultra-conservative Home Office Secretary, William Joynson-Hicks, proposed the creation of a National Transport Service of "private motors" to mitigate the impact of transport strikes.[24] Similarly, Lord Montagu of Beaulieu suggested that motorists could be properly organised and deployed to limit the consequences of a general railway strike.[25] Such schemes for recruiting and mobilising volunteer labour were evidently attractive to the patriotic middle classes. Dismayed by the gravity of industrial unrest and its potential revolutionary escalation, many of them had already served as special constables during the summer strike crisis. In Liverpool, during the August riots, justices swore in 4,142 citizens, of which "over 1,200 did actual street duty in the disturbed areas".[26] In London, many hundreds of volunteers proved "ready to take a baton" for the preservation of public peace and the protection of property.[27] The petit-bourgeois composition of the special constabulary helped exacerbate tensions.[28] "In 1911 we had Bluebottles on top of the meat vans", Labour MP John Johns recalled, "they were special constables, and very special constables. They were not used to break the strike, but to break people's heads".[29]

The government attempted to forestall such securitarian pressures by institutionalising them.[30] In mid-September 1911, the chairman of the Sheffield Watch Committee, Alfred Cattell, announced before the City Council that the Home Secretary, Winston Churchill, was working hard to arrange the formation of a permanently organised special constabulary in the most populated cities to cope with emergencies similar to those that had arisen during the transport strikes and to preclude the use of the military to repress civil disorders. The chairman praised the Home Office's scheme, pointing out that "the ordinary police forces were totally inadequate for the recent troubles", and to have a volunteer force ready for times of great stress could be a necessary arrangement to contain industrial unrest.[31]

While labour representatives expressed their legitimate concern over the strikebreaking nature of a civilian police force dedicated to the defence of property, the Home Office issued the seminal Circular 214312, a document that pressed police authorities to persist in the enrolment of special constables and to keep a classified register of trusted persons who could be mobilised to deal with future emergencies. The Home Secretary also suggested the creation of a two-tier police reserve: the First Police Reserve was to consist of men accustomed to military discipline and trained in the police or in the army, while the Second Police Reserve was to be made up of regular special constables. The proposed scheme for a new reserve police force, which came under severe criticism from municipal authorities as it would entail further cost to the taxpayer, was only systematised at the onset of the war and remained fundamentally unmodified until the end of World War II.[32]

In London, a movement in support of a volunteer police force had earlier gained traction after the Chief Commissioner of Police, Edward Henry, recommended setting up a permanent register of citizens who would be available for Special Constable service in every borough.[33] In relation to this proposal, the future founder of the VPF, W. M. Power, who had offered to raise a company of special constable cyclists during the London Dock Strike, began making preparatory arrangements for the formation of a civilian police.[34] Power, who had joined the Queen's Westminster Volunteers as far back as 1874 and was the first attested member of the 16th (County of London) Battalion, The London Regiment, envisaged a national organisation of "volunteer police clubs" whose main purpose was to assist the regular police during emergencies arising from industrial disputes and to make local authorities independent of military aid in maintaining order and protecting life and property. These corps, organised in a decentralised structure, much on the lines of volunteer clubs and, at least initially, funded by private contributions, were to be subordinate to the Chief Commissioner and to Chief Constables. Volunteers had to take the special constable's oath and were provided with a badge or a warrant. Former Army and Navy servicemen, Territorials, professionals and youths in the quest for an "adrenaline rush" were expected to constitute the primary recruiting pool for the new organisation. Labour training and periods of drilling, including boxing, wrestling, gymnastics and athletics, were to be arranged for the members.[35]

The proposal to form a civilian force, with no formal connection to the Special Constable scheme, attracted the suspicion of the Home Office. On 16 September, Churchill received a letter from Power, accompanied by a memorandum, in which the mission and objectives of the proposed Volunteer Police Force were outlined.[36] It specified that the formation of a "Volunteer Auxiliary Body" responded to the desire of citizens not only to support the police in maintaining law and order during outbreaks of "industrial warfare", but also to prevent a repetition of such occurrences. Power hoped to secure the cooperation, or at least the acquiescence, of the Home Office in establishing such a force. The Home Office declined to express any support whatsoever for a private body that unreservedly misconceived the Home Secretary's recommendations apropos the organisation of police reserves under the control of public authorities. Furthermore, Churchill, who was preparing to switch offices with Reginald McKenna and move to the Admiralty, refused to meet Power and distanced himself from any possible association of his name with the movement.[37]

Despite the government's hostility, the VPF was set up. The Duke of Abercorn accepted to become its president, while a loose assemblage of right-wing conservatives, businessmen, financiers, clerics and other contemptuous opponents of the Liberal government, expressed public support for the new civilian body.[38] Power wrote on the eve of the inauguration of the VPF:

> The government must do something. . . . The first instinct of man is "self-defence". On to this civilization has grafted the great motto of "Peace", while experience has shown us that the only method . . . that works smoothly is "be prepared".[39]

"England expects every man to do his duty": the Volunteer Police Force[40]

The Volunteer Police Force was established in London on Trafalgar Day, 1911. For the inaugural meeting, which was held in the central transept of the Crystal Palace, the Victorian opera diva Emma Albani had consented to sing "Home Sweet Home" and "God Save the King". Other noted artists of the time, including Violet Oppenshaw, Walter Hedgcock, Dalton Baker and Herbert Godfrey, were also engaged for the musical entertainment of the public. Throughout the previous days, the major railway companies had been advertising the event and "running excursions" in London.[41]

In the midst of a noisy crowd, for the most part drawn to the Palace by the prospect of hearing Albani sing, Viscount Templeton opened the meeting by stating that there was no political bias in the movement and that the new civilian police was not intended to replace, but rather to supplement the regular police during national emergencies.[42] After this preamble, the body's organising chairman, Arnold Statham, a well-known barrister, delivered an aggressive speech in which trade union solidarity action was labelled as "a mere cloak for class warfare to extort surrender to unjustifiable demands", and the peaceful picket "a kind of State-protected highway robber with violence". He argued that Labour leaders and their threat to call a national strike of railway and transport workers were "holding England by the throat". In consequence, he stressed the right of citizens to come together in self-defence and "to take a firm stand against anarchy". "What Britain wants today", he concluded "is not weak-kneed local authorities, but a

Bismarck with a will of iron".[43] After this extravagant praise of authoritarian rule, Statham moved the first resolution:

> that this Mass Meeting of citizens from all parts of the United Kingdom, impressed with the urgent necessity of quelling lawlessness and disorder from time to time in case of need, resolves to form, without casting any additional burden upon the taxpayer, a Volunteer Police Force of private citizens to cooperate with the Regular Forces in the protection of life, property and liberty, where the same are assailed, and for the maintenance of general transport, whensoever the public carriers of the people's food are threatened with violent interference.[44]

After unanimous approval of the first resolution by an impromptu Grand Council,[45] F. C. Morgan, president of the Central Association of Accountant, moved the second resolution. This set out in detail the constitution and organisational principles of the force. In 14 points, it declared that the VPF was a force of private citizens, which, in cooperation with the regular forces of the United Kingdom, was committed to the protection of "life and property" and to the maintenance of essential services of public utility during disputes. The force was to submit to the orders of the heads of the Police Departments, although it was stated that

> it shall be free to act . . . where attempts are threatened to wreck trains or signal boxes, set fire to warehouses, loot shops, or do other malicious injury to public methods of locomotion, transport, or private property without awaiting the initiative of absentee officials.

The national character of the Volunteer Police Force was to be firmly established and its units made available during "any sudden crisis . . . like a force of light infantry for rapid transit to areas where rioting, arson, or scenes of violence are being enacted". The organisation, whose recruitment processes included physical fitness screening, was to be maintained by private contributions with no demands made upon the state.[46]

Once the forms of the organisation were fixed, it was announced to the public that branches of the VPF were to be formed in Wales, Scotland and Ireland.[47] The force, one of its secretaries, Wilfrid E. Myers, declared to a correspondent of the *London Daily News*, was not a strikebreaking organisation, but "when as happened in Swansea, rioters start setting fire to houses and damaging property, then we think it is time for the ordinary citizen to step in". "Our scheme", Myers bizarrely added, "is really a form of Socialism – citizens themselves looking after the common welfare".[48]

As early as 13 November, the press reported that the London Brighton and South Coast, the London and New Western, the Great Eastern, the London and South-Western, and the Central London railway companies had engaged the services of the VPF in anticipation of a renewal of labour disturbances on the railways.[49] Corps of patriotic volunteers, complemented by technical experts in railway and engineering work, were to be mobilised to protect labour replacements and railway materials. Each man dispatched to the strike areas was expected to wear a uniform and to be equipped with a blackjack (or life preserver).[50] To meet all contingencies, the administrators of the VPF proposed that manufacturers of commercial vehicles provide assistance in transporting supplies from the railway termini to distribution centres. Car makers Dodson Motors Ltd responded to the appeal by placing a car at the disposal of the movement.[51] "This organization", the Home Office laconically commented on the VPF's strikebreaking plans, "is likely to give trouble".[52]

At the end of November, the VPF had received over 30,000 applications at its headquarter on Victoria Street.[53] Membership was "largely composed of wealthy young men, who might, intentionally or unintentionally, fail to distinguish between hooliganism and legitimate forms of working-class protest", historian Veronica Cicely Wedgwood wrote many years later.[54] While the peer's sons volunteered, as they did against the Boers, "to stamp on the restless workers", the Duke of Abercorn repeatedly appealed for funds to help meet the organisation's growing expenses.[55] "In order for the force to be effective in rendering substantial assistance to the public services", he wrote, "a highly efficient organization of the force must be built", and this evidently required money.[56]

If the conservative press lauded the VPF for its avowal to protect general transportation, working-class organisations had grown increasingly alarmed by the decision of local commercial and industrial personalities to set up volunteer police corps. In Yorkshire, it was reported that members of the VPF had held meetings with local businessmen and plans for the formation of a civilian police force had been positively received.[57] In Derby, the presidents of the Chamber of Commerce and the Chamber of Trade informed the VPF's organising secretary, W. M. Myers, of their decision to form a similar private organisation on the banks of the river Derwent.[58]

"Efforts are being made in many directions", the pseudonymous *Labourite* complained in the *Derbyshire Courier*, "to undermine the power of the workers, intimidatory forces are being organized under one disguise or another".[59] Leftist papers bluntly defined the VPF as a strikebreaking group organised along the lines of the Pinkertons in America. The *Justice* wrote significantly:

> There are two movements now going on by which the master class are now endeavouring to ensure themselves against any dislocation of business in the event of a strike. . . . One is the Home Office movement for the enrolment of special constables . . . and the other is the organization of a "volunteer police force" by the capitalist themselves.[60]

Under the pen name "Trade Unionist", a commentator for the Bournemouth-based *Christchurch Times* wrote:

> A number of busybodies, almost entirely prominent Tories, are going about the country seeking to establish what they call a Volunteer Police Force . . . a

> private venture. . . . This new body is to have a uniform, and it is quite certain that it will be composed of men who are strongly anti-trade unionist. Thus, if such a force were to become numerous, there is all the material for class antagonism of the worst kind. It is to be hoped that Mr. McKenna will keep his eye on these amateur policemen, who are likely to cause more trouble to the regular police than to assist them to maintain order. These Tory strike-breakers may easily become a greater danger than any strikers.[61]

The propagation of the VPF across the country kindled talk of self-defence among workers. The Bradford branch of the Amalgamated Society of Railway Servants passed a resolution stating that the formation of such a force, "organized and controlled by the capitalist classes outside and above the law of the land and openly supported by railway companies", was a serious menace to the liberties of working men. They therefore agreed to form a "physical protection league", whose objective would be to train and equip selected trade unionists "to meet on equal terms the bullies of organized capital".[62]

Meanwhile, at the House of Commons, Labour MPs raised questions about the legality of a private uniformed volunteer force, "purposely armed with bludgeons to break people's heads" and to be used as a strikebreaking force in the event of industrial disputes. Home Secretary Reginald McKenna replied that the Volunteer Police Force was a private and self-governing organisation which had not received any government approval. He cautioned that the formation of an independent organisation, whose purpose usurped the functions of the police, aroused reasonable "suspicion", and therefore was inimical to the safety of the state. Furthermore, the use of uniforms and badges that resembled those of ordinary police forces was illegal and per se objectionable. McKenna concluded by deploring what he termed a "perilous venture".[63] The *Irish News* observed:

> The Home Secretary's hint is to be hoped of hav[ing] the effect of calming the martial ardour of the zealous patriots who are anxious to be invested with the nimble truncheon and teach the mere hack policeman how much better they could bring about peace by cracking skulls.[64]

In answer to the observations made in the House of Commons, Statham – in his capacity as chairman of the Grand Council – denied that the intention of the force was to imitate the functions of the regular police, but rather it was intended to render "practical assistance to the public in times of necessity":

> The services to the public, such as the assistance of electric light, power and other public undertakings by mechanical engineers, electrical engineers, and other trained members of the force were functions entirely different from the ordinary police, and it was considered absolutely necessary in the interests of the public services that an organization should exist for their succour when they might otherwise be paralyzed.[65]

The hostile stance of the Home Office prompted the VPF to publish a booklet in order to publicly clarify the "aims and objects" of the organisation. It stated that the underlying principle of the force was that all law-abiding and loyal citizens owed a duty to assist the state – the guardian of the "common good" – in protecting the rights and liberties of citizens threatened with tumult, intimidation and violence. Among members' duties were the preservation of peace, either in cooperation or in partnership with the regular police, the protection of non-union workers and public vigilance.[66]

In spite of all the controversies, organisation of the VPF continued to push forward. A Southend and County branch of the force was inaugurated and "a company of 120 men was enrolled among scenes of great enthusiasm".[67] Investment broker and estate agent, Aitken Tweedale, began making preparations for the formation of the VPF in Bristol. Large employers and prominent citizens were invited to help the new force by funding equipment and materials. In return they might have had a company named after them.[68] In mid-December, an "at home" was given by Mrs. Holcombe Ingleby to raise funds for the force and was attended by influential figures, including Major General Sterling, Admiral de Courcy Hamilton, Lieutenant Colonel Driscoll and the pioneer of aircraft design, Lieutenant Edward Busk. At the event, Statham stated that a "great number of men", some trained in electrical and mechanical engineering, retired civil servants, men of the Royal Artillery and the Field Artillery and others who served on the railways during the time of the Boer war had been recruited. Major-General Sterling also addressed the gathering, deprecating the use of the military during the strikes and lauding the movement as a great patriotic one. "A body of guardsmen", he said, "in their shirtsleeves with big sticks might be useful in a street riot".[69]

Two days later, at a meeting of the Grand Council, a proposal was made by Lord Lonsdale, and approved unanimously, to rename the Volunteer Police Force the Civilian Force. It was understood that the change was aimed at preventing any possibility of confusion between the Volunteer Police Reserve, which was being established by the Home Office with police functions, and the Volunteer Police Force whose purpose was "the maintenance of public services and other purely civic duties".[70] This resolution did not dispel the suspicion that the force was nothing more than a strikebreaking outfit and the concurrent news that its members were being hired *en bloc* by companies added to this presentiment.[71] Speaking before the executives of the National Sailors' and Firemen's Union, syndicalist Madame Sorgue, the "most dangerous woman in Europe", commenting on the labour unrest of summer 1911 and the new challenges facing the British labour movement, stated:

> I see there is a volunteer police force being organized [in England]. That is the most serious blunder. I knew those volunteer police. I have seen them at work at Parma. There they pursued deliberately a policy of exasperation. It will lead to civil war.[72]

At the end of the year, the Civilian Force released a new, detailed booklet. The objectives and aims of the force were restated, and the right and duty of citizens to protect their liberty and the inviolability of property, without statutory approval, was repeated. In pursuing these objectives, volunteers would assist "Railways, Ships, Docks, Tramways, Electric Power, Light Sanitary, or other Public Services" and would ensure the movement of essential supplies. The force was also directed to recruit Special Constables and to supplement them and the fire and ambulance services and provide safeguards for the protection of animals from acts of cruelty. Finally, the Civilian Force was "to provide a system of physical and moral training for young men, to render them proficient in some branch of public spirit and patriotism, and equip them for the full discharge of the responsibilities of citizenship".[73]

The organisational structure of the Civilian Force was streamlined and functionally differentiated. Beneath the Grand Council, members were divided into "special service members", who would act as flying columns throughout the Kingdom; "trade service members", who were assigned to prescribed industries "for the protection of their business or employment, or with the consent of their employers for the protection of other concerns of a similar kind"; and, finally, "service members", who operated in a specific district and were organised into companies of 120 men commanded by a captain, who was in turn appointed by the district headquarters. In addition to the regular companies, mounted cyclists and motor cyclists were in the process of being organised. The Civilian Force's equipment consisted of a helmet, armlet, whistle, collar numbers and unspecified "weapons of defence". The men received training in boxing, walking-stick defence and a method of attack known as the Vigny system, which had been devised to combat "Les Apaches" of Paris. The uniform was grey with fawn facings and a distinctive aluminium badge. The members of the Civilian Force did not receive any monetary reward for their services. However, when engaged in duty, members were covered by a special insurance that paid out a sum of £200 in the event of death or permanent disability. For temporary or partial disability, up to £2 per week was paid.[74]

District staffs, which consisted of a chief of staff, a medical officer, an enrolment officer, a principal mobilisation officer, a director of supplies and transport, a signalling instructor and a veterinary officer, had the authority to conduct all of the Civilian Force's affairs, including fundraising, recruitment, and training, equipping and mobilising the service's operating forces. To ensure compliance with the applicable laws, members of the Civilian Force were sworn in as special constables "before going on duty in any public place". They were exonerated from taking the special constable's oath when they acted on "behalf of the Proprietor as his friends or servants for the purpose of protecting his property from forcible trespass".[75]

The Civilian Force's undertaking "to assist the community at large" under the cover of the law did not soften the Home Office's opposition. The Permanent Under-Secretary, Sir Edward Troup, considered it intolerable for any "government which stands for law, order and impartiality, and not for punching the heads of strikers, to have anything to do it".[76] In spite of Abercorn's reassurances to the Home Office that there was no intention of the Civilian Force "being a privately controlled or directed organization",[77] at the beginning of the year its associates continued looking for financial backers and businesses willing to either hire them or set up their own companies. In London, a delegation of the force approached the representatives of the Shipping Federation to offer them their protection services. The shipowners, who staunchly opposed trade unionism, agreed to make a donation of £500 to Abercorn's force, which would be increased to £1,000 if the organisation developed along promised lines.[78] Harrods Limited pledged to form a full company from among their employees and to open a recruiting depot at their stores in London.[79] In Oxford, a Strike Emergency Committee was formed with the intention of joining the Civilian Force. "It is hoped", *The Times* wrote, "the example of the undergraduates there will lead to similar action in other University towns and elsewhere".[80]

In the meantime, at the Civilian Force's headquarters, retired cavalrymen, colonials and members the Legion of Frontiersmen were enrolled "as a flying squadron", while retired army offices were assigned to the coordination of service members. Arrangements were made to train volunteers in operating electrical power stations and railways.[81] A correspondent from the *London Evening News* described one of the first public appearances of the force thus:

> If you were in Victoria-street . . . on Monday evening, you must have noticed a number of men, dressed in an odd mixture of police and military-looking uniform, patrolling the pavement or standing on guard. They were London's new policemen. In their grey military helmets, long, dark coloured police overcoats, shiny black waterproof capes, blue and white armlets and ordinary workday trousers, forty men and officers of this new civilian force were out on duty for the first time.[82]

While new companies of the Civilian Force were formed around the country,[83] the press reported that Abercorn's "amateur police" had been engaged to guard the Victoria Street branch of the London and South Western Bank to prevent suffragettes carrying out window-smashing protest.[84] Also at this time the new secretary, Pirie Gordon, unsuccessfully approached Sir Robert Baden Powell to propose enlisting 18-year-old boy scouts in the Civilian Force.[85]

At the beginning of March, perhaps after consultation with Sir Theodore Morison, a member of the Council of India, the Duke of Abercorn announced that

> in view of the serious possibilities which may be in store for the country, the Civilian Force has decided to try to enlist the assistance of those officers of the Indian Army, Indian Police, and other Indian services who are home on furlough in the Civilian Force.[86]

In response to Abercorn's proposal to raise a company for special service to be known as the "Indian Service Company", the Under-Secretary of State for

India, Edwin Samuel Montagu, sought legal advice from the Home Office as he entertained "grave doubts" over the legality of the matter.[87] The Home Office replied that while the government could not support the policies and methods of the Civilian Force, it recognised that it could not interfere with the citizen's right to offer his services to police authorities. These officers in the service of the government of India could, therefore, have been employed on public duty, but only after being sworn in as Special Constables.[88] After fresh questions on the activities of the Civilian Force were raised in the House of Commons, Abercorn cautiously ordered that the "Indian Services Company" should not be involved in the maintenance of any branch of public services during labour disputes.[89]

With the miners' strike spreading nationwide, the Civilian Force was alerted for possible mobilisation. If deployed, the force was expected to guard the pitheads and pumping installations and to feed the pit ponies. The strike was described in a pamphlet circulated by the Civilian Force as "the first stage of the revolutionary scheme" and a step towards the "syndicalist ideal" which would bring employers to their knees, coerce the government and by "one grand coup d'état" collectivise property. To deal with such a revolutionary threat, "patriotic citizens" should be mobilised for the protection of society:

> The hour appears to be approaching when the long intended blow will be struck by organized Labour against an unorganized community, and it is of urgent importance that every patriotic citizen should hasten the assistance of the only body [the Civilian Force] that has been organized to assist the forces of the Crown to cope with such an INSURRECTION IN THE LABOUR WORLD.[90]

Although the Civilian Force's strikebreaking services were not requested by the coal mine owners, and would in any case have been of little or no value to them considering the scale of the dispute, the fear of a revolutionary strike was drawing an unnegotiable line between good and bad citizenship in the minds of Abercorn and his associates. The "socialist trade unionist" could not have been a good citizen nor could he have been acknowledged as a member of the national community.

At the beginning of the London Dock Strike of 1912, the Shipping Federation, which had complained of the Home Office's decision to refuse police protection for imported labour, hired the services of the Civilian Force. On 28 May, *The Times* reported that

> an urgency call was received for a detachment of the Civilian Force to escort labourers to the docks where already many members of the force had been engaged in discharging cargoes of food. By midnight, an officered and fully-equipped company supplied with rations were at work. By 4.30 yesterday morning the whole body were stationed at places indicated by the Shipping Federation at whose instance their services were requisitioned.[91]

At Greenhithe, where the Shipping Federation's notorious frigate, Lady Jocelyn, was lying along the pier with 600 blacklegs housed on board ready to be dispatched by several tugs to the various London docks, members of the Civilian police clashed with pickets. The confrontations resulted in many injuries on both sides. The shipowners recognised that the presence of the Civilian Police "largely contributed towards a feeling of security on the part of the imported men".[92] According to an unnamed trade unionist, Abercorn's volunteers were "unprepossessing and mostly unshaven men, in grey helmets, long coats with belts, corduroy trousers and dirty boots. They were all armed with heavy sticks and revolvers".[93] In several instances, there was actual or threatened use of these firearms, conceivably supplied by the shipping companies, against the strikers. At the beginning of June, the Civilian Force released a statement declaring that it had assisted the Shipping Federation in the

> transportation of food supplies for London, protected free labourers from molestation, escorted large bodies of willing workers to the docks and guarded vessels from damage by strikers, and some detachments have, in addition to protection duty, worked hard in discharging cargoes of food.[94]

The practice of substituting a private for the public police authority spawned a lively debate in parliament and in the press.[95] For MP Wedgwood, the Civilian Force appeared to be not only an unnecessary reflection upon the regular police, but also an imitation of those private police organisations in America "which were largely responsible for the bloodshed which marks labour trouble in that country".[96] The *Daily Herald* criticised the Civilian Force as "the new slave guards",[97] while *The Syndicalist and Amalgamation News* would later speak of a "Capitalists' Private Army of Armed Strike Breakers".[98] Trade union leader Ben Tillett vigorously protested the use of the Civilian Police and told Lord Haldane that "if he permitted the capitalists to arm their blacklegs with revolvers and truncheons, they would arm their men with similar weapons".[99]

During the summer, amidst ongoing polemics on the purposes and functions of Abercorn's organisation, the Home Office pressed those stipendiary magistrates who had been associated with the Grand Council of the Civilian Force to sever their connections with that organisation.[100] At the end of the year, vice-president and chief of staff, William M. Power, had his membership revoked by unanimous resolution of the Grand Council following accusations by other executive members of administrative and financial malfeasance.[101] A short time later, Power would establish a new organisation, the Volunteer Civil Force (VCF), on much the same lines as the Civilian Force. After the sudden death of the Duke of Abercorn on 3 January 1913, proceedings were brought against Power in the Chancery Division to restrain him from presenting the VCF as the direct successor or replacement of the Civilian Force or from persuading the public that the Civilian Force had ceased to exist. A series of legal squabbles virtually paralysed the new organisation up to the summer of 1914, when Power began publication of the monthly V.C.F. Notes.[102]

Although, as the Board of Trade reported in its annual report on Strikes and Lock-outs, the year 1913 “was remarkable for the number of disputes which occurred during its course, far exceeding the number recorded in any previous year”,[103] the activities of the Civilian Force appear to have been sporadic. A scarcity of funds and, perhaps, a decline in membership because of internal disagreements were very likely the causes of this lack of activity. However, at the end of the free speech demonstration in Trafalgar Square on 29 June, which was attended by trade unionists, suffrage societies and the Free Speech Defence League, members of the Civilian Force violently clashed with “dockers and socialists” who were marching to Downing Street.[104] In defending Britain from “subversion”, the extreme anti-socialist ideology of the Civilian Force easily amalgamated with anti-feminism and anti-suffragism.[105]

At the end of October, James A. E. Hamilton, 3rd Duke of Abercorn, who had succeeded his father as president of the Civilian Force and commanded the Tyrone Regiment of the newly formed Ulster Volunteer Force, appealed for money. “It is abundantly evident”, he argued, “that our organisation may be badly needed in the near future, and committee is anxious to raise an assured income to enable them to maintain the Force on substantial scale, and ready to meet any emergency”.[106] About a week later, a detachment of the Civilian Force was dispatched to Dublin for “protection duty” in the midst of the lockout and was quartered on the Shipping Federation’s depot ships. By mid-November, hundreds of strikebreakers were regularly working in the guarded docks under the protective eye of volunteers.[107]

On the outbreak of war, the Civilian Force, like the other patriotic organisations that had sprung up with perplexing rapidity in the turbulent summer of 1911 to safeguard Britain from the evils that the self-appointed saviours of society dreaded, began to volunteer for the various forms of war service. This led to the establishment of a hospital for the wounded, assistance with recruitment and fundraising for Belgian refugees. The Civilian Force was not reconstituted at the end of the war.[108]

Conclusions

In the post-war years, the Volunteer Police Force (then the Civilian Police) had only survived in the tenacious memory of some Labour MPs, to then fall into oblivion. In his memoirs, much influenced by the years of fascism and war, Josiah Wedgwood went so far as to define the VPF as an “abortive forerunner of the Nazis”.[109] Aside from hyperbolic comparisons, the meteoric rise of Abercorn’s amateur police reveals the apprehension and disquiet afflicting British elites and upper middle classes in the face of extended political, social and industrial citizenship. At the same time, the formation of a private body organised on quasi-military lines for the maintenance of civil order and for the preservation of individual liberty, freedom of contract and “national efficiency” suggests a certain deterioration of trust on the part of vested interests and conservative elements in the ability of state authorities to suppress deviance. In addition, the wearing of uniforms, the organisation and training of members and the carrying of offensive weapons drew attention to the distorting effects of the militarisation of society and the risk of legitimising violence perpetrated by civil actors, where this was deemed to be in the national interest. In this context, the principles and practices of the VPF embodied an exclusionary concept of citizenship, which tended to relegate demands for collective bargaining and industrial democracy to the status of "social treason". The government's firm opposition to the VPF inhibited its development and prevented potential imitative spirals, and at the same time might have cautioned certain sectors of British capital against unlawful, if not seditious, conduct against trade unionism and calmed their push towards the privatisation of security. The mobilisation for total war absorbed those "patriotic excesses", traces of which were to resurface as fears of revolt spread following the Russian Revolutions of 1917 and in the turbulent post-war years.[110]

Notes

* Research for this article received funding from the European Research Council (ERC) under the European Union's Horizon 2020 Research and Innovation program (G.A. 677199 – ERC-StG2015 "The Dark Side of the Belle Époque. Political Violence and Armed Associations in Europe before the First World War").

1 Geoffrey Searle, "'The Revolt from the Right' in Edwardian Britain," in *Nationalist and Racialist Movements in Britain and Germany Before 1914*, ed. Paul Kennedy and Anthony Nicholls (London: Palgrave Macmillan, 1981), 21–39; John Douglas Pratten, *The Reaction to Working Class Unrest 1911–1914* (PhD thesis, Sheffield University PhD, 1975).

2 On 21 August 1911, *The Daily Mail* labelled the transport dispute in 1911 as a "strike against society" which "could only succeed by the destruction of society itself". Quoted in Charles Townshend, *Making the Peace. Public Order and Public Security in Modern Britain* (Oxford: Oxford University Press, 1993), 44.

3 On the Liverpool Civic Service League, The Liverpool Athenaeum Archives, Civic Service League, Minute Book, Vol. 1 (29 August 1911–19 September 1913). On the Leeds Citizen's League of Law and Order, J. E. Williams, "The Leeds Corporation Strike in 1913," in *Essays in Labour History 1886–1923,* ed. Asa Briggs and John Saville (London: Palgrave Macmillan, 1971), 70–95.

4 Hansard Parliamentary Debate, 9 April 1923, Vol. 162 cc. 943–1019.

5 On the Special Constables Act 1923, see, Clare Katherine Leon, "From special constables to special constabularies," in The Special Constabulary: Historical Context, International Comparisons and Contemporary Themes, ed. by Karen Bullock and Andrew Millie (United Kingdom: Taylor & Francis, 2017), 51–55.

6 Standish Meacham, "The Sense of an Impending Clash," *American Historical Review* 77 (December 1972): 1346. On the psychological dimension of the "Great Unrest", Henry Phelps Brown, *The Growth of British Industrial Relations* (London: Palgrave Macmillan, 1959), 332.

7 On the Great Unrest, see, generally, Hugh Clegg, *A History of British Trade Unions since 1889, Vol. 2: 1911–1933* (Oxford: Oxford University Press, 1985). See also a first-hand account of the industrial troubles written by Lord Askwith, *Industrial Problems and Disputes* (London: J. Murray, 1920).

8 Robert J. Holton, "Revolutionary Syndicalism and the British Labour Movement," in *The Development of Trade Unionism in Great Britain and Germany 1880–1914*, ed. Wolfgang J. Mommsen and Hans Gerhard Husung (London and Boston: George Allen and Unwin, 1985), 270.

9 David Smith, "Tonypandy, 1910: Definitions of Community," *Past and Present* 87 (May 1980): 158–84.

10 Élie Halévy, *A History of the English People in the Nineteenth Century,* VI*: The Rule of Democracy, 1905–1914, Book II* (London: P. Smith, 1952), 479.
11 On the 1911 uprising of seamen and dockers in the English ports, see, generally, Ken Coates and Anthony Topham, *The Making of the Labour Movement: The Formation of the Transport and General Workers' Union, 1870–1922* (Nottingham: Spokesman, 1994).
12 Halévy, *The Rule of Democracy, 1905–1914,* 441–556.
13 Eric Taplin, *Near to Revolution. The Liverpool General Transport Strike of 1911* (Liverpool: Bluecoat, 1994); H. R. Hikins, "The Liverpool General Transport Strike, 1911," *THSLC* 113 (1961): 169–96.
14 On the Llanelli riot, see John Edwards, *Remembrance of a Riot: The Story of the Llanelli Railway Strike Riots of 1911* (Llanelli: Llanelli Borough Council, 2010); Deian Hopkin, "The Llanelli Riots, 1911," *Welsh History Review* 11 (1983): 488–513.
15 Geoffrey Alderman, "The Anti-Jewish Riots of August 1911 in South Wales," *Welsh History Review* 6 (1972): 190–200.
16 "The Strikes," *The Times*, August 8, 1911.
17 On the crisis of Edwardian Britain, see George Dangerfield, *The Strange Death of Liberal England* (New York: Capricorn Books, 1961; 1st ed., 1935).
18 General Manager of H. L. Raphaels' Refinery to Home Office, 11 August 1911, in PRO HO 144/5491/212342/28.
19 Hansard Parliamentary Debate, 13 March 1911, Vol. 22 cc. 1862–3.
20 "News of Day," *The Liverpool Daily Post and Mercury*, August 30, 1911.
21 Liverpool Athenaeum, Civil Service League, CSL/1/1 and CSL/4 (Membership).
22 W. T. Stead, "What We Have Learned from the Railway Strike. Hints from the Hague for the Regulation of Industrial War," *The Review of Reviews* 44 (September 1911): 249–55.
23 "General Strikes and General Strike-Breakers," *The Times,* August 26, 1911.
24 [Letter to the Editor] "The Strike Peril," *Dorking and Leatherhead Advertiser*, September 16, 1911.
25 Montagu of Beaulieu, "Road Transport During Strikes," *The Times*, August 23, 1911.
26 Parliamentary Papers, Employment of Military during the Railway Strike. Correspondence between the Home Office and Local Authorities relating to the Employment of the Military during the Railway Strike in August 1911, 22.
27 "Our London Correspondent," *Forres Elgin and Nairn Gazette*, September 20, 1911.
28 On the class character of the Special Constabulary, see Tony Bunyan, *The History and Practice of the Political Police in Britain* (London: Julian Fiedmann Publishers, 1976), 98.
29 Hansard Parliamentary Debate, 7 May 1923, Vol. 163 cc. 1973–2010.
30 For a comprehensive examination of policing in the pre-war years, see Clive Emsley, *The English Police: A Political and Social History* (London: Harvester Wheatsheaf, 1991); Roger Geary, *Policing Industrial Disputes: 1893–1985* (Cambridge: Cambridge University Press, 1985); Jane Morgan, *Conflict and Order: The Police and Labour Disputes in England and Wales, 1900–1939* (Oxford: Oxford University Press, 1987); Barbara Weinberger, *Keeping the Peace? Policing Strikes in England and Wales 1906–1926* (Oxford: Oxford University Press, 1991).
31 "Citizen Police: Home Secretary Seeks to Raise Volunteer Force," *Birmingham Mail,* September 14, 1911.
32 On the setting up of police reserve, see Clare Katherine Leon, *Special Constables: An Historical and Contemporary Survey* (PhD thesis, University of Bath, 1991).
33 "Special Constables as Reservists," *Tower Hamlets Independent and East End Local Advertiser*, September 2, 1911.
34 For biographical information on William Mailes Power, see PRO, WO 339/93876. Also, see his profile in *The Business World: Men & Methods of the New Georgian Era. Imperial Interests, Pen Sketches and Illustrations* (London: DoD Publications, 1913), 130–31.

35 "A Volunteer Police Force," *The Standard*, September 8, 1911.
36 Letter from W. M. Power to Home Secretary Winston Churchill, 16 September 1911, in PRO, HO 45.10666.216733, Volunteer Police Force, 1911–14.
37 Letter from (Sd) E. Blackwell to W.M. Power, 2 October,1911, in Ibid.
38 "The Duty of a Citizen," *Pall Mall Gazette*, October 11, 1911.
39 "A Volunteer Police," *Pall Mall Gazette*, October 12, 1911. In response to Power, Edward Johns Urwick, at the time professor of economic science at King's College, criticised the VPF as a potential source of hooliganism and mob-justice. See Edward Urwick, "The Manners of Pavement," *Pall Mall Gazette*, October 13, 1911.
40 The Nelsonian quote was made the motto of the Volunteer Police Force.
41 "Volunteer Police: To-day's Demonstration at the Crystal Palace," *Pall Mall Gazette*, October 21, 1911.
42 The proceedings of the inaugural meeting were printed and circulated in a booklet titled *The Volunteer Police Force*. Copy of the booklet is in PRO HO 45.10666.216733
43 Ibid., p. 10. This passage is also quoted in Clive Emsley, *The English and Violence since 1750* (London: A&C Black, 2007), 109.
44 "A Volunteer Police Force," 3.
45 The Grand Council of the VPF included, among others, the Earl of Meath, the Earl of Lonsdale, the Viscount Templeton, Lord Cheylesmore, Lord Ninian Stuart, the Archdeacon Sinclair, the stipendiary magistrates John De Grey Albert de Rutzen and William Chichele Plowden, the Major A.J.N Tremearne, Captain Walter Waring, the mayors of Peterborough, Guilford and Basingstoke, Joseph Lyons, and several prominent London lawyers.
46 Ibid., 14–15.
47 Ibid., 18.
48 "Unofficial Scheme of Citizen Service," *London Daily News*, October 14, 1911.
49 "Unrest Among Railway Employees," *The Railway Times*, November 18, 1911.
50 "Volunteer Police and a Railway Strike. Directions to Commanding Officers," *The Times*, November 13, 1911.
51 "The Need for Motors," *Pall Gazette*, November 14, 1911.
52 Home Secretary's Minutes, 16 November 1911, HO 45.10666.216733/2, Volunteer Police Force, 1911–1914.
53 [no title], *Henley & South Oxford Standard*, December 1, 1911.
54 Cicely V. Wedgwood, *The Last of the Radicals: Josiah Wedgwood, M.P.* (London: Cape, 1951), 89–90.
55 Quote in Josiah Wedgwood, "The Honorary Strikebreakers," *The Eyewitness*, December 21, 1911, 16–17.
56 "A Volunteer Police Force," *The Times*, November 23, 1911.
57 "The Volunteer Police Force: To the editor of the Yorkshire Post," *Yorkshire Post and Leeds Intelligencer*, November 22, 1911.
58 "Derby and the Volunteer Force Movement," *Derbyshire Advertiser and Journal*, November 17, 1911.
59 Labourite, "Labour Topics," *Derbyshire Courier*, October 20, 1911.
60 "A British 'Pinkertons' Organization," *Justice*, November 18, 1911.
61 [By a Trade Unionist], "The Labour Movement," *Christchurch Times*, December 2, 1911.
62 "The Railway Situation: Men in Militant Mood," *The Manchester Guardian*, December 4, 1911.
63 Hansard Parliamentary Debate, 4 December 1911, Vol. 32 cc. 1009–10.
64 "Volunteer Police," *Irish News and Belfast Morning News*, December 5, 1911.
65 "The Volunteer Police Force: A Reply to Criticism," *The Times*, December 6, 1911.
66 Aims and Objects of the Volunteer Police Force. Volunteer Police Force, afterwards Civilian Force, London, [1911], in PRO, HO 45.10666.216733.
67 "The Volunteer Police Force," *Chard and Ilminster News*, December 9, 1911.
68 "The Volunteer Police Force," *Bristol Times and Mirror*, December 4, 1911.

69 "Volunteer Police Force," *The Times*, December 12, 1911.
70 "The Volunteer Police Force," *Globe*, December 16, 1911.
71 "Civilian Police London. Functions explained by Mr. Statham," *London Daily News*, December 20, 1911.
72 "London Letter," *Irish News and Belfast Morning News*, December 29, 1911.
73 The Civilian Force. Founded on Trafalgar Day as the "Volunteer Police Force," 7–8. A copy of the booklet is in PRO, HO 45.10666.216733, Volunteer Police Force, 1911–14.
74 Ibid., 11–24.
75 Ibid., 4.
76 Letter from Edward Troup to Russell Scott, 12 March 1912, in PRO HO 45.10666.216733, Volunteer Police Force, 1911–14.
77 Letter of the Duke of Abercorn to the Home Secretary, 8 March 1912, in PRO HO 45.10666.216733, Volunteer Police Force, 1911–14.
78 Modern Record Centre, Shipping Federation, General and Executive Council Meetings, Proceedings at General and Executive Council Meetings. Bound volume. May 1912–November 1914, Annual General Meeting Friday, 17 May 1912, 8.
79 "Civilian Force: Organization to Protect Property," *Pall Mall Gazette*, March 8, 1912.
80 "The Civilian Force: Oxford Undergraduate Offer," *The Times*, March 7, 1912. Students at the University of Cambridge followed the example by forming their own anti-strike service division.
81 "London Letter: Civilians for Public Protection," *Aberdeen Press and Journal*, January 19, 1912.
82 "Amateur Police: Over a Thousand Enrolled in London," *London Evening News*, March 6, 1912.
83 "The Civilian Force," *Near and Far Newcastle Daily Chronicle*, April 3, 1912.
84 [no title], *Illustrated London News*, March 9, 1912. The manager of the London and South Western Bank was the Stephen Trott, who was also a member of the Grand Council of the Volunteer Police Force.
85 "North Devon Scout Notes," *North Devon Journal*, March 7, 1912.
86 PRO HO 45.10666.216733/12, Volunteer Police Force, 1911–1914. For the proposal of the Duke of Abercorn to raise an "Indian Service Company" in connection with the Civilian Force see "The Civilian Police. An Appeal to Indian Officers," *The Times*, March 7, 1912.
87 Letter from the Under-Secretary of State for India to the Under-Secretary of State Home Office, 9 March 1912, in PRO, HO 45.10666.216733/12, Volunteer Police Force, 1911–1914.
88 Reply of the Undersecretary of State Home Office to the Under-Secretary of State for India, 11 March 1912 in Ibid.
89 Letter of the Duke of Abercorn to the Secretary of State Home Office 13 March 1912, in PRO HO 45.10666.216733/14.
90 Civilian Force: The Danger of a National Strike, in PRO HO 45.10666.216733/15.
91 "Food Supplies at the Markets," *The Times*, May 30, 1912.
92 Modern Record Centre, Shipping Federation, Policy and Administration, Grey Books, Transactions of the Federation, 1911–1914. Report of the General Purposes Committee to the Executive Council, 29 November 1912, 2–3.
93 "Blackleg Outrage. Revolver Shots fired at Gravesend Pickets," *Daily Herald*, June 7, 1912.
94 "The Civilian Force," *The Times*, June 6, 1912.
95 Hansard Parliamentary Debate, 12 June 1912, Vol. 39 cc. 872–995.
96 "Mr. Wedgwood, M.P. and Strikes," *Staffordshire Sentinel*, June 24, 1912.
97 "The New Slave Guards," *Daily Herald*, August 28, 1912.
98 "The Menace to the Workers," *The Syndicalist and Amalgamation News* IL, no. 2, February 1913.

99 "Mr. Tillett's Ultimatum: Use of Arms by Blacklegs Severely Condemned," *Daily Herald*, June 7, 1912.
100 PRO HO 45.10666.216733/21.
101 "Founder's Suit Against Committee," *Pall Mall Gazette*, July 28, 1913.
102 The V.C.F. Notes was later renamed the Volunteer Civil Force (July 1914 – February/March 1916).
103 Report on Strikes and Lock-Outs and on Conciliation and Arbitration Boards in the United Kingdom in 1913, with comparative statistics (London: Printed for H.M. Stationery Office by Darling & Son [etc.], 1914), X.
104 "Another Riot," *Daily Herald*, June 30, 1913.
105 "How England is Ruined. Salvation against Socialists and Suffragists," *Daily Herald*, July 30, 1914.
106 "Now Gaol Abercorn," *Daily Herald*, October 28, 1913.
107 "Civilian Force for Dublin," *Belfast Newsletter*, November 12, 1913.
108 "Gifts for Child Refugees," *The Bystander*, December 2, 1914.
109 On the interpretation of the Volunteer Police Force as a failed precursor of fascist paramilitarism see Josiah Clement Wedgewood, *Memoirs of a Fighting Life* (London: Hutchinson & Co., Ltd., 1940), 80.
110 R. C. Maguire, "The Fascists . . . are . . . to be Depended Upon. The British Government, Fascists and Strike-breaking during 1925 and 1926," in *British Fascism, the Labour Movement and the State*, ed. N. Copsey and D. Renton (Basingstoke: Palgrave Macmillan, 2005), 6–26.

14 From "state protection" to "private defence"

Strikebreaking, civilian armed mobilisation and the rise of Italian fascism*

Matteo Millan

On 14 July 1919, the Italian Parliament was discussing a vote of confidence in Francesco Saverio Nitti's cabinet. Often accused of being an opportunistic politician and a cold-hearted economist, unable to grasp the passions and the new situation created by the end of the war, Nitti's legacy has often been surrounded by a general antipathy.[1] However, at the time, the government that Nitti was going to lead was seen with great hope. It was born with the ambitious purpose of moving the country away from the legacies of the First World War towards a new future of prosperity.[2] Nitti's internal policy reflected his economics-oriented background and was well exemplified in the motto "consume less, produce more", that he repeated again and again during his parliamentary speeches. Usually tolerant and neutral in economic disputes, Nitti's government was nonetheless harsh and repressive against any real or perceived political demonstrations, often interpreted as the prelude to social revolution and a waste of energies and productive resources.[3]

While parliament was discussing the vote of confidence, Nitti, in his capacity as minister of the interior, issued a circular letter to all the prefects of the Kingdom of Italy. The circular was part of a broad set of measures that the government was taking in response to the impending "super strike" (*scioperissimo*) called by left-wing organisations, parties and unions in solidarity with the Bolsheviks and against the intervention of western powers in Russia.[4] Nitti invited the prefects to "keep in touch" with reliable members of liberal "groups [*fasci*] and veterans' associations" in order to obtain their "collaboration at times when public authorities cannot remain isolated and only rely on public officials and the public force". Nitti also invited the prefects to prevent any autonomous initiative:

> if such groups want to cooperate to enforce law and order and to repress violence and attempts at revolution, they will act patriotically by voluntarily observing the orders of the authorities and by accepting their leadership in accordance with the regulations, which cannot be but unique.[5]

Interestingly, Mussolini's newly established *Fasci di combattimento* were among those patriotic organisations that the authorities considered potentially useful for deployment in strikebreaking services.[6]

Nitti's instructions came at a time of panic over the potential revolutionary consequences of the general strike. In March, the leadership of the Italian Socialist Party asserted that the general strike was the main instrument for establishing a socialist republic.[7] Despite these proclamations, however, the strike was a general fiasco for reasons both international and domestic in nature. Not only did other international organisations, and in particular the French General Confederation of Labour, refuse to join the international mobilisation, but, more importantly, leading Italian unions, such as the railway workers' unions, kept working.

Many historians have considered Nitti's 14 July dispatch as part of a political strategy to obtain the approval of ultra-nationalist movements and associations both within and outside parliament.[8] Others saw in it tangible proof that the political authorities of the liberal state had given up the Weberian state monopoly of physical violence.[9] According to Emilio Gentile, such "patriotic" groups reflected a process of "secondary mobilisation" in reaction to the primary mobilisation of left-wing parties and unions. Although they could not be put down to any actual attempt at revolution, nonetheless mass mobilisation during strikes and other demonstrations, requests for wage increases and better working conditions, the contractual power of left-wing organisations and their significant success at general and local elections "were perceived as a real danger by the bourgeoisie and the middle-classes, prompting them to mobilise".[10]

There is no doubt that these forms of secondary mobilisation were fertile ground for the development of fascism, in terms of both political cultures and membership. At the same time, the huge impact and massive scale of later fascist violence helped cast a shadow on the concrete organisational and violent practices of these former associations, and their cultural and political background has been generally described in the light of a vague anti-socialism.[11]

This chapter argues that strikebreaking – in terms of both work replacement and auxiliary police functions – was a veritable obsession for significant sectors of the middle classes and was at the heart of their armed political mobilisation. Within a broader framework the focus is on the two paradigmatic cases of Bologna and Milan in the immediate post-war years (1919–20).[12] The first two sections show how the founding of strikebreaking groups reflected the crucial role played by work replacement and anti-strike activities in shaping outlooks and mentalities in broad sectors of Italian society. In this regard, the concluding section claims that post-war forms of bourgeois mobilisation can be fully appreciated only by situating them within a longer tradition of armed civilian cooperation between the state authorities and discrete social sectors, especially in the case of major strikes involving public services. This long-term interpretative perspective offers new insights into the origins of the crisis in the Italian liberal state and ultimately can help explain the consensus enjoyed by the armed fascist reaction.[13]

Looking for the support of honest citizens

The circular letter of 14 July was a response to the genuine panic that had spread among the political elites and large sections of the bourgeoisie following a dramatic series of popular protests against the high cost of living, the so-called *moti per il caroviveri*. In such a state of affairs, Nitti's entire policing policy was ambitious but also extremely difficult to implement. In his directives, he always stressed the need to rigorously repress social disorder, but at the same time to also "avoid making people think that we want reaction". "I approve whatever has to be done against reckless strikes", he told the prefects, "as long as this does not give the impression that we are carrying out a reactionary policy". His policy may be summarised not so much as "anti-popular and anti-socialist" but rather as "anti-revolutionary"[14] and resulted in the issuing of uncertain and contradictory directives which did nothing but upset everyone. It was with these directives in mind that police authorities dealt with a number of incidents, upheavals, small revolts, riots and lootings. The response usually fell under the banner of bloody repression. In the first two weeks of July 1919 alone – that is, in the period immediately before the circular was sent – about 30 people were killed by police forces; many were wounded and hundreds arrested.[15] This was largely the result of the panic and fear which invested police forces, who were largely undertrained and deficient in number.[16]

Nitti's 14 July circular aimed to be a response to the serious lack of available forces by resorting to the complementary assistance and support of trustworthy social sectors of civil society. This was conceived as an emergency response prior to full implementation of a civilian police force, the Royal Guard of Public Security, that Nitti and the chief of police, Vincenzo Quaranta, worked to establish and that became fully operational in January 1920.[17]

Although determined to obtain the support of reliable citizens, Nitti was also fully aware of the risk that he was taking and was worried – with good reason – that things might get irretrievably out of control. In an "urgent telegram" sent just five days after the original circular letter, he insisted that "cooperation must be regulated and follow obediently the orders of local political authorities"; autonomous initiatives would be "illegal and reckless" as these "would do nothing but fuel dangerous reactions". The prefect, he concluded, "is the only one who has the duty and responsibility to defend public order in the exclusive interests of the country".[18] The effectiveness of such measures is, of course, debatable. Nitti's insistence on local police and political authorities having exclusive control and leadership over forms of civilian collaboration indicates a full awareness of the state's prerogatives. However, he was also convinced that state forces alone would be insufficient to deal with the massive disorders and demonstrations that the country would probably experience. That being so, the support of patriotic citizens and associations in law enforcement and strikebreaking operations was deemed necessary, though extremely dangerous, given the extreme counter-positions and panic over an impending revolution. Nevertheless, Nitti and other government officers decided to play that card, maybe in the hope that this would strengthen the loyal classes' support for the government. At the same time, Nitti's frequent letters and telegrams are telling of his worries over the actual capacity of the authorities to control delegation of the power to enforce law and order to private citizens that he had unleashed.[19]

Although the *scioperissimo* of July 1919 was a flash in the pan, Nitti and other government officials did not abandon the idea of seeking the support of good citizens. On 19 January 1920, the minister of justice and acting prime minister (Nitti was at that time in London), Ludovico Mortara, issued a circular letter to all the prefects in preparation for an upcoming massive railway and postal workers strike. Mortara invited prefects to act with the "most absolute rigour" in order to protect rail infrastructures and passengers. "Using weapons in cases like these", he added, "is a form of self-defence on the part of the homeland [*Patria*] and civilisation against any wild aggression". Faced with the "too scarce presence of deployable military units", Mortara requested prefects to establish "volunteer vigilance squads to effectively enforce public order". "Such squads", he stated, should be formed of "honest citizens" and "could be armed, if necessary".[20]

Mortara's initiative was soon taken up by other ministers and state officials. Minister of Transport Roberto De Vito invited former railway workers to join the anti-strike squads comprising Navy sailors and engineers, though with little success.[21] Government directives were immediately implemented in many Italian cities. On 20 January, the prefect of Milan, Angelo Pesce, invited industrialists, employers and local politicians to "foster citizens' reactions against the strike and collaboration with government authorities to overcome deficiencies in public services, and establish squads of volunteers to support the public force". When the strike broke out the following day, Pesce and the local chief of police (*questore*) organised a corps of about 40 volunteers to take on public order functions.[22] Over 50 volunteer engineers were recruited in southern Italy and dispatched to the north to replace the striking workers.[23] There were also attempts to recruit retired engineers as strikebreakers.[24] Secondary school and university students were particularly keen to offer their time and energies as strikebreakers. In Venice, students, boy scouts and women of the Red Cross worked on trains to secure passenger services.[25] In Florence, 160 volunteers from the Alliance of City Defence took up service in post offices to substitute for strikers.[26] The young black-shirt Mario Piazzesi was proud – though a little bit fatigued – to act as a *crumiro*, a derogative Italian term to indicate a blackleg.[27] He also mentioned, with a touch of envy, that volunteers armed with regular Army rifles had been sent to Bologna to act as strikebreakers.[28]

In Bologna, Mortara's directive was indeed followed to the letter. From 24 to 29 January, "volunteer vigilance squads" were set up to perform "public order duties", enjoying the full support of the local military command, the prefect and police authorities. The 123 volunteers, led by "9 officials", were deployed to protect a train depot and coal yard, substituting for regular troops, which could then be deployed for patrol and public order services. The volunteers were all armed with carbines provided by the military authorities and wore civilian clothes with a "white and red armband". Improvisation and lack of proper training led to a couple of accidental injuries resulting from the misuse of firearms. Despite such incidents, official reports all agreed that the volunteers were quite effective in preventing thefts of coal and other materials.[29] According to the prefect of Bologna, "their action has been broadly appreciated and should be further encouraged".

Students from the "pre-military training battalion" also cooperated to substitute for striking postal workers.[30] Military authorities committed to responding to the strike in a similar fashion. General Ugo Sani, the local military commander, issued a wall poster calling for volunteer motorists to transport food and other supplies during the strike. Sani invited "veterans" and "citizens" to enlist in special corps "for the exclusive interest of the country", in the name of the same "patriotism" that they had shown during the war.[31] Sani's words are particularly interesting, as they indicate a substantial overlap between external and internal enemies.

The establishment of civilian-government cooperation initiatives stemmed from joint bottom-up and top-down efforts. Patriotic associations dedicated to strikebreaking and work replacement were autonomously mushrooming throughout the country. These included the Permanent Committee for National Defence in Vicenza,[32] the National Alliance in Venice, the Alliance of City Defence in Florence, the Association of Volunteers for Public Services in Rome, the Association for Social Renewal and Defence led by future Prime Minister Ivanoe Bonomi in Mantua and, as we will see, the Association of Social Defence in Bologna and the Committee of Civil Organisation in Milan.[33] These largely spontaneous forms of mobilisation had several points in common with the government's outlook and actions. While the postal and railway workers strike was still going on, Nitti sent the umpteenth circular letter explaining how to manage the protesters and enforce law and order. The prime minister exhorted prefects to "try to encourage a spirit of resistance in all kinds of forms". He added that

> Citizens in the first place must resist abuses. If people understand the dangers of the present situation, then they have the duty to organise themselves and react. Repression can be avoided only if resistance increases. I approve anything people do in response to excessive strikes, as far as people do not want to merely react.[34]

As Nitti explained, one of the main reasons for preventing and, if necessary, repressing strikes lay in the weakness of the Italian economic system, still largely subject to foreign imports and credits.

It is no surprise then, that what were, for certain sectors of the middle classes and for the authorities, manifestations of patriotism in a collaborative and collective effort to preserve peace and order, for socialist organisations were mere acts of strikebreaking and reaction. According to the Socialist Party's newspaper *L'Avanti!*, the capitalist bourgeoisie, the government, the conservative press and the bourgeois parties were all working together to call for "the support of self-styled citizens of order to restore public services". These "so-called citizens" were invited to act as *crumiri*. Some of them, the "daddy's boys", "students" and other "loafers by definition", were deployed for work replacement, substituting for rubbish collectors, stokers and tramway drivers, often inefficiently or unsafely. Others, the newspaper claimed, the more "violent men", were instead called upon to collaborate in quashing the emancipation of the working classes.[35]

The January 1920 strike in many ways paved the way for new forms of bourgeois mobilisation. From then onwards, civilian volunteering in the case of a strike had two forms. On the one side, there was the defence of public order through the organisation of units of armed volunteer auxiliary police with the aim of supporting and assisting ordinary state police and military forces. On the other side, the mobilisation of citizens responded to the imperative of securing public services, from train and tram services to sanitation, food supplies and street lighting. Strike-breaking practices and volunteer work replacement were, therefore, considered vital to the defence of the social fabric and public order, along with more direct and confrontational forms of repressive intervention. These attitudes mirrored deep-seated and long-standing outlooks and political cultures in large sectors of the Italian middle classes.

Loss of support

Faced with the perceived threat of complete disruption to the foundations of the social order, various sectors of Milan civil society established a Committee of Civil Organisation (*Comitato di organizzazione civile*) in January 1920. The committee was an "association based on the principles of order and aimed to fight any kind of social movement acting against the principle of state authority and social peace and preventing public services from operating". It fostered inter-class cooperation to prevent social struggle and, at the same time, claimed to help "the poorest people". It gathered together veteran groups, monarchical and liberal clubs, professional associations of shopkeepers and tenants, industrial associations and Benito Mussolini's *Fasci di combattimento*.[36] Following the great postal and railway workers' strike in January 1920, the committee "organised and provided personnel to replace workers on strike"[37] and became the main "reservoir" of patriotic citizens from which volunteers could be recruited. On 19 February 1920, the prefect of Milan, Angelo Pesce, put out a call to raise a corps of "Volunteers of Order". Their aim would be to cooperate with police forces to prevent and repress crimes against "persons and properties" and so quash the wave of criminality that was plaguing the city, also as a consequence of the continuous social disorder. Both private citizens and patriotic associations could apply to become volunteers. All members would be armed with "revolvers or rifles", and those without "gun licences" were provided with "special authorisations". The volunteers were to be organised under the command and responsibility of police officers. Although open to "upright and courageous citizens belonging to any social class and political party", the volunteers received no remuneration and were to patrol the streets in their spare time, so that despite claims of inter-class cooperation, it is somewhat doubtful that the working class played any part in the initiative.[38] The prefect's proposal was warmly received by employers, patriotic associations and politicians.[39] The newspaper *Corriere della Sera* enthusiastically welcomed his commitment to fighting crime and saw in it a prelude to the establishment of a real "city militia [*milizia comunale*]" that could enforce law and order more effectively and more promptly than the ordinary police forces.[40] Others agreed: a private citizen asked the prefect to create a "corps of Citizens' Patrols, like those operating in other cities".[41] As we will see in the last section, these references to militias and Citizens' Patrols are not accidental.

Although the Volunteers had the approval of the local bourgeoisie, the prefect's initiative immediately provoked the opposition of Milan's socialist mayor, Emilio Caldara. In Caldara's view the Volunteers were a serious threat: "in an atmosphere of passion and high tension [*elettricità*]", in which people continuously "fire revolver or rifle shots", arming volunteer citizens and giving them "the authority to use weapons" was an extreme danger in itself, not to mention a serious embarrassment to "the authority of the state". The creation of the Volunteers, Caldara prophesied, would mean "the reactionary elements, who had carried out the most provocative strikebreaking actions during working-class agitations, will be able to get a foot in the door of the state police". This, Caldara concluded, might result in "civil war". In linking the activities of the Volunteers with those of strikebreakers, Caldara was not simply resorting to the usual socialist argumentation but was stressing the crucial role that the newly established militia would play in social conflicts and, therefore, their implicit partiality.[42] Just a few days after the calls for volunteers to enlist had been put out, Minister of Justice Mortara aligned himself with Caldara's positions. In fact, given the strong presence of an "anti-socialist party" in Milan, Mortara feared that direct, institutional support for the recruitment of volunteers would have severe political repercussions for the government. At the same time, loyal to his long-lasting commitment to recruiting auxiliary volunteers, Mortara invited Pesce to leave these sorts of initiatives to private citizens and associations, so that the government would not be deemed accountable for their actions.[43] This is a crucial turning point in the attitude of the government. Without formally delegating a portion of the state monopoly to recognised private organisations, but by simply turning a blind eye to forms of vigilantism, Mortara only unleashed forms of organised private violence against the so-called subversives. The consequences would be felt for a long time.

The need to maintain good relations with Milan's moderate and reformist socialist city administration eventually obliged the government to appoint a new prefect to replace Angelo Pesce.[44] His successor, Enrico Flores, nevertheless pursued the same policy of collaboration with the city's patriotic forces as his predecessor had done. In June 1920, it was again an impending railway-workers' strike that pushed the government to look for the collaboration and support of "experienced citizens willing to operate in the public interest".[45] Nitti asked prefects to collaborate with industrialists and employers, who "are among those most affected by the strike", in order to create "squads of volunteers" to replace the striking railway workers. Moreover, the support of "citizens willing to cooperate with the authorities to enforce law and order" was extremely welcome as long as they remained under the orders of police officials, Nitti concluded.[46]

In Milan, prefect Flores soon started organising "squads of volunteers" to serve both as replacement workers and as "armed squads" to protect infrastructures, industrial premises, banks and warehouses.[47] Again, however, collaboration with local patriotic associations under the auspices of government directives was frustrated by political qualms and perplexity. On 17 June, just three days after issuing his first order, the national chief of police, Vincenzo Quaranta, urged the prefect to avoid establishing a "special corps of volunteers to support the police forces" as it was deemed politically compromising for political authorities to take full responsibility for the action. Again, Quaranta suggested not giving "official character to the institution" of the volunteers and "letting private citizens take the initiative".[48]

Despite advice to the contrary, prefect Flores made further agreements with the local military authorities to establish "a civil organisation against popular upheavals". Again, the "civil organisation" would be formed of two branches. A first group, composed of "elements with technical functions" to be recruited with the support of the Regional Federation of Industrialists, would serve as a work-replacement unit to be deployed in case of "interruption to public services". A second group, the "military auxiliaries", would be in charge of enforcing public order under the command of military personnel; all members of this group would be armed with regular military rifles. When popular upheavals broke out on 24 June, a first unit of 200 auxiliaries was recruited.[49] As Flores stated, the "use of every single piece of civilian energy" and the "spirit of initiative", shown by the city's "social organisations", "in support of state powers against any form of public disturbance" had been "my first concern since taking office". The "patriotism", proof of which the good citizens of Milan had demonstrated during the war, had now, according to the prefect, to be redirected in support of "state authority" against internal enemies.[50] The case of Milan clearly shows how the government's contradictory policies and attitudes towards bourgeois mobilisation contributed to create subversive attitudes among the middle classes.

Milan was not the only city were such dynamics occurred. The Association of Social Defence in Bologna is also a somewhat paradigmatic case. It is usually analysed by scholars as a forerunner of local fascism,[51] although its strikebreaking activities have been generally overlooked. Again, this is not to underestimate its connections with the first fascist squads in the city, but rather to stress that those connections were made possible first and foremost by the common ground of anti-strike mobilisation.

The association's early origins lay in the spontaneous reaction to a massive strike. In April 1920 local trade unions and the Chamber of Labour called a general strike in protest at the massacre of Decima di Persiceto (5 April 1920), in which eight day labourers were killed and 45 wounded by the Army. The strike immediately progressed into an almost complete stoppage of public services and factory work, which was on a much wider scale than the railway strike of January. Tired of "those who wanted to suppress the most elementary liberties", a group of citizens established a Civic Committee and prepared an exonerating report to be presented to the government.[52] In the document delivered to Nitti and Quaranta, the citizens stated that the recent strike was "the last event in which we are prepared to take part without the vigorous engagement of volunteer defence and protection". What made them furious, in particular, was the tolerant attitude of the authorities towards strikes that interrupted public services: they had, they claimed, to suffer the "outrageous event of the suspension of public lighting at night". The complete interruption of public services and production was considered dangerous not only for economic reasons, but also because "it created a situation of anxiety and distress, made worse by the spread of false news (*voci fantastiche*)". Panic also spread as soon as the workers at the city bake-house went on strike, as they were immediately accused of starving children. "What else should we wait for", clamoured one of the leaders of the committee, "no bread can be bought", "the city has been in darkness for three nights", "trains have stopped", there is "no mail", "no sanitation".[53]

In the face of such a state of affairs, the report condemned the change in government policy: "not having been invited to give a show of civilian resistance", as in the past, the "citizens" had no other option than to organise themselves.[54] Faced with the government's impotence, many citizens started to think they would exercise their natural right of "self-defence". If the good citizens had so far been "trustful in the very concept of liberty" and "had yielded to the government their means of defence", now these means had to be "created by ourselves", the committee declared.[55] According to the supporters of the Civic Committee, the rise of "civil conscience" was first and foremost because of their "loss of confidence" in government action.[56] As soon as the report spread across the city, conservative and socialist newspapers alike spoke of the return of the so-called *pattuglioni* (big patrols),[57] although the committee deemed this a "fantasy".[58] As we will see, the *pattuglioni* referred to were vigilante formations which had been organised in the pre-war period and had clear connections with the Citizens' Patrols, a long-established militia that had been cooperating with police forces in patrolling the streets of the city since the early nineteenth century. The issue reached parliament, where the socialist member Lionello Grossi asked the government to explain why a "Committee of citizens in Bologna" wanted to create "organisations with the same duties as those of the State, including those of armed police". The answer from the under-secretary for home affairs was telling: while he excluded any informal or formal authorisation by the government, "civilian volunteering . . . responded to a free and fully legal individual activity" that the government had to protect from interference.[59]

Established in June 1920, the Association of Social Defence represented the institutionalisation of these first forms of civilian mobilisation. Its statute clearly stated the aims and objectives of the association: "to cooperate . . . in continuing absolutely necessary public services in case of major general or partial strikes, thus making the authorities' tasks easier". Strikes were not to be banned, but the freedom to work had to be secured along with the "freedom to strike", the only "exception" being public service strikes, which had to be absolutely outlawed and repressed.[60] In the following months, the association was involved in multiple propagandistic activities as well as concrete strikebreaking mobilisation. In November 1920, for example, the association created a substitute urban public transport service using lorries supplied by local employers and agricultural entrepreneurs to be deployed in case of strike.[61]

Feelings of betrayal and disdain towards the government did not change when seasoned politician Giovanni Giolitti took office as the new prime minister in

June 1920. In July 1920, the association warned that if the prefect did not prevent a socialist rally from taking place, the "healthiest segments of the citizens would rise up and act in self-defence" against the enemies of "social coexistence".[62] In October, an implicit threat was made by several members of the association and local politicians: they repeatedly stated that in the name of "self-defence" they were ready to react against the "State within the State" represented by socialist local administrations. That these were not just words soon became clear. In a memorandum to the authorities, the leaders of the association publicly stated that their aim was to gather, "always in arms, and always together", all those men who were ready to "defend with any means our principles and our sacred right".[63] On at least one occasion, in November 1920, members of the nationalist paramilitary formation, *Sempre pronti* (Always Ready), guarded the premises of the association.[64] To bolster their propaganda efforts and even their strikebreaking activities, in September the association decided to hire a group of "300 young men, to be armed".[65] The association also made contact with the local fascists led by former anarchist Leandro Arpinati, although it, is unlikely they recruited any of them. The local black-shirts soon assumed a role as the armed wing of fearful citizens. As many historians have reconstructed it, the Association of Social Defence in some way paved the way for the full development of local fascism, which found spaces of initiative and a broad consensus for its violent and brutal methods among wide sectors of the respectable bourgeoisie. The so-called massacre of Palazzo D'Accursio, in which fascist action squads from Bologna, Ferrara and other cities of the Po Valley provoked a series of incidents and violent confrontations on the day Bologna's new socialist administration was inaugurated (21 November 1920), left 11 people dead: ten socialist militants and one nationalist councillor, Giulio Giordani, who quickly rose to become a "fascist martyr". According to the national chief of police, the event was the starting point of a process of legal and illegal dismantling of socialist presence in the economic, political and social life of the province and, more generally, the beginning of a mass campaign of destruction carried out by fascist squads throughout northern and central Italy in the months to come.[66]

Long-lasting self-defence of the bourgeoisie

As the examples cited have shown, strikes were not merely economic manifestations but a genuine obsession and a real nightmare for large segments of the Italian middle classes. The Association of Civil Defence's report clearly outlined the true panic that strikes aroused. References to dark cities without public lighting, dark hospitals where patients were left without care, fathers unable to feed hungry children, the spread of false news that "nobody can confirm", conjured powerful images of a social order shaken to its foundations.[67] The very same Volunteers of Order in Milan were (allegedly) established to counter the spread of crime that was making the city unsafe. Right-wing newspapers, civilian associations and state authorities alike used highly politicised and almost apocalyptic terms. The Volunteers were needed to carry out the "sound work of civil preservation" in order to "eradicate once and for all the evil tree" of criminality, claimed prefect Pesce.[68] Mortara, in urging prefects to organise corps of volunteers, contrasted the efforts of "honest citizens" with the "wild aggression" of subversives.[69]

While Italian authorities did not underestimate the potential threat represented by the strike wave that hit the country in the immediate post-war months, they probably failed to fully grasp what the strikes, disorder and protests represented for "honest citizens" and certainly failed to appreciate the lack of trust held by these good bourgeois citizens in how the state was dealing with the increasing social conflicts. This contributed to a significant underestimation of the inherent psychological and emotional power of the strikes. Those involving public services, in particular, were seen as a threat to the entire foundation of society, not only because their supposed aim was to ignite revolution, but also because they prevented the orderly functioning of society and caused a waste of public money. Behind the interruption of the electricity supply, many saw the spread of criminality in dark cities; behind the stoppage of local trains and tramways, a blow to individual freedom of movement; behind the strike of municipal bakeries, a threat to children and the sanctity of the family; behind the strike of agricultural day labourers, the first step towards collectivisation and a threat to national wealth. Such fears could not simply be considered propagandistic claims; they in fact mirrored deep-seated political cultures and outlooks that made it almost impossible to see strikes anything other than clashes of "civilisation".

Faced with what they believed was an impending revolution, local associations and committees and state authorities spoke of the necessity for "self-defence". Self-defence soon became a social imperative, totally unrelated to the very rigorous and limited specimens of criminal law.[70] Referring to popularised versions of the social contract and natural law doctrines, honourable citizens always insisted on their right to defend themselves where the state failed to provide protection and defence. In a letter to the local prefect, the Association for Social Defence spoke of the need to act in "self-defence against the wounded dignity" of "citizens".[71] An article in the conservative newspaper *Il Progresso* was even more explicit:

> in the same way the Law forbids individuals to use weapons, but allows it for legitimate self-defence, so, too, should the community be allowed legitimate self-defence. The bourgeoisie, stifled by insane and criminal people, see their own existence as being in great danger. . . . They have not only the right but the duty to resist and fight.[72]

Mortara himself – despite his legal education and his position as a senior magistrate – stated that "using weapons" in cases of major strike was a "form of self-defence to protect the homeland (*Patria*) and civilisation against any wild aggression".[73]

Undoubtedly, the deep political crisis that affected Italy in the aftermath of the Great War was largely the result of huge problems inherited from the war period. However if we look at it from a specifically strikebreaking angle, interesting continuities with the pre-war period emerge. The introduction of the 1889 Penal Code recognised workers as having both the right to strike and the right to work. After some years in which the code was not substantially implemented in terms of concrete protection of workers' rights, Prime Minister Giovanni Giolitti introduced a new policing policy based on state neutrality in social conflicts. There were, however, significant exceptions. Pasquale Arena, a professor of law, claimed in 1908 that the state should act according to the "holy right of self-defence" and use both repression and replacement workers in response to public service strikes. "No one can deny the state the opportunity to ban public service strikes in order to defend its own existence", stated his colleague Guglielmo Sabatini.[74]

Continuities also emerged in terms of actual practices of civilian mobilisation. Throughout the chapter we have seen that in Bologna, in particular, but also in Milan, patriotic citizens or organisations referred several times to patrols or *pattuglioni* (i.e. big patrols). The terms come from a very specific institution particular to Bologna, the so-called Citizens' Patrols (*Pattuglie cittadine*). Established in 1827, under papal rule, the Patrols were intended to support local police forces in patrolling the streets at night, a task they retained after Italian unification. Although largely ineffective and disorganised, they nevertheless represented an institutional opportunity for the grouping of bourgeois reaction during the major strikes of 1906 and 1908 and again during the so-called Red Week of 1914. The *pattuglioni* were in fact groups of "good citizens" which took to the streets shoulder to shoulder with members of the Citizens' Patrols, forming indeed "big patrols". They performed strikebreaking tasks, which soon degenerated into vigilante activities. They made arrests and carried out searches autonomously and on one occasion tried to destroy the local Chamber of Labour.[75]

In the new and highly conflictual context of the immediate post-war years, it is interesting that references were made to Patrols and *pattuglioni* to justify legitimised forms of strikebreaking and vigilantism. According to the conservative, but pro-government, newspaper, *Il resto del Carlino*, the Association of Social Defence had tried to resurrect the *pattuglioni* of 15 years earlier. True "liberal consciousness", the newspaper claimed, "rejects this: it rejects this because it is against the very conception of state authority and the modern state".[76] Others, in contrast, wholeheartedly praised the re-establishment of *pattuglioni* as the sole and unique reaction against impotent authorities.[77] The "myth" of the Patrols helped place the new phenomenon of fascist *squadrismo* within a longer tradition of civilian mobilisation and violence. Writing a few weeks after the March on Rome, a semi-unknown law scholar, Ettore Vulterini, resorted to the example of the Citizens' Patrols ("a private armed corps") in Bologna to justify the violent actions perpetrated by fascist squads. According to Vulterini, to save the state and social order, citizens had the right to organise themselves and, weapons in hands, to react against "delinquency and thugs". This was what citizens in Bologna had done as members of the Patrols and the *pattuglioni* before the war and immediately after the end of the conflict, and what fascists had done in more recent times, Vulterini sustained. Such forms of self-organisation were considered a fully legitimate reaction to mortal threats to the nation once the ordinary police forces proved to be impotent and weak.[78]

By looking at the interplay and mutual relationships between state authorities and patriotic associations through the lens of armed voluntarism, this chapter has highlighted the crucial role played by strikebreaking in radicalising the social struggle and making private intervention a fully legitimised course of action. The persistence of patterns, experiences and models, for example in terms of the debate on state intervention in public service strikes or anti-strike activities, made post-war strikebreaking a plausible, thinkable and ultimately legitimate course of action.

Mortara's and Nitti's attempts to involve "honest citizens" in the defence of order and "civilisation" was a huge political gamble. However, this did not necessarily represent a dismissal on the part of the Italian authorities of the state monopoly on physical violence. As many scholars have shown, forms of cooperation between legal authorities and good citizens precisely in the case of major strikes were common throughout Europe, both before and after the Great War.[79] However, civilian mobilisation in Italy took on quite strong vigilante implications, as the recurrent references to self-defence testimony.[80] Members of the Association of Social Defence or the Committee of Civil Organisation were not hotheads or ultra-reactionary mobs; they were men wholly concerned with the need to restore order and the correct functioning of society and the economy disrupted by strikes and popular upheavals. While they wanted to restore law and order and strengthen state authority, their very existence was the consequence of a derogation from the principle of state monopoly on physical violence. We have seen that Nitti's and Mortara's instructions, as well as those given by prefects at the local level, clearly testify to an acknowledgement of the state's prerogative to have exclusive and full control over the civilian volunteers. However, this prerogative could in many cases be ignored in the light of contradictory instructions and political opportunism, as happened in Milan after Mayor Caldara's protests. This had the effect of paving the way for forms of autonomous mobilisation by "honourable citizens", completely outside state control and legitimisation. After all, calling for the support of patriotic citizens was a risky political gamble: if the state was strong, credible and legitimised, then both state authorities and private citizens would feel themselves part of the same community of destiny; if the state was de-legitimised and there was a wide discrepancy between rulers and civil society, then a call for help and support would be perceived as a sign of weakness and would encourage vigilante (i.e. anti-state) initiatives. What is paradoxical is that Nitti and other government officers justified their contradictory attitude towards supporting civilian mobilisation in the name of political impartiality, electoral opportunism and, ultimately, respect for the state's role as a neutral and impartial mediator in social conflicts. It was this perceived betrayal in the name of democratic and liberal principles (no matter how opportunistic they might be) that pushed the now mobilised "honest citizens" to go it alone, precisely in the name of self-defence. In the face of a weak state and an impending socialist threat, breaking the law was the only way, they believed, to restore law and order. It was in the grey zone between the defence of public order and fears of subversion that fascism could prosper.

This does not mean, however, that the ultimate convergence of these "good citizens" into fascism was inevitable. The contradictory attitudes of the political elites towards the involvement of private citizens in public order and strikebreaking tasks helped shed light on the difficulties the liberal elites encountered in finding a credible balance between order and freedom in times of rapid social and political change. The political system was "incapable of answering citizens' requests for change but nevertheless capable of preserving and reproducing itself".[81] Nitti's attempt to involve private citizens in the defence of the state was just the last stage in a long and conflictual relationship between the Italian state and its "loyal classes". In the context of the liberal state's enduring crisis of legitimisation, solutions were extremely hard to find, if they might be found at all. In a speech in 1914, Alfredo Rocco, a law scholar and future minister of justice during the fascist dictatorship, spoke of the necessity to substitute "state protection" with "private defence". "The private intervenes", Rocco argued, "when the State has broken down. . . . Therefore, what should be condemned is not private defence in itself but the return of the State to past eras of juridical evolution".[82] In the light of these words, we may wonder whether the involvement of private citizens in public functions might have had some chance of success in strengthening the shaken legitimacy of the liberal state.

Nitti's gamble was an attempt to bring the country out of political stalemate. In the end, all it did was open a Pandora's box. Paradoxically, the fragile legitimacy of the liberal state was ultimately destroyed by neither popular upheaval nor the consequences of full democratisation but by those forces mobilised to oppose them.

Notes

* Research for this article received funding from the European Research Council (ERC) under the European Union's Horizon 2020 Research and Innovation program (G.A. 677199 – ERC-StG2015 'The Dark Side of the Belle Époque. Political Violence and Armed Associations in Europe before the First World War').

1 Roberto Vivarelli, *Storia delle origini del fascismo: l'Italia dalla grande guerra alla marcia su Roma*, Vol. 1 (Bologna: il Mulino, 1991), 462–89. On Nitti, see, among others, Francesco Barbagallo, *Francesco S. Nitti* (Torino: Unione tipografico-editrice torinese, 1984); Michele Cento, *Tra capitalismo e amministrazione: il liberalismo atlantico di Nitti* (Bologna: il Mulino, 2017).

2 See the circular letter of 27 June 1919 to the prefects of the kingdom, in Vivarelli, *Storia delle origini del fascismo*, 1, 622–23.

3 Vivarelli, *Storia delle origini del fascismo*, 1, 471.

4 Guido Neppi Modona, *Sciopero, potere politico e magistratura, 1870–1922* (Roma-Bari: Laterza, 1979), 221–22; Vivarelli, *Storia delle origini del fascismo*, 1:478–89. On 1919 social conflicts see, among others, Roberto Bianchi, *Bocci Bocci. I Tumulti Annonari Nella Toscana Del 1919* (Firenze: Olschki, 2001); Roberto Bianchi, *Pace, pane e terra. Il 1919 in Italia* (Roma: Odradek, 2006); Roberto Bianchi, *1919: piazza, mobilitazioni, poteri* (Milano: Egea, 2019); Fabio Fabbri, *Le origini della guerra civile. L'Italia dalla Grande Guerra al Fascismo (1918–1921)* (Torino: Utet, 2009).

5 The circular letter is transcribed in Vivarelli, *Storia delle origini del fascismo*, 1:623. See also in Archivio di Stato di Bologna, Gabinetto di prefettura (thereafter, ASBo, GP), 1305.

6 See Renzo De Felice, *Mussolini. Il Rivoluzionario: 1883–1920* (Torino: Einaudi, 1965), 538–39.

7 Neppi Modona, *Sciopero, potere politico e magistratura*, 217. See also Pietro Nenni, *Storia di quattro anni: 1919–1922* (Roma: Einaudi, 1946), 32–33.
8 Vivarelli, *Storia delle origini del fascismo*, 1:488–89; Bianchi, *Bocci Bocci*, 303.
9 See, for example, Marco Mondini, *La politica delle armi. Il ruolo dell'esercito nell'avvento del Fascismo* (Roma-Bari: Laterza, 2006), 61; Fabbri, *Le origini della guerra civile*, 91–92, 159–61.
10 Emilio Gentile, *Storia del Partito fascista 1919–1922: movimento e milizia* (Roma-Bari: Laterza, 1989), 78.
11 There are few exceptions, though: Angelo Ventrone, *La seduzione totalitaria: guerra, modernità, violenza politica: 1914–1918* (Roma: Donzelli, 2003); Silvia Becherini, "'Borghesi fiorentini, muovetevi! Insorgete!': L'Alleanza di Difesa cittadina e la mobilitazione antisocialista a Firenze nel primo dopoguerra," *Rassegna Storica Toscana* LXIII, no. 2 (2017): 335–83.
12 The examination of similar dynamics in the rural context, in Matteo Millan, "'The Public Force of the Private State' – Strikebreaking and Visions of Subversion in Liberal Italy (1880s to 1914)," *European History Quarterly* 49, no. 4 (2019): 625–49.
13 Fabbri, *Le origini della guerra civile*, 96.
14 Nitti to prefects, 29 April 1920 and 23 January 1920, in ASBo, GP, 1319.
15 Fabbri, *Le origini della guerra civile*, 87.
16 Lorenzo Donati, "La Guardia Regia," *Storia Contemporanea* 8 (1977): 441–87; Marco Mondini, "L'Arma dei Carabinieri," in *Gli italiani in guerra. Conflitti, identità, memorie del Risorgimento ai giorni nostri, IV, Il Ventennio fascista*, ed. Giulia Albanese and Mario Isnenghi (Torino: Utet, 2008), 159–65.
17 Luca Madrignani, *La guardia regia: la polizia italiana nell'avvento del fascismo (1919–1922)* (Milano: UNICOPLI, 2014).
18 Nitti to prefects, 19 July 1919, ASBo, GP, 1305.
19 Copy of the telegram from Nitti to prefects, 14 July 1919, in ASBo, GP, b. 1305.
20 Mortara to prefects, 19 January 1920, in Archivio Centrale dello Stato, Ufficio Cifra, Telegrammi in partenza. On Mortara see Massimiliano Boni, *Il figlio del rabbino: Lodovico Mortara, storia di un ebreo ai vertici del Regno d'Italia* (Roma: Viella, 2018).
21 Boni, *Il figlio del rabbino*, 171.
22 Gerardo Padulo, "Un Prefetto Conservatore: Angelo Pesce," *Annali dell'Istituto per gli Studi Storici*, no. VI (1979–1980): 303–4.
23 *L'Avanti!*, 22 January 1920.
24 See various records in ASBo, GP, b. 1319.
25 Raffaele A. Vicentini, *Il Movimento fascista veneto attraverso il diario di uno squadrista* (Venezia: Zanetti, 1935), 26.
26 Becherini, "Borghesi fiorentini, muovetevi! Insorgete!," 367.
27 On the origin of the word "crumiri" or "krumiri", see Millan, "'The Public Force of the Private State'," 632.
28 Mario Piazzesi, *Diario di uno Squadrista Toscano: 1919–1922* (Roma: Bonacci, 1981), 64.
29 Prefect to Army Corps of Bologna (22 January 1920), Report on the services of a "group of citizens", in ASBo, GP, b. 1319.
30 Prefect to the Army corps commander (3 February 1920), in ASBo, GP, b. 1319.
31 Billboard, signed by general Ugo Sani, in ASBo, GP, 1319. On Sani see also Mondini, *La politica delle armi*.
32 Mario Passuello and Nevio Furegon, *Le origini del fascismo a Vicenza e le lotte sociali fra il 1919 e il 1922* (Vicenza: Neri Pozza, 1981), 81; Francesco Benacchio, "Le leghe rosse nel Vicentino del primo dopoguerra," in *La classe, gli uomini e i partiti, Storia del movimento operaio e socialista in una provincia bianca: il Vicentino: 1873–1948*, ed. Emilio Franzina (Vicenza: Odeonlibri, 1982), 656–60.
33 Gentile, *Storia del Partito fascista*, 73–77. See also Roberto Cantagalli, *Storia del Fascismo fiorentino 1919–1925* (Firenze: Vallecchi, 1972). On the Alliance of City

Defence of Florence see Bianchi, *1919*, 140–44; Becherini, "Borghesi fiorentini, muovetevi! Insorgete!"

34 Nitti to prefects, 23 January 1920, in ASBo, GP, b. 1319.

35 Anonymous, "Tristizie Borghesi," *L'Avanti!* January 22, 1920; anonymous, "Quei cari studenti!," *L'Avanti!* January 23, 1920.

36 List of patriotic associations, 22 July 1920, in Archivio di Stato di Milano, Gabinetto di prefettura (hereafter ASMi, GP), 192.

37 Questore of Milan to prefect, 5 July 1920 and 22 July 1920, in ASMi, GP, 192.

38 Decree of the prefect, 19 February 1920, and Letter of the prefect to various patriotic associations (20 February 1920), in ASMi, GP, 192. A partial reconstruction of the role of the volunteers also in Padulo, "Un Prefetto Conservatore."

39 Senator to prefect, 20 February 1920, Popular Liberal Association to prefect, 20 February 1920, Association of Traders, Shopkeepers and Industrialists to prefect, 23 February 1920, in ASMi, GP, 192.

40 Anonymous, "Il Corpo dei Volontari dell'ordine," *Corriere della Sera*, February 21, 1920.

41 Astorre Alessandri to prefect, 24 February 1920.

42 Letters of Caldara to prefect Angelo Pesce, 20 and 21 February 1920, in ASMi, GP, 192. See also, Anonymous, "La guardia bianca," *L'Avanti!* February 22, 1920.

43 Mortara to prefect of Milan, 27 February 1920, in ASMi, GP, 192.

44 Padulo, "Un Prefetto Conservatore."

45 Chief of police Vincenzo Quaranta to all the prefects, 14 June 1920, in ASBo, GP, 1319.

46 Nitti to all the prefects, 12 June 1920, in Archivio Centrale dello Stato, Ufficio Cifra, Telegrammi in partenza.

47 Prefect of Milan to Minister of Interior (19 June 1920), in ASMi, GP, 192.

48 Chief of police to prefect, 17 June 1920, in ASMi, GP, 192.

49 Prefect Flores to general De Albertis, 2 July 1920, general De Albertis to prefect, 23 June 1920, in ASMi, GP, 192.

50 Prefect Flores to general De Albertis, 2 July 1920, in ASMi, GP, 192.

51 Nazario Sauro Onofri, *La strage di Palazzo d'Accursio. Origine e nascita del fascismo bolognese 1919–1920* (Milano: Feltrinelli, 1980), 205–18; Nazario Sauro Onofri, "1913–1922, Un decennio storico per Bologna: dalla rivoluzione rossa alla reazione near," in *Bologna 1920. Le origini del Fascismo*, ed. Luciano Casali (Bologna: Cappelli, 1982), 57–92; Fiorenza Tarozzi, "Dal primo al secondo Fascio di combattimento: note sulle origini del Fascismo a Bologna (1919–1920)," in *Bologna 1920: Le origini del Fascismo*, ed. Luciano Casali (Bologna: Cappelli, 1982), 93–114; Jonathan Dunnage, *The Italian Police and the Rise of Fascism: A Case Study of the Province of Bologna, 1897–1925* (London: Praeger, 1997).

52 *Avvenire d'Italia*, 17 April 1920.

53 Letter of Masetti Zannini, *L'avvenire d'Italia*, 24 April 1920.

54 According to Onofri, this led to an immediate reinstatement of the 14 July 1919 circular letter: Onofri, *La strage di Palazzo d'Accursio*, 208.

55 Memorial of 10 April 1920, in ASBo, GP, 1322.

56 Ibid.

57 *Il resto del carlino*, 17–18 April 1920; *La squilla*, 17 April 1920.

58 *Avvenire d'Italia*, 20 April 1920.

59 *Atti parlamentari*, 5 May 1920, 1777 and *Atti parlamentari*, 24 June 1920, 2362.

60 Questore to prefect, Statute of the Association of Social Defence, 26 June 1920, in ASBo, GP, 1322.

61 Prefect to Minister of Finance, 18 November 1920, in ASBo, GP, 1322.

62 Association of Social Defence to prefect, 30 July 1920, and Proclaim of the Association, 29 July 1920, in ASBo, GP, 1322.

63 Camera dei deputati, Commissione parlamentare per l'accertamento dei fatti avvenuti a Bologna, 1921, Legislatura XXV 1919–1921, Allegato 27, 146–47.

64 Camera dei deputati, Commissione parlamentare per l'accertamento dei fatti avvenuti a Bologna, 1921, Legislatura XXV 1919–1921, Allegato 8, 56.
65 Questore to prefect, 17 September 1920, in ASBo, GP, b. 1322. Conversely to Onofri, *La strage di Palazzo D'Accursio*, 215; Mondini, *La politica delle armi*, 68; Dunnage, *The Italian Police and the Rise of Fascism*, 102, I found no evidence that the 300 armed men were actually recruited and that the initiative had the placet of the prefect. Onofri, who first stated this, gives no evidence of the statement.
66 Memoriale Vigliani, in Archivio Centrale dello Stato, Ps 1921, b. 90. See also Fabbri, *Le origini della guerra civile*, 349–58; Gentile, *Storia del Partito fascista*, 149–52; Onofri, *La strage di Palazzo d'Accursio*.
67 See, "Istigazione a delinquere," *Il* Progresso, 21 April 1920. See, different examples, in Mark Jones, *Founding Weimar: Violence and the German Revolution of 1918–1919* (Cambridge: Cambridge University Press, 2016); Matteo Millan, "The Shadows of Social Fear: Emotions, Mentalities and Practices of the Propertied Classes in Italy, Spain and France (1900–1914)," *Journal of Social History* 50, no. 2 (2016): 336–61.
68 Prefect to patriotic associations, 20 January 1920, in ASMi, GP, 192.
69 Mortara to prefects, 19 January 1920, in ASBo, GP, 1319.
70 According to the Italian penal code, self-defence was an exceptional and extreme necessity to preserve life and goods in case of impossible intervention by the state to enforce law and order (art. 49 of the 1889 Penal Code). On the different meanings of self-defense in pre-WWI Italy, see Matteo Millan, "Sostituire l'autorità, Riaffermare la Sovranità. Legittima Difesa, Corpi Armati e Crisi dello Stato nell'Italia Giolittiana," *Studi Storici*, no. 1 (2019): 139–66.
71 Association for Social Defence to prefect, 30 July 1920, in ASBo, GP, 1322.
72 "Istigazione a delinquere," *Il Progresso*, April 21, 1920.
73 Mortara to prefects, 19 January 1920, in ASBO, GP, 1319. See also Gianfranco Faina, *Lotte di classe in Liguria dal 1919 al 1922* (Firenze: Nuova Italia, 1965), 37; Padulo, "Un Prefetto Conservatore," 303.
74 Pasquale Arena, *Dei delitti contro la liberta del lavoro* (Torino: Bocca, 1908), 286; Guglielmo Sabatini, *I delitti contro la libertà del lavoro: nella sociologia, nella legislazione e nella psicologia collettiva* (Catanzaro: Tipografia del Tramonto, 1904), 136–37. On this see also Millan, "The Public Force of the Private State".
75 On the Citizens Patrols and *pattuglioni* see Matteo Millan, "In Defence of Freedom? The Practices of Armed Movements in Pre-1914 Europe: Italy, Spain and France," *European History Quarterly* 46, no. 1 (2016): 48–71; Matteo Millan, "Milizie Civiche Prima Della Grande Guerra. Violenza Politica e Crisi Dello Stato in Italia e Spagna (1900–1915)," *Storica* 20, no. 58 (2014): 49–84; Dunnage, *The Italian Police and the Rise of Fascism*.
76 "Il volontariato civile," *Il resto del carlino*, 18 April 1920.
77 Letter of Masetti Zannini, *L'avvenire d'Italia*, 24 April 1920.
78 Ettore Vulterini, "Arditi Comunisti e Squadre d'azione Fasciste," *Rivista di Psicologia* XVIII–XIX (1923/1922): 40–42.
79 See the Introduction to this volume.
80 See Christopher Joseph Nicodemus Capozzola, *Uncle Sam Wants You: World War I and the Making of the Modern American Citizen* (Oxford and New York: Oxford University Press, 2008), 140–43; Les Johnston, "What Is Vigilantism?" *The British Journal of Criminology* 36, no. 2 (1996): 220–36; David Kowalewski, "Vigilantism," in *International Handbook of Violence Research*, ed. Wilhelm Heitmeyer and John Hagan (Dordrecht: Kluwer Academic Publisher, 2003).
81 Luigi Bonanate, "Some Unanticipated Consequences of Terrorism," *Journal of Peace Research* 16, no. 3 (1979): 205.
82 A. Rocco, "Contro la politica dei dubbi, delle incertezze e della rinuncia vile. I nazionalisti in piazza (1914)," in Id., *Scritti e discorsi politici*, Vol. I (Milano: Giuffrè, 1938), 189.

15 Conclusion

Strikebreaking and the fault lines of mass society, 1880–1930

Martin Conway

History is often best viewed from the margins. That would certainly seem to be true of the forms of strikebreaking that occurred in the half-century from the 1880s to the 1930s. As the fascinating studies contained in this collection demonstrate, strikebreaking – and the myriad activities associated with it – were a pervasive feature of the many societies which experienced disruptive economic transformations, along with consequent social upheavals and crises of state authority, across the globe in this period. And yet as the novelty of this collection equally indicates, it is not a phenomenon which until recently has attracted sustained attention from historians.[1]

Part of the explanation of this neglect lies in the simple difficulty of recovering its history from the archival record. As a number of the contributors to this volume remark, the activities of strikebreakers, of company trade unions, of volunteer vigilante groups and of groups committed to the defence of the freedom of honest workers (and, more especially, of employers) are an elusive historical subject. This was partly by design. Those operating on the edges of legality and illegality preferred to keep a low profile, often changing their location and identity with rather bewildering frequency. But it also reflects the discontinuous history of instances of strikebreaking. They were, in every sense, circumstantial phenomena, the transient character of which reflected the episodic nature of the strike or other incident that had caused them to come into existence. The history of labour relations is a notoriously challenging subject of research, which demands a close familiarity with the complexities of workplace structures, that is rendered all the more challenging by frequent gaps in the archival documentation.[2] But that difficulty is all the greater when one is dealing with the actions of those whose effectiveness often relied on their evasion of responsibility. Those who instigated confrontations with strikers or pickets, intimidated smallholders with threats of violence or recruited replacement labour to break an industrial dispute, left little by way of paper records and have to be glimpsed through the allegations of their opponents, or the often one-sided accounts provided by newspapers or state authorities.

This is all the more so when the actions of the strikebreakers and their allies occurred in distant, often marginal, locations. Disputes in mines and on rural estates in remote corners of Spain or Portugal, on the ranching lands of Wyoming and still more on the ships of the *Messageries* sailing from Marseille to the Far East occurred out of sight of a mass public, or the visibility provided by press coverage. Moreover, even when the actions of strikebreakers occurred in more accessible locations, as in the case of the strikes in the ports of colonial-era Bengal, or the tobacco factories of Cairo or Athens, they remained opaque events, in which much about their genesis and true dynamics was hidden from view. The actions of strikebreakers and their allies consequently flit across the historical record, lacking the legibility and continuity of their socialist or communist opponents, or of the police or state authorities.

To these archival difficulties are added the relative anonymity of the actors themselves. There were few outstanding figures in the ranks of the strikebreakers, the volunteer civilian guards and the short-lived employers' associations, which proliferated in the early years of the twentieth century. The media celebrity transiently enjoyed by strikebreaking gang leaders in late Wilhelmine Germany was in this respect the exception to the rule; but even they were less significant in themselves than for the way in which the press attention given to their activities served as a means of giving voice to wider fears about criminality and the fragility of the legal order. Much more commonplace was the way that many of these anti-socialist activists and self-declared defenders of freedom proved to be opportunists, publicists and in a good number of cases simple rogues and criminals, whose grand rhetorical posturing belied the emphatically self-interested nature of their actions. Of course, in some contexts, the struggle against organised trade unionism and revolutionary socialism drew in more significant political forces, such as the nascent right-wing nationalist groups in Russia in the first decade of the twentieth century, or the communal politicians of interwar Bengal. But, as the studies in this collection demonstrate, these were essentially marriages of convenience that disintegrated as political circumstances changed. The history of strikebreaking in its manifold local forms was much more generally populated by a repertoire of figures of secondary importance, whose efforts at economic or political entrepreneurism, and unoriginal manipulation of rather empty slogans, served to display the opportunism of men – and they were overwhelmingly men – seeking to gain advantage from the rapidly changing winds of social and economic circumstance.[3]

And what was true of the leaders was of course even more true of the rank and file. The replacement workforces recruited during industrial disputes to work in Egyptian cigarette factories, to unload ships in the port of Calcutta, or to staff the boiler rooms and kitchens of the ships of the *Messageries*, remain for the most part obstinately anonymous in the archival records. At most, we can occasionally detect their confessional or ethnic character: foreign workers brought in to replace those on strike, but whose value and reliability for their employers rarely proved to be especially durable. These "scabs" – to use the offensive term of abuse invariably thrown at them in a multitude of linguistic variants – were the mute foot soldiers of these social disputes, imprisoned within the negative social resonances of community betrayal and the most basic motives of economic opportunism imputed to them by those on the other side of the picket lines.[4] Those who broke strikes were in this respect the necessary antithesis. For the activists in labour movements, the scab worker was always the opposite against which they defined their ethics of commitment, and more especially of kinship with their fellow strikers and union militants.[5]

The most profound cause of the marginalisation of strikebreaking in the history of the era is however perhaps not so much archival as historiographical. For all of the mediocrity of its actors and the litany of failed ventures and broken lives which it left behind it, strikebreaking had a global ubiquity and a scale which demands attention. And yet it sits uneasily within the established paradigms of the history of the era as one of globalisation, projects of political revolution, and mass warfare on an unprecedented scale. Amidst the tall trees of the emergence of a global economy, world war and the powerful surges in revolutionary socialism, it is tempting to regard strikebreaking as of no more than anecdotal significance, part of the undergrowth generated by other more powerful forces. This is perhaps especially so, given the dominant political template that is often applied to the era from the emergence of mass politics in the 1880s, through the revolutionary transitions of the early decades of the twentieth century to the bitter conflicts generated by the Great Depression of the 1930s. This template implicitly accords priority to the forces of the left in the social and political conflicts of the final years of the nineteenth century, and the first two decades of the twentieth century.[6] Consequently, historians of the early twentieth century have, on the whole, been more preoccupied by the actions and motivations of those who went on strike, demonstrated or even marched on the citadels of state power, than those who remained loyal to the established structures of economic and political authority.[7] But the same is also true of the subsequent development during the 1920s and 1930s of movements of the extreme right. The historiography of the right has long neglected the continuity of cultures of conservatism to focus on the specifically political and ideological dynamics of fascism, which within a few years propelled this new form of politics to the centre of state power.[8]

And yet as much recent work on left revolution and extreme-right counter-revolution in this era has served to elucidate, these instances of political success and failure were above all products of contexts that were much more than political in nature. Movements of left and right gained their definition and momentum less through their own actions than through the way that they were moulded by the complex interaction of economic, social and institutional forces that were specific to the contexts of place and time.[9] This localising of historical perspectives challenges the generalisations inherent to phraseology such as "the Russian Revolution of 1917", or "the rise of Italian Fascism" or of German Nazism and brings to the fore instead the irreducible diversity of the local contexts out of which they arose. Rather than a zero-sum game of the victory of one political force at the expense of the other, political outcomes were defined by the economic ruptures, social conflicts and challenges to state authority, out of which they arose.[10]

***

It is within this context-specific perception of European and global history of the era from the 1880s to the 1930s that strikebreaking and related activities acquire their importance. All of the essays in this volume are deeply embedded in the particularities of place and time; and yet all demonstrate, too, the prevalence of a broader pattern of social, economic and institutional conflict. This is revealed above all by their remarkable synchronicity. The specific nature of the events was highly varied and not in any meaningful sense interconnected. And yet it is striking that the same chronologies return again and again within the individual chapters: the new forces of mass socialist organisation and trade unionism took shape in the 1880s, prompting a new era of labour militancy over the subsequent years, notably in key industries and public services, which reached an initial peak in the general strikes that occurred in many locations during the first decade of the twentieth century.[11] The fears (and hopes) that these generated of a wider social and political explosion were initially deferred by the outbreak of war in 1914. But they returned all the more intensely during the crescendo of state collapse, economic and ethnic conflicts and political polarisation that occurred in the era of military demobilisation (and political remobilisations) that accompanied the end of the formal military conflict in 1917–18 and continued to reverberate powerfully into the post-war years.[12]

The various forms of strikebreaking, volunteer vigilantism and semi-formal and informal acts of violence that multiplied across this period were direct, often jagged, manifestations of the conflicts that characterised this most chaotic era of global modernisation. They owed little to central direction, as the failure of the various attempts at federating vigilante groups within a national framework demonstrated, at least until Mussolini's partial unification of the *squadristi* groups within his Fascist movement in Italy in 1920–21.[13] But they were all closely tied to the highly disruptive – and on occasions traumatic – impact of capitalist economic transformations. The emergence of long-distance global marketplaces, sensitive to all of the vagaries inherent to the circumstances of production as well as to shifts in demand, led to booms and crashes in the prices of basic commodities (including land) as well as of manufactured or semi-manufactured goods. Their impact was reinforced by the rapid pace of technological changes, which abruptly rendered craft-based processes of production obsolete, while creating new commercial opportunities for machine-based mass production. But they were exacerbated too by the volatility of stock-market prices and more especially of a banking sector, to which many individuals and companies were heavily indebted. The consequence was an economic context in which nothing could be regarded as certain, and where the exploitation of advantage, or at least the averting of disaster, depended on moving swiftly, and often ruthlessly.

These processes of change were directly visible in the patterns of strikebreaking which occurred. It was in sectors such as railways, ports or shipping, where time was everything, and the ability of workers to exploit their power to block trade was often most tangible, that the incentive was greatest for employers to resort to direct action. Strikers had to removed, by force if necessary, and replaced by those who as a consequence of their dependence would be more reliably quiescent.[14] But in other sectors too, notably mining and iron and steel production, as well as the commercial exploitation of agriculture, many of the same forms of economic conflict developed. Everywhere, it seemed, workers were alert to the possibilities to exploit whatever transient leverage they possessed to demand higher rates of pay, less oppressive working conditions or the dismissal of unpopular foremen or managers. In response employers resorted to a wide repertoire of techniques to reinforce labour discipline, including the intimidation of union organisers or political militants, the recruitment of factory guards and the procuring of the services of groups of vigilantes or local members of the bourgeoisie. Direct physical conflict was never far away and was reinforced by the relatively easy availability in many locations of the guns and pistols being produced in unprecedented volumes by the small-arms industry. The consequence was a new militancy among employers. Convincing themselves they were confronted by the danger of a socialist revolution, they acted with more individual force within and without the law, but also with more collective resolve, creating sectoral and national federations to protect their interests and to make their voices heard in the arenas of state decision making.

The state was the third element in this volatile relationship of forces. Far from acting as the neutral arbiter between the interests of workers and employers, the state at its various hierarchical levels generally opted to side with the employers in the interest of the maintenance of economic production, or the wider and less tangible goal of the defence of the social order. Thus, the state authorities in tsarist Russia or colonial Bengal, but also in Wilhelmine Germany, deployed their judicial and administrative powers to prosecute union activists or deport them to distant locations, as well as using the uniformed ranks of the police, the national guard or *gendarmerie*, or *in extremis* the army, to break picket lines, protect replacement workers or forcibly clear agricultural day labourers off the land. The state was, however, rarely a reliable guarantor of social order and economic peace. The growth of modern police forces was too recent, their skills and resources too limited, and the willingness of populations to accept their authority too uncertain, for the state to be able to exercise its writ without challenge. Moreover, state officials were too jealous of their self-image as the impartial guardians of the national or public interest to rush too readily or visibly to act as the lackeys of the employers in an industrial dispute.[15] A certain prudence, reinforced by the lobbying of elected Social Democratic officials, led policemen and army officers to hold back, notably in various areas of Austria-Hungary, from the unrestrained deployment of the forces of order. Consequently employers and landowners were obliged to appeal for the assistance of a wide range of less formal groups. This was the era of civil leagues, bourgeois associations, and after the First World War, of military reservists, *Freikorps* and *squadristi*, transferring their mentalities and practices of the defence of order from the military sphere to the town squares, factory gates and agricultural estates, of the post-war world.

Strikebreaking was therefore never a specific form of action, but a shorthand expression for the much larger reality of an era when economic power was fiercely challenged, contested and defended. The phenomenon was neither universal nor continuous. On the contrary, it tended to come to the fore at moments of economic crisis and along the fault lines of economic change, at the nodes constituted by transport hubs or in areas of recent and intense industrialisation. These were often distant from more long-established locations of industry and of state authority – the wild west and the wild east of the global economy. But the underlying reality was everywhere the same, as was demonstrated by the multiplication of forms of vigilantism and paramilitary mobilisation which occurred in Catalonia, in the provinces of northern Italy and across the post-imperial territories of central-eastern Europe in the years following 1918.

It is this pervasiveness which also explains to a large degree why it came to an end. The forms of action analysed in this volume never went away. They continued through the prolonged economic depression of the 1930s and returned again in the 1970s and 1980s, most notably during the bitter Miners' Strike of 1984–85 in Britain. Moreover the authority of the state to regulate social and economic order was directly challenged through the actions of Resistance groups and trade unions in liberated Europe during the mid-1940s, and amidst the social upheavals of the later 1960s.[16] But there was something distinctly different about these later practices. They operated within a structure of industrial relations which, though it certainly did not exclude the use of force and the infiltration and subversion of trade unions by employers and the state, was much more institutionalised, and on the whole predictable. Unions and employers alike had been drawn into a structure of corporatist negotiation, with each other and with the state, which had blunted the frontal confrontations that had taken place during the early twentieth century.[17] In large part, this evolution was the consequence of changes in the structure of capitalism, which at least in the economies of the Global North had replaced individual structures of ownership with joint-stock companies, in which financial institutions often had the predominant influence. The obstinate individualism and preoccupation with short-term profit maximisation, which had long hindered attempts at coordination among employers gave way to the more cautious and corporate mentality of a professionalised class of managers. Only when this attitude changed once again in response to the economic crisis of the 1970s, and the dissemination of neo-liberal ideologies of the market, did employers revert to much more direct attacks on the authority of trade unions, including a return to the use of alternative labour forces, and the partisan deployment of the police in industrial disputes.[18]

The role of the state too had changed. The improvised and fragile forces of law and order evident in the early decades of the twentieth century were replaced by much more professionalised and better resourced police forces, at least in Europe, that could confront most challenges to their authority without recourse to large-scale violence. Nor were they challenged so directly. The stateless societies that developed in some areas of Spain during the early period of the Civil War in 1936–37, and more generally across many areas of occupied and liberated Europe during the latter years of the Second World War,[19] were the last occasion when state authority was swept away within Europe. Thereafter such insurrectionary strategies were displaced from Europe to territories such as Palestine and Algeria, where the dwindling power exercised by European powers was contested by those imbued with the legitimacy of national liberation.[20] Within Europe, but also across Western states more generally, challenges to state power were replaced by a pragmatic tendency on the part of individuals, communities and interest groups to seek their advantage by working within a state-defined regime of legality.[21] The mentality of the state, and of those who staffed it, had changed too. The nervous concern of state officials to assert their authority at all costs had been replaced by a policy – well exemplified in this volume by the case of Sweden – of encouraging unions and employers' organisations to collaborate in a wider process of social and economic managerialism. This creation of what Zygmunt Bauman termed the "social engineering state"[22] was the dominant reality in Western Europe in the decades following 1945, creating a technocratic ethos which privileged Keynesian economic management and the construction of an inclusive welfarism over the brutal assertions of state power described in this volume.[23]

These differences rest on a distinctive Western perspective. In many other areas of the world, and perhaps most notably in South Asia and Latin America, the direct confrontations described in this volume remained the norm. However, the more regulated and legalistic structure of industrial relations that emerged in Europe and in a number of other Western economies from the middle decades of the twentieth century onwards serves to underline the distinctiveness of the era from the 1880s to the 1930s. During that half-century, the volatility of the global economy, but also the uncertain relationships of power within it, created a potential for violence and conflict that often spilled beyond the formal frontiers of industrial disputes. Recent historical research has served to emphasise the importance of this phenomenon of unstructured violence in the military and political spheres. The warfare conducted on the battlefields of the First World War, and its many ancillary conflicts, notably in imperial territories, formed merely one part of a much more generalised culture of informal military violence which endured on a smaller scale in many areas of the world until at least the end of the 1940s. Similarly, in politics, the rituals of electoral contests and parliamentary politics coexisted with a much wider sphere of informal politics, where practices of streetfighting, ethnic violence and social intimidation were commonplace.[24] The prevalence of strikebreaking and other violent actions within the global economy across the same period extends this perspective into the sphere of labour relations. Thus, by reorientating attention towards the confrontations, social violence, and simple chaos that characterised many industrial disputes in these formative decades of the twentieth century, this volume brings what had formerly seemed marginal or secondary emphatically to the centre of the picture.

Notes

1 See, however, the special issue of *European History Quarterly* 49, no. 4 (2019), which arises from the same research project as this volume.

2 See, for examples of such work, D. Kalb, *Expanding Class: Power and Everyday Politics in Industrial Communities, The Netherlands, 1850–1950* (Durham, NC and London: Duke University Press, 1997); H. H. Chenut, *The Fabric of Gender. Working Class Culture in Third Republic France* (University Park, PA: Pennsylvania State University Press, 2005); D. Reid, *Opening the Gates: the Lip Affair 1968–1981* (New York and London: Verso, 2018); J. Clarke, "Work, Consumption and Subjectivity in Postwar

France: Moulinex and the Meanings of Domestic Appliances 1950s – 70s," *Journal of Contemporary History* 47 (2012): 838–59.

3 See also the portrayal of the fluid borders of espionage, criminality and commercial opportunism, in M. B. Miller, *Shanghai on the Metro: Spies, Intrigue, and the French between the Wars* (Berkeley, CA: University of California Press, 1994). For a vivid fictional description of a similar reality, see E. Ambler, *Cause for Alarm* (London: Hodder and Stoughton, 1938).

4 Matteo Millan, "Introduction: Strikebreaking during Europe's Belle Epoque," *European History Quarterly* 49, no. 4 (2019): 558.

5 See the intelligent reflections in S. Lazar, *The Social Life of Politics. Ethics, Kinship and Union Activism in Argentina* (Stanford, CA: Stanford University Press, 2017), esp. 12–17.

6 See, for example, G. Eley, *Forging Democracy. The History of the Left in Europe, 1850–2000* (New York and Oxford: Oxford University Press, 2002), esp. 13–229.

7 E.g. Victoria E. Bonnell, *Roots of Rebellion: Workers' Politics and Organizations in St Petersburg and Moscow, 1900–1914* (Berkeley, CA and London: University of California Press, 1983); T. Kaplan, *Red City, Blue Period. Social Movements in Picasso's Barcelona* (Berkeley, CA: University of California Press, 1992); Leopold Haimson and Charles Tilly, eds., *Strikes, Wars and Revolution in an International Perspective: Strikes Waves in the Late Nineteenth and Early Twentieth Centuries* (Cambridge: Cambridge University Press, 1989).

8 S. Payne, *Fascism: Comparison and Definition* (Madison, WI and London: University of Wisconsin Press, 1980); R. Griffin, *The Nature of Fascism* (London: Pinter, 1991). But see also M. Blinkhorn, ed., *Fascists and Conservatives: The Radical Right and the Establishment in Twentieth-Century Europe* (London: Unwin Hyman, 1990).

9 K. Passmore, *From Liberalism to Fascism: The Right in a French Province, 1928–1939* (Cambridge: Cambridge University Press, 1997); R. O. Paxton, *French Peasant Fascism: Henry Dorgères's Greenshirts and the Crises of French Agriculture, 1929–1939* (New York and Oxford: Oxford University Press, 1997); J. Osmond, *Rural Protest in the Weimar Republic: The Free Peasantry in the Rhineland and Bavaria* (New York and Basingstoke: Palgrave Macmillan, 1993).

10 This approach, much influenced by sociological concepts, is evident in G. Luebbert, *Liberalism, Fascism, or Social Democracy: Social Classes and the Political Origins of Regimes in Interwar Europe* (New York and Oxford: Oxford University Press, 1991); M. Mann, *Fascists* (Cambridge: Cambridge University Press, 2004). For a stimulating study of the primacy of the local in socialist politics, see M. Van Ginderachter, *The Everyday Nationalism of Workers. A Social History of Modern Belgium* (Stanford, CA: Stanford University Press, 2019).

11 That this effectively negates any lingering notion of a pre-1914 era of social peace is a point well made in M. Millan, "The Shadows of Social Fear: Emotions, Mentalities and Practices of the Propertied Classes in Italy, Spain and France (1900–1914)," *Journal of Social History* 50, no. 2 (2016): 336–61.

12 Robert Gerwarth and John Horne, eds., *War in Peace: Paramilitary Violence in Europe after the Great* War (Oxford: Oxford University Press, 2012); R. Gerwarth, *The Vanquished: Why the First World War Failed to End* (London: Allen Lane, 2016).

13 See G. Albanese, *The March on Rome: Violence and the Rise of Italian Fascism* (London: Routledge, 2019).

14 For the analogous case of the recruitment of Polish miners to work in French mines in the interwar years, see the analysis in G. S. Cross, *Immigrant Workers in Industrial France: The Making of a New Laboring Class* (Philadelphia, PA: Temple University Press, 1983). I am grateful to Owen Coughlan for this reference.

15 See the comments of Millan, "Introduction: Strikebreaking during Europe's Belle Epoque," 562.

16 T. Behan, *The Long-Awaited Moment. The Working Class and the Italian Communist Party in Milan, 1943–1948* (New York: Peter Lang, 1997); R. Hemmerijckx, *Van Verzet tot Koude Oorlog* (Brussels: Vrije Universiteit Brussel Press, 2003); G-R Horn, *The Spirit of '68. Rebellion in Western Europe and North America, 1956–1976* (Oxford: Oxford University Press, 2007), 100–18.

17 M. Conway, *Western Europe's Democratic Age 1945–1968* (Princeton, NJ and Oxford: Princeton University Press, 2020), 138–42.

18 R. Franzosi, *The Puzzle of Strikes: Class and State Strategies in Postwar Italy* (Cambridge: Cambridge University Press, 1995), 301–42. I am indebted to Matt Myers for his assistance with this point.

19 M. Vincent, *Spain 1833–2002: People and State* (Oxford and New York: Oxford University Press, 2007), 137–43; C. Pavone, *A Civil War: A History of the Italian Resistance* (London and New York: Verso, 2013); M. Koreman, *The Expectation of Justice. France 1944–46* (Durham, NC and London: Duke University Press, 1999); M. Conway, *The Sorrows of Belgium. Liberation and Political Reconstruction 1944–47* (Oxford: Oxford University Press, 2012), 48–51.

20 W. R. Louis and R. W. Stookey, eds., *The End of the Palestine Mandate*, 2nd ed. (London: I.B. Tauris, 2012); M. Evans, *Algeria: France's Undeclared War* (Oxford: Oxford University Press, 2012). But see also J. House and N. Macmaster, *Paris 1961: Algerians, State Terror and Memory* (Oxford: Oxford University Press, 2006).

21 Conway, *Western Europe's Democratic Age*, 221–23.

22 Z. Bauman, *Memories of Class: The Pre-History and After-Life of Class* (London and Abingdon: Routledge, 1982), 165–67.

23 P. Nord, *France's New Deal: From the Thirties to the Post-War Era* (Princeton, NJ and Oxford: Princeton University Press, 2010); H. Chapman, *France's Long Reconstruction. In Search of the Modern Republic* (Cambridge, MA and London: Harvard University Press, 2018).

24 R. Gerwarth and M. Conway, "Revolution and Counter-Revolution," in *Political Violence in Twentieth-Century Europe*, ed. D. Bloxham and R. Gerwarth (Cambridge: Cambridge University Press, 2011), 140–75; C. Millington, *Fighting for France. Violence in Interwar French Politics* (Oxford: Oxford University Press, 2018); S. Kalyvas, *The Logic of Violence in Civil War* (Cambridge and New York: Cambridge University Press, 2006).

Index

Note: Page numbers in *italic* indicate a figure and page numbers in **bold** indicate a table on the corresponding page.

Taylor & Francis Group
an informa business

Taylor & Francis eBooks

www.taylorfrancis.com

A single destination for eBooks from Taylor & Francis with increased functionality and an improved user experience to meet the needs of our customers.

90,000+ eBooks of award-winning academic content in Humanities, Social Science, Science, Technology, Engineering, and Medical written by a global network of editors and authors.

TAYLOR & FRANCIS EBOOKS OFFERS:

- A streamlined experience for our library customers
- A single point of discovery for all of our eBook content
- Improved search and discovery of content at both book and chapter level

REQUEST A FREE TRIAL

support@taylorfrancis.com

Routledge
Taylor & Francis Group

CRC Press
Taylor & Francis Group